MILLER

GAAP

IMPLEMENTATION MANUAL

1999

MILLER

GAAP
IMPLEMENTATION MANUAL

Restatement and Analysis of Other Current FASB and AICPA Pronouncements

JAN R. WILLIAMS, Ph.D., CPA
JOSEPH V. CARCELLO, Ph.D., CPA

HARCOURT BRACE PROFESSIONAL PUBLISHING

A Division of
Harcourt Brace & Company
SAN DIEGO NEW YORK CHICAGO LONDON

This publication is designed to provide accurate and authoritative information in regard to the subject matter covered. It is sold with the understanding that the publisher is not engaged in rendering legal, accounting, or other professional service. If legal advice or other expert assistance is required, the services of a competent professional person should be sought.

The publisher has not sought nor obtained approval of this publication from any other organization, profit or not-for-profit, and is solely responsible for its contents.

Copyright © 1998 by Harcourt Brace & Company

All rights reserved. No part of this publication may be reproduced or transmitted in any form or by any means, electronic or mechanical, including photocopy, recording, or any information storage and retrieval system, without permission in writing from the publisher.

Permission is hereby granted to reproduce the CPE Answer Sheet in this publication in complete pages, with the copyright notice, for professional use and not for resale.

Portions of this work were published in previous editions.

IMPRESS and logo is a registered trademark of Harcourt Brace & Company.

HARCOURT BRACE and Quill is a registered trademark of Harcourt Brace & Company.

Printed in Canada.

ISBN: 0-15-606247-X

98   99   00   01   FR   4   3   2   1

1999 *Miller GAAP* Implementation Manual

Contents

Contents of Other Titles in the 1999 **Complete Miller GAAP Library for Business**	
1999 *Miller GAAP Guide*	vii
1999 *Miller Implementation Manual: EITF*	ix
Preface	xi
About the Authors	xiv
About the GAAP Hierarchy	xv
Accounting Resources on the Web	xvii
IMPRESS™ Comprehensive Table of Contents	xix
Cross-Reference—Original Pronouncements to *Miller GAAP Implementation Manual*	xxxiii

Generally Accepted Accounting Principles

Accounting Policies and Standards	1.01
Advertising	2.01
Balance Sheet Classification	3.01
Bankruptcy and Reorganization	4.01
Business Combinations	5.01
Changing Prices	6.01
Contingencies, Risks, and Uncertainties	7.01
Equity Method	8.01
Extinguishment of Debt	9.01
Financial Instruments	10.01
Foreign Operations and Exchange	11.01
Income Taxes	12.01
Intangible Assets	13.01
Interest on Receivables and Payables	14.01
Interim Financial Reporting	15.01
Inventory Pricing and Methods	16.01
Investment Tax Credit	17.01
Investments in Debt and Equity Securities	18.01
Leases	19.01
Long-Term Construction Contracts	20.01

Nonmonetary Transactions	**21.01**
Pension Plans—Employers	**22.01**
Pension Plans—Settlements and Curtailments	**23.01**
Personal Financial Statements	**24.01**
Postemployment and Postretirement Benefits Other Than Pensions	**25.01**
Research and Development Costs	**26.01**
Results of Operations	**27.01**
Revenue Recognition	**28.01**
Segment Reporting	**29.01**
Stockholders' Equity	**30.01**
Stock Issued to Employees	**31.01**
Troubled Debt Restructuring	**32.01**
Self-Study CPE Program	**33.01**
Index	**34.01**

OTHER TITLES IN THE COMPLETE MILLER GAAP LIBRARY FOR BUSINESS

★

1999 *Miller GAAP Guide*
Contents

Generally Accepted Accounting Principles

Accounting Changes
Accounting Policies
Business Combinations
Cash Flow Statement
Changing Prices
Consolidated Financial Statements
Contingencies, Risks, and Uncertainties
Convertible Debt and Debt with Warrants
Current Assets and Current Liabilities
Deferred Compensation Contracts
Depreciable Assets and Depreciation
Development Stage Enterprises
Earnings per Share
Equity Method
Extinguishment of Debt
Financial Instruments
Foreign Operations and Exchange
Futures Contracts
Government Contracts
Impairment of Loans and Long-Lived Assets
Income Taxes
Installment Sales Method of Accounting
Intangible Assets
Interest Costs Capitalized
Interest on Receivables and Payables
Interim Financial Reporting
Inventory Pricing and Methods
Investment Tax Credit
Investments in Debt and Equity Securities
Leases
Long-Term Construction Contracts
Long-Term Obligations
Nonmonetary Transactions
Pension Plans—Employers

Pension Plans—Settlements and Curtailments
Postemployment and Postretirement Benefits Other Than Pensions
Product Financing Arrangements
Property Taxes
Quasi-Reorganizations
Related Party Disclosures
Research and Development Costs
Results of Operations
Revenue Recognition
Segment Reporting
Stockholders' Equity
Stock Issued to Employees
Transfer and Servicing of Financial Assets
Troubled Debt Restructuring

Specialized Industry Accounting Principles

Banking and Thrift Institutions
Entertainment Industry
   Broadcasters
   Cable Television
   Motion Picture Films
   Records and Music
Franchise Fee Revenue
Insurance Industry
   Insurance Enterprises
   Title Plant
Mortgage Banking Industry
Not-for-Profit Organizations
Oil and Gas Producing Companies
Pension Plan Financial Statements
Real Estate Transactions
   Real Estate Costs and Initial Rental Operations
   Real Estate—Recognition of Sales
Regulated Industries

Disclosure Index

Self-Study CPE Program

Index

1999 *Miller GAAP Implementation Manual: EITF*
Contents

Generally Accepted Accounting Principles

Accounting Changes
Balance Sheet Classification
Business Combinations
Capitalization and Expense Recognition Concepts
Cash Flow Reporting
Consolidation and the Equity Method
Contingencies
Convertible Debt, Debt with Warrants, and Convertible Equity Securities
Earnings per Share
Extinguishment of Debt
Financial Instruments
Foreign Currency Transactions
Impairment of Long-Lived Assets
Income Taxes
Intangible Assets
Interest on Receivables and Payables
Interim Financial Reporting
Inventory
Investments in Debt and Equity Securities
Leases
Nonmonetary Transactions
Nonrefundable Loan Fees and Costs
Pension Accounting
Postemployment and Postretirement Benefits Other Than Pensions
Results of Operations
Revenue Recognition
Stockholder's Equity
Stock Compensation to Employees and Others
Transfers of Financial Assets
Troubled Debt Restructuring

Specialized Industry Accounting Principles

Banking and Thrift Institutions
Computer Software Industry
Insurance Enterprises
Mortgage Banking Industry

Rate-Regulated Industries
Real Estate Transactions

Self-Study CPE Program

Index

Preface

The 1999 *Miller GAAP Implementation Manual* shows you how AICPA and FASB accounting pronouncements apply to specific business transactions. It is designed with one goal in mind: To give you what you need to find complete, correct answers quickly. We have taken the complex and often lengthy technical implementation guidance contained in the original text of these pronouncements and have restated and analyzed it in clear, understandable terms.

Coverage of GAAP Hierarchy of Accounting Standards

As part of Harcourt Brace Professional Publishing's **Complete Miller GAAP Library for Business**, this innovative Manual covers authoritative GAAP contained in Levels B through D of the GAAP hierarchy, which was established by Statement on Auditing Standards No. 69. (See "About the GAAP Hierarchy" for complete information on this structure.) Pronouncements in these levels include:

- Technical Bulletins issued by the FASB (Level B)
- Statements of Position of the AICPA's Accounting Standards Executive Committee (Level B)
- Industry Audit and Accounting Guides of the AICPA (Level B)
- Practice Bulletins of the AICPA's Accounting Standards Executive Committee (Level C)
- Accounting Interpretations of the AICPA associated with Accounting Principles Board Opinions that remain in effect (Level D)
- Implementation Guides (Q&A) issued by the FASB (Level D)

Statements of Position (SOPs) of the AICPA Accounting Standards Executive Committee are the primary source of generally accepted accounting principles for a number of significant business events for which there is no accounting guidance in Level A of the GAAP hierarchy. That is, they must be applied if no higher-level GAAP exists. AICPA Statements of Position are the primary source of accounting guidance for the following topics and transactions:

- Accounting for start-up costs (SOP 98-5)
- Environmental remediation liabilities (SOP 96-1)
- Disclosure of certain risks and uncertainties (SOP 94-6)
- Reporting on advertising costs (SOP 93-7)

- Employers' accounting for employee stock option plans (SOP 93-6)
- Financial reporting by entities in reorganization under the Bankruptcy Code (SOP 90-7)
- Accounting and financial reporting for personal financial statements (SOP 82-1)
- Accounting for performance of construction-type and certain production-type contracts (SOP 81-1)

Three types of pronouncements in the Implementation Manual answer specific questions that have arisen from the application of GAAP in practice:

- FASB Technical Bulletins (FTBs) address a limited number of narrow financial accounting and reporting issues in a question and answer format. For example, FTB 85-6 presents accounting guidance when an entity repurchases its own stock at a price significantly in excess of the prevailing market price prior to the purchase.
- Practice Bulletins, issued by the Accounting Standards Executive Committee, address a limited number of narrow accounting issues.
- Accounting Interpretations, issued by the Accounting Principles Board, are similar to FASB Technical Bulletins in that they address a limited number of narrow accounting issues in a question and answer format.
- A significant feature of this Manual is our coverage of Implementation Guides issued by the FASB. Implementation Guides tend to be lengthy; they provide detailed financial accounting and reporting guidance, in a question and answer form, as well as additional examples for some of the more complex accounting standards that the FASB has issued. These Implementation Guides are issued on a stand-alone basis, and no existing commercial publication provides in-depth coverage of the material contained in them. The FASB Implementation Guides covered in this Manual provide implementation guidance and additional examples for the following FASB Statements:
    — FAS-87 (Employers' Accounting for Pensions)
    — FAS-88 (Employers' Accounting for Settlements and Curtailments of Defined Benefit Pension Plans and for Termination Benefits)
    — FAS-106 (Employers' Accounting for Postretirement Benefits Other Than Pensions)

— FAS-109 (Accounting for Income Taxes)

— FAS-115 (Accounting for Certain Investments in Debt and Equity Securities)

Format and Practical Features

The 1999 *Miller GAAP Implementation Manual* organizes accounting pronouncements alphabetically by topic. Pronouncements covering the same subject are compiled and incorporated in a single chapter so that the authoritative information is immediately accessible.

The *Miller GAAP Implementation Manual* is written in clear, understandable language. Each pronouncement is discussed in a comprehensive format that makes it easy to understand and apply. Abundant illustrations demonstrate and clarify specific accounting principles.

The Self-Study CPE Program offers a low-cost opportunity to put to additional use the knowledge gained from reading this *Miller GAAP Implementation Manual*. The Index provides quick, accurate reference to needed information.

Three other features of the 1999 *Miller GAAP Implementation Manual* also provide tools for finding the correct, complete answer quickly. First, the Tables of Contents of all three volumes in the **Complete Miller GAAP Library for Business** are included at the beginning of each volume so you can locate pertinent topics in the Library easily. Second, the Cross-Reference gives the chapter location of each AICPA and FASB original pronouncement covered in this Manual. Pronouncements are listed in chronological and GAAP hierarchical order. Finally, the GAAP hierarchy's logic and the Miller Library's comprehensiveness can be accessed instantly through the IMPRESS™ system of cross-references, described below.

IMPRESS™ Cross-References

IMPRESS™ stands for the Integrated Miller Professional Reference and Engagement Series System. It is the system by which all Miller publications are thoroughly cross-referenced to one another on a chapter-by-chapter basis. The system is designed to facilitate comprehensive research and to assure that you will always find the complete answers you need. The IMPRESS™ Comprehensive Table of Contents shows the system in its entirety across all Miller publications. The IMPRESS™ Cross-References at the beginning of each chapter refer you to corresponding chapters in other Miller publications as well as to related chapters in the 1999 *Miller GAAP Implementation Manual*.

The foundation of the IMPRESS™ system is the GAAP hierarchy of authoritative accounting pronouncements, established by Statement on Auditing Standards No. 69 (The Meaning of "Present Fairly in Conformity with Generally Accepted Accounting Principles" in the Independent Auditor's Report). (See "About the GAAP Hierarchy for more details.)

The three volumes of the Complete Miller GAAP Library for Business are based on the GAAP hierarchy. The 1999 *Miller GAAP Guide* covers Level A pronouncements—the highest level in the hierarchy. The 1999 *Miller GAAP Implementation Manual* covers Levels B through D, and the 1999 *Miller GAAP Implementation Manual: EITF* focuses on the guidance from the Emerging Issues Task Force contained in Level C.

Abbreviations

The following abbreviations are used throughout the text to represent the various sources of authoritative literature covered in this book:

AIN-APB	AICPA Accounting Interpretations
FIG-FAS	FASB Implementation Guides
FTB	FASB Technical Bulletins
PB	AICPA AcSEC Practice Bulletins
SOP	AICPA Statements of Position

Acknowledgments

The authors and publisher thank Wayne R. Borkowski, CPA, CMA, CFM, of Borkowski & Associates, Olympia, Washington, for suggesting many improvements to the 1999 *Miller GAAP Implementation Manual*. Many thanks are due to Sidney Bernstein, Rachel de la Vega, Cate DaPron, and JoAnn Koppany of Harcourt Brace Professional Publishing. Jan Williams would like to thank his wife, Elaine, for her willingness to adjust to the time required to write this book. Many hours that could have been spent with her have been spent writing, and for her understanding he is eternally grateful. Joe Carcello would like to thank his wife, Terri, and children, Janie, Stephen, Karen, and Sarah, for their patience and understanding during the writing of this book.

About the Authors

Jan R. Williams, Ph.D., CPA, is the Ernst & Young Professor of Accounting and Associate Dean in the College of Business Administration at the University of Tennessee, Knoxville, where he has been on the faculty since 1977. Formerly, he was on the faculties of the University of Georgia and Texas Tech University. He received a Ph.D. in business administration, major in accounting, from the University of Arkansas and is a CPA licensed in Arkansas and Tennessee.

Dr. Williams has, for many years, been actively involved in the American Institute of Certified Public Accountants, the Tennessee Society of Certified Public Accountants, and several other professional organizations. Throughout his career, he has taught continuing professional education for CPAs. In 1994, Dr. Williams received both the Tennessee Society of CPAs and the AICPA Outstanding Accounting Educator Award. At the time this book is being printed, he has been nominated for the position of president of the American Accounting Association.

Joseph V. Carcello, Ph.D., CPA, CMA, CIA, is an Associate Professor in the Department of Accounting and Business Law at the University of Tennessee. Dr. Carcello has published extensively in numerous academic and practitioner journals, and he is the co-author of *Current FASB Standards: A Review for Industry,* published by the AICPA. He has taught continuing education/professional development courses for the Tennessee Society of CPAs, the Florida Society of CPAs, the Institute of Management Accountants, and two of the major national accounting firms.

About the GAAP Hierarchy

The meaning of the term *generally accepted accounting principles* (GAAP) has varied over time. Originally, GAAP referred to accounting policies and procedures that were widely used in practice. As standards-setting bodies and professional organizations increasingly became involved in recording practices and recommending preferred practices, the term came to refer more and more to the pronouncements issued by particular accounting bodies, such as the Committee on Accounting Procedure and the Accounting Principles Board, both committees of the AICPA, and more recently the FASB. Today, many different series of authoritative literature exist, some of which are still in effect but are no longer being issued, like APB Opinions and AICPA Accounting Research Bulletins. Others—such as FASB Statements and Interpretations—continue to be issued by accounting organizations.

To better organize and make clear what is meant by GAAP, Statement on Auditing Standards (SAS) No. 69 (The Meaning of "Present Fairly in Conformity with Generally Accepted Accounting Principles" in the Independent Auditor's Report) established what is commonly referred to as the GAAP hierarchy. The purpose of the hierarchy is to instruct financial statement preparers, auditors, and users of financial statements concerning the relative priority of the different sources of GAAP used by auditors to judge the fairness of presentation in financial statements. While the GAAP hierarchy appears in the professional auditing literature, its importance goes beyond auditors: preparers, users, and others interested in financial statements must understand the sources of GAAP that underlie those statements.

SAS-69 defines the GAAP hierarchy by outlining four categories of established accounting principles. Because these sources of accounting principles arose over five decades and were promulgated by different groups, some conflicts exist among them. The four categories of GAAP as set forth by SAS-69 correspond to these principles' relative authoritativeness. Sources of accounting principles in higher categories carry more weight and must be followed when conflicts arise. When two or more sources of GAAP within a given level of the hierarchy disagree on the accounting for a particular type of transaction, the approach that better portrays the substance of the transaction should be followed.

In addition to the four levels of established accounting principles, the GAAP hierarchy recognizes other types of accounting literature that may be useful in resolving financial reporting problems when issues have not been covered in established sources of GAAP.

The following figure displays the GAAP hierarchy's four levels of established principles that are supported by authoritative accounting literature, as well as the additional sources of GAAP. The *Miller GAAP Implementation Manual* is based on Levels B, C, and D.

Hierarchy of Generally Accepted Accounting Principles

Level A
- FASB Statements of Financial Accounting Standards (FAS)
- FASB Interpretations (FIN)
- APB Opinions (APB)
- Accounting Research Bulletins (ARB)

Level B
- FASB Technical Bulletins (FTB)
- AICPA Industry Audit and Accounting Guides
- AICPA Statements of Position (SOP)

Level C
- Consensus Positions of the Emerging Issues Task Force (EITF)
- AICPA AcSEC Practice Bulletins (PB)

Level D
- AICPA Accounting Interpretations (AIN)
- FASB Implementation Guides (FIG)
- Industry practices widely recognized and prevalent

Other Accounting Literature
- FASB Concepts Statements (CON)
- APB Statements
- AICPA Issues Papers
- International Accounting Standards Committee Statements
- GASB Statements, Interpretations, and Technical Bulletins
- Pronouncements of other professional associations and regulatory bodies
- AICPA Technical Practice Aids
- Accounting textbooks, handbooks, and articles

Accounting Resources on the Web

The following World Wide Web addresses are just a few of the resources on the Internet that are available to practitioners. Because of the evolving nature of the Internet, some addresses may change. In such a case, refer to one of the many Internet search engines, such as Yahoo! (http://www.yahoo.com).

AICPA   http://www.aicpa.org/

American Accounting Association   http://www.rutgers.edu/accounting/raw/aaa/

FASB   http://www.rutgers.edu:80//Accounting/raw/fasb/

Federal Tax Code Search   http://www.tns.lcs.mit.edu:80/uscode/

Fedworld   http://www.fedworld.gov

GASB   http://www.rutgers.edu/Accounting/raw/gasb/

General Accounting Office   http://www.gao.gov/

Harcourt Brace Professional Publishing   http://www.hbpp.com

House of Representatives   http://www.house.gov/

IRS Digital Daily   http://www.irs.ustreas.gov/prod/cover.html

Library of Congress   http://lcweb.loc.gov/homepage/

Office of Management and Budget   http://www.gpo.gov/omb/omb001.html

Securities and Exchange Commission   http://www.sec.gov/

Thomas Legislative Research   http://thomas.loc.gov/

INTEGRATED MILLER PROFESSIONAL REFERENCE AND ENGAGEMENT SERIES SYSTEM

IMPRESS stands for the Integrated Miller Professional Reference and Engagement Series System. It is the system by which all Miller publications are thoroughly cross-referenced to one another on a chapter-by-chapter basis. The system is designed to facilitate comprehensive research and to assure that you will always find the complete answers you need.

Comprehensive Table of Contents
GENERALLY ACCEPTED ACCOUNTING PRINCIPLES

MILLER GUIDE CHAPTER

IMPRESS™ Topic	1999 Miller GAAP Guide	1999 Miller GAAP Implementation Manual: EITF	1999 Miller GAAP Implementation Manual	1999 Miller Governmental GAAP Guide	1999 Miller GAAS Guide	1999 Miller GAAP for Not-for-Profit Organizations
Accounting Changes	1	1	—	—	3, 8, 11	1
Accounting Policies	2	—	1	—	3	—
Advertising	—	—	2	—	—	2

xx   IMPRESS Table of Contents

IMPRESS™ Topic	1999 Miller GAAP Guide	1999 Miller GAAP Implementation Manual: EITF	1999 Miller GAAP Implementation Manual	1999 Miller Governmental GAAP Guide	1999 Miller GAAS Guide	1999 Miller GAAP for Not-for-Profit Organizations
Balance Sheet Classification	—	2	3	—	—	2
Bankruptcy and Reorganization	—	—	4	—	—	—
Business Combinations	3	3	5	—	11	2, 7
Capitalization and Expense Recognition Concepts	—	4	—	—	—	5, 6, 16
Cash Flow Statement	4	5	—	5, 6	—	10
Changing Prices	5	—	6	—	—	—
Consolidated Financial Statements	6	6	—	—	8	2, 7

IMPRESS Table of Contents **xxi**

IMPRESS™ Topic	1999 Miller GAAP Guide	1999 Miller GAAP Implementation Manual: EITF	1999 Miller GAAP Implementation Manual	1999 Miller Governmental GAAP Guide	1999 Miller GAAS Guide	1999 Miller GAAP for Not-for-Profit Organizations
Contingencies, Risks, and Uncertainties	7	7	7	20	11	2
Convertible Debt and Debt with Warrants	8	8	—	—	—	—
Current Assets and Current Liabilities	9	—	—	9, 13, 16	—	2
Deferred Compensation Contracts	10	—	—	27	—	—
Depreciable Assets and Depreciation	11	—	—	13, 24, 30	—	5

IMPRESS™ Topic	1999 Miller GAAP Guide	1999 Miller GAAP Implementation Manual: EITF	1999 Miller GAAP Implementation Manual	1999 Miller Governmental GAAP Guide	1999 Miller GAAS Guide	1999 Miller GAAP for Not-for-Profit Organizations
Development Stage Enterprises	12	—	—	—	—	—
Earnings per Share	13	9	—	—	—	—
Equity Method	14	6	8	13	8	7
Extinguishment of Debt	15	10	9	16	—	2, 6, 11
Financial Instruments	16	11, 29	10	13	11	2
Foreign Operations and Exchange	17	12	11	13	—	2, 11

IMPRESS™ Topic	1999 Miller GAAP Guide	1999 Miller GAAP Implementation Manual: EITF	1999 Miller GAAP Implementation Manual	1999 Miller Governmental GAAP Guide	1999 Miller GAAS Guide	1999 Miller GAAP for Not-for-Profit Organizations
Futures Contracts	18	—	—	—	—	—
Government Contracts	19	—	—	—	—	15
Impairment of Loans and Long-Lived Assets	20	13	—	—	—	—
Income Taxes	21	14	12	—	—	2, 13
Installment Sales Method of Accounting	22	—	—	—	—	—
Intangible Assets	23	15	13	—	—	2
Interest Costs Capitalized	24	—	—	—	—	6

IMPRESS™ Topic	1999 Miller GAAP Guide	1999 Miller GAAP Implementation Manual: EITF	1999 Miller GAAP Implementation Manual	1999 Miller Governmental GAAP Guide	1999 Miller GAAS Guide	1999 Miller GAAP for Not-for-Profit Organizations
Interest on Receivables and Payables	25	16	14	—	—	2
Interim Financial Reporting	26	17	15	—	13	—
Inventory Pricing and Methods	27	18	16	13	8	—
Investment Tax Credit	28	—	17	—	—	—
Investments in Debt and Equity Securities	29	19	18	13, 14, 15	8	2, 5, 9
Leases	30	20	19	19, 29, 30	—	—

IMPRESS™ Topic	1999 Miller GAAP Guide	1999 Miller GAAP Implementation Manual: EITF	1999 Miller GAAP Implementation Manual	1999 Miller Governmental GAAP Guide	1999 Miller GAAS Guide	1999 Miller GAAP for Not-for-Profit Organizations
Long-Term Construction Contracts	31	—	20	24	8, 18	—
Long-Term Obligations	32	—	—	29	—	2, 6, 11
Nonmonetary Transactions	33	21	21	—	—	2, 10, 14
Pension Plans—Employers	34	23	22	21, 28	8, 20	16
Pension Plans—Settlements and Curtailments	35	—	23	17	—	—
Personal Financial Statements	—	—	24	—	—	—

IMPRESS™ Topic	1999 Miller GAAP Guide	1999 Miller GAAP Implementation Manual: EITF	1999 Miller GAAP Implementation Manual	1999 Miller Governmental GAAP Guide	1999 Miller GAAS Guide	1999 Miller GAAP for Not-for-Profit Organizations
Postemployment and Post-retirement Benefits Other Than Pensions	36	24	25	22	8, 20	—
Product Financing Arrangements	37	—	—	—	—	—
Property Taxes	38	—	—	—	9	—
Quasi-Reorganizations	39	—	—	—	—	—
Related Party Disclosures	40	—	—	—	8	2
Research and Development Costs	41	—	26	—	—	—

IMPRESS™ Topic	1999 Miller GAAP Guide	1999 Miller GAAP Implementation Manual: EITF	1999 Miller GAAP Implementation Manual	1999 Miller Governmental GAAP Guide	1999 Miller GAAS Guide	1999 Miller GAAP for Not-for-Profit Organizations
Results of Operations	42	25	27	5	—	2, 11
Revenue Recognition	43	26	28	9	—	2, 3, 9
Segment Reporting	44	—	29	26	—	7, 11
Stockholders' Equity	45	27	30	—	—	—
Stock Issued to Employees	46	28	31	—	—	—
Transfer and Servicing of Financial Assets	47	29	—	—	—	—
Troubled Debt Restructuring	48	30	32	—	—	2, 6

xxviii IMPRESS Table of Contents

IMPRESS™ Topic	1999 Miller GAAP Guide	1999 Miller GAAP Implementation Manual: EITF	1999 Miller GAAP Implementation Manual	1999 Miller Governmental GAAP Guide	1999 Miller GAAS Guide	1999 Miller GAAP for Not-for-Profit Organizations
SPECIALIZED INDUSTRY ACCOUNTING PRINCIPLES						
Agricultural Producers and Co-ops	—	—	—	—	—	—
Airlines and Aircraft Manufacturers	—	—	—	—	—	—
Computer Software	41	32	—	—	—	—
Entertainment *Broadcasters*	50	—	—	—	—	—
Cable Television	51	—	—	—	—	—
Motion Picture Films	52	—	—	—	—	—

IMPRESS™ Topic	1999 Miller GAAP Guide	1999 Miller GAAP Implementation Manual: EITF	1999 Miller GAAP Implementation Manual	1999 Miller Governmental GAAP Guide	1999 Miller GAAS Guide	1999 Miller GAAP for Not-for-Profit Organizations
Records and Music	53	—	—	—	—	—
Financial Institutions						
Banking and Thrift Institutions	49	22, 31	—	—	19	—
Mortgage Banking Industry	57	34	—	—	—	—
Franchising	54	—	—	—	—	—
Health Care	—	—	—	—	21	—
Insurance Insurance Enterprises	55	33	—	—	—	—

IMPRESS™ Topic	1999 Miller GAAP Guide	1999 Miller GAAP Implementation Manual: EITF	1999 Miller GAAP Implementation Manual	1999 Miller Governmental GAAP Guide	1999 Miller GAAS Guide	1999 Miller GAAP for Not-for-Profit Organizations
Title Plant	56	—	—	11	—	—
Investment Companies	—	—	—	—	—	—
Not-for-Profit Organizations	58	—	—	34	22	2, 8
Oil and Gas Producing Companies	59	—	—	—	—	—
Pension Plan Financial Statements	60	—	—	27	—	—
Real Estate Costs and Initial Rental Operations	61	36	—	—	—	—

IMPRESS™ Topic	1999 Miller GAAP Guide	1999 Miller GAAP Implementation Manual: EITF	1999 Miller GAAP Implementation Manual	1999 Miller Governmental GAAP Guide	1999 Miller GAAS Guide	1999 Miller GAAP for Not-for-Profit Organizations
Recognition of Sales	62	36	—	—	—	—
Regulated Industries	63	35	—	—	—	—

CROSS-REFERENCE

ORIGINAL PRONOUNCEMENTS TO *1999 MILLER GAAP IMPLEMENTATION MANUAL* CHAPTERS

This locator provides instant cross-reference between an original pronouncement and the chapter(s) in this publication in which a pronouncement is covered. Original pronouncements are listed chronologically on the left and the chapter(s) in which they appear in the *1999 Miller GAAP Implementation Manual* are listed on the right.

FASB TECHNICAL BULLETINS

ORIGINAL PRONOUNCEMENT	IMPLEMENTATION MANUAL REFERENCE
FTB 79-1 (R) Purpose and Scope of FASB Technical Bulletins and Procedures for Issuance	Accounting Policies and Standards, ch. 1
FTB 79-3 Subjective Acceleration Clauses in Long-Term Debt	Balance Sheet Classification, ch. 3
FTB 79-4 Segment Reporting of Puerto Rican Operations	Segment Reporting, ch. 29
FTB 79-5 Meaning of the Term "Customer" as It Applies to Health Care Facilities Under FASB Statement No. 14	Segment Reporting, ch. 29
FTB 79-8 Applicability of FASB Statements 21 and 33 to Certain Brokers and Dealers in Securities	Segment Reporting, ch. 29
FTB 79-9 Accounting in Interim Periods for Changes in Income Tax Rates	Interim Financial Reporting, ch. 15
FTB 79-10 Fiscal Funding Clauses in Lease Agreements	Leases, ch. 19

FTB 79-12
Interest Rate Used in Calculating the Present Value of Minimum Lease Payments

Leases, ch. **19**

FTB 79-13
Applicability of FASB Statement No. 13 to Current Value Financial Statement

Changing Prices, ch. **6**

FTB 79-14
Upward Adjustment of Guaranteed Residual Values

Leases, ch. **19**

FTB 79-15
Accounting for Loss on a Sublease Not Involving the Disposal of a Segment

Leases, ch. **19**

FTB 79-16 (R)
Effect of a Change in Income Tax Rate on the Accounting for Leveraged Leases

Leases, ch. **19**

FTB 79-17
Reporting Cumulative Effect Adjustment from Retroactive Application of FASB Statement No. 13

Leases, ch. **19**

FTB 79-18
Transition Requirement of Certain FASB Amendments and Interpretations of FASB Statement No. 13

Leases, ch. **19**

FTB 79-19
Investor's Accounting for Unrealized Losses on Marketable Securities Owned by an Equity Method Investee

Equity Method, ch. **8**

FTB 80-1
Early Extinguishment of Debt through Exchange for Common or Preferred Stock

Extinguishment of Debt, ch. **9**

FTB 80-2
Classification of Debt Restructurings by Debtors and Creditors

Troubled Debt Restructuring, ch. **32**

FTB 81-6
Applicability of FASB Statement 15 to Debtors in Bankruptcy Situations

Troubled Debt Restructuring, ch. **32**

FTB 82-1
Disclosure of the Sale or Purchase of Tax Benefits Through Tax Leases

Accounting Policies and Standards, ch. **1**

FTB 84-1
Accounting for Stock Issued to Acquire the Results of a Research and Development Arrangement

Research and Development Costs, ch. 26

FTB 85-1
Accounting for the Receipt of Federal Home Loan Mortgage Corporation Participating Preferred Stock

Nonmonetary Transactions, ch. 21

FTB 85-3
Accounting for Operating Leases with Scheduled Rent Increases

Leases, ch. 19

FTB 85-4
Accounting for Purchases of Life Insurance

Balance Sheet Classification, ch. 3

FTB 85-5
Issues Relating to Accounting for Business Combinations

Business Combinations, ch. 5

FTB 85-6
Accounting for a Purchase of Treasury Shares at a Price Significantly in Excess of the Current Market Price of the Shares and the Income Statement Classification of Costs Incurred in Defending against a Takeover Attempt

Stockholders' Equity, ch. 30

FTB 86-2
Accounting for an Interest in the Residual Value of a Leased Asset

Leases, ch. 19

FTB 88-1
Issues Relating to Accounting for Leases

Leases, ch. 19

FTB 90-1
Accounting for Separately Priced Extended Warranty and Product Maintenance Contracts

Revenue Recognition, ch. 28

FTB 94-1
Application of Statement 115 to Debt Securities Restructured in a Troubled Debt Restructuring

Troubled Debt Restructuring, ch. 32

FTB 97-1
Accounting under Statement 123 for Certain Employee Stock Purchase Plans with a Look-Back Option

Stock Issued to Employees, ch. 31

AICPA STATEMENTS OF POSITION

ORIGINAL PRONOUNCEMENT	IMPLEMENTATION MANUAL REFERENCE
SOP 76-3 Accounting Practices for Certain Employee Stock Ownership Plans	Stock Issued to Employees, ch. 31
SOP 81-1 Accounting for Performance of Construction-Type and Certain Production-Type Contracts	Long-Term Construction Contracts, ch. 20
SOP 82-1 Accounting and Financial Reporting for Personal Financial Statements	Personal Financial Statements, ch. 24
SOP 90-3 Definition of the Term *Substantially the Same for Holders of Debt Instruments*, as Used in Certain Audit Guides and a Statement of Position	Investments in Debt and Equity Securities, ch. 18
SOP 90-7 Financial Reporting by Entities in Reorganization Under the Bankruptcy Code	Bankruptcy and Reorganization, ch. 4
SOP 92-3 Accounting for Foreclosed Assets	Bankruptcy and Reorganization, ch. 4
SOP 93-3 Rescission of Accounting Principles Board Statements	Accounting Policies and Standards, ch. 1
SOP 93-4 Foreign Currency Accounting and Financial Statement Presentation of Investment Companies	Foreign Operations and Exchange, ch. 11
SOP 93-6 Employers' Accounting for Employee Stock Ownership Plans	Stock Issued to Employees, ch. 31
SOP 93-7 Reporting on Advertising Costs	Advertising, ch. 2
SOP 94-6 Disclosure of Certain Significant Risks and Uncertainties	Contingencies, Risks, and Uncertainties, ch. 7

SOP 96-1
Environmental Remediation Liabilities
    Contingencies, Risks, and Uncertainties, ch. 7

SOP 98-5
Reporting on the Costs of Start-Up Activities
    Results of Operations, ch. 27

AICPA AcSEC PRACTICE BULLETINS

ORIGINAL PRONOUNCEMENT   *IMPLEMENTATION MANUAL REFERENCE*

PB-1
Purpose and Scope of AcSEC Practice Bulletins and Procedures for Their Issuance
    Accounting Policies and Standards, ch. 1

PB-2
Elimination of Profits Resulting from Intercompany Transfers of LIFO Inventories
    Inventory Pricing and Methods, ch. 16

PB-4
Accounting for Foreign Debt/Equity Swaps
    Financial Instruments, ch. 10

PB-5
Income Recognition on Loans to Financially Troubled Countries
    Troubled Debt Restructuring, ch. 32

PB-11
Accounting for Preconfirmation Contingencies in Fresh-State Reporting
    Bankruptcy and Reorganization, ch. 4

PB-12
Reporting Separate Investment Fund Option Information of Defined-Contribution Pension Plans
    Pension Plans—Employers, ch. 22

PB-13
Direct-Response Advertising and Probable Future Benefits
    Advertising, ch. 2

PB-14
Accounting and Reporting by Limited Liability Companies and Limited Liability Partnerships
    Stockholders' Equity, ch. 30

ACCOUNTING INTERPRETATIONS OF THE ACCOUNTING PRINCIPLES BOARD

ORIGINAL PRONOUNCEMENT   *IMPLEMENTATION MANUAL REFERENCE*

AIN-APB 4

Accounting for the Investment Tax Credit: Accounting Interpretations of APB Opinion No. 4

Investment Tax Credit, ch. **17**

AIN-APB 9

Reporting the Results of Operations: Unofficial Accounting Interpretations of APB Opinion No. 9

Results of Operations, ch. **27**

AIN-APB 16

Business Combinations: Accounting Interpretations of APB Opinion No. 16

Business Combinations, ch. **5**

AIN-APB 17

Intangible Assets: Unofficial Accounting Interpretations of APB Opinion No. 17

Intangible Assets, ch. **13**

AIN-APB 18

The Equity Method of Accounting for Investments in Common Stock: Accounting Interpretations of APB Opinion No. 18

Equity Method, ch. **8**

AIN-APB 21

Interest on Receivables and Payables: Accounting Interpretations of APB Opinion 21

Interest on Receivables and Payables, ch. **14**

AIN-APB 25

Accounting for Stock Issued to Employees: Accounting Interpretations of APB Opinion No. 25

Stock Issued to Employees, ch. **31**

AIN-APB 26

Early Extinguishment of Debt: Accounting Interpretations of APB Opinion No. 26

Extinguishment of Debt, ch. **9**

AIN-APB 30

Reporting the Results of Operations: Accounting Interpretations of APB Opinion No. 30

Results of Operations, ch. **27**

FASB IMPLEMENTATION GUIDES

ORIGINAL PRONOUNCEMENT   *IMPLEMENTATION MANUAL REFERENCE*

FIG-FAS 87

A Guide to Implementation of Statement 87 on Employers' Accounting for Pensions

Pension Plans—Employers, ch. **22**

FIG-FAS 88

A Guide to Implementation of Statement 88 on Employers' Accounting for Settlements and Curtailments of Defined Benefit Pension Plans and for Termination Benefits

Pension Plans—Settlements and Curtailments, ch. **23**

FIG-FAS 106

A Guide for Implementation of Statement 106 on Employers' Accounting for Postretirement Benefits Other Than Pensions

Postemployment and Postretirement Benefits Other Than Pensions, ch. **25**

FIG-FAS 109

A Guide to Implementation of Statement 109 on Accounting for Income Taxes

Income Taxes, ch. **12**

FIG-FAS 115

A Guide to Implementation of Statement 115 on Accounting for Certain Investments in Debt and Equity Securities

Investments in Debt and Equity Securities, ch. **18**

CHAPTER 1
ACCOUNTING POLICIES AND STANDARDS

CONTENTS

IMPRESS™ Cross-References	1.02
Overview	1.03
FTB 79-1 (R): Purpose and Scope of FASB Technical Bulletins and Procedures for Issuance	1.04
Background	1.04
Standards	1.04
FTB 82-1: Disclosure of the Sale or Purchase of Tax Benefits through Tax Leases	1.05
Background	1.05
Standards	1.05
SOP 93-3: Rescission of Accounting Principles Board Statements	1.05
Background	1.05
Standards	1.06
PB-1: Purpose and Scope of AcSEC Practice Bulletins and Procedures for Their Issuance	1.07
Background	1.07
Standards	1.07
ACRS Lives and GAAP	1.08
Accounting by Colleges and Universities for Compensated Absences	1.08
ADC Arrangement	1.09

CROSS-REFERENCES

1999 MILLER GAAP GUIDE: Chapter 2, "Accounting Policies"

1999 MILLER GAAS GUIDE: Chapter 3, "Generally Accepted Accounting Principles"

CHAPTER 1
ACCOUNTING POLICIES AND STANDARDS

OVERVIEW

Accounting policies are important considerations in understanding the content of financial statements. FASB (Financial Accounting Standards Board) and APB (Accounting Principles Board) standards require the disclosure of accounting policies as an integral part of financial statements when those statements are intended to present financial position, cash flows, and results of operations in conformity with GAAP.

The following pronouncement is the primary source of promulgated GAAP concerning disclosure of accounting policies that is included in the highest level of authority in the SAS-69 GAAP hierarchy.

APB-22 Disclosure of Accounting Policies

The following additional sources of GAAP that are in lower levels of the SAS-69 GAAP hierarchy are discussed in this Manual:

FTB 79-1 (R) Purpose and Scope of FASB Technical Bulletins and Procedures for Issuance (Level B)

FTB 82-1 Disclosure of the Sale or Purchase of Tax Benefits through Tax Leases (Level B)

SOP 93-3 Rescission of Accounting Principles Board Statements (Level B)

PB-1 Purpose and Scope of AcSEC Practice Bulletins and Procedures for Their Issuance (Level C)

FTB 79-1 (R): Purpose and Scope of FASB Technical Bulletins and Procedures for Issuance

BACKGROUND

The FASB has authorized its staff to prepare Technical Bulletins to provide timely guidance on certain financial accounting and reporting issues. FTB 79-1 (R) describes the purpose and scope of Technical Bulletins and the procedures for their issuance.

STANDARDS

FASB Technical Bulletins provide guidance in applying Accounting Research Bulletins, APB Opinions, and FASB Statements and Interpretations and guidance for resolving issues that are not directly addressed in those pronouncements. The following kinds of guidance are provided in Technical Bulletins:

- To clarify, explain, or elaborate on an underlying standard
- To provide guidance for a particular situation (e.g., a specific industry) in which application of a standard may differ from its general application
- To address areas not directly covered by existing standards

Problems and issues that are brought to the FASB's attention are the basis for issuing a Technical Bulletin if the financial reporting problem or issue can be resolved within all of the following guidelines:

- The guidance is not expected to cause a major change in accounting practice for a large number of entities.
- The administrative cost that may be involved in implementing the guidance is not expected to be significant for most affected entities.
- The guidance does not conflict with a broad fundamental principle or create a new accounting practice.

Proposed Technical Bulletins are available to the public, and interested individuals may comment in writing to the FASB. Issues proposed for Technical Bulletins are discussed by the FASB at a public meeting, and FASB members are provided copies of all proposed Bulletins before their issuance. FASB members are also provided copies of a summary of the comments that are received before a Technical Bulletin is issued. Technical Bulletins are generally in a question and answer format.

FTB 82-1: Disclosure of the Sale or Purchase of Tax Benefits through Tax Leases

BACKGROUND

The term *tax lease*, as used in FTB 82-1, refers to leases that are entered into to transfer certain tax benefits as allowed by the leasing provisions of the Economic Recovery Act of 1981. The tax benefits that can be transferred are deductions under the Accelerated Cost Recovery System (ACRS) and credits such as the investment tax credit and energy credit.

STANDARDS

Question: What disclosures are required for the sale or purchase of tax benefits through tax leases?

Answer: APB-22 (Disclosure of Accounting Policies) requires disclosure of all significant accounting policies where alternative accounting principles or practices exist, including methods of application that affect an enterprise's financial position, results of operations, and cash flows. Because alternative accounting practices may exist with regard to the sale or lease of tax benefits, the accounting policy and practice followed should be disclosed. This disclosure should include the method of accounting for those transactions and the method of recognizing revenue and allocating income tax benefits and asset costs to current and future periods.

SOP 93-3: Rescission of Accounting Principles Board Statements

BACKGROUND

Statements of Position present the conclusions of at least two-thirds of the Accounting Standards Executive Committee (AcSEC). The

AcSEC is a senior technical body of the AICPA authorized to represent the AICPA on matters involving accounting and financial reporting.

The FASB's predecessor, the APB, issued both Opinions and Statements. The APB issued thirty-one Opinions between 1959 and 1973. Any of these Opinions that has not been superseded by an FASB Statement is part of the literature encompassed by Rule 203 of the AICPA's Code of Professional Conduct. A member is precluded from issuing an unmodified report on financial statements that contain a material departure from a non-superseded APB Opinion.

The APB also issued four Statements. These Statements never were considered rules or standards that AICPA members had to follow (i.e., they were not encompassed by the Code of Professional Conduct). In addition, SAS-69 (The Meaning of "Present Fairly in Conformity with Generally Accepted Accounting Principles" in the Independent Auditor's Report), listed APB Statements as a source of "other accounting literature." Practitioners may choose to follow items included in this category; they are not required to do so. However, even though APB Statements never represented a source of authoritative literature, some practitioners erroneously viewed APB Statements as authoritative. SOP 93-3 was issued to rectify this situation.

STANDARDS

SOP 93-3 rescinds the four Statements issued by the APB. This action was taken to eliminate any confusion as to whether APB Statements represented a source of authoritative literature. Also, FASB pronouncements have effectively superseded each of the four APB Statements. The following APB Statements were rescinded:

- APB Statement No. 1 (Statement by the Accounting Principles Board)
- APB Statement No. 2 (Disclosure of Supplemental Financial Information by Diversified Companies)—effectively superseded by FAS-14
- APB Statement No. 3 (Financial Statements Restated for General Price-Level Changes)—partially superseded by FAS-89
- APB Statement No. 4 (Basic Concepts and Accounting Principles Underlying Financial Statements of Business Enterprises)—effectively superseded by the various FASB Statements of Financial Accounting Concepts

APB Statement No. 3 (Financial Statements Restated for General Price-Level Changes) provided guidance for a comprehensive application of price-level adjusted financial statements. FAS-89 (Financial

Reporting and Changing Prices) effectively superseded a portion of APB Statement No. 3. However, FAS-89 addresses the presentation of partial price-level data only. Although SOP 93-3 rescinds APB Statement No. 3, it does not preclude an entity from following the guidance presented in APB Statement No. 3 for preparing a comprehensive set of price-level adjusted financial statements (assuming the statements are not inconsistent with the guidance in FAS-89 regarding historical cost/constant purchasing power accounting, such as the classification of assets and liabilities as monetary or nonmonetary).

PB-1: Purpose and Scope of AcSEC Practice Bulletins and Procedures for Their Issuance

BACKGROUND

Practice Bulletins are issued to disseminate the views of the AcSEC on narrow financial accounting and reporting issues. The AcSEC is a senior technical body of the AICPA authorized to represent the AICPA on matters involving accounting and financial reporting. Practice Bulletins address issues that are not addressed and are not expected to be addressed by either the FASB or the Governmental Accounting Standards Board (GASB).

STANDARDS

Before the issuance of Practice Bulletins (which commenced during 1987), similar guidance was provided as "Notices to Practitioners." These Notices typically were published in either *The CPA Letter* or the *Journal of Accountancy*. Practice Bulletins are designed to convey information that will enhance the quality and comparability of financial statements.

Drafts of proposed Practice Bulletins, which are discussed in open meetings of the AcSEC, are available to the public as part of the agenda for meetings of the AcSEC. However, Practice Bulletins are not exposed for public comment, and their issuance does not involve holding hearings.

A Practice Bulletin is issued if both of the following conditions exist. First, two-thirds or more of AcSEC members must vote in favor of the proposed Bulletin. Second, after reviewing the proposed Bulletin, the FASB and GASB must indicate that they have no plans to address the particular issue.

Practice Bulletins do not fall under the rubric of Rule 203 of the AICPA Code of Professional Conduct. However, per SAS-69, Practice Bulletins are Level C pronouncements in the GAAP hierarchy.

Most of the Notices to Practitioners that preceded the issuance of Practice Bulletins have been superseded. However, three Notices to Practitioners continue to be in effect and are discussed in the appendix to PB-1. A brief discussion of these three non-superseded Notices to Practitioners follows.

ACRS Lives and GAAP

In most cases, the number of years specified by the ACRS for recovery deductions will not bear any reasonable resemblance to the asset's useful life. In these cases, ACRS recovery deductions cannot be used as the depreciation expense amount for financial reporting purposes. Rather, depreciation for financial reporting purposes should be based on the asset's useful life.

Accounting by Colleges and Universities for Compensated Absences

When FAS-43 (Accounting for Compensated Absences) was issued, there was some discussion as to whether it would apply to colleges and universities. The FASB decided not to exempt colleges and universities from the provisions of this standard. A Notice to Practitioners was issued to assist colleges and universities in applying FAS-43. The essential conclusions of this Notice were as follows:

1. In recognizing the liability, and the associated charge, for compensated absences in the current and prior years, the unrestricted current fund is to be used (use of the plant fund is specifically prohibited).

2. In some cases the liability for compensated absences might be recoverable from future state appropriations and/or from grants and contracts for funded research. A receivable, and the associated revenue, can be recognized to offset a portion of the liability only in limited situations. More specifically, a receivable can be recognized only if it meets the definition of an *asset* in Statement of Financial Accounting Concepts No. 6 (Elements of Financial Statements of Business Enterprises). In evaluating the receivable, the college or university should consider the measurability and collectibility of the receivable and the institution's legal right to it.

3. The reduction in the unrestricted current fund balance caused by recognizing the liability for compensated absences may be

reduced by interfund transfers. These interfund transfers may be recognized only if (*a*) unrestricted assets are available for permanent transfer and (*b*) payment (or other settlement) to the unrestricted current fund is expected within a reasonable period.

ADC Arrangement

This Notice to Practitioners addresses the funding provided by financial institutions for real estate acquisition, development, and construction (ADC). In some cases, financial institutions enter into ADC agreements where the institution has essentially the same risks and rewards as an investor or a joint venture participant. In these cases, treating the ADC funding as a loan would not be appropriate.

This notice applies to only those ADC arrangements where the financial institution is expected to receive some or all of the residual profit. Expected residual profit is the amount of funds the lender is expected to receive—whether these funds are referred to as interest, as fees, or as an equity kicker—above a customary amount of interest and fees normally received for providing comparable financing.

The profit participation between the lender and the developer is not always part of the mortgage loan agreement. Therefore, the auditor should be cognizant that such side agreements may exist and should design the audit to detect such profit participation agreements between the lender and the developer.

A number of characteristics, in addition to the sharing of the expected residual profit, indicate that the ADC arrangement is more akin to an investment or a joint venture than to a loan. These characteristics are as follows:

1. The financial institution provides all, or substantially all, of the funds necessary to acquire, develop, and construct the project. The developer has title but little or no equity investment in the project.
2. The financial institution rolls into the loan any commitment and/or origination fees.
3. The financial institution adds to the loan balance all, or substantially all, interest and fees during the term of the loan.
4. The financial institution's only security for the loan is the ADC project. There is no recourse to other assets of the borrower. Also, the borrower does not guarantee the debt.
5. The financial institution recovers its investment in one of three ways: (*a*) the project is completed and sold to an independent third party, (*b*) the borrower obtains refinancing from another source, or (*c*) the project is completed and placed in service,

and cash flows are sufficient to fund the repayment of principal and interest.
6. Foreclosure during the development period due to delinquency is unlikely, because the borrower is not required to make any payments during this period.

In some cases, even though the lender is expected to participate in the residual profit from the project, the facts and circumstances of the borrowing arrangement are consistent with a loan. The following characteristics of an ADC arrangement are consistent with a loan:

1. The lender's participation in the expected residual profit is less than 50%.
2. The borrower has a substantial equity investment in the project, not funded by the lender. This equity investment can be either in the form of cash or in the form of the contribution of land to the project.
3. Either (*a*) the lender has recourse to other substantial, tangible assets of the borrower, which have not already been pledged under other loans, or (*b*) the borrower has secured an irrevocable letter of credit from a creditworthy, independent third party for substantially all of the loan balance and for the entire term of the loan.
4. A take-out commitment for the entire amount of the loan has been secured from a creditworthy, independent third party. If the take-out commitment is conditional, the conditions should be reasonable and their attainment should be probable.

Some ADC loans contain personal guarantees from the borrower or from a third party. The AcSEC believes that such guarantees are rarely sufficient to support classifying the ADC arrangement as a loan.

In evaluating the substance of a personal guarantee, the following factors should be considered: (1) the ability of the guarantor to perform under the guarantee, (2) the practicality of enforcing the guarantee in the applicable jurisdiction, and (3) a demonstrated intent on the part of the lender to enforce the guarantee. Factors that might indicate the ability to perform under the guarantee include placing liquid assets in escrow, pledging marketable securities, and obtaining irrevocable letters of credit from a creditworthy, independent third party.

In the absence of the support discussed above for a guarantee, financial statements of the guarantor need to be evaluated. In evaluating the financial statements of the guarantor, the auditor should consider both the guarantor's liquidity and net worth. A guarantee has little substance if its only support is assets already pledged as security for other debt. Also, guarantees made by the guarantor on other projects should be considered.

If the lender expects to receive more than 50% of the residual profit from the project, the lender should account for the income or loss from the arrangement as a real estate investment. The guidance in FAS-67 (Accounting for Costs and Initial Rental Operations of Real Estate Projects) and in FAS-66 (Accounting for Sales of Real Estate) should be followed.

If the lender expects to receive less than 50% of the residual profit from the project, the ADC arrangement should be accounted for as a loan or as a joint venture, depending on the applicable circumstances. If the ADC arrangement is classified as a loan, interest and fees may be recognized as income if they are recoverable. In assessing the recoverability of loan amounts and accrued interest, both SOP 75-2 (Accounting Practices of Real Estate Investment Trusts) and the AICPA Audit and Accounting Guide titled *Savings and Loan Associations* might prove useful. If the ADC arrangement is classified as a joint venture, the primary accounting guidance is found in SOP 78-9 (Accounting for Investments in Real Estate Ventures) and in FAS-34 (Capitalization of Interest Cost).

ADC arrangements classified as investments in real estate or as joint ventures should be combined and reported separately from those ADC arrangements treated as loans for balance sheet reporting purposes.

In some cases, the lender's share of the expected residual profit is sold before the project is completed. The applicable accounting in these cases hinges on whether the ADC arrangement was treated as a loan, as an investment in real estate, or as a joint venture. If the ADC arrangement was treated as a loan, proceeds received from the sale of the expected residual profit should be recognized as additional interest income over the remaining term of the loan. If the ADC arrangement was treated as a real estate investment or a joint venture, any gain to be recognized upon sale of the expected residual profit is determined by reference to FAS-66.

The accounting treatment of an ADC project should be periodically reassessed. For example, an ADC arrangement originally classified as an investment or a joint venture might subsequently be classified as a loan if the lender is not expected to receive more than 50% of the residual profit and if the risk to the lender has decreased significantly. It is important to note that a change in the accounting for an ADC arrangement depends on a change in the facts that were relied upon when the ADC arrangement was initially classified. The absence of, or a reduced participation in, a residual profit is not sufficient to change the categorization of the ADC arrangement. In addition, it is possible for an ADC arrangement initially classified as a loan to be reclassified as a real estate investment or a joint venture. The lender may take on additional risks and rewards of ownership by releasing collateral to support a guarantee and by increasing its percentage of profit participation. An improvement in the economic prospects for the project does not justify a change in how the ADC arrangement is categorized. A change in classification is expected to be rare and needs to be supported by adequate documentation.

Finally, regardless of the accounting treatment for an ADC arrangement, it is necessary to continually assess the collectibility of principal, accrued interest, and fees. Also, ADC financing often entails a heightened risk of related party transactions. The auditor needs to design the audit accordingly.

CHAPTER 2
ADVERTISING

CONTENTS

Overview	2.03
SOP 93-7: Reporting on Advertising Costs	2.03
Background	2.03
Standards	2.04
Illustration of Expensing Advertising Costs	2.04
Direct-Response Advertising	2.05
Generation of Sales and Traceability to Direct-Response Advertising	2.05
Illustration of Direct-Response Advertising	2.05
Illustration of Advertising Costs Not Capitalized	2.06
Probable Future Economic Benefits of Direct-Response Advertising	2.06
Illustration of Capitalizing Costs of Subsequent Products	2.07
Measurement of the Costs of Direct-Response Advertising	2.07
Amortization of Capitalized Advertising Costs	2.08
Illustration of Amortizing Advertising Costs	2.08
Assessment of Realizability of Capitalized Advertising Costs	2.09
Illustration of Write-Off of Unamortized Advertising Costs	2.09
Miscellaneous Issues	2.10
Disclosures	2.10
Effect on Other Related Pronouncements	2.10
PB-13: Direct-Response Advertising and Probable Future Benefits	2.11
Background	2.11
Standards	2.12

CHAPTER 2
ADVERTISING

OVERVIEW

Although advertising is a common business expenditure, before 1993 there were no stand-alone authoritative accounting pronouncements on the treatment of advertising costs. Given this lack of authoritative guidance, a wide diversity in practice developed as to how these costs were treated. Some entities expensed advertising costs as incurred; other entities deferred these costs, with subsequent amortization, in an attempt to match revenues with expenses. The AcSEC issued SOP 93-7 (Reporting on Advertising Costs) to narrow the range of acceptable practices in reporting advertising costs. There are no stand-alone pronouncements on advertising costs in Level A of the SAS-69 GAAP hierarchy.

The following pronouncements establish accounting and reporting standards for advertising costs:

SOP 93-7   Reporting on Advertising Costs (Level B)

PB-13   Direct-Response Advertising and Probable Future Benefits (Level C)

In general, advertising expenditures are to be expensed either as incurred or the first time the advertisement appears. There are two exceptions to this general rule. First, direct-response advertising, which meets certain conditions, is to be capitalized and amortized against revenues in future periods. Second, expenditures for advertising costs that are made after the recognition of revenues related to those costs are to be capitalized and charged to expense when the related revenues are recognized.

SOP 93-7: Reporting on Advertising Costs

BACKGROUND

Before SOP 93-7 was issued, there was a lack of broad authoritative guidance on the treatment of advertising costs. Entities accounted for these costs in diverse ways. Some entities charged advertising expenditures to expense as incurred. Other entities, believing that advertising created a probable future economic benefit that was sufficiently measurable, capitalized these costs and amortized them against future revenues.

Advertising is defined as the promotion of an industry, company, brand, product name, or specific product or service for the purpose of improving an entity's image and/or increasing future revenues. Advertising is typically distributed via one or more media outlets (e.g., television, radio, magazines, direct-mail).

STANDARDS

In most cases, the costs of advertising should be expensed as incurred or the first time the advertisement appears. There are two exceptions to this general rule. First, entities are to capitalize certain direct-response advertising. Second, expenditures for advertising costs that are made subsequent to the recognition of revenues related to those costs are to be capitalized and charged to expense when the related revenues are recognized. For example, some entities enter into an arrangement whereby they are responsible for reimbursing some or all of their customers' advertising costs. In most cases, revenues related to the transactions creating these obligations are earned before the reimbursements are made. The entity responsible for reimbursing advertising expenditures would recognize a liability and the related advertising expense concurrently with the recognition of revenue.

There are two general types of advertising costs: the costs of producing advertisements and the costs of communicating them. Costs of communicating advertisements should not be expensed until the dissemination service has been received. For example, the costs of purchasing television or radio airtime should not be expensed until the advertisement is aired (the costs of communicating certain direct-response advertisements will be charged to expense as the advertising benefit is received).

Illustration of Expensing Advertising Costs

Ace Motor Company plans to introduce a series of new cars (the A series). Ace Motor agrees to reimburse dealerships for advertising costs they incur during January of 19X8 to promote this new series of cars. The reimbursement rate is set at 20% of the value of orders placed by the dealership for cars in the A series (up to 50% of the advertising costs incurred by the dealership). Russell Ace, a dealership in Waterbury, Connecticut, incurs $100,000 of advertising costs during January 19X8 and places $300,000 of orders for cars from the A series during that month. When the automobiles are shipped, Ace Motor will record $300,000 of revenue. Concurrently with recognizing the revenue, Ace Motor is to record a liability and a charge to advertising expense for $50,000 (Ace's reimbursement obligation to the Russell Ace dealership).

Direct-Response Advertising

Direct-response advertising must meet two conditions in order to be capitalized. First, the primary purpose of the advertising must be to generate sales, and these sales must be capable of being traced specifically to the advertising. Second, the direct-response advertising must result in probable future economic benefits.

Generation of Sales and Traceability to Direct-Response Advertising

In order for the costs of direct-response advertising to be capitalized, sales derived therefrom must be traceable directly to the advertising. The entity must maintain records that identify customers making purchases and the advertisement that customers responded to. Acceptable documentation includes the following examples:

- Files indicating customer names and the applicable direct-response advertisement
- A coded order form, coupon, or response card, included with an advertisement, which includes the customer name
- A log of customers placing phone orders in response to a number appearing in an advertisement, linking those calls to the advertisement

Illustration of Direct-Response Advertising

Fantastic Systems, Inc., has developed a new product—an aerobic exercise machine called the Air Flyer. In order to elicit sales of this product, Fantastic Systems produces a 30-minute infomercial. Fantastic Systems has obtained a unique toll-free telephone number to facilitate sales that result from the airing of this infomercial. This toll-free number is displayed frequently throughout the infomercial. Assuming this infomercial results in probable future economic benefits to Fantastic Systems (discussed below in the section titled "Probable Future Economic Benefits of Direct-Response Advertising"), the cost of producing and airing this infomercial would be capitalizable as direct-response advertising. Given the targeted toll-free number used, the resultant sales and the customer names can be traced to a specific advertisement (i.e., the infomercial).

Certain advertising costs may be related to a direct-response advertising campaign and yet still not be capitalizable. If the subsequent sale cannot be traced to the direct-response advertising, the related advertising costs cannot be capitalized.

Illustration of Advertising Costs Not Capitalized

Fleet Foot, Inc., a large athletic-shoe manufacturer, incurs costs to produce and air a television advertisement for a new running shoe. The commercial states that order forms, with discount coupons, will soon be distributed to certain consumers (this is the direct-response advertisement). The costs of producing and airing the television commercial are not capitalizable, since there is not a link to trace subsequent sales directly to the television commercial. However, the cost of producing and distributing the order forms would be capitalizable (assuming this direct-response advertisement provided Fleet Foot with future economic benefits).

Probable Future Economic Benefits of Direct-Response Advertising

Probable future economic benefits are expected future revenues from direct-response advertising minus the costs to be incurred in generating those revenues. In order for the costs of direct-response advertising to be capitalized, there must be *persuasive evidence* that the effect of the current advertising campaign will be similar to that of previous advertising campaigns that generated future economic benefits. In terms of probable future benefits, attributes to consider in evaluating the similarity between the current direct-response advertising campaign and prior campaigns include audience demographics, the advertising method, the product, and economic conditions.

A specific entity needs to base its decision about whether to capitalize direct-response advertising costs on its past results with other direct-response advertising campaigns. In the absence of prior experience with direct-response advertising, an entity cannot rely on industry statistics as support for capitalizing advertising costs. The most persuasive type of evidence in support of the capitalization of direct-response advertising costs is a prior history of similar advertising for similar products that resulted in future economic benefits. Although an entity may not have a prior history of advertising a similar product, it may have used direct-response advertising to promote a related product or service. An entity may be able to support the capitalization of direct-response advertising for the new product or service if it can document that the results from a prior advertising campaign for a related product or service are likely to be highly correlated with the current advertising campaign. Test market results may suggest that the reaction of prospective consumers to the advertising campaign for a new product or service is likely to be similar to consumer reaction to a similar campaign for a different product or service. In the absence of a high degree of correlation between the current campaign and advertising campaigns for other products in the past, a success rate based on the historical ratio of successful products or services to total products or services introduced to the marketplace would not be sufficient to support capitalization.

Illustration of Capitalizing Costs of Subsequent Products

As discussed in a previous illustration, Fantastic Systems, Inc., marketed a new fitness product, the Air Flyer, via a direct-response television campaign. This product was introduced in 19X7, and the costs of the campaign were capitalized as direct-response advertising. Fantastic Systems plans to introduce a new product, the Magic Club, in 19X8. The Magic Club, which is a new type of golf club, clearly represents a different product than the Air Flyer. On the basis of test market results, however, Fantastic Systems believes that there will be a high degree of correlation between the response of consumers to the ads for the Air Flyer and the response to the ads for the Magic Club. Therefore, Fantastic Systems can capitalize the costs of producing and distributing an infomercial for the Magic Club.

Direct-response advertising that is not capitalized, because future economic benefits are uncertain, should not be retroactively capitalized if future results indicate that the advertisement did produce economic benefits.

Measurement of the Costs of Direct-Response Advertising

Each separate direct-response advertising campaign that meets the capitalization criteria represents a *separate stand-alone cost pool.*

The costs of direct-response advertising that should be capitalized include both of the following:

1. Incremental direct costs of direct-response advertising incurred in transactions with independent third parties (e.g., idea development, writing advertising copy, artwork, printing, magazine space, and mailing).
2. Payroll and payroll-related costs for the direct-response advertising activities of employees who are directly associated with and devote time to the advertising reported as assets (e.g., idea

development, writing advertising copy, artwork, printing, and mailing). The costs of payroll and fringe benefits for these employees should be capitalized only to the extent of the time spent working on the particular advertising project (i.e., if 10% of an employee's time is spent working on a direct-response advertising campaign that is subject to capitalization, 10% of that employee's compensation and fringe benefit costs would be included among the costs to be capitalized).

If the criteria for capitalization are met, the entire cost of the direct-response campaign, not just a pro rata share of the cost based on the expected response rate of consumers to the campaign, is capitalizable. For example, an entity distributes one million order forms and coupons to target customers and expects to receive 10,000 orders as a result of this mailing. In this case, orders can be directly traced to the advertisement. If this advertising campaign is likely to generate future economic benefits, the cost of the entire mailing campaign should be capitalized (not just the cost of mailing to the 10,000 individuals who are likely to place an order).

Amortization of Capitalized Advertising Costs

Amortization of direct-response advertising costs for a particular cost pool is as follows: Current Period Revenues Attributable to the Direct-Response Advertising Cost Pool/(Current Period Revenues Attributable to the Direct-Response Advertising Cost Pool + Estimated Future Revenues Attributable to the Direct-Response Advertising Cost Pool). Estimated future revenues may change over time, and the amortization ratio is to be recalculated each period.

Direct-response advertising costs are typically amortized over a period of not more than one year or one operating cycle. This suggests that future revenues attributable to the advertisement are limited to those likely to result within the next year (or within the next operating cycle). The AcSEC bases this recommendation on the belief that the reliability of future revenue estimates decreases as the length of time for which such estimates are made increases. However, a possible exception to this general recommendation is illustrated below.

Illustration of Amortizing Advertising Costs

An entity undertakes a direct-response advertising campaign, via a series of television commercials and a dedicated toll-free number, to sell classic works of literature (e.g., *Moby Dick* and *A Tale of Two Cities*). Because sales can be tied directly to the advertisement, the costs of this campaign will be capitalized if the campaign is likely to generate probable future economic benefits. For this entity such benefits exist. Customers who buy the first book are sent a response card on a monthly basis thereafter, asking them if they would like to order another book in the set (there are 24 books in the collection). These future advertising efforts (mailing the response card on a monthly basis) are viewed as minimal. The entity also knows that a certain percentage of the customers who buy the first book will buy a quantifiable percentage of the remaining books. In this case, the amortization ratio used will include total revenues expected from all sales, including an estimate of future book sales. If a significant advertising effort was necessary for each book sold, however, each of these advertising efforts would be treated separately—in terms of both initial capitalization and subsequent amortization.

Assessment of Realizability of Capitalized Advertising Costs

The realizability of capitalized direct-response advertising costs should be evaluated at each reporting date on a cost-pool-by-cost-pool basis. The unamortized direct-response advertising costs are to be compared to probable future *net* revenues that are expected to be generated directly from such advertising. *Net revenues* are gross revenues less costs to be incurred in generating those revenues, excluding the amortization of advertising costs. Examples of costs to be included in making this evaluation are cost of goods sold, sales commissions, and payroll and payroll-related costs.

If the carrying amount of unamortized direct-response advertising exceeds probable future net revenues, the difference should be charged to advertising expense in the current period.

Illustration of Write-Off of Unamortized Advertising Costs

MMX Enterprises has $400,000 of unamortized direct-response advertising costs at December 31, 19X8; probable future net revenues are $300,000. This difference—$100,000—would be reported as advertising expense in 19X8.

Any later-period increase in probable future net revenue cannot be used to increase the carrying amount of the unamortized advertising costs (i.e., the write-down cannot be reversed on the basis of a subsequent increase in probable net revenues).

Miscellaneous Issues

Certain tangible assets (e.g., blimps and billboards) may be used in a number of different advertising campaigns. These tangible assets are to be capitalized and depreciated over their estimated useful lives. The related depreciation charge is a cost of advertising to the extent that the tangible asset was used for an advertising-related purpose.

Costs to produce film or audio, and video tape used to communicate advertising, do not constitute tangible assets under the provisions of SOP 93-7. Sales materials, such as brochures and catalogs, should be classified as prepaid supplies until they are no longer owned or expected to be used. At that point, the related cost would be considered a cost of advertising.

Disclosures

The notes to the financial statements should contain the following disclosures:

1. The accounting policy selected for non-direct-response advertising costs. The two choices are to (a) expense these costs as incurred or (b) expense them the first time the advertising takes place.
2. A description of the direct-response advertising reported as assets (if any), the related accounting policy, and the amortization period.
3. The total amount charged to advertising expense for each income statement presented, with a separate disclosure (if any) of amounts representing a write-down to net realizable value.
4. The total amount of advertising expenditures reported as an asset for each balance sheet presented.

Effect on Other Related Pronouncements

Statements of Position are considered a Level B pronouncement in the GAAP hierarchy, per SAS-69. Therefore, the following sections of Level A pronouncements addressing advertising expenditures take precedence over the conclusions expressed in SOP 93-7. These pronouncements and the relevant sections are as follows:

- APB-17 (Intangible Assets), paragraphs 24 and 28
- APB-28 (Interim Financial Reporting), paragraphs 15(a) and 16(d)

- FAS-91 (Accounting for Nonrefundable Fees and Costs Associated with Originating or Acquiring Loans and Initial Direct Costs of Leases), paragraphs 7 and 24
- FAS-51 (Financial Reporting by Cable Television Companies), paragraph 17 of Appendix A
- FAS-53 (Financial Reporting by Producers and Distributors of Motion Picture Films), paragraph 15
- FAS-60 (Accounting and Reporting by Insurance Enterprises), paragraph 29
- FAS-67 (Accounting for Costs and Initial Rental Operations of Real Estate Projects), paragraphs 19, 20, 21, and Appendix A, paragraph 28

PB-13: Direct-Response Advertising and Probable Future Benefits

BACKGROUND

Under the provisions of SOP 93-7 (Reporting on Advertising Costs), a direct-response advertisement must provide an entity with probable future economic benefits in order for the related advertising costs to be capitalized. In determining whether an advertisement provides an entity with probable future economic benefits, an entity estimates future revenues (derived from the advertisement) less costs incurred in generating those revenues. There has been diversity in practice as to which revenues are considered in making this determination.

Some entities have limited their consideration of future revenues to primary revenues, that is, revenues derived from sales to customers receiving and responding to the direct-response advertisement. Other entities have taken a more expansive view of the appropriate revenues to consider. These entities consider both primary and secondary revenues in evaluating whether the advertisement provides probable future economic benefits. Secondary revenues are revenues other than those derived from sales to customers receiving and responding to the direct-response advertisement. For example, revenues that publishers receive from subscriptions are considered primary revenues. Revenues resulting from advertisements placed in the magazine are secondary revenues.

STANDARDS

In determining probable future revenues, an entity should consider only primary revenues—revenues expected from customers receiving and responding to the direct-response advertisement. In addition, only primary revenues should be considered for purposes of amortizing direct-response advertising costs and for assessing realizability of these same costs.

CHAPTER 3
BALANCE SHEET CLASSIFICATION

CONTENTS

IMPRESS™ Cross-References	3.02
Overview	3.03
FTB 79-3: Subjective Acceleration Clauses in Long-Term Debt Agreements	3.04
Background	3.04
Standards	3.04
FTB 85-4: Accounting for Purchases of Life Insurance	3.04
Background	3.04
Standards	3.05

CROSS-REFERENCES

1999 MILLER GAAP GUIDE: Chapter 9, "Current Assets and Current Liabilities"

1999 MILLER GAAP IMPLEMENTATION MANUAL: EITF: Chapter 2, "Balance Sheet Classification"

1999 MILLER GOVERNMENTAL GAAP GUIDE: Chapter 13, "Assets"; Chapter 16, "Liabilities"

1999 MILLER GAAP FOR NOT-FOR-PROFIT ORGANIZATIONS: Chapter 2, "Overview of Current Pronouncements"

CHAPTER 3
BALANCE SHEET CLASSIFICATION

OVERVIEW

The balance sheet (i.e., statement of financial position) is presented in three major categories: assets, liabilities, and equity (stockholders' equity for the equity form of ownership). In a classified balance sheet, the distinction between current and noncurrent assets and liabilities is particularly important. There is considerable interest in the liquidity of the reporting enterprise, and the separate classification of current assets and liabilities is an important part of liquidity analysis.

GAAP concerning current assets and current liabilities are found in the following pronouncements that are included in the highest level of authority in the SAS-69 GAAP hierarchy:

ARB-43	Chapter 1A, Receivables from Officers, Employees, or Affiliated Companies
	Chapter 3A, Current Assets and Current Liabilities
APB-10	Omnibus Opinion—1966
FAS-6	Classification of Short-Term Obligations Expected to Be Refinanced
FAS-43	Accounting for Compensated Absences
FAS-78	Classification of Obligations That Are Callable by the Creditor
FIN-8	Classification of a Short-Term Obligation Repaid Prior to Being Replaced by a Long-Term Security
FIN-39	Offsetting of Amounts Related to Certain Contracts

The following additional sources of GAAP that are in lower levels of the SAS-69 GAAP hierarchy are discussed in this Manual:

FTB 79-3	Subjective Acceleration Clauses in Long-Term Debt Agreements (Level B)
FTB 85-4	Accounting for Purchases of Life Insurance (Level B)

FTB 79-3: Subjective Acceleration Clauses in Long-Term Debt Agreements

BACKGROUND

FAS-6 (Short-Term Obligations Expected to Be Refinanced) indicates that a subjective acceleration clause in a financing arrangement that would otherwise permit a short-term obligation to be refinanced on a long-term basis precludes that obligation from being classified as noncurrent. FAS-6 does not, however, address agreements other than those related to short-term obligations.

STANDARDS

Question: Should long-term debt be classified as a current liability if the long-term debt agreement includes a subjective acceleration clause?

Answer: The circumstances dictate the answer to this question. In some circumstances, such as recurring losses or liquidity problems, the long-term debt should be classified as current. Other situations, however, would require disclosure of only the acceleration clause. If the likelihood of the acceleration of the due date is considered remote, neither reclassification nor disclosure would be required.

FTB 85-4: Accounting for Purchases of Life Insurance

BACKGROUND

The premium paid by a purchaser of life insurance serves several purposes. Part of it pays the insurer for assumption of mortality risk and provides for recovery of the insurer's contract acquisition, initiation, and maintenance costs. Part of the premium contributes to the accumulated contract value. The relative amounts of premium payment credited to various contract attributes change over time as the age of the insured person increases and as earnings are credited to previously contracted values. An insurance contract is significantly different from other investment agreements. The various attributes of the policy could be obtained separately through term insurance and the purchase of separate investments, but the combination of benefits and contract values typically could not be acquired without the insurance contract.

STANDARDS

Question: How should an entity account for an investment in life insurance?

Answer: The amount that could be realized under the contract at the date of the financial statements (i.e., the contract's cash surrender value) should be reported as an asset. The change in that value during the period is an adjustment to the amount of premium paid in recognizing expense or income for that period.

CHAPTER 4
BANKRUPTCY AND REORGANIZATION

CONTENTS

IMPRESS™ Cross-References	4.02
Overview	4.03
SOP 90-7: Financial Reporting by Entities in Reorganization Under the Bankruptcy Code	4.04
Background	4.04
Standards	4.04
Legal Summary of the Reorganization Process	4.04
Accounting and Financial Aspects of the Reorganization Process	4.06
Illustration of Estimating Reorganization Value	4.06
Need for and Scope of SOP 90-7	4.07
Financial Reporting—Entity Operating Under Chapter 11 Protection	4.07
Balance Sheet Reporting	4.08
Illustration of Balance Sheet Presentation	4.08
Income Statement	4.10
Statement of Cash Flows	4.10
Other Issues	4.11
Fresh-Start Reporting—Emergence from Chapter 11	4.11
Implementing Fresh-Start Reporting	4.12
Transitioning to Fresh-Start Reporting	4.12
Disclosures Required by Fresh-Start Reporting	4.13
Other Issues	4.13
Illustration of Fresh-Start Reporting	4.14
SOP 92-3: Accounting for Foreclosed Assets	4.22
Background	4.22
Standards	4.22
Scope	4.22
Held-for-Sale Assumption	4.22
Foreclosed Assets Held for Sale	4.23

Illustration of Valuation of Foreclosed Assets	**4.24**
Other Issues	**4.24**
PB-11: Accounting for Preconfirmation Contingencies in Fresh-Start Reporting	**4.25**
Background	**4.25**
Standards	**4.25**

CROSS-REFERENCES

1999 MILLER GAAP IMPLEMENTATION MANUAL: Chapter 32, "Troubled Debt Restructuring"

1999 MILLER GAAP GUIDE: Chapter 48, "Troubled Debt Restructuring"

1999 MILLER GAAP IMPLEMENTATION MANUAL: EITF: Chapter 30, "Troubled Debt Restructuring"

CHAPTER 4
BANKRUPTCY AND REORGANIZATION

OVERVIEW

Before 1990, there was little authoritative accounting and reporting guidance for entities that were operating under Chapter 11 protection or that had recently reorganized under the provisions of the Federal Bankruptcy Code. As a result, great diversity in practice developed. The two Statements of Position and the one Practice Bulletin discussed in this chapter were issued to provide guidance to entities in bankruptcy that are attempting to reorganize under Chapter 11 of the Federal Bankruptcy Code and to provide guidance to those entities that have emerged from Chapter 11 protection with a confirmed reorganization plan. There are no Statements on bankruptcy and reorganization in Level A of the SAS-69 hierarchy.

The following pronouncements establish accounting and reporting standards for entities in bankruptcy or reorganization:

SOP 90-7   Financial Reporting by Entities in Reorganization Under the Bankruptcy Code (Level B)
SOP 92-3   Accounting for Foreclosed Assets (Level B)
PB-11   Accounting for Preconfirmation Contingencies in Fresh-Start Reporting (Level C)

These pronouncements discuss presentation in the balance sheet, income statement, and statement of cash flows. They require that liabilities on the balance sheet be segregated into prepetition liabilities subject to compromise, prepetition liabilities not subject to compromise (e.g., fully secured liabilities), and postpetition claims. The reporting of assets is not affected by these pronouncements. Items of revenue, expense, gain, or loss that occur because the entity is operating in reorganization proceedings are to be reported separately. In a similar fashion, cash flows from operating, investing, and financing activities that relate to the reorganization should be shown separately. The statement of cash flows is viewed as providing the most useful information for an entity operating under bankruptcy-law protection.

In many cases, entities emerging from Chapter 11 protection will implement fresh-start reporting. The adoption of fresh-start reporting gives rise to a new reporting entity, which has no retained earnings or deficit when it begins operations. Any deficit of the predecessor entity would be eliminated before the new entity begins operations. The detailed requirements for implementing fresh-start reporting are discussed in this chapter.

There is a rebuttable presumption that foreclosed assets are held for sale. Foreclosed assets held for sale are to be carried at the lower of (*a*) fair value less estimated costs to sell or (*b*) cost.

SOP 90-7: Financial Reporting by Entities in Reorganization Under the Bankruptcy Code

BACKGROUND

Entities experiencing severe financial distress may file for protection from creditors under Chapter 11 of the Bankruptcy Code. An entity filing for protection under Chapter 11 seeks to reorganize and to emerge from bankruptcy as a viable business. The primary objective of the reorganization is to maximize the recovery of creditors and shareholders by preserving the going concern value of the entity.

STANDARDS

Legal Summary of the Reorganization Process

To begin the process of bankruptcy reorganization, an entity would file a petition with the Bankruptcy Court, an adjunct of the United States District Courts. The entity filing the bankruptcy petition typically prepares a reorganization plan, which it submits to the Court for confirmation. This plan specifies the treatment of the entity's assets and liabilities, and it may result in debt being forgiven. For the reorganization plan to be confirmed, the consideration to be received by parties in interest under the plan must exceed what would be received if the entity liquidated under Chapter 7 of the Bankruptcy Code. In most cases, the debtor has the exclusive right to file a reorganization plan during the first 120 days after the bankruptcy filing (this right is lost if the Court appoints a trustee).

In general, the provisions of a confirmed reorganization plan bind all parties connected with the entity. This includes (1) the entity itself (i.e., the debtor), (2) any entity issuing securities under the plan, (3) any entity acquiring assets under the plan, and (4) any creditor, stockholder, or general partner of the debtor. This is the case regardless of whether the claim of any of these parties is impaired by the reorganization plan and irrespective of whether the party accepted the plan.

The requirements that must be met for the Bankruptcy Court to approve a reorganization plan include the following:

1. The technical requirements of the Bankruptcy Code have been met.
2. In soliciting acceptance of the plan, the entity has provided adequate disclosures.
3. A class of individuals whose claims are impaired might consent to the plan and yet have some individual members who dissent from this action. These dissenting members must receive at least as much under the plan as they would receive in a Chapter 7 liquidation.
4. Priority claims under the terms of the Bankruptcy Code will be paid in cash.
5. If the plan is confirmed, it is not likely to be followed by liquidation or further reorganization.
6. At least one class of impaired claims, not including insiders, has accepted the plan.
7. The plan proponent, typically the debtor, has obtained the consent of all parties with impaired claims or equity securities, or the plan proponent can comply with the "cram-down" provisions of the Bankruptcy Code. (This means that the plan can be forced on non-assenting creditors by the Court.) The Court can confirm a plan even if one or more parties with impaired claims or equity securities do not accept it. In order for the Court to confirm a plan under these circumstances, the plan cannot unfairly discriminate against a nonconsenting class impaired by the plan, and it must treat nonconsenting classes in a fair and equitable manner.
    a. A secured claim is treated in a fair and equitable manner if it remains adequately collateralized and if the present value of the payments it is to receive equals the amount of the secured claim when the plan becomes effective.
    b. An unsecured claim is treated in a fair and equitable manner if the discounted assets it is to receive equal the allowed amount of the claim or if any claim junior to it will not receive or retain any assets.
    c. An equity interest is treated in a fair and equitable manner if the discounted assets it is to receive equal the greatest of (1) any fixed liquidation preference, (2) any fixed redemption price, or (3) the value of such interest. Alternatively, the

equity interest is treated fairly and equitably if no junior equity security interest will receive or retain any assets under the plan.

Accounting and Financial Aspects of the Reorganization Process

A central feature of the reorganization plan is to determine the reorganization value of the entity that seeks to emerge from Bankruptcy Court protection. The reorganization value is designed to approximate the fair value of the entity's assets, and it should conform with the amount that a willing buyer would pay for these assets.

The reorganization value is generally determined through the following steps:

1. Consideration of the amount to be received for assets that will not be needed by the reconstituted business
2. Computation of the present value of cash flows that the reconstituted business is expected to generate for some period into the future
3. Computation of the terminal value of the reconstituted business at the end of the period for which future cash flows are estimated

---

Illustration of Estimating Reorganization Value

ERT, Inc., is a debtor-in-possession operating under the protection of Chapter 11 of the Bankruptcy Code. In order to prepare a reorganization plan, ERT needs to estimate its reorganization value. ERT has $150,000 of cash above its likely needs as an ongoing business. (It is not unusual for entities operating under Chapter 11 protection to accumulate excess cash; these entities do not pay most claims during the period of time they are operating under Chapter 11 protection.) Also, ERT is expected to generate $40,000 of net cash flows per month, each year, during the first five years after it emerges from Chapter 11. ERT's terminal value is estimated to be $1,910,456. ERT's reorganization value of approximately $2,816,667 represents the $150,000 of excess cash on hand, the present value of receiving $40,000 per month for the next five years ($1,575,211 discounted at 18%), and the terminal value of the enterprise.

After the entity's reorganization value is determined, it is allocated to parties in interest in accordance with their respective legal priorities. Secured claims have first priority, to the extent of the value of their collateral. Following secured claims are those claims specifically granted priority under the provisions of the Bankruptcy Code. Finally, distributions are made to various classes of unsecured debt and equity interests in accordance with their respective legal priorities, or otherwise as the parties may agree.

Before the reorganization plan is submitted to creditors, equity holders, etc., these groups are provided with a disclosure statement. The disclosure statement must be approved by the Court, and it should contain adequate information for interested parties to make an informed decision as to the appropriateness of the reorganization plan.

The disclosure statement typically contains (1) a description of the reorganization plan, (2) historical and prospective financial information, and (3) a pro forma balance sheet that presents the reorganization value and the capital structure of the new entity. A valuation of the emerging entity is not required for the disclosure statement to be approved by the Bankruptcy Court. Normally, however, such a valuation would be performed unless (1) the reorganization value of the emerging entity exceeds its liabilities or (2) holders of existing voting shares will own a majority of the emerging entity.

Need for and Scope of SOP 90-7

Before the issuance of SOP 90-7, there was no specific guidance for entities operating in reorganization proceedings. This led to wide diversity in practice.

SOP 90-7 applies to both (1) entities that are operating under Chapter 11 protection and that expect ultimately to emerge from such protection as a going concern and (2) entities that have emerged from Chapter 11 protection under a confirmed reorganization plan. It does not apply to (1) entities that restructure their debt outside of the Chapter 11 process, (2) entities that liquidate or that plan to do so, and (3) governmental entities.

Financial Reporting—Entity Operating Under Chapter 11 Protection

For the most part, filing for Chapter 11 protection does not change the application of generally accepted accounting principles. One difference is that transactions or events that are directly associated with the reorganization proceedings should be kept separate from ongoing operations.

Balance Sheet Reporting

Prepetition liabilities (i.e., liabilities incurred by the enterprise before the Chapter 11 filing) may be subject to compromise. A liability is compromised when it ultimately is settled for less than its allowed amount. The *allowed* amount is that which is permitted by the Bankruptcy Court, even though such liabilities may not be paid in full. Prepetition liabilities subject to compromise should be separated from prepetition liabilities not subject to compromise (e.g., fully secured liabilities) and from postpetition claims. These two latter amounts are combined and reported as one amount. All liabilities should be reported at the amount allowed by the Bankruptcy Court, even though they ultimately may be settled for less than the allowed amount.

Some secured liabilities may be undersecured. An undersecured liability exists when the fair value of the collateral may be less than the allowed liability. In this case, the entire liability should initially be classified as a prepetition claim subject to compromise. The liability would not be reclassified unless it became clear that the secured claim in question would not be compromised. Certain prepetition liabilities may not become known until after the bankruptcy petition is filed. These liabilities are to be reported at the expected amount of the allowed claims (per the framework of FAS-5 (Accounting for Contingencies)). If the existence of the liability is at least reasonably possible, this information should be disclosed in the notes to the financial statements even if the amount of the prepetition liability cannot be estimated.

In certain cases, the allowed amount of a prepetition liability may differ from its recorded amount. When this circumstance occurs, the carrying amount of the liability should be adjusted to the allowed amount. If unamortized debt discounts, premiums, or debt issue costs exist, these accounts are used in making the adjustment to record the liability at its allowed amount. Any resulting gain or loss is classified as a reorganization item and, as such, will be reported separately in the income statement.

Details of claims subject to compromise are to be reported in the financial statement notes. Finally, if a classified balance sheet is presented, claims not subject to compromise are to be categorized as current or noncurrent.

Illustration of Balance Sheet Presentation

Hale & Carter filed for protection from creditors under Chapter 11 of the Bankruptcy Code on February 15, 19X8. Its first set of annual financial statements prepared after this date is prepared on December 31, 19X8. The details of Hale & Carter's liabilities and stockholders' equity are as follows:

Prepetition liabilities subject to compromise

Secured debt, 12%, secured by a first mortgage on equipment (the fair value of the collateral is less than the claim)	$200,000
Senior subordinated secured notes, 16%	300,000
Subordinated debentures, 19%	200,000
Trade and other miscellaneous claims	100,000
Priority tax claims	50,000

Prepetition liabilities not subject to compromise

Secured debt, 11%, secured by a first mortgage on a building ($50,000 of principal due on 6/30/X9)	$700,000

Postpetition claims

Accounts payable—trade	$120,000
Short-term borrowings	180,000

Stockholders' equity

Preferred stock	$150,000
Common stock	100,000
Retained earnings (deficit)	(500,000)

In its December 31, 19X8, balance sheet Hale & Carter reports total assets of $1,600,000. (The presentation of the asset side of the balance sheet for an entity operating under Chapter 11 does not present any unique issues.) The right-hand side of Hale & Carter's balance sheet would look as follows:

Liabilities and Shareholders' Deficit

Liabilities Not Subject to Compromise	
Current liabilities:	
Short-term borrowings	$ 180,000
Accounts payable	120,000
Total current liabilities	$ 300,000
Noncurrent liabilities:	
11%, Long-term note (see Note xx)	$ 700,000
Liabilities Subject to Compromise	$ 850,000[a]
Total liabilities	$1,850,000
Shareholders' (deficit):	
Preferred stock	$ 150,000
Common stock	100,000
Retained earnings (deficit)	(500,000)
Total liabilities & shareholders' deficit	$ 1,600,000

(a) Liabilities subject to compromise consist of the following:

Secured debt, 12%, secured by a first mortgage on equipment (the fair value of the collateral is less than the claim)	$200,000
Senior subordinated secured notes, 16%	300,000
Subordinated debentures, 19%	200,000
Trade and other miscellaneous claims	100,000
Priority tax claims	50,000
	$850,000

Income Statement

Items of revenue, expense, gain, or loss that occur because the entity is operating in reorganization proceedings are to be reported separately. However, under the provisions of APB-30 (Reporting the Results of Operations), this requirement does not apply to an item required to be reported separately as a discontinued operation or as an extraordinary item.

SOP 90-7 specifically discusses the treatment of three items on the income statement. First, professional fees related to the reorganization are to be recognized as incurred and categorized as a reorganization expense. Before SOP 90-7 was issued, some entities would establish a liability for professional fees upon filing for bankruptcy; other entities capitalized these fees when incurred and ultimately offset them against debt discharge when the reorganization plan was confirmed. Neither of these treatments is now acceptable. Second, interest expense is *not* a reorganization item. It should be reported only to the extent that interest is paid during the reporting period or to the extent that it will be an allowed claim. In many cases, the interest expense reported will be significantly less than contractual interest. Any difference between reported interest expense and contractual interest is to be disclosed. SEC registrants must disclose this difference on the face of the income statement. Third, any interest income above that which would normally be earned on invested working capital is to be reported as a reorganization item. Entities operating under Chapter 11 protection often generate large amounts of interest income. The entity continues to generate cash flows from operations, and payments under many liabilities are stayed by the bankruptcy proceedings.

Statement of Cash Flows

SOP 90-7 states that the most beneficial information that can be provided for an entity operating under Chapter 11 protection is the information contained in the statement of cash flows. Cash flows from operating, investing, and financing activities that relate to the reorganization should be shown separately. This treatment is facilitated if the entity uses the direct method of preparing the statement. If the indirect method is used, a supplementary schedule (or a note) containing information on operating cash flows due to the reorganization proceedings must be provided.

Other Issues

A company presenting consolidated results may have one or more entities in reorganization proceedings. Assuming that this hypothetical company also has other entities that are not operating under Chapter 11 protection, condensed combined financial statements for the units operating under Chapter 11 must accompany the consolidated financial statements. Those units operating under Chapter 11 must present intercompany receivables and payables in the condensed combined financial statements. In addition, those entities that are not in reorganization proceedings must evaluate the propriety of reporting an intercompany receivable from a unit that is operating in Chapter 11.

In general, earnings per share for entities in reorganization are calculated in a manner similar to the calculation for any other entity. However, if it is probable that additional shares of stock or common stock equivalents will be issued under the reorganization plan, that fact should be disclosed.

Fresh-Start Reporting—Emergence from Chapter 11

For an entity emerging from Chapter 11 protection to employ fresh-start reporting, two conditions must exist. First, the value of the emerging entity's assets immediately before the reorganization plan is confirmed must be less than the amount of postpetition liabilities and prepetition allowed claims. Second, persons holding existing voting shares immediately before the reorganization plan is confirmed must receive less than 50% of the voting shares of the new entity. Note that the loss of control experienced by the former shareholders must be substantive and not temporary. Fresh-start reporting is to be applied as of the confirmation date, or at a later date when all material conditions precedent to the reorganization plan becoming binding has been resolved.

If an entity emerging from reorganization proceedings does not meet *both* of the criteria outlined in the previous paragraph, the entity is precluded from adopting fresh-start reporting. However, even in this case, the entity needs to ensure that (1) liabilities adjusted as a result of a confirmed reorganization plan are stated at present value and (2) any debt forgiveness received is reported as an extraordinary item.

Implementing Fresh-Start Reporting

In implementing fresh-start reporting, the reorganization value of the emerging entity is allocated among the tangible and specifically identifiable intangible assets of the entity (this process is similar to that used in recording a business combination using the purchase method—see APB-16 (Business Combinations). Any excess of reorganization value over that which can be assigned to tangible and specifically identifiable intangible assets is reported as *reorganization value in excess of amounts allocable to identifiable assets*. This intangible asset is to be allocated to expense in future years, per the provisions of APB-17 (Intangible Assets). In virtually all cases, this intangible asset would be amortized over a period substantially shorter than 40 years.

With the exception of deferred taxes, each liability of the emerging entity should be reported at the present value of the amounts to be paid (determined using current interest rates). Deferred income taxes are to be measured in conformity with GAAP.

Any tax benefits from preconfirmation net operating loss carryforwards are to be credited against the intangible asset account titled "reorganization value in excess of amounts allocable to identifiable assets." If any amount remains, any other intangible assets of the emerging entity are credited. If any tax benefits from preconfirmation net operating loss carryforwards remain after both of these steps are carried out, the remaining balance is credited to additional paid-in capital.

If any changes in accounting principles will be required within the first 12 months of the entity having adopted fresh-start reporting, such changes are to be implemented at the time fresh-start reporting is adopted.

Transitioning to Fresh-Start Reporting

Before the confirmation date of the reorganization plan, the accounting should follow that which is required when an entity is operating under Chapter 11 protection. Any adjustments to the recorded asset and liability amounts that result from the adoption of fresh-start reporting would be reported in the predecessor entity's final statement of operations. Also, the effects of debt forgiveness, which is to be shown as an extraordinary item, are to be reported in the predecessor entity's final statement of operations. The adoption of fresh-start reporting gives rise to a new reporting entity, which has no retained earnings nor deficit when it begins operations. Any deficit of the predecessor entity would be eliminated before the new entity begins operations.

Disclosures Required by Fresh-Start Reporting

A number of disclosures are required for entities that are exiting Chapter 11 proceedings and are adopting fresh-start reporting. These disclosures are as follows:

1. Adjustments to the historical amounts of assets and liabilities.
2. The amount of debt that has been forgiven.
3. The amount of prior retained earnings or deficit that is eliminated.
4. Significant matters in determining reorganization value. These include the following:
   a. The method or methods used to determine reorganization value. This includes disclosing information such as discount rates, tax rates, the number of years for which cash flows are projected, and the method of determining terminal value.
   b. Sensitive assumptions. These are assumptions made where there is a reasonable possibility of divergence from the assumption that could materially affect the estimate of reorganization value.
   c. Assumptions about anticipated conditions that are expected to be different from current conditions (unless these differences are already apparent).

Other Issues

Assume a calendar-year-end entity has its reorganization plan confirmed on June 30, 19X9, and that it adopts fresh-start reporting on July 1, 19X9. At December 31, 19X9, this new entity should *not* prepare comparative financial statements. The financial statements presented would be limited to capturing the activity of the new entity for the latter half of 19X9. The AcSEC believed that presenting comparative financial statements that straddle a confirmation date would be misleading; therefore, such statements should not be presented.

Illustration of Fresh-Start Reporting

Background

Edison, Inc., filed for protection from creditors under Chapter 11 of the Bankruptcy Code on March 1, 19X8. Edison's reorganization plan was confirmed by the applicable Bankruptcy Court on May 1, 19X9.

Reorganization Value

Edison's reorganization value immediately before the confirmation of the reorganization plan was as follows:

Cash in excess of normal operating requirements generated by operations	$ 85,000
Net realizable value expected from asset dispositions	130,000
Present value of discounted cash flows of the emerging entity	525,000[1]
Terminal value	1,250,000[2]
Reorganization value	$1,990,000

---

[1] The present value of discounting estimated yearly cash flows, $250,000, over the forecast period, 3 years, by the appropriate interest rate, 20%.

[2] Terminal value is determined via an independent business valuation.

Applicability of Fresh-Start Reporting

Holders of Edison's existing voting shares before the confirmation of the reorganization plan will receive less than 50% of the voting shares in the emerging entity (in fact, these former shareholders will have no interest in the new entity). This meets the first requirement for use of fresh-start reporting. The second requirement, that reorganization value must be less than total postpetition liabilities and allowed claims, is also met, as illustrated below:

Postpetition current liabilities	$ 400,000
Liabilities deferred pursuant to Chapter 11 proceeding	1,700,000
Total postpetition liabilities and allowed claims	$ 2,100,000
Reorganization value	(1,990,000)
Excess of liabilities over reorganization value	$ 110,000

Computing the Total Assets of the Emerging Entity

Total assets of the emerging entity are computed by subtracting assets that will be distributed before or simultaneously with the confirmation of the reorganization plan—in this case, the $85,000 of excess cash—from the new entity's reorganization value. Therefore, the total assets of Edison – New Entity at May 1, 19X9, are $1,905,000 ($1,990,000 – $85,000).

Beginning Capital Structure—Emerging Entity

After consideration of the emerging entity's debt capacity, projected earnings to fixed charges, earnings before interest and taxes to interest, free cash flow to interest, etc., the following capital structure for the new entity has been agreed upon:

Capital Structure for the Emerging Entity

Postpetition current liabilities	$ 400,000
IRS note	75,000
Senior debt	610,000[1]
Subordinated debt	420,000
Common stock	400,000

---

[1] $100,000 due each year for the next five years, at 14% interest; $110,000 due in the sixth year.

Distributions to Be Received by Parties in Interest

Secured Debt—The company's $600,000 of secured debt was exchanged for $85,000 in cash, $400,000 of new senior debt, and $115,000 of subordinated debt. The senior debt carries an interest rate of 14%, and principal payments of $65,574 are due during each of the next five years (the first payment is due on June 30, 19X9). The final payment of $72,130 is due in the sixth year.

Priority Tax Claims—Payroll and withholding taxes of $75,000 are payable in five equal annual installments, with the first payment due on May 31, 19X0. The annual interest rate is 11%.

Senior Debt—The company's $400,000 of senior debt was exchanged for $150,000 of new senior debt, $175,000 of subordinated debt, and 15% of the new issue of voting common stock. The senior debt carries an interest rate of 14%, and principal payments of $24,590 are due during each of the next five years (the first payment is due on June 30, 19X9). The final payment of $27,050 is due in the sixth year. Payments under the subordinated debentures are due in equal annual installments over seven years. The first payment is due September 30, 19X0, and the interest rate is 17%.

Trade and Other Claims—The holders of $200,000 of trade and other claims received the following for their stake: (a) $60,000 of senior debt, (b) $70,000 of subordinated debentures, and (c) 10% of the new issue of voting common stock. The senior debt carries an interest rate of 14%, and principal payments of $9,836 are due during each of the next five years (the first payment is due on June 30, 19X9). The final payment of $10,820 is due in the sixth year. Payments under the subordinated debentures are due in equal annual installments over seven years. The first payment is due September 30, 19X0, and the interest rate is 17%.

Subordinated Debentures—The company's $425,000 of subordinated debt was exchanged for $60,000 of new subordinated debentures and 75% of the new issue of voting common stock. Payments under the subordinated debentures are due in equal annual installments over seven years. The first payment is due September 30, 19X0, and the interest rate is 17%.

Common Stock—Edison had 200,000 shares of $1 par value common stock outstanding immediately before the confirmation of its reorganization plan. None of these stockholders will have any interest in the emerging entity. Four hundred thousand shares of new voting common stock, $1 par value, will be issued. These shares will be issued as follows: (a) 60,000 shares to holders of the former entity's senior debt, (b) 40,000 shares to holders of trade and other claims from the former entity, and (c) 300,000 shares to holders of the former entity's subordinated debentures.

Plan of Reorganization—Recovery Analysis

It is necessary to prepare a schedule detailing what the claims of the parties in interest are, and how and to what extent these claims are being satisfied. This schedule facilitates the preparation of the journal entries necessary to implement fresh-start reporting. This type of schedule is included either as a note to the financial statements or as supplementary information to the financial statements.

The following points should be noted about this schedule:

1. All of Edison's liabilities, both prepetition and postpetition, and shareholders' equity accounts are listed in column (a) of the table.
2. Column (b), elimination of debt and equity, represents the difference between the claim held (column (a) amount) and the consideration received for the claim (total recovery listed in column (j)).
3. Columns (c)–(g) represent the book value, which at the date of fresh-start reporting would also equal fair value, of the various items of consideration issued to settle the Chapter 11 claims (e.g., surviving debt, cash, new secured debt).
4. Column (h), common stock percentage, represents the percentage of the voting shares of the emerging entity issued to various parties.
5. Column (i), the value of the common stock issued, is computed by multiplying the net assets of the emerging entity by the percentage of voting shares of common stock received. For instance, the emerging capital structure for Edison will have only $400,000 of common stock (a deficit or retained earnings is always eliminated as part of the fresh-start process). Multiplying this amount by the percentage of common

stock received produces the common stock value. Also, although this is not the case for Edison, some entities will have a beginning balance in additional paid-in capital as a result of the fresh-start process.

6. Column (j), total recovery, represents the total of the various types of consideration received.
7. Column (k), total recovery percentage, is computed by dividing the total recovery amount (column (j)) by the amount of the claim.

Journal Entries—Needed to Implement Fresh-Start Reporting

Entry to record debt discharge:

Liabilities subject to compromise	$1,700,000	
Cash		$ 85,000
IRS note		75,000
Senior debt—current		100,000
Senior debt—long-term		510,000
Subordinated debt		420,000
Common stock—new		400,000
Extraordinary item—gain on debt discharge		110,000[1]

[1] The gain on debt discharge can be calculated as follows:

Using the recovery analysis schedule, column (b)—elimination of debt and equity, add the amounts in this column for liabilities that have been compromised. In the case of Edison, the $400,000 of senior debt was settled for $385,000, a $15,000 gain. In a similar fashion, there were $30,000 and $65,000 gains on the settlement of trade claims and subordinated debentures, respectively. The sum of these three amounts is $110,000.

Entry to retire Edison's (old) common stock:

Common stock—old	200,000	
Additional paid-in capital		200,000

Entry to record the adoption of fresh-start reporting and to eliminate the deficit in retained earnings:

Inventory	50,000 [1]	
Property, plant, and equipment	200,000 [1]	
Reorganization value in excess of amounts allocable to identifiable assets	375,000 [2]	
Gain on debt discharge	110,000 [3]	
Additional paid-in capital	200,000 [4]	
Goodwill		400,000 [2]
Deficit		535,000 [2]

4.18 *Bankruptcy and Reorganization*

EDISON, INC.
PLAN OF REORGANIZATION
RECOVERY ANALYSIS

	(a)	(b) Elimination of Debt and Equity	(c) Surviving Debt	(d) Cash	(e) IRS Note	(f) Senior Debt	(g) Sub-ordinated Debt	(h) Common Stock Percentage	(i) Common Stock Value	(j) Total Recovery	(k) Total Recovery Percentage
Postpetition liabilities	$ 400,000		$400,000							$ 400,000	100
Claim/Interest											
Secured debt	600,000			$85,000		$400,000	$115,000			600,000	100
Priority tax claim	75,000				$75,000					75,000	100
Senior debt	400,000	$ (15,000)				150,000	175,000	15%	$ 60,000	385,000	96
Trade and other claims	200,000	(30,000)				60,000	70,000	10%	40,000	170,000	85
Subordinated debentures	425,000	(65,000)					60,000	75%	300,000	360,000	85
	1,700,000	(110,000)									
Common shareholders	200,000	(200,000)								0	0
Deficit	(535,000)	535,000									
	$1,765,000	$225,000	$400,000	$85,000	$75,000	$610,000	$420,000	100%	$400,000	$1,990,000	

(1) The fair values of inventory and property, plant, and equipment immediately before the confirmation of Edison's reorganization plan have increased by $50,000 and $200,000, respectively. To implement fresh-start reporting, the recorded values of these assets are written up to their fair values. Note that the staff of the SEC, in their interpretation of *Financial Reporting Release* Section 210 (ASR 25), believes that the recognition of reorganization value in the balance sheet of an emerging entity that meets the criteria for fresh-start reporting should be limited to no net write-up of assets.

(2) To eliminate goodwill and the deficit of the predecessor entity and to record the excess of the emerging entity's reorganization value over amounts allocated to tangible and identified intangible assets. These amounts are obtained from the Balance Sheet Worksheet (see next page).

(3) This amount represents the difference between Edison's allowed liabilities of $2,100,000 (see column (a) of Edison's plan of reorganization—recovery analysis) and the amount paid to settle these same liabilities, $1,990,000 (see column (j) of Edison's plan of reorganization—recovery analysis).

(4) The entry to additional paid-in capital is used to balance the entry. In this case, it represents the book value of Edison's former stockholders that is being forfeited as part of the reorganization plan.

Balance Sheet Analysis—Needed to Implement Fresh-Start Reporting

The table that follows illustrates the implementation of Edison's reorganization plan and the preparation of Edison's initial balance sheet as a reorganized entity.

4.20 *Bankruptcy and Reorganization*

	Precon-firmation	Adjustments to Record Confirmation of Plan			Edison, Inc.'s Reorganized Balance Sheet
		Debt Discharge	Exchange of Stock	Fresh Start	
ASSETS					
Current Assets					
Cash	$ 120,000	$ (85,000)			$ 35,000
Receivables	250,000				250,000
Inventory	350,000			$ 50,000	400,000
Assets to be disposed of valued at market, which is lower than cost	30,000				30,000
Other current assets	15,000				15,000
Total current assets	$ 765,000	$ (85,000)		$ (50,000)	$ 730,000
Property, plant, and equipment	500,000			200,000	700,000
Assets to be disposed of valued at market, which is lower than cost	100,000				100,000
Goodwill	400,000			(400,000)	0
Reorganization value in excess of amounts allocable to identifiable assets				375,000	375,000
Total assets	$1,765,000	$ (85,000)		$ 225,000	$1,905,000
LIABILITIES AND SHAREHOLDERS' DEFICIT					
Current Liabilities Not Subject to Compromise					
Short-term borrowings	$ 250,000				$ 250,000
Current maturities of senior debt		$ 100,000			100,000
Accounts payable—trade	150,000				150,000
Total current liabilities	$ 400,000	$ 100,000			$ 500,000

Liabilities Subject to Compromise

Prepetition liabilities	1,700,000	(1,700,000)	0
IRS note		75,000	75,000
Senior debt, less current maturities		510,000	510,000
Subordinated debt		420,000	420,000
Total Liabilities	$2,100,000	$ (595,000)	$1,505,000
Shareholders' Deficit			
Common stock—old	200,000	(200,000)	-0-
Common stock—new		400,000	400,000
Additional paid-in capital		200,000	-0-
Retained earnings (deficit)	(535,000)	110,000	425,000[1]	-0-
Total liabilities in shareholders' deficit	$ (335,000)	$ 510,000	$ -0-	$ 225,000	$ 400,000
Total liabilities and shareholder's deficit	$1,765,000	$ (85,000)	$ -0-	$ 225,000	$1,905,000

[1] Represents the net effect of the elimination of the deficit in retained earnings, via a $535,000 credit to this account, and the debit to retained earnings to eliminate the $110,000 gain on debt discharge.

SOP 92-3: Accounting for Foreclosed Assets

BACKGROUND

Before the issuance of SOP 92-3, accounting by creditors for foreclosed assets—particularly accounting for foreclosed real estate assets—was diverse. This diversity was partly due to inconsistencies in the authoritative literature (e.g., AICPA Audit and Accounting Guides and Statements of Position) regarding the treatment of foreclosed assets. The AcSEC's primary objective in issuing SOP 92-3 was to reduce diversity in practice. In addition, the AcSEC wanted to eliminate the inconsistencies in the authoritative literature related to the treatment of foreclosed assets.

STANDARDS

Scope

SOP 92-3 addresses the balance sheet treatment of foreclosed assets after foreclosure. It does not provide guidance on how operating results related to these assets are to be treated in the income statement. *Foreclosed assets* are defined as all assets received in satisfaction of a receivable in a troubled debt restructuring. This includes both real and personal property; interests in other corporations, partnerships, and joint ventures; and interests in trusts.

SOP 92-3 applies to all reporting entities except those that account for assets at fair value (e.g., broker-dealers, futures commission merchants, and investment companies). It also applies to all assets received through foreclosure or repossession, except for the following: (1) inventories that are covered by Chapter 4 of ARB-43 (Restatement and Revision of Accounting Research Bulletins), (2) marketable securities that are covered by FAS-115 (Accounting for Certain Investments in Debt and Equity Securities), and (3) foreclosed real estate that was previously owned by the lender and that is accounted for under FAS-67 (Accounting for Costs and Initial Rental Operations of Real Estate Projects).

Held-for-Sale Assumption

The assumption of SOP 92-3 is that foreclosed assets are held for sale. This assumption conforms with the intent of most entities that receive foreclosed assets. In fact, some states require that assets received through foreclosure and repossession be sold. However, the held-for-sale assumption can be rebutted through a *preponderance of evidence*.

In order to rebut the held-for-sale assumption, the following three conditions must be met:

1. The intent of management is to hold the foreclosed asset for the production of income.
2. Management has the ability to hold the foreclosed asset for the production of income, and holding the asset is not prohibited by applicable laws and regulations (including the manner in which applicable laws and regulations are implemented by administrative bodies).
3. Management's intent is supported by the preponderance of evidence. The held-for-sale assumption is not necessarily rebutted just because management plans to hold and operate the foreclosed asset for a period of time before disposition. This is the case even if the holding period exceeds one year. To summarize, the length of the holding period of a foreclosed asset is not sufficient, in and of itself, to rebut the held-for-sale assumption.

Foreclosed Assets Held for Sale

Foreclosed assets held for sale should be carried at the lower of (*a*) fair value less estimated costs to sell or (*b*) cost. The *fair value* of the foreclosed asset is defined in SOP 92-3 as the amount that would be received in a sale between a willing buyer and a willing seller. In making this determination, the entity should first determine if there is an active secondary market for the foreclosed asset in question. If there is, the fair value of the foreclosed asset can be determined relatively directly. If no active secondary market for the foreclosed asset exists, the entity should look to prices in the secondary market for similar assets. These prices may be useful in estimating the fair value of the foreclosed asset. Finally, if no applicable secondary market exists, the entity should determine the fair value of the asset by discounting estimated cash flows from the foreclosed asset at an appropriate interest rate.

At the time of foreclosure, the cost of an asset is equal to its fair value. Therefore, since SOP 92-3 requires (held-for-sale) foreclosed assets to be carried at the lower of fair value less costs to sell or cost, and since cost at the date of foreclosure equals fair value, foreclosed assets will initially be carried at fair value less costs to sell. After the foreclosure date, the fair value of the foreclosed asset and its cost may diverge.

Illustration of Valuation of Foreclosed Assets

On April 1, 19X8, McBee Brothers LP repossesses a 15-acre tract of undeveloped land that it had sold and financed. Based on what other comparable properties are selling for, McBee estimates the fair value of this land to be $1,500,000. Selling costs are estimated at $150,000. On the foreclosure date, April 1, 19X8, the land would be recorded at the net amount of $1,350,000 (a $150,000 valuation allowance account would be offset against $1,500,000). On December 31, 19X8, the fair value of the land has risen to $2,000,000, and estimated selling costs are $200,000. Therefore, the land would be valued at $1,500,000 at December 31, 19X8 (the lower of the land's cost; its $1,500,000 fair value on the date of foreclosure; or its fair value less costs to sell, $1,800,000 ($2,000,000 − $200,000)). The $150,000 balance in the valuation allowance account established on April 1, 19X8, would be reversed, and the net effect of this series of transactions on the income statement would be zero.

The valuation of foreclosed assets should be determined on an individual asset basis. When fair value less costs to sell is less than cost, the foreclosed asset should be written down, via the use of a valuation allowance account, to this lower amount. Subsequent recoveries in the fair value of the foreclosed asset should be recognized, and any valuation allowance should be commensurately reduced. In no case should the valuation allowance be reduced below zero (i.e., a foreclosed asset cannot be carried at an amount greater than cost). Changes in the valuation allowance account are to flow through the income statement.

Other Issues

In many cases foreclosed assets will be subject to unpaid debt (both principal and accrued interest). Any such debt to which the foreclosed asset is subject at the time of foreclosure should be accrued as a liability. It is not acceptable to offset the amount of any such liability against the asset.

If the held-for-sale assumption is rebutted, the foreclosed asset is viewed as being held for the production of income. In this case, the foreclosed asset is to be reported and accounted for in the same way as if the asset had been acquired in some way other than foreclosure.

In some cases a foreclosed asset being treated as held-for-sale will be reclassified as being held for the production of income. If this is the case, the asset is to be reclassified from the held-for-sale category at the amount at which the asset would be recorded if it had been treated as an asset held for the production of income from the date of foreclosure. Any selling costs included in the valuation allowance account are to be reversed. The net effect of the reclassification should be reported in determining income from continuing operations in the period in which the decision not to sell the asset is made.

PB-11: Accounting for Preconfirmation Contingencies in Fresh-Start Reporting

BACKGROUND

SOP 90-7 (Financial Reporting by Entities in Reorganization Under the Bankruptcy Code) provides guidance for financial reporting by entities that file bankruptcy petitions and expect to reorganize as going concerns under Chapter 11 of Title 11 of the United States Code. SOP 90-7 does not provide specific guidance on accounting for contingencies existing at the date fresh-start reporting is adopted.

One alternative is to include the effects of adjusting or resolving these contingencies by including them in preconfirmation earnings. Others believe that accounting similar to that in FAS-38 (Accounting for Preacquisition Contingencies of Purchased Enterprises) should be applied. This could result in adjustments to reorganization value in excess of amounts allocable to identifiable assets.

STANDARDS

Certain contingencies that were not resolved during an entity's Chapter 11 proceedings may continue to exist at the confirmation date. Under SOP 90-7, for an entity that emerges from Chapter 11 reorganization and applies fresh-start reporting, *preconfirmation contingencies* are those contingencies that exist at the date of confirmation of the plan. A preconfirmation contingency can be a contingent asset, a contingent liability, or a contingent impairment of an asset.

Preconfirmation contingencies include uncertainties concerning the following:

- Amounts to be realized upon the disposition of assets designated for sale by the confirmed plan
- Nondischargeable claims (e.g., environmental issues)
- Claims that are disputed, unliquidated, or contingent and that are unresolved at confirmation

Preacquisition contingencies do not include the allocation of reorganization value to the entity's assets or deductible temporary differences or net operating loss and tax credit carryforwards that exist at confirmation.

After the entity adopts fresh-start reporting, adjustments that result from a preconfirmation contingency should be included in the determination of net income in the period in which the adjustment is determined. Such adjustments should be included in income or loss from continuing operations and separately disclosed.

CHAPTER 5
BUSINESS COMBINATIONS

CONTENTS

IMPRESS™ Cross-References	5.02
Overview	5.03
FTB 85-5: Issues Relating to Accounting for Business Combinations	5.04
Background	5.04
Standards	5.04
AIN-APB 16: Business Combinations: Accounting Interpretations of APB Opinion No. 16	5.06
Background	5.06
Standards	5.06
Illustration of Termination of Combination Plan	5.09
Illustration of Issuing Warrants in a Combination	5.10
Illustration of Combining Parts of a Single Business	5.17
Illustration of Combining Commonly Owned Separate Businesses	5.17
Illustration of the Impact of a Compensation Contract	5.20

CROSS-REFERENCES

1999 MILLER GAAP IMPLEMENTATION MANUAL: Chapter 13, "Intangible Assets"

1999 MILLER GAAP GUIDE: Chapter 3, "Business Combinations"

1999 MILLER GAAP IMPLEMENTATION MANUAL: EITF: Chapter 3, "Business Combinations"

1999 MILLER GAAP FOR NOT-FOR-PROFIT ORGANIZATIONS: Chapter 2, "Overview of Current Pronouncements"; Chapter 7, "Organizational Issues"

1999 MILLER GAAS GUIDE: Chapter 11, "Auditor's Reports"

CHAPTER 5
BUSINESS COMBINATIONS

OVERVIEW

A business combination occurs when two or more entities combine to form a single entity. An *asset combination* results when one company acquires the assets of one or more other companies, or when a new company is formed to acquire the assets of two or more existing companies. In an asset combination, the target companies cease to exist as operating entities and may be liquidated or become investment companies. An *acquisition of stock combination* occurs when one company acquires more than 50% of the outstanding voting common stock of one or more target companies, or when a new company is formed to acquire controlling interest in the outstanding voting common stock of two or more target companies.

There are two basic methods of accounting for the above types of business combinations: (1) the purchase method and (2) the pooling of interests method. The pooling method is required when certain criteria regarding the nature of the consideration given and the circumstances of the exchange are met. If the pooling criteria are not met, the purchase method of accounting must be used to record the combination.

In a purchase method combination, the combined entity reports the assets and liabilities of the target company at fair market value on the date of acquisition. Any excess of the fair market value of the consideration given over the fair market value of the net assets acquired is reported as goodwill. If the fair market value of the consideration given is less than the fair market value of the net assets acquired, the resulting negative goodwill is immediately written off against identifiable long-term assets before a deferred credit for negative goodwill is recorded. The operating statements for purchase method combinations report combined results only for the period subsequent to the combination.

In a pooling of interests combination, the combined entity reports the assets and liabilities of the target company at the book values previously reported by the combining entities. In a pooling transaction, only voting common stock may be given as consideration, and it is recorded in an amount equal to the net book value of the combined assets and liabilities; thus, no goodwill is recorded in a pooling transaction. The operating statements for pooling of interests combinations are combined for the full year in the year of the combination regardless of the specific date the pooling occurs. Comparative prior years' financial statements are restated retroactively to reflect the pooled status.

The following pronouncements are the sources of GAAP for business combinations that are included in the highest level of authority in the SAS-69 hierarchy:

APB-16	Business Combinations
APB-17	Intangible Assets
FAS-38	Accounting for Preacquisition Contingencies of Purchased Enterprises
FAS-72	Accounting for Certain Acquisitions of Banking or Thrift Institutions
FAS-79	Elimination of Certain Disclosures for Business Combinations by Nonpublic Enterprises
FIN-9	Applying APB Opinions No. 16 and 17 When a Savings and Loan Association or a Similar Institution Is Acquired in a Business Combination Accounted for by the Purchase Method

The following additional sources of GAAP that are in lower levels of the SAS-69 GAAP hierarchy are discussed in this Manual:

FTB 85-5	Issues Relating to Accounting for Business Combinations (Level B)
AIN-APB 16	Business Combinations: Accounting Interpretations of APB Opinion No. 16 (Level D)

FTB 85-5: Issues Relating to Accounting for Business Combinations

BACKGROUND

FTB 85-5 responds to five questions in specific areas related to business combinations in accordance with APB-16 (Business Combinations).

STANDARDS

Question 1: Are the costs incurred to close duplicate facilities of an acquiring company recognized as part of the costs of acquisition in a business combination that is accounted for by the equity method?

Answer: No. Only the direct costs of an acquisition are included in the cost of a purchased company. Expenses of closing duplicate facilities should be charged to expense in determining net income.

Question 2: How should a parent company account for minority interest in an exchange of stock between two of its subsidiaries if one or both of the subsidiaries are partially owned?

Answer: The proper accounting depends on whether the minority shareholders are party to the exchange of shares. If some or all of the shares owned by minority shareholders are exchanged for shares of ownership in another subsidiary of the parent, or in a new subsidiary that is formed by combining two or more subsidiaries of the parent, the transaction is accounted for by the parent as the acquisition of shares from the minority interest and is based on fair value. This accounting is based on the fact that the previous minority interest is purchased and a new minority interest is established in a different subsidiary. If the minority interest does not change, however, the transaction is not a purchase and should be accounted for based on existing carrying amounts rather than fair value.

Question 3: Are there circumstances in which an exchange of a partially owned subsidiary's common stock for the outstanding voting common stock of its parent (i.e., a downstream merger) can be accounted for as a pooling of interests?

Answer: No. This situation is specifically addressed in AIN-APB 16, Interpretation 26 (Acquisition of Minority Interest).

Question 4: Does the issuance of common shares that are identical to other outstanding common shares, except that the issuer retains a right of first refusal to repurchase the shares issued in certain specific circumstances, preclude the issuer from accounting for the combination as a pooling of interests?

Answer: Yes. APB-16, paragraph 47(b), states that the shares that are issued by a combining company to effect a business combination must have rights identical to those of the majority of its outstanding voting common stock in order for the business combination to qualify for accounting as a pooling of interests.

Question 5: Does the conversion of a mutual or cooperative enterprise to stock ownership within two years before a plan of combination is initiated, or between the dates a combination is initiated and consummated, preclude accounting for the combination as a pooling of interests?

Answer: No. The changes in the equity interests of the combining companies that are indicated in APB-16 for a business combination to qualify as a pooling of interests are those that might be used to circumvent the intent of APB-16—namely, that the combination is effected through an exchange of voting interests. In a conversion from mutual ownership to stock ownership, the change to stock ownership may be necessary to effect a combination, in which case it does not preclude the use of the pooling of interests method.

AIN-APB 16: Business Combinations: Accounting Interpretations of APB Opinion No. 16

BACKGROUND

AIN-APB 16 responds to 38 questions in specific areas related to business combinations in accordance with APB-16.

STANDARDS

Question 1: Per the terms of paragraph 46(a), does the announcement of a formula by which the ratio of exchange will be determined in the future constitute the initiation of a plan of combination?

Answer: Yes. The actual exchange ratio need not be known in order for a business combination to be initiated, as long as the exchange ratio is absolutely determinable by objective means in the future. The formula may permit lower and upper limits for the exchange ratio, and these limits may be adjusted based on appraisals, audits of financial statements, etc.

If a formula is used to initiate a business combination that is intended to be accounted for by the pooling of interests method, the terms of the exchange offer must be finalized within one year after the initiation date of the combination (under paragraph 47a of APB-16, the business combination must be consummated within one year after the initiation date in order to be accounted for as a pooling of interests).

Question 2: Under the terms of paragraph 46(a), if a corporation communicates in writing to its own stockholders that it plans a future exchange offer to another company, but it does not disclose the terms, does this communication constitute initiation of a business combination?

Answer: No. The above question refers to the initiation of a tender offer. In a tender offer, a plan is not initiated until the stockholders of the target company are made aware of the offer and its major terms, including the exchange ratio (or the formula for determining such).

Question 3: Under paragraph 46(b), in order to apply the pooling of interests method to their business combination, the combining companies are prohibited from owning 10% or more of the outstanding voting common stock of any combining company at either the initiation or the consummation date of the combination. Would an intercorporate investment of 10% or more between the initiation and consummation dates, but less than 10% on both the initiation and consummation dates, preclude the use of the pooling of interests method?

Answer: Yes. The pooling of interests method is precluded if a combining company owns 10% or more of the outstanding voting common stock of any company involved in the combination at any time from the initiation date through the consummation date. However, note that stock acquired after the initiation date in exchange for the voting common stock issued to effect the combination is not included in making this 10% computation.

Question 4: If certain conditions specified in paragraphs 46–48 of APB-16 are met, the business combination must be accounted for using the pooling of interests method. Among these conditions are quantitative measurements that are to be made on the consummation date of the transaction (pars. 46b and 47b). What is the consummation date for a business combination?

Answer: The consummation date is the date the combination is completed. This date occurs when assets are transferred to the issuing corporation. Physical transfer of stock certificates need not be accomplished by the consummation date; however, this transfer must be in process.

As a practical accommodation, paragraph 93 permits the combining parties to designate the end of an accounting period, falling between the initiation date and the consummation date, as the effective date of the combination. However, this substitute date cannot be used in lieu of the consummation date to determine whether the purchase method or the pooling of interests method is more appropriate for the combination. Therefore, using a date before the consummation date as the effective date for the combination implies that the entities anticipate accounting for the combination as a purchase. This is due to the fact that a combination accounted for as a pooling of interests must be recorded as of the consummation date.

Question 5: A business combination must be completed within one year from the initiation date in order to utilize the pooling of interests method. However, delays that are beyond the control of the combining parties can be used to extend this one-year time frame. If completion of a business combination is delayed beyond one year, how would the offering of new exchange terms during the delay period meet the condition of paragraph 47(a) for a business combination to utilize the pooling of interests method?

Answer: New terms may be offered beyond one year from the initiation date if (*a*) the delay is beyond the control of the combining parties and (*b*) earlier exchanges of stock are adjusted to the new terms. Per paragraph 47(a), the only delays permitted are proceedings of a governmental authority or litigation.

Question 6: Would the exchange of unrestricted voting common stock of the issuing corporation for the shares owned by a substantial common stockholder of a combining company whose stock was restricted as to voting or public sale invalidate the use of the pooling of interests method?

Answer: No. The exchange of *registered* voting common stock of the issuing corporation for *restricted* voting common stock of the combining corporation would not negate the use of the pooling of interests method. It is also acceptable to exchange unrestricted voting common stock for stock previously held in a voting trust.

Question 7: Business combinations initiated before November 1, 1970, could follow the provisions of either APB-16 or the applicable previous pronouncements. Must a business combination initiated before November 1, 1970, be completed within one year in order to be accounted for as a pooling of interests under the pre-APB-16 rules?

Answer: No. Any business combination initiated before November 1, 1970, need only be completed under the terms in effect as of October 31, 1970, in order to be accounted for under the pre-APB-16 rules. However, if the terms of the combination are changed after October 31, 1970, the provisions of APB-16 would now apply to the entire combination.

Question 8: Does APB-16 apply when one corporation acquires less than 90% of the voting common stock of another corporation?

Answer: Yes. An investment by a corporation in the voting common stock of another corporation must be accounted for as a purchase. In addition, subsequent acquisitions of stock in the same company are to be accounted for by the purchase method. Finally, acquisition of a minority interest remaining after an acquisition accounted for using the pooling of interests method (a 90% or greater acquisition) is to be handled using the purchase method of accounting.

Question 9: To meet the requirements for the pooling of interests method of accounting, each combining company must be autonomous for two years before the initiation of the combination, and each company must not have had a change in its equity interests during this time. Since APB-16 applies to combinations initiated after October 31, 1970, must these two conditions be met for a combination initiated in November 1970 in order to apply the pooling of interests method?

Answer: No. A change in the equity interest or a change in the autonomy of combining parties that occurred before November 1, 1970, would not preclude the use of the pooling of interests method.

Question 10: What is the effect of two parties terminating a plan of combination before it is approved by stockholders and subsequent resuming negotiations?

Answer: If negotiations are formally terminated after a plan has been initiated, the subsequent resumption of negotiations constitutes a new plan. This is the case even if the new plan is identical to the old plan. Any shares exchanged under the provisions of the old plan affect the new plan's conformity with the requirements of paragraphs 46(b) and 47(b) of APB-16. Paragraph 46(b) requires the combining companies to be independent of each other. No combining company can hold more than 10% of the outstanding voting common stock of another combining company. Paragraph 47(b) requires one of the combining companies to issue its voting common stock in exchange for at least 90% of another combining company's voting common stock that is outstanding on the date the combination is consummated.

Illustration of Termination of Combination Plan

ABC Co. announces a plan to merge with XYZ, Inc., on July 1, 19X8. ABC offers to acquire 100% of the outstanding shares of XYZ (500,000 shares outstanding) by issuing two of its shares for every share of XYZ tended. The initiation date of this proposed combination is July 1, 19X8. The planned merger between ABC and XYZ is terminated on August 1, 19X8. During July 80,000 shares of XYZ were tended to and acquired by ABC. On September 1, 19X8, these two entities announce that the merger is on again—under the same terms as announced on July 1, 19X8. The plan announced on September 1, 19X8, represents a new acquisition plan. Also, because ABC owns more than 10% of the outstanding voting stock of XYZ as of September 1, 19X8, this merger must be accounted for using the purchase method of accounting.

Question 11: In order to utilize the pooling of interests method, a corporation must issue common stock with rights that are identical to those of its existing common stock (par. 47b). Would restrictions on the sale of shares of common stock issued result in different rights for these shares?

Answer: It depends on the nature of the restriction on the sale of the common stock issued. In general, the "rights" referred to in paragraph 47(b) relate to the relationship between the shareholder and the corporation. A shareholder receiving new shares as a result of the combination must not be disadvantaged in regard to voting rights, dividends, or liquidation preference. A restriction on the sale of stock received in a business combination that results from government regulations would not indicate that the shares received were not identical to those already outstanding. However, in the absence of a governmental regulation pertaining to the sale of the stock, a prohibition on such sale would probably indicate that the newly issued shares were not identical to the shares already outstanding. In addition, if new shareholders can sell their shares to only the issuing corporation or an affiliate, this would constitute a *planned transaction*. Planned transactions are incompatible with the use of the pooling of interests method (par. 48a).

Question 12: May a business combination be accounted for by the pooling of interests method if the issuing corporation exchanges voting common stock and warrants for the voting common stock of a combining company?

Answer: No. In order to utilize the pooling of interests method, a corporation must issue only voting common stock for at least 90% of the common stock of another company. Therefore, a pro rata distribution of warrants of the issuing corporation to the stockholders of the combining corporation would not meet this condition, and the pooling method could not be used.

Warrants, cash, or debt may be used to acquire up to 10% of the common stock of a combining company. However, in this case, the other 90% of the combining company must be acquired through the issuer's use of its own common stock. It is also acceptable for the issuer to exchange warrants for the preferred stock or debt of the combining company.

Any warrants issued cannot provide for the purchase of a greater number of shares than could be obtained if the warrants were exercised.

Illustration of Issuing Warrants in a Combination

TMT Enterprises has announced a plan to merge with MOT, Inc. TMT plans to issue two shares of its common stock for each share of MOT received. MOT has warrants outstanding that allow the holder to convert the warrant for three of MOT's common shares. TMT plans to issue warrants in exchange for the outstanding MOT warrants. The warrants issued by TMT can be convertible for up to six shares of TMT (the equivalent number of shares of TMT that could be acquired if the original MOT warrants had been converted).

Finally, warrants issued by either company in contemplation of a merger may violate the prohibition against changes in the equity interests of the combining companies (par. 47c).

Question 13: In order to utilize the pooling of interests method, the issuer must issue common stock with rights identical to those of its outstanding voting common stock. Could the common stock issued be designated as a class of stock different from the majority class (e.g., Class B if the majority class is designated Class A) and still meet this condition?

Answer: There is no prohibition against designating the stock issued differently from the stock already outstanding. However, the rights of the newly issued stock must be identical to those of the existing voting common stock. Therefore, simply giving the newly issued common stock a different name does not appear to serve any useful purpose. In addition, such a designation may arouse suspicion that the parties have secretly agreed to change the rights of the newly issued shares in the future.

Question 14: Can a corporation issue some maximum number of shares to stockholders of the combining company under an agreement that part of the shares would be returned if future earnings are below a certain amount or the future market price of the stock is above a stipulated price and still use the pooling of interests method?

Answer: No. Contingent shares based on earnings, stock prices, etc., require the combination to be accounted for as a purchase. The only contingent arrangements compatible with a pooling involve (*a*) settlement of a contingency that existed at the time of consummation and (*b*) audits of "open" income tax returns.

Question 15: To allow for intercorporate investments that existed at October 31, 1970, paragraph 99 discusses how certain combinations are *part-purchase, part-pooling*. Is the application of paragraph 99 mandatory for a business combination meeting the conditions of that paragraph?

Answer: No. The accounting treatment discussed in paragraph 99—part-purchase, part-pooling—is an election available to the issuing corporation because of intercorporate investments held at October 31, 1970.

Question 16: How do sales of investments in another corporation's voting common stock owned at October 31, 1970, and acquisitions of additional investments of the same class of stock after that date affect computations that are made under the grandfather clause (i.e., part-purchase, part-pooling) in paragraph 99?

Answer: Sales after October 31, 1970, of investments in another corporation's voting common stock that was owned at that date are always considered as reductions of the common stock to which the grandfather clause in paragraph 99 applies (FIFO basis).

Question 17: Does paragraph 99 also apply to the issuing company's stock that is owned by the other combining company on October 31, 1970?

Answer: Yes. The grandfather clause of paragraph 99 was designed to apply to all intercorporate investments (both of the issuing company and of the combining company) owned as of October 31, 1970. Stock of the issuing company held by the combining company on October 31, 1970, can essentially be ignored in determining whether the combination can be treated as a pooling.

Question 18: Paragraph 46(a) states that a wholly owned subsidiary may distribute voting common stock of its parent to effect a combination that can be accounted for as a pooling if its parent would have met the pooling criteria had the parent consummated the combination. If a parent company owns substantially all of the outstanding voting stock of a subsidiary, will the subsidiary be considered wholly owned for purposes of applying paragraph 46(a)?

Answer: Yes. A subsidiary is considered wholly owned under paragraph 46(a) if the parent owns substantially all of the subsidiary's outstanding voting stock. In most cases, it is expected that the parent would own all but an insignificant number of the subsidiary's shares. For example, some state laws require a certain number of directors to own some of the corporation's shares. This is one reason why the parent may not own 100% of the subsidiary's shares. In other cases, the parent might not be able to locate all of the subsidiary's shareholders, or some shareholders of the subsidiary may not be willing to sell at a reasonable price. However, in no case can the parent own less than 90% of the subsidiary and yet be considered to own substantially all of that entity. In most cases, the percentage of the subsidiary owned by the parent would be expected to be much higher than 90%.

In addition, the reason why the subsidiary rather than the parent is making the acquisition has some bearing on evaluating whether substantially all of the subsidiary is owned by the parent. For example, if the acquisition is equally feasible for either the parent or the subsidiary, the parent should own all but a very limited number of shares. However, if only the subsidiary can make the acquisition (e.g., both the subsidiary and the target company are licensed to operate in a particular state; the parent is not), the parent can own less of the subsidiary and still be viewed as having substantial ownership (in no case can the parent own less than 90%).

Question 19: Paragraph 47(b) states that the issuing company may exchange only voting common stock for outstanding equity and debt securities of the other combining company that have been issued in exchange for voting common stock of that company (the combining company) during a period beginning two years before the date a pooling combination is initiated. What is the purpose of this provision?

Answer: A business combination cannot be accounted for as a pooling if any equity or debt securities are issued in exchange for or to retire voting common stock, by either combining company, within two years before the initiation date of the combination or between the initiation and consummation dates. The issuing corporation may be able to cure this pooling violation by issuing its voting common stock to the holders of the equity or debt securities of the other combining company in exactly the same ratio as their former holdings of voting common stock in the other combining company. The objective is to restore the holders of these securities in the combining company to their former position.

Question 20: For what purposes may treasury stock be reacquired during the two years before the initiation of a combination, or between initiation and consummation?

Answer: Purchases of treasury stock for specific purposes that are not undertaken to effect an acquisition to be accounted for as a pooling are not prohibited. However, in the absence of persuasive evidence to the contrary, it is assumed that all acquisitions of treasury stock during this period are for the purpose of effecting a business combination to be accounted for as a pooling.

Specific reasons why treasury shares might be reacquired before the consummation of a pooling include (a) that shares are granted under stock option or compensation plans and (b) that stock dividends are declared. Also, treasury shares may be reacquired to resolve an existing contingent share agreement under a prior business combination. Treasury shares reacquired for these purposes should be reissued before the consummation of the combination, or they should be specifically reserved for these purposes.

What if treasury shares reacquired within the period two years before the initiation of the consummation plan, or between initiation and consummation, are not reissued or specifically reserved? An equivalent number of treasury shares can be sold before consummation of the combination to cure this violation of the pooling requirements.

If the number of treasury shares not reissued or reserved before consummation (referred to as "tainted shares") are material in relation to the number of shares to be issued to effect the combination, the combination should be accounted for as a purchase. However, if the number of tainted shares is not material in relation to the number of shares to be issued to effect the combination, these tainted treasury shares can be issued to effect the combination. These shares should first be accounted for as though retired.

Question 21: In order to account for a business combination using the pooling of interests method, the combining company is not permitted to agree to either directly or indirectly retire or reacquire the shares used to effect the combination (par. 48a). Also, in order to utilize the pooling method, the combined corporation is not permitted to enter into financial arrangements for the benefit of former stockholders. Would an arrangement whereby a third party buys all or part of the voting common stock issued to stockholders of a combining company immediately after consummation of a business combination cause a combination to not meet these conditions?

Answer: No. The central issue is whether the voting common stock that was issued to effect the combination continues to be held by individuals and/or entities different from the combining companies. There can be no provision for any of the combining companies to bail out former stockholders or to induce another party to do so. However, it is permissible for one or more of the combining companies to help former stockholders find an unrelated buyer for their shares.

Question 22: In order for a business combination to be accounted for using the pooling of interests method, significant asset disposals by the combined companies are prohibited for two years after the consummation of the combination (asset sales in the ordinary course of business and to dispose of duplicate facilities are permitted) (par. 48c). In addition, changes in the equity interests of voting common stock (e.g., a spin-off of a division or a subsidiary) are prohibited within two years before the initiation of a combination, or between the initiation and consummation dates. Does a prior or planned disposition of a significant part of the assets of a combining company to comply with an order of a governmental authority or judicial body constitute a violation of this condition?

Answer: No. A disposition of a significant part of the assets of a combining company does not invalidate use of the pooling method if the disposition is undertaken to comply with the terms of an order issued by a governmental authority or judicial body. Such a disposition is also acceptable to comply with an order that is likely to be issued, based on all available evidence.

Any material gain or loss resulting from such a disposition that occurs within two years of the consummation date of the combination is to be accounted for as an extraordinary item (and reported net of tax on the face of the income statement).

Question 23: A business combination recorded using the pooling of interests method is to be recorded as of the date the combination is consummated. In some cases a business combination, accounted for as a pooling, will be consummated between the date of the financial statements and the date of the auditor's report. In this case, the combining company is precluded from retroactively reflecting the effects of the combination in the financial statements for the year under audit. However, the entity is required to disclose, as supplemental information, the nature of the combination and its effects on financial position and results of operations. Could this disclosure be in the form of a statement with side-by-side columns reporting financial data for (a) the issuing corporation, (b) the combined corporations, and, perhaps, (c) the other combining company?

Answer: Yes. For handling the disclosure requirement for a combination accounted for as a pooling that occurs between the balance sheet date and the date of the auditor's report, a side-by-side columnar format approach is permitted. However, the columns presenting information for the issuing corporation must be designated as primary; columns for the combined entity and for the other combining company must be designated as supplemental information.

This side-by-side columnar presentation presents more information than is required. The required disclosures are the effects on revenue, net income, earnings per share, and accounting policies as a result of the combination.

The auditor should be aware that these supplemental disclosures are considered part of the financial statements. The auditor's opinion, unless appropriately modified, would encompass supplemental disclosures on the effect of a combination consummated between the balance sheet date and the audit report date. If the auditor has not examined this supplemental information, the auditor's opinion would normally be modified.

Question 24: A combination cannot be accounted for as a pooling of interests if it involves a subsidiary. However, certain subsidiaries with significant minority-interest stockholders may have been contemplating a pooling transaction on October 31, 1970. APB-16 was not intended to be retroactive. Are subsidiaries with significant minority-interest stockholders as of October 31, 1970, precluded from accounting for a combination as a pooling?

Answer: No. If the subsidiary had a significant outstanding minority interest at October 31, 1970 (20% or more owned by persons not affiliated with the parent company), the subsidiary may utilize the pooling method, provided the significant minority interest also exists at the initiation of the consummation. This grandfathering does not permit a pooling between a parent and its subsidiary.

Question 25: In order to utilize the pooling of interests method, the issuing corporation must issue its voting common stock for at least 90% of the voting common stock of the combining company. Assuming the issuing corporation exchanges common stock for at least 90% of the common stock of the combining company, may individual common stockholders of the combining company exchange some of their shares for shares of the issuing corporation and either retain the balance of their shares or sell the shares to the issuing corporation for cash?

Answer: No. In order to treat the combination as a pooling, individual common shareholders of the combining company must exchange all of their shares for shares of the issuing company or exchange none of their shares. There can be no partial exchange of shares, with the remaining shares either retained or sold for cash. However, shareholders of the combining company can receive cash in lieu of fractional shares in the issuing company.

Question 26: How should a corporation account for the acquisition of all or part of the minority interest of a subsidiary?

Answer: The acquisition of all or part of the minority interest of a subsidiary should be accounted for as a purchase. This treatment is the same whether the acquisition is by the parent itself, by the subsidiary, or by another affiliate of the parent.

In general, pooling is precluded when the combining companies hold as intercorporate investments more than 10% of the outstanding voting common stock of any combining company (see Question 15 for an exception to this general rule).

Pooling is precluded in the exchange of a subsidiary's common stock for the outstanding voting common stock of its parent. This type of transaction should be accounted for as a purchase, as if the parent had exchanged its common stock for the common stock held by minority shareholders of its subsidiary.

Question 27: In general, the provisions of APB-16 should be applied to combinations involving one or more unincorporated businesses. Each of the combining parties must be autonomous in order to use the pooling method. How does APB-16 apply to a combination involving one entity controlled by one or a few individuals who control several other entities?

Answer: First, a business combination accounted for under the terms of APB-16 can encompass a proprietorship or a partnership. Second, considerable judgment is typically necessary when a combination involves one (or more) of several companies under common control.

For example, if one individual owns two separate businesses organized as corporations, the individual owner is technically the parent and has two separate subsidiaries. In reality, the relationship between the two separate businesses is the more important issue. It is not acceptable to fragment a similar business and to account for the resultant combination as a pooling.

Illustration of Combining Parts of a Single Business

Howard Varny owns 100% of two separate unincorporated businesses. Mr. Varny owns two automobile dealerships in California: one in Long Beach, the other in Pasadena. Mr. Varny is planning to merge his Pasadena dealership with another dealership located in Century City. This combination cannot be accounted for as a pooling of interests, because the two automobile dealerships Mr. Varny owns are part of a single kind of business. The two separate legal organizations that Mr. Varny has created are ignored, and paragraph 46(a) precludes fragmenting a business and pooling only part of that business.

Illustration of Combining Commonly Owned Separate Businesses

Dawn Russell owns 100% of two unincorporated businesses. Ms. Russell owns a used car dealership and a new boat dealership. Both entities are located in Jonesboro, Georgia. Ms. Russell is planning to merge her boat dealership with another boat dealership located in Griffin, Georgia. Assuming the other requirements for pooling accounting are met, this proposed combination would not run afoul of the pooling guidelines, because Ms. Russell is operating two unrelated businesses.

In a combination, the two or more businesses owned by a single individual must be accounted for using the same method. For example, if Ms. Russell plans to combine her used auto dealership and her boat dealership with another, unrelated company, both combinations must be accounted for using the same accounting method (i.e., one combination could not be accounted for as a purchase, the other as a pooling).

In general, the guidelines discussed above apply to a business with a few owners rather than with just one owner.

Question 28: In some cases a single individual may control other corporations through a personal holding company, a form of ownership that may be employed for federal income tax purposes. The pooling requirements mandate that each company to a combination be autonomous. A pooling is not permitted if a party to the combination has been a subsidiary or a division of another entity during the past two years. Does this preclude a pooling by a corporation that is controlled by a personal holding company?

Answer: Not necessarily. In some cases, the legal form may be ignored if the combination involves a subsidiary of a personal holding company. A personal holding company may be a device established purely for federal income tax purposes. The reality may be that the various subsidiaries are operated by the owners as if the holding company does not exist. If this is the case, the personal holding company may be disregarded and the various subsidiaries considered autonomous for purposes of applying the pooling of interests criteria.

Question 29: If the shareholders of a closely held company grant another company an option to exchange substantially all of their shares at a future date, does this constitute the initiation of a business combination?

Answer: It depends. If the option requires either unilateral performance by either party or bilateral performance, the initiation date of the combination is the date the option is granted. For example, if one party is required to issue its shares upon the tender of shares by stockholders in the other entity, a unilateral performance requirement exists. In order for the combination to be accounted for as a pooling, the option must be exercised within one year from the initiation date (and the combination must be consummated during this time).

An agreement that grants an entity the right of first refusal does not constitute initiation of a combination. For example, an entity may have been granted the right to negotiate with the stockholders of a closely held company if the closely held company considers entering into a combination in the future. Such an option right does not represent the initiation of a combination.

If the right of first refusal discussed in the preceding paragraph is acquired through a cash payment made by the entity acquiring this right, this type of payment is inconsistent with accounting for a subsequent combination as a pooling. However, individual shareholders may pay cash for the right of first refusal without prejudicing any future combination from pooling treatment, as long as the entity's resources are not directly or indirectly involved.

Question 30: In order for a combination to be accounted for as a pooling, there can be no provision to issue additional shares of stock or other consideration at a later date. There also can be no escrowing of shares until a contingency is resolved. However, upon the resolution of a contingency it is permissible to revise the number of shares issued in a combination for an amount different from that recorded by the combining company. May an issuing company reserve or escrow some shares against the representations of the management of a combining company in a pooling?

Answer: A contingency agreement that is not prohibited in a pooling may be handled in a number of ways. These include (*a*) the reservation by the issuing company of a portion of the shares being issued, (*b*) the issuance of additional shares, (*c*) the return of shares already issued, and (*d*) the holding of shares by an escrow agent (with these shares to be distributed to the former shareholders of the issuing and combining companies depending upon the resolution of the contingency). For the combination to meet the pooling requirements, any shares held by an escrow agent until the contingency is resolved must be subject to the voting control of the combining company's shareholders. However, it is acceptable to specify that any dividends on these contingent shares are to "follow" the shares when the contingency is resolved.

The most common type of a contingency that does not run afoul of the pooling rules is a contingency for "general management representations." Most combinations are structured to address the possibility that representations made by management of the combining company may not be accurate. These representations include (*a*) the nature and value of assets and (*b*) the completeness and valuation of liabilities. The contingency typically permits for a small adjustment in the total number of shares issued by the issuing company (typically around 10%) for discrepancies in the representations made by management of the combining company.

A contingency for general management representations must be limited to a reasonable period of time in order to be acceptable. This period gives the management of the issuing company an opportunity to verify the veracity of the representations made by the combining company. In most cases, this reasonable period would be a few months from the date the combination is consummated. In no case can a general management representation contingency extend beyond the date of the first audit report on the combined entity's financial statements. An undue delay in resolving a general management representation contingency may indicate that, in reality, what exists is an earnings contingency agreement. An earnings contingency would invalidate the use of the pooling method to record the combination.

There are certain types of contingencies (not general management representations) that cannot be determined for even up to a few years after the consummation of a combination. These types of contingencies are acceptable, and they do not preclude the use of the pooling of interests method.

Any adjustment in the number of shares issued as the result of resolving either a general or a specific contingency is recorded as an adjustment to stockholders' equity of the combined entity. The effect of the resolution of a contingency involving either an asset or a liability is reflected currently in net income or as a prior-period adjustment.

Question 31: In order for a combination to be accounted for as a pooling, there can be no provision to issue additional shares of stock or other consideration at a later date to former shareholders of the combining company. Would the granting of an employment contract or a deferred compensation plan by the combined corporation to former stockholders of a combining company cause this condition not to be met?

Answer: Not necessarily. An employment contract and/or deferred compensation plan that is reasonable and that is restricted to continuing management personnel would not preclude the use of the pooling method of accounting. Conversely, employment contracts granted to stockholders of the combining company with no expectation of future service would most likely represent a veiled attempt to provide these individuals with a contingent payment. Consulting contracts with former stockholders that lack substance (i.e., no work is required, or the former stockholder is not a qualified consultant) would also run afoul of the pooling rules.

Illustration of the Impact of a Compensation Contract

FRG Enterprises has entered into a business combination with Schultz Enterprises. The entities plan to account for this combination using the pooling method. The initiation date of the combination is July 1, 19X8, and the combination is consummated on October 1, 19X8. During this three-month interval, management of Schultz Enterprises enters into a consulting agreement with a stockholder, Mr. Izzie, who owns 20% of Schultz's outstanding voting common stock. The terms of the consulting agreement call for Mr. Izzie to receive $100,000 from Schultz Enterprises, or any successor corporation, for a period of 10 years. Mr. Izzie is 62 years old. He has had no experience in managing Schultz, no prior experience in Schultz's industry, and no substantive business expertise (he received his shares through an inheritance). This consulting agreement would preclude the use of the pooling method to account for the combination between FRG Enterprises and Schultz. The consulting contract with Mr. Izzie lacks substance; it represents nothing more than an attempt to provide Mr. Izzie with additional consideration from the forthcoming merger. APB-16 precludes a combining company from entering into a contingency-type compensation agreement in contemplation of the combination if a similar agreement entered into by the issuing company would preclude the use of the pooling method.

Question 32: In order for a combination to be accounted for as a pooling, there can be no provision to issue additional shares of stock or other consideration at a later date to former shareholders of the combining company. Would this condition be violated if the combined corporation granted stock options to stockholders of the combining company?

Answer: Not necessarily. Former stockholders of the combining company who are employees or directors of the combined entity may participate in a general stock option plan adopted by the combined entity. However, in some cases, the specific facts may indicate that the option plan represents nothing more than a way to transfer to former stockholders of the combining company an option to buy additional shares of stock at a low cost. This type of stock option plan would preclude the use of the pooling method. In addition, a similar stock option plan adopted by the combining company in contemplation of the combination would preclude the use of the pooling method.

Question 33: A corporation maintains a department to search for and evaluate potential acquisition candidates. The cost records of this department are excellent, and each acquisition investigation is costed separately (i.e., a job order costing approach). What is the appropriate accounting for these types of costs?

Answer: All internal costs associated with acquisitions, whether the acquisition is accounted for as a purchase or as a pooling, are deducted as incurred in determining net income.

Direct acquisition costs associated with an acquisition accounted for as a purchase are added to the acquisition price. However, these direct acquisition costs are incremental, out-of-pocket costs, not internal costs. Examples of direct acquisition costs include finder's fees and legal and accounting fees. Both direct acquisition costs and internal costs related to a pooling are charged to expense as incurred.

Question 34: Can a combination that requires shareholders to sell some of their stock after the combination is consummated be accounted for as a pooling?

Answer: No. Any requirement imposed on shareholders to either sell or not sell shares received in a combination is contrary to the pooling concept.

Question 35: How should a corporation account for the costs of registering previously unregistered equity securities that are to be issued in a combination? The registration of these securities will not occur until after the securities are issued.

Answer: A publicly held company issuing unregistered securities, which will be subsequently registered, should credit its equity accounts at the fair value of the securities less the future registration costs. The present value of the estimated registration costs should be recorded as a liability on the date of acquisition, with the offsetting debit typically to goodwill. Any difference between the actual registration costs and the estimated costs at the time the liability was initially recorded, plus accrued interest, would be recorded as an adjustment to goodwill.

It is not unusual to plan to register the unregistered securities as part of a future offering of other securities. In such a case, only the incremental cost of registering the equity securities issued in the acquisition would be accrued as a liability.

Question 36: Company A offers to exchange its voting common stock for 100% of the voting common stock of Company B on a one-for-one basis. This offer is announced on January 1, 19X8 (i.e., the initiation date). On that date, Company C owned 30% of the outstanding voting common stock of Company B. On April 1, 19X8, Company C acquired the 70% of Company B that it did not already own. November 1, 19X8, Company C tended all of the shares of Company B to Company A. APB-16 requires that both companies to a combination be independent for two years before the initiation date to qualify for pooling treatment. Company B was independent on the initiation date of the combination; however, it became a subsidiary of Company C between the initiation date and the consummation date. Does the fact that Company B became a wholly owned subsidiary of Company C following initiation of the combination by Company A preclude use of the pooling method?

Answer: Yes. The effect of what has happened here is that Company C has sold its wholly owned subsidiary to Company A. The only way in which a wholly owned subsidiary can use the pooling method is by distributing the stock of its parent company.

Although APB-16 refers to being independent during the two years before the initiation date of the combination, the intent is that the combining company has not been a subsidiary during the period beginning two years before the initiation date and ending on the consummation date.

Question 37: In a combination accounted for as a pooling, it is acceptable for former shareholders of the combining company to sell shares received in the business combination. The combined entity may even help these former shareholders locate an unrelated buyer for their shares (see Question 21). Would the accounting for a combination be affected by the fact that its consummation is contingent upon a third party or parties purchasing all or part of the voting common stock to be issued in the combination?

Answer: Yes. Any business combination that is contingent upon the subsequent sale of shares received in effecting the combination cannot be accounted for as a pooling.

Question 38: How does APB-16 apply when more than two companies are involved in a single business combination?

Answer: A business combination that is dependent on more than two companies agreeing to the terms of the combination is deemed a single combination. In order for the combination to be accounted for as a pooling, each company to the combination must meet all 12 of the pooling criteria (specified in pars. 46–48 of APB-16). If any one company to the combination fails to meet one of the pooling criteria, the entire combination must be accounted for as a purchase.

It is possible for an entity to be involved in multiple, unrelated business combinations at the same time. Different accounting methods can be used to record these unrelated business combinations.

Question 39: APB-16 does not apply to a transfer of net assets or to an exchange of sales of entities under common control. What are some examples of the types of transactions excluded from APB-16 by this provision, and what accounting should be applied?

Answer: In general, transfers or exchanges that do not involve outsiders are not subject to the provisions of APB-16. Examples include the following:

1. A parent may transfer the net assets of a wholly owned subsidiary and liquidate the subsidiary.

2. A parent may transfer its interest in several partially owned subsidiaries to a new wholly owned subsidiary.

3. A parent may transfer its ownership or the net assets of a wholly owned subsidiary for additional shares issued by a partially owned subsidiary of the parent.

All of these transactions would be accounted for at historical cost, in a manner similar to a pooling of interests.

Purchase accounting must be used when the effect of a transaction is to acquire shares from a minority shareholder in a subsidiary (see Question 26).

CHAPTER 6
CHANGING PRICES

CONTENTS

IMPRESS™ Cross-References	6.02
Overview	6.03
FTB 79-13: Applicability of FASB Statement No. 13 to Current Value Financial Statements	6.04
Background	6.04
Standards	6.04

CROSS-REFERENCES

1999 Miller GAAP Implementation Manual: Chapter 19, "Leases"

1999 Miller GAAP Guide: Chapter 5, "Changing Prices"

CHAPTER 6
CHANGING PRICES

OVERVIEW

Financial statements prepared in conformity with GAAP are based on the assumption of a stable monetary unit. That is, the assumption is made that the monetary unit used to convert all financial statement items into a common denominator (i.e., dollars) does not vary sufficiently over time that distortions in the financial statements are material. Also, financial statements prepared in conformity with GAAP are primarily historical-cost based (i.e., the characteristic of most financial statement items that is measured and presented is the historical cost of the item).

Over the years, two approaches have been proposed and procedures developed to compensate for changes in the monetary unit and changes in the value of assets and liabilities after their acquisition—current value accounting and general price-level accounting. *Current value accounting* substitutes a measure of current value for historical cost as the primary measurement upon which the elements of financial statements are based. *General price-level accounting* adheres to historical cost, but substitutes a current value of the dollar for historical dollars through the use of price indexes. Neither current value accounting nor general price-level accounting is required at the present time. Procedures are established in the accounting literature for use by those enterprises that choose to develop either general price-level or current value financial statements. In FAS-89, the FASB has developed disclosure standards that are optional for dealing with the problem of the impact of changing prices on financial statements.

Promulgated GAAP in the area of changing prices are found in the following pronouncement that is included in the highest level of the SAS-69 GAAP hierarchy:

FAS-89   Financial Reporting and Changing Prices

The following additional source of GAAP that is in a lower level of the SAS-69 GAAP hierarchy is discussed in this Manual:

FTB 79-13   Applicability of FASB Statement No. 13 to Current Value Financial Statements (Level B)

FTB 79-13: Applicability of FASB Statement No. 13 to Current Value Financial Statements

BACKGROUND

Uncertainty has existed concerning the applicability of FAS-13 (Accounting for Leases) in current value financial statements.

STANDARDS

Question: Are financial statements prepared on a current value basis subject to the provisions of FAS-13?

Answer: FAS-13 is not inapplicable merely because financial statements are prepared on a current value basis. Under FAS-13, the carrying amount of a capitalized lease would be adjusted in accordance with the valuation techniques employed in the preparation of the financial statements on a current value basis.

CHAPTER 7
CONTINGENCIES, RISKS, AND UNCERTAINTIES

CONTENTS

IMPRESS™ Cross-References	7.02
Overview	7.03
SOP 94-6: Disclosure of Certain Significant Risks and Uncertainties	7.03
Background	7.03
Standards	7.04
Nature of Operations	7.04
Use of Estimates	7.04
Significant Estimates	7.04
Vulnerability from Concentrations	7.05
SOP 96-1: Environmental Remediation Liabilities	7.06
Background	7.06
Standards	7.08
Recognition of Environmental Remediation Liabilities	7.08
Probability That a Liability Has Been Incurred	7.08
Ability to Make a Reasonable Estimate	7.09
Illustration of Estimating an Environmental Remediation Liability	7.09
Measurement of Environmental Remediation Liabilities	7.10
Costs to Be Included	7.11
Effects of Expected Future Events or Developments	7.12
Allocation of the Liability Among PRPs	7.13
Financial Statement Presentation and Disclosure	7.15
Financial Statement Presentation	7.15
Disclosure	7.16
Illustration of Accounting Policy Note	7.16
Illustration of Disclosures for Loss Contingencies	7.18

CROSS-REFERENCES

1999 MILLER GAAP GUIDE: Chapter 7, "Contingencies, Risks, and Uncertainties"

1999 MILLER GAAP IMPLEMENTATION MANUAL: EITF: Chapter 7, "Contingencies"

1999 MILLER GOVERNMENTAL GAAP GUIDE: Chapter 20, "Risk Financing and Related Insurance Issues"

1999 MILLER GAAP FOR NOT-FOR-PROFIT ORGANIZATIONS: Chapter 2, "Overview of Current Pronouncements"

1999 MILLER GAAS GUIDE: Chapter 11, "Auditor's Reports"

CHAPTER 7
CONTINGENCIES, RISKS, AND UNCERTAINTIES

OVERVIEW

Accounting for contingencies is an important feature of the preparation of financial statements in accordance with GAAP, because of the many uncertainties that may exist at the end of each accounting period. Standards governing accounting for loss contingencies require accrual and/or note disclosure when specified recognition and disclosure criteria are met. Gain contingencies generally are not recognized in financial statements but may be disclosed.

GAAP concerning accounting for contingencies are provided in the following pronouncements that are included in the highest level in the SAS-69 GAAP hierarchy:

FAS-5	Accounting for Contingencies
FAS-38	Accounting for Preacquisition Contingencies of Purchased Enterprises
FIN-14	Reasonable Estimation of the Amount of a Loss
FIN-34	Disclosure of Indirect Guarantees of Indebtedness of Others

The following additional sources of GAAP that are in lower levels of the SAS-69 GAAP hierarchy are discussed in this Manual:

SOP 94-6	Disclosure of Certain Significant Risks and Uncertainties (Level B)
SOP 96-1	Environmental Remediation Liabilities (Level B)

SOP 94-6: Disclosure of Certain Significant Risks and Uncertainties

BACKGROUND

Volatility and uncertainty in the business and economic environment result in the need for disclosure of information about the risks and uncertainties confronted by reporting entities. SOP 94-6 requires disclosure of significant risks and uncertainties that confront entities in the following areas: nature of operations, use of estimates in the preparation of financial statements, certain significant estimates, and current vulnerability due to certain concentrations.

STANDARDS

Nature of Operations

Financial statements should include a description of the major products or services an entity sells or provides and its principal markets and locations of those markets. Entities that operate in more than one market must indicate the relative importance of their operations in each market. Disclosures concerning the nature of operations are not required to be quantified, and relative importance may be described by terms such as *predominantly, about equally, major,* and *other*.

Use of Estimates

Financial statements should include an explanation that their preparation in conformity with GAAP requires the application of management's estimates.

Significant Estimates

Disclosure regarding an estimate is required when *both* of the following conditions are met:

1. It is at least reasonably possible that the estimate of the effect on the financial statements of a condition, situation, or set of circumstances that existed at the date of the financial statements will change in the near term due to one or more future confirming events.
2. The effect of the change would have a material effect on the financial statements.

The disclosure requirements of FAS-5 for contingencies are supplemented by SOP 94-6 as follows:

- If an estimate requires disclosure under FAS-5 or another pronouncement, an indication also shall be made that it is at least

reasonably possible that a change in the estimate will occur in the near term.
- An estimate that does not require disclosure under FAS-5 (such as estimates associated with long-term operating assets and amounts reported under profitable long-term contracts) may meet the standards described above and, if so, requires the following:
  — Disclosure of its nature
  — An indication that it is reasonably possible that a change in the estimate will occur in the near term

Following are examples of the types of situations that may require disclosure in accordance with SOP 94-6, assuming the conditions stated above are present:

- Inventory subject to rapid technological obsolescence
- Specialized equipment subject to technological obsolescence
- Valuation allowances for deferred tax assets based on future taxable income
- Capitalized motion picture film production costs
- Capitalized computer software costs
- Deferred policy acquisition costs of insurance enterprises
- Valuation allowances for commercial and real estate loans
- Environmental remediation-related obligations
- Litigation-related obligations
- Contingent liabilities for obligations of other entities
- Amounts reported for long-term obligations (e.g., pensions and other post-retirement benefits)
- Estimated net proceeds recoverable, the provisions for expected loss to be incurred, etc., on disposition of a business or assets
- Amounts reported for long-term contracts

Vulnerability from Concentrations

Vulnerability from concentrations exists because of an enterprise's greater exposure to risk than would be the case if the enterprise had mitigated its risk through diversification. Financial statements should disclose concentrations if *all* of the following conditions are met:

1. The concentration existed at the date of the financial statements.

2. The concentration makes the enterprise vulnerable to the risk of a near-term severe impact.
3. It is reasonably possible that the events that could cause the severe impact will occur in the near term.

Information sufficient to inform financial statement users of the general nature of the risk associated with the concentration is required for the following specific concentrations:

1. Concentrations in the volume of business transacted with a particular customer, supplier, lender, grantor, or contributor
2. Concentrations in revenue from particular products, services, or fund-raising events
3. Concentrations in the available sources of supply of materials, labor, or services, or of licenses or other rights used in the entity's operations
4. Concentrations in the market or geographic area in which an entity conducts its operations

In addition, for concentrations of labor subject to collective bargaining agreements, disclosure shall include both the percentage of the labor force covered by a collective bargaining agreement and the percentage of the labor force covered by a collective bargaining agreement that will expire within one year. For concentrations of operations located outside the entity's home country, disclosure shall include the carrying amounts of net assets and the geographic areas in which they are located.

SOP 96-1: Environmental Remediation Liabilities

BACKGROUND

SOP 96-1 provides accounting guidance for environmental remediation liabilities that relate to pollution resulting from some past act. Generally, these liabilities result from one of the following:

- Superfund provisions
- The corrective-action provisions of the Resource Conservation and Recovery Act (RCRA)
- State and non–U.S. laws and regulations that are analogous to the RCRA

SOP 96-1 applies to all entities that prepare financial statements in conformity with generally accepted accounting principles applicable to nongovernmental entities. The provisions of SOP 96-1 are intended to be applied on a site-by-site basis.

SOP 96-1 is written in the context of operations taking place in the United States, although the guidance provided is applicable to all the operations of the reporting entity. SOP 96-1 is *not* intended to provide guidance for the following:

- Accounting for pollution control costs with respect to current operations
- Accounting for costs of future site restoration or closure that are required upon the cessation of operations or sale of facilities
- Accounting for environmental remediation actions that are undertaken at the sole discretion of management and that are not induced by the threat of litigation or of assertion or by a claim of assessment by governments or other parties
- Recognizing liabilities of insurance companies for unpaid claims
- Asset impairment issues

SOP 96-1 is intended to provide guidance for "clean-up" activities rather than preventative or other activities. For example, it does not cover situations in which remediation is required only at the time of sale of a property.

SOP 96-1 is effective for fiscal years beginning after December 15, 1996, with earlier application encouraged. The effect of initially applying SOP 96-1 is to be reported as a change in accounting estimate in accordance with APB-20 (Accounting Changes), which precludes restatement of previously issued financial statements for this type of accounting change.

The following discussion is drawn primarily from Part II of SOP 96-1, which provides detailed accounting guidance on accounting and disclosure for environmental remediation liabilities. Three other sections of SOP 96-1 that are not covered here are particularly important for entities applying this standard or auditing entities that are applying this standard. The first is Part I, which presents an overview of environmental laws and regulations that relate to environmental liabilities. The second is Appendix B, which includes an environmental remediation case study that works through a six-year period to illustrate the application of the recognition and measurement guidance provided by SOP 96-1. The third is Appendix C, which provides auditing guidance with respect to SOP 96-1. Familiarity with these sections of the standard is highly recommended before implementation of the accounting guidance summarized here is attempted.

STANDARDS

Recognition of Environmental Remediation Liabilities

SOP 96-1 builds on the recognition criteria of FAS-5 by requiring accrual of a liability when *both* of the following conditions are met:

- Information available before issuance of the financial statements indicates that it is probable that an asset has been impaired or a liability has been incurred at the date of the financial statements.
- The amount of the loss can be reasonably estimated.

A liability related to environmental remediation often results over a period of time rather than as a distinct event. The underlying cause of such a liability is the past or present ownership or operation of a site, or the contribution or transportation of waste to a site, at which remedial actions must take place. For the criteria for recognizing a liability to be met, this underlying cause must have occurred on or before the date of the financial statements.

Probability That a Liability Has Been Incurred

Applying the criteria of FAS-5 to environmental remediation liabilities requires the following:

- It has been asserted (or it is probable that it will be asserted) that the entity is responsible for participating in a remediation process because of a past event. This usually means that litigation has begun, a claim or an assessment has been asserted, or commencement of litigation or assertion of a claim or assessment is considered probable.
- Available evidence indicates that the outcome of such litigation, claim, or assessment will be unfavorable (i.e., the entity will be held responsible for participating in a remediation process because of the past event).

In light of the legal framework in which most environmental remediation liabilities arise, SOP 96-1 is based on a presumption that if litigation has commenced (or a claim or an assessment has been asserted or is considered probable), and the reporting entity is associated with the site, the outcome will be unfavorable for the entity.

Ability to Make a Reasonable Estimate

Developing an estimate of environmental remediation liabilities involves a consideration of many factors, such as the following:

- The extent and types of hazardous substances at the site
- The range of technologies that can be used for remediation
- Evolving standards of what constitutes acceptable remediation
- The number and financial condition of other potentially responsible parties and the extent of their responsibility for the remediation

---

Illustration of Estimating an Environmental Remediation Liability

Foster, Inc., has determined that its environmental remediation obligation meets the recognition criteria of SOP 96-1. The company is in the process of estimating the amount of the obligation that will be recognized. The company has further determined that the liability consists of four components, described as follows:

Component	Description
A	Estimated at $750,000
B	Estimated to be within a range of $500,000 to $900,000, with the most likely amount at $625,000
C	Estimated to be within a range of $275,000 to $400,000, with no amount within that range more likely than any other amount
D	Unable to estimate

The environmental remediation liability that should be recognized at this time, subject to adjustment in the future as additional information becomes available, is determined as follows:

Component A	$ 750,000
Component B	625,000
Component C	275,000
Component D	None
	$1,650,000

FIN-14 (Reasonable Estimation of the Amount of a Loss) is particularly important in estimating the amount of an environmental remediation liability. In the early stages of the remediation process, liabilities are not easily quantified. The range and ultimate amount of the liability will be determined as events occur over time. The range of an environmental remediation liability typically is estimated by first estimating the various components of the liability—which may themselves be ranges. As suggested in FIN-14, if an amount within a range is a better estimate than any other amount within the range, that figure should be used. If no amount within the range is a more reliable estimate than any other, the minimum amount in the range should be used. Thus, the amount of the environmental remediation liability will be a combination of most likely amounts and minimum amounts of the components of the liability. Even if a range for certain components of the liability cannot be estimated, a liability still should be recognized and recorded at the appropriate amount for those components that can be estimated. SOP 96-1 describes the various stages (benchmarks) involved in the remediation process and when costs generally should be accrued.

A complexity that arises in estimating environmental remediation liabilities is the assignment and allocation among the various potentially responsible parties (PRPs). The final allocation may not be known until the remediation effort is substantially complete and may depend on factors such as the PRPs' willingness to negotiate a cost allocation. This should not preclude an entity from recognizing its best estimate of its share of the liability if the probability criterion is met. Any change in the estimate of the environmental remediation liability, including those due to negotiations with other PRPs, is accounted for as a change in accounting estimate in accordance with APB-20.

Measurement of Environmental Remediation Liabilities

Once an entity determines that it is probable that an environmental remediation liability has been incurred, it must estimate the amount of that liability based on available evidence. The estimate of the liability includes the allocable share of the liability for a specific site, and the share of amounts related to the site that will not be paid by other PRPs or the government.

SOP 96-1 identifies the following four issues that must be addressed in the measurement of an entity's environmental remediation liability; each is discussed below.

1. Costs that should be included in the measurement
2. Whether the measurement should consider the effects of expected future events or developments
3. How the measurement should be affected by the existence of other PRPs

4. How the measurement should be affected by potential recoveries

Costs to Be Included

Costs to be included in the measurement of the environmental remediation liability include (a) incremental direct costs of the remediation effort and (b) costs of compensation and benefits for those employees who are expected to devote a significant amount of time on the remediation effort (e.g., in-house lawyers and engineers).

The remediation effort is considered on a site-by-site basis and includes the following:

- Precleanup activities (e.g., the performance of a remedial investigation, risk assessment, or feasibility study and the preparation of remedial action plan)
- Performance of remedial actions under Superfund, corrective actions under RCRA, and analogous actions under state and non–U.S. laws
- Government oversight and enforcement activities
- Operation and maintenance of the remedy

The following are examples of incremental direct costs of a remediation effort:

- Fees paid to outside law firms for work related to remedial actions
- Costs related to completing the remedial investigation/feasibility study
- Fees to outside engineering and consulting firms for site investigations and the development of remedial action plans and designs
- Costs of contractors performing remedial actions
- Government oversight costs
- Costs of machinery and equipment related to the remedial effort that do not have alternative uses
- The PRP's assessments of the costs it incurred in dealing with a site
- Operating costs and remedial action maintenance

The costs of the following are included in the measurement of the remediation liability:

- Determining the extent of the remedial actions that are required
- Determining the types of remedial actions to be used
- Allocating the costs among PRPs

The costs of routine environmental compliance matters and litigation costs involved with potential recoveries are *not* part of the remediation effort. Further, SOP 96-1 does not require that the cost of defense against assertions of liability be included in the measurement of the environmental remediation liability. It notes that the current practice in this regard is diverse: some include legal defense costs in the measurement of liability under FAS-5, while most companies treat litigation costs as period costs.

Effects of Expected Future Events or Developments

Remediation of a site may extend over several years. As a result, the laws that govern the remediation process and the technology available may change during the remediation process. Other factors that may affect estimates of costs to be incurred are the impact of inflation and productivity improvements.

Enacted laws and adopted regulations and policies should provide the basis for measuring a remediation liability. Changes in these factors should not be anticipated, and the impact of changes that are enacted or adopted should be recognized only when they occur. Concerning remediation technology, the remediation plan should be based on the methodology that is expected to be approved, and the liability should be based on that methodology and technology, which should continue to be the basis for the liability until it is probable that a revised methodology will be accepted.

The measurement of environmental remediation liabilities should be based on the reporting entity's estimate of what it will cost to perform each of the elements of the remediation effort (identified earlier) when those elements are expected to be performed. As such, the entity should take into account productivity improvements due to experience, as well as inflation. When it is not practicable to estimate inflation, the cost estimate should include the minimum in the range of the liability until these costs can be more reasonably estimated.

If the amount and timing of cash payments is (reasonably) fixed or reliably determinable, the measurement of the liability, or a component of the liability, may be discounted to reflect the time value of money. The discount rate that should be used is that rate (*a*) that will produce an amount at which the environmental liability theoretically could be settled in an arm's-length transaction with a third party and (*b*) that does not exceed the interest rate on monetary assets that are essentially risk-free and have maturities comparable to that of the environmental liability.

Allocation of the Liability Among PRPs

The environmental remediation liability recorded by an entity should be based on the entity's estimate of its allocable share of the joint and several remediation liability. This requires an identification of the PRPs for the site, an assessment of the likelihood that other PRPs will pay their share of the liability, and a determination of the portion of the liability that will be allocated to the entity.

Identification of PRPs SOP 96-1 identifies five categories of PRPs:

1. *Participating PRPs*—PRPs that acknowledge their potential involvement with the site. These PRPs also are referred to as "players."
2. *Recalcitrant PRPs*—PRPs that adopt an attitude of non-responsibility, even though evidence suggests their involvement in the site. Typically, parties in this category must be sued in order for their allocable share of the remediation liability to be collected.
3. *Unproven PRPs*—Parties that have been identified as PRPs by the Environmental Protection Agency (EPA) but that do not acknowledge their potential involvement because no substantive evidence currently links them to the site. These PRPs eventually will be reclassified based on evidence that is later discovered.
4. *Parties that have not been identified as PRPs*—As the investigation progresses, additional PRPs may be identified. These PRPs will later be reclassified to the participating category or the recalcitrant category.
5. *PRPs that cannot be identified or have no assets*—PRPs from which no contributions will be received because they are not found or have no assets. These PRPs are sometimes referred to as "orphan PRPs."

Allocation Process The environmental remediation liability is allocated only among participating PRPs. There are several ways to allocate the liability among PRPs. The following are the four principal factors that are considered in a typical allocation process:

1. *Elements of fair share*—Examples are the amount of waste based on volume, mass, type, and toxicity and the length of time the site was used.

2. *Classification of PRP*—Examples are site operator, transporter of waste, and generator of waste.
3. *Limitations on payments*—Any statutory or regulatory limitations on contributions.
4. *Degree of care*—Refers to the degree of care exercised in selecting the site or in selecting a transporter.

The environmental remediation liability may be allocated according to any of the following methods: (1) PRPs may agree among themselves as to the allocation, (2) they may hire an allocation consultant whose conclusions may or may not be binding, or (3) they may request a nonbinding allocation of responsibility from the EPA. The allocation method or percentages may change as the project moves forward.

An entity should determine its allocable share of the remediation liability based on its estimate of the allocation method and its percentage of the amount that will ultimately be used for the entire remediation effort. Sources for this estimate should be the allocation method and the percentages that the PRPs have agreed to, the method and percentages that have been assigned by a consultant, or the method and percentages determined by the EPA, depending on the method that is chosen (as described in the preceding paragraph). If the entity's estimate of the ultimate liability differs significantly from the method or percentage from these primary sources, the entity's estimate should be based on objective, verifiable evidence, such as the following:

- Existing data about the kinds and quantities of waste at the site
- Experience with allocation approaches in comparable situations
- Reports of environmental specialists
- Internal data refuting EPA allegations about the entity's contribution of waste to the site

A consideration in estimating an entity's allocable share of the liability is the financial condition of the participating PRPs, including their ability to pay. The entity should include in its liability its share of amounts that are not expected to be paid by other PRPs or by the government.

Impact of Potential Recoveries   Potential recoveries may come from a number of sources, such as insurers, PRPs other than participating PRPs, and government or third-party funds. The environmental remediation liability should be determined without regard to potential recoveries. An asset related to recoveries should be separately recognized only when realization is considered probable. If the claim is subject to litigation, the realization of the recovery claim is not considered probable.

Fair value should be the basis for measuring the potential recovery. This requires consideration of both the transaction costs related to the recovery and the time value of money. The time value of money should not be considered, however, if the liability is not discounted and if the timing of the recovery depends on the timing of the payment of the liability. Usually the point in time when the liability is both probable and reasonably estimable precedes the point in time when any related recovery is probable of realization.

Financial Statement Presentation and Disclosure

This section discusses SOP 96-1 guidelines for financial statement presentation and disclosure. Entities that are subject to the rules and regulations of the Securities and Exchange Commission (SEC) also are required to adhere to various SEC rules that apply to environmental matters.

Financial Statement Presentation

Several assets may result from an environmental remediation obligation, including the following:

- Receivables from other PRPs that are not providing initial funding
- Anticipated recoveries from insurers
- Anticipated recoveries from prior owners as a result of indemnification agreements

FIN-39 (Offsetting of Amounts Related to Certain Contracts) specifies that offsetting assets and liabilities is appropriate only when a right of setoff exists, which requires *all* of the following:

- Each of the two parties owes the other party a determinable amount.
- The reporting entity has the right to set off the amounts owed with the amount owed by the other party.
- The reporting entity intends to set off.
- The right of setoff is enforceable at law.

For environmental remediation assets and liabilities these rules apply, although SOP 96-1 indicates that it would be rare for the facts and circumstances surrounding environmental remediation liabilities and related assets to meet these conditions.

Recording an environmental remediation liability usually results in a charge to income. Such a charge does not meet the criteria of APB-30 (Reporting the Results of Operations) for extraordinary classification, because it does not result from an event that is unusual in nature and infrequent in occurrence. Furthermore, it is difficult to substantiate the classification of environmental remediation costs as a component of nonoperating expenses, because the events underlying the obligation are part of the entity's operations. Thus, environmental remediation–related expenses should be reported as a component of operating income in an income statement that separates operating and nonoperating items. Credits (i.e., gains or loss recoveries) that are recognized in the entity's financial statements should be presented in the income statement in the same manner. Any earnings on assets that are reflected in the entity's balance sheet and are reserved for its environmental liabilities should be reported as investment income. Environmental remediation–related expenses and recoveries that are associated with disposals of a segment of a business that are accounted for in accordance with APB-30 should be classified as discontinued operations.

Disclosure

Accounting Policies APB-22 (Disclosure of Accounting Policies) provides guidance concerning information that must be disclosed about the accounting policies employed by an entity in the preparation of its financial statements. With regard to environmental remediation liabilities, that disclosure should include an indication of whether the accrual is measured on a discounted basis.

Environmental remediation liabilities are increasingly significant and involve subjective judgment. As a result, entities are encouraged, but not required, to disclose the event, situation, or set of circumstances that generally triggers recognition of loss contingencies that arise out of the entity's environmental remediation–related obligations. Entities also are encouraged to disclose their policy with regard to the timing of recognition of recoveries. An example of an accounting policy note is presented in the following Illustration.

Illustration of Accounting Policy Note

Environmental remediation costs—Company X accrues losses associated with environmental remediation obligations when they are probable and reasonably estimable, which usually is no later than the time of completion of the remedial feasibility study. These accruals are adjusted as additional information is available or if circumstances change. Costs of future expenditures for environmental remediation obligations are [not] discounted to their present value. Expected recoveries of environmental remediation costs from other parties are recognized as assets when their receipt is judged to be probable.

Loss Contingencies The disclosure requirements of FAS-5 and SOP 94-6 are particularly important for environmental remediation liabilities. FAS-5 requires disclosure of loss contingencies as follows:

- If accrual is possible, the nature of an accrual for a loss contingency and, in some circumstances, the amount accrued to keep financial statements from being misleading
- If no accrual is possible because the loss is either not probable or estimable, or if an exposure to loss exists in excess of the accrued amount, the reasonable possibility of loss, the nature of the loss, and an estimate of the possible range of loss, or a statement that such an estimate cannot be made

Disclosure requirements of SOP 94-6 that are particularly important for an environmental remediation liability are the following:

- Estimates used in determining the carrying amount of assets or liabilities or gain or loss contingencies
- Information regarding an estimate when information known before issuance of the financial statements indicates that both of the following are met:
  — It is at least reasonably possible that the estimate of the effect on the financial statements of a condition, situation, or set of circumstances that existed at the date of the financial statements will change in the near term due to one or more future confirming events.
  — The effect of the change would be material to the financial statements.
- Information regarding the nature of the uncertainty and an indication that it is at least reasonably possible that a change in the estimate will occur in the near term. (If the estimate involves a loss contingency covered by FAS-5, the disclosure also should include an estimate of the possible loss or range of loss or state that such an estimate cannot be made.)

Uncertainties associated with environmental remediation loss contingencies are pervasive and may result in wide ranges of reasonably possible loss contingencies. These contingencies may occur over many years. As a result, SOP 96-1 encourages but does not require additional specific disclosures with respect to environmental remediation loss contingencies that would be useful in better understanding the entity's financial statements.

The following Illustration summarizes the disclosure requirements of FAS-5, SOP 94-6, and SOP 96-1 for loss contingencies related to environmental remediation liabilities.

Illustration of Disclosures for Loss Contingencies

Related to Recorded Accruals

1. The nature of the accrual (if required to keep financial statements from being misleading), including the total amount accrued
2. If any portion of the accrued obligation is discounted, the undiscounted amount of the obligation and the discount rate used in the present value calculation
3. If the criteria of SOP 94-6 are met with respect to the accrued obligation or to any recognized asset for third-party recoveries, an indication that it is at least reasonably possible that a change in the estimate, obligation, or asset will occur in the near term

Related to Reasonably Possible Loss Contingencies

1. The nature of the reasonably possible loss contingency; also, an estimate of the possible loss exposure, or the fact that such an estimate cannot be made
2. If the criteria of SOP 94-6 are met with respect to estimated gain or loss contingencies, an indication that it is at least reasonably possible that a change in the estimate will occur in the near term

Disclosures Encouraged But Not Required

1. The estimated time frame of disbursements for recorded amounts if expenditures are expected to continue over a long period of time
2. The estimated time frame for realization of recognized probable recoveries if those recoveries are not expected in the near term
3. If the criteria of SOP 94-6 are met with respect to the accrued obligation, to any recognized asset for third-party recoveries, or to reasonably possible loss exposures or disclosed gain contingencies, the factors that cause the estimate to be sensitive to change
4. If an estimate of the probable or reasonably possible loss or range of loss cannot be made, the reasons why
5. If information about the reasonably possible loss or the recognized and additional reasonably possible loss for an environmental remediation obligation related to an individual site is relevant to an understanding of the financial statements, the following with respect to that site:
    a. The total amount accrued for the site

b. The nature of any reasonably possible loss contingency or additional loss, and an estimate of the possible loss or the fact that such an estimate cannot be made and why
   c. Whether other PRPs are involved, and the entity's estimated share of the obligation
   d. The status of regulatory proceedings
   e. The estimated time frame for resolution of the contingency

Probable But Not Reasonably Estimable Losses

1. If the environmental remediation liability may be material, a description of the remediation obligation and the fact that a reasonable estimate cannot be made
2. Disclosure of the estimated time frame for resolution of the uncertainty about the amount of the loss (encouraged, but not required)

Unasserted Claims

1. If an entity is required by existing laws and regulations to report the release of hazardous substances and to begin a remediation study, or if assertion of a claim is considered probable, the matter represents a loss contingency subject to the disclosure requirements for unasserted claims of FAS-5.

Environmental Remediation Costs Currently Recognized

Entities are encouraged, but not required, to disclose the following details concerning environmental remediation costs:

1. The amount recognized for environmental remediation loss contingencies for each period
2. The amount of any recovery from third parties that is credited to environmental remediation costs in each period
3. The income statement caption in which environmental remediation costs and credits are included

CHAPTER 8
EQUITY METHOD

CONTENTS

IMPRESS™ Cross-References	8.02
Overview	8.03
FTB 79-19: Investor's Accounting for Unrealized Losses on Marketable Securities Owned by an Equity Method Investee	8.04
Background	8.04
Standards	8.04
AIN-APB 18: The Equity Method of Accounting for Investments in Common Stock: Accounting Interpretations of APB Opinion No. 18	8.04
Background	8.04
Standards	8.04
Illustration of Intercompany Profit Elimination	8.05

IMPRESS™
CROSS-REFERENCES

1999 MILLER GAAP GUIDE: Chapter 14, "Equity Method"

1999 MILLER GAAP IMPLEMENTATION MANUAL: EITF: Chapter 6, "Consolidation and the Equity Method"

1999 MILLER GOVERNMENTAL GAAP GUIDE: Chapter 13, "Assets"

CHAPTER 8
EQUITY METHOD

OVERVIEW

The equity method of accounting for investments in common stock is appropriate if an investment enables the investor to influence the operating or financial decisions of the investee. In these circumstances, the investor has a degree of responsibility for the return on its investment, and it is appropriate to include in the investor's results of operations its share of the earnings or losses of the investee. The equity method is not intended as a substitute for consolidated financial statements when the conditions for consolidation are present.

The following pronouncements are the sources of GAAP concerning the equity method that are included in the highest level of authority in the SAS-69 GAAP hierarchy:

APB-18	The Equity Method of Accounting for Investments in Common Stock
FAS-94	Consolidation of All Majority-Owned Subsidiaries
FIN-35	Criteria for Applying the Equity Method of Accounting for Investments in Common Stock

The following additional sources of GAAP that are in lower levels of the SAS-69 GAAP hierarchy are discussed in this Manual:

FTB 79-19	Investor's Accounting for Unrealized Losses on Marketable Securities Owned by an Equity Method Investee (Level B)
AIN-APB 18	The Equity Method of Accounting for Investments in Common Stock: Accounting Interpretations of APB Opinion No. 18 (Level D)

FTB 79-19: Investor's Accounting for Unrealized Losses on Marketable Securities Owned by an Equity Method Investee

BACKGROUND

A subsidiary or investee may be required to account for investments at market value with an associated adjustment made directly to stockholders' equity.

STANDARDS

Question: How should a parent or investor account for its share of the accumulated changes in the valuation allowance for investments included in stockholders' equity of an investee accounted for by the equity method?

Answer: If a subsidiary or other investee that is accounted for by the equity method is required to include accumulated changes in a valuation allowance for a portfolio of investments in stockholders equity, the parent or investor shall adjust its investment by its proportionate share of the accumulated allowance and the same amount shall be included in the stockholders' equity of the parent or investor.

AIN-APB 18: The Equity Method of Accounting for Investments in Common Stock: Accounting Interpretations of APB Opinion No. 18

BACKGROUND

AIN-APB 18 provides guidance on three implementation issues associated with APB-18: (1) elimination of intercompany profit or loss, (2) its applicability to partnerships and joint ventures, and (3) transition issues in applying APB-18.

STANDARDS

Question 1: APB-18 and ARB-51 (Consolidated Financial Statements) require that intercompany profits or losses on assets still remaining with an investor or an investee at a reporting date are to be eliminated. Should all of the intercompany profit or loss be eliminated, or should only that portion related to the investor's common stock interest in the investee be eliminated?

Answer: The extent of the intercompany profit or loss to be eliminated depends on the relationship between the investor and the investee. Given certain relationships between the investor and the investee, none of the intercompany profit or loss should be recognized by the investor until it has been realized through transactions with third parties. The following are examples of situations where this accounting treatment would be appropriate:

1. The investor owns a majority of the voting shares of the investee and enters into a transaction with the investee that is not on an arm's-length basis.

2. An investee is established with the cooperation of the investor, and the investor controls the investee through guarantees of indebtedness, through extension of credit by the investor for the benefit of the investee, or through warrants or convertible securities of the investee owned by the investor. An example of this type of arrangement is where the investee is established for the financing and operation of property that the lessor sells to the lessee.

In other cases, it is acceptable for the investor to eliminate intercompany profit based on its percentage ownership of the investee; the elimination of intercompany profit would be the same regardless of whether the transaction is "downstream" (a sale by the investor to the investee) or "upstream" (a sale by the investee to the investor). The elimination of intercompany profit is to be performed on a net-of-tax basis.

Illustration of Intercompany Profit Elimination

On December 31, 19X8, an investor holds $800,000 worth of inventory items that were sold to it during the year by the investee. The investee's gross profit rate on sales of inventory is 25%. Both the investor and the investee face a 36% tax rate. The investor owns 40% of the outstanding voting stock of the investee. At year-end, the investor holds inventory items for which the investee recognized $200,000 of gross profit ($800,000 x 25%). In computing the investor's equity "pickup," $128,000 would be deducted from the investee's net income [$200,000 x (1 − 36%)]. The investor's share of the intercompany gross profit after tax, $51,200, would be eliminated from the investor's equity income ($128,000 x 40%). The offsetting credit recorded by the investor would be either to the investor's investment account (the most common method) or to the inventory account.

8.06 Equity Method

Question 2: Do the provisions of APB-18 apply to investments in partnerships and joint ventures?

Answer: Not directly. APB-18 applies only to investments in common stocks of corporations. It does not pertain to partnerships or unincorporated joint ventures. However, many of the provisions of APB-18 would be applicable in accounting for these unincorporated ventures. For example, partnership profits and losses accrued by investor-partners are generally reflected in their financial statements at a single amount. In addition, and consistent with APB-18, the following additional provisions would apply to a partnership: (1) the elimination of intercompany profits and losses and (2) the accrual of income taxes on the profits accrued by investor-partners regardless of the tax basis employed in the partnership return.

For the most part, the preceding discussion as to the applicability of APB-18 to partnerships would also apply to unincorporated joint ventures. However, in one divergence from APB-18, where it is established industry practice, the investor-venturer may account in its financial statements for its pro rata share of the assets, liabilities, revenues, and expenses of the venture.

Question 3: If a company owns an investment in 1971 for which it does not adopt the equity method until 1972 (the mandatory effective date of APB-18), when the retroactive application will materially change the originally reported 1971 net income, should the amount of the change be disclosed in the 1971 financial statements when they are first issued?

Answer: Yes. At a minimum the company should disclose in its 1971 financial statements the effect that later retroactive application of APB-18 will have on its 1971 net income.

CHAPTER 9
EXTINGUISHMENT OF DEBT

CONTENTS

IMPRESS™ Cross-References	**9.02**
Overview	**9.03**
FTB 80-1: Early Extinguishment of Debt through Exchange for Common or Preferred Stock	**9.04**
Background	**9.04**
Standards	**9.04**
AIN-APB 26: Early Extinguishment of Debt: Accounting Interpretations of APB Opinion No. 26	**9.05**
Background	**9.05**
Standards	**9.05**

IMPRESS™

CROSS-REFERENCES

1999 MILLER GAAP GUIDE: Chapter 15, "Extinguishment of Debt"

1999 MILLER GAAP IMPLEMENTATION MANUAL: EITF: Chapter 10, "Extinguishment of Debt"

1999 MILLER GOVERNMENTAL GAAP GUIDE: Chapter 16, "Liabilities"

1999 MILLER GAAP FOR NOT-FOR-PROFIT ORGANIZATIONS: Chapter 2, "Overview of Current Pronouncements"; Chapter 6, "Liabilities"; Chapter 11, "Display of Certain GAAP Transactions"

CHAPTER 9
EXTINGUISHMENT OF DEBT

OVERVIEW

An *extinguishment of debt* is the reacquisition of debt, or removal of debt from the balance sheet, prior to or at the maturity date of that debt. Gain or loss on the extinguishment is the difference between the total reacquisition cost of the debt to the debtor and the net carrying amount of the debt on the debtor's books at the date of extinguishment.

GAAP for the extinguishment of debt are found in the following authoritative pronouncements that are included in the highest level of authority in the SAS-69 GAAP hierarchy:

APB-26	Early Extinguishment of Debt
FAS-4	Reporting Gains and Losses from Extinguishment of Debt
FAS-22	Changes in the Provisions of Lease Agreements Resulting from Refundings of Tax-Exempt Debt
FAS-64	Extinguishments of Debt Made to Satisfy Sinking-Fund Requirements
FAS-125	Accounting for Transfers and Servicing of Financial Assets and Extinguishments of Liabilities

The authoritative literature carefully defines when debt has been extinguished and generally requires any gain or loss on extinguishment of debt to be included in the determination of net income in the period of the extinguishment transaction.

The following additional sources of GAAP that are in lower levels of the SAS-69 GAAP hierarchy are discussed in this Manual:

FTB 80-1	Early Extinguishment of Debt through Exchange for Common or Preferred Stock (Level B)
AIN-APB 26	Early Extinguishment of Debt: Accounting Interpretations of APB Opinion No. 26 (Level D)

FTB 80-1: Early Extinguishment of Debt through Exchange for Common or Preferred Stock

BACKGROUND

Under APB-26 (Early Extinguishment of Debt), conversion of debt to common or preferred stock is not an extinguishment if the conversion represents the exercise of a conversion right contained in the terms of the debt issue. Other exchanges of common or preferred stock for debt would constitute extinguishment.

STANDARDS

Question: Does APB-26 apply to extinguishments of debt effected by issuance of common or preferred stock, including redeemable and fixed-maturity preferred stock?

Answer: All extinguishments must be accounted for in accordance with either FAS-15 (Accounting by Debtors and Creditors for Troubled Debt Restructurings) or APB-26. Thus, APB-26 applies to all extinguishments except those subject to the requirements of FAS-15. In accordance with APB-26, the difference between the net carrying amount of the extinguished debt and the reacquisition price is recognized currently in income of the period of extinguishment. In this situation, the reacquisition price of the extinguished debt is the value of the common or preferred stock issued or the value of the debt, whichever is more clearly evident. FAS-4 (Reporting Gains and Losses from Extinguished Debt) requires extraordinary classification for gains or losses from the extinguishment of debt.

AIN-APB 26: Early Extinguishment of Debt: Accounting Interpretations of APB Opinion No. 26

BACKGROUND

AIN-APB 26 clarifies the applicability of APB-26 (Early Extinguishment of Debt) to debt tendered to exercise warrants.

STANDARDS

Question: APB-26 indicates that gain or loss should be recognized currently in income when a debt security is reacquired by the issuer except through conversion by the holder. Does APB-26 apply to debt tendered to exercise warrants that were originally issued with that debt, but which were detachable?

Answer: APB-26 does not apply to debt tendered to exercise detachable warrants that were originally issued with that debt if the debt is permitted to be tendered toward the exercise price of the warrants under the terms of the securities at issuance. In this circumstance, the debt is considered a conversion. (APB-26 does not apply to conversion of debt. In practice, however, the carrying amount of the debt, including any unamortized premium or discount, is transferred to capital accounts when the debt is converted. No gain or loss is recognized.)

CHAPTER 10
FINANCIAL INSTRUMENTS

CONTENTS

IMPRESS™ Cross-References	**10.02**
Overview	**10.03**
PB-4: Accounting for Foreign Debt/Equity Swaps	**10.04**
Background	**10.04**
Standards	**10.04**
Illustration of Loss on Debt/Equity Swap	**10.05**
Other Issues	**10.05**

CROSS-REFERENCES

1999 MILLER GAAP IMPLEMENTATION MANUAL: Chapter 18, "Investments in Debt and Equity Securities"

1999 MILLER GAAP GUIDE: Chapter 16, "Financial Instruments"; Chapter 29, "Investments in Debt and Equity—Securities"

1999 MILLER GAAP IMPLEMENTATION MANUAL: EITF: Chapter 11, "Financial Instruments"; Chapter 30, "Troubled Debt Restructuring"

1999 MILLER GOVERNMENTAL GAAP GUIDE: Chapter 13, "Assets"

1999 MILLER GAAP FOR NOT-FOR-PROFIT ORGANIZATIONS: Chapter 2, "Overview of Current Pronouncements"

1999 MILLER GAAS GUIDE: Chapter 11, "Auditor's Reports"

CHAPTER 10
FINANCIAL INSTRUMENTS

OVERVIEW

The FASB is involved in a long-term project intended to improve GAAP for financial instruments. Because of the complexity of the issues surrounding financial instruments, the project has been separated into several phases. The project's final output is expected to be broad standards that will assist in resolving financial reporting and other issues about various financial instruments and other related transactions.

GAAP established by the FASB for financial instruments are contained in the following pronouncements that are included in the highest level of authority in the SAS-69 GAAP hierarchy:

FAS-105	Disclosure of Information about Financial Instruments with Off-Balance-Sheet Risk and Financial Instruments with Concentrations of Credit Risk
FAS-107	Disclosures about Fair Value of Financial Instruments
FAS-119	Disclosures about Derivative Financial Instruments and Fair Value of Financial Instruments
FAS-126	Exemption from Certain Required Disclosures about Financial Instruments for Certain Nonpublic Entities
FIN-39	Offsetting of Amounts Related to Certain Contracts
FIN-41	Offsetting of Amounts Related to Certain Repurchase and Reverse Repurchase Agreements

The following additional source of GAAP that is in a lower level of the SAS-69 GAAP hierarchy is discussed in this Manual:

PB-4	Accounting for Foreign Debt/Equity Swaps (Level C)

3. Market value (if available) of similar equity investments

PB-4: Accounting for Foreign Debt/Equity Swaps

BACKGROUND

Certain foreign countries, particularly those with rapidly developing economies, may experience periodic financial difficulties. These financial difficulties may call into question the ability of these countries to service debt that they have issued. As a method of dealing with these financial difficulties, foreign countries experiencing financial difficulties may permit U.S. lending institutions to convert dollar-denominated debt, issued by these same countries, into approved local equity investments.

These foreign debt/equity swaps are generally structured as follows. First, holders of the U.S. dollar-denominated debt are credited with an amount of the local currency approximately equal to the amount of the outstanding debt. This conversion is performed at the official exchange rate, with a discount from the exchange rate imposed as a transaction fee. Second, the local currency so credited to the lender must be used to make an approved equity investment—the currency can be used for no other purpose. Third, capital usually cannot be repatriated for several years. In some cases, it may be permissible to sell the investment. However, the proceeds from such a sale are generally subject to the same repatriation restrictions.

STANDARDS

These types of foreign debt/equity swaps represent the exchange of a monetary asset for a nonmonetary asset. The transaction should be measured at its fair value on the date it is agreed to by both parties. Determining fair value for these types of transactions can be challenging. In some cases, the fair value of the equity investment received is unclear, and the fair value of the debt surrendered may be equally difficult to determine. It is not unusual for debt of foreign countries experiencing financial difficulty to be thinly traded.

Regarding the fair value of the exchange, both the secondary market value of the loan surrendered and the fair value of the equity investment/net assets received should be considered. The following factors should be considered in determining the fair value of the equity investment/net assets received:

1. Similar transactions for cash
2. Estimated cash flows from the equity investment or net assets received

4. Currency restrictions affecting (*a*) dividends, (*b*) the sale of the investment, or (*c*) the repatriation of capital

If the fair value of the equity investment/net assets received is less than the recorded amount of the loan, the resulting difference should be reflected in income as a loss at the time the transaction is consummated. The amount of any resulting loss recognized is to be charged against the allowance for loan losses. This treatment is not affected even if some portion of the loan loss may have been due to changes in the interest rate environment (i.e., the fair value of the loan had declined due to an increase in interest rates). It is assumed that the causal factor leading to the debt/equity swap, which precipitates the loss, is the adverse financial condition of the foreign debtor.

Illustration of Loss on Debt/Equity Swap

Countries Bank, Inc., has a long-term $10 million dollar-denominated loan outstanding to the Mexican government. As a result of adverse financial conditions, the Mexican government is having difficulty making payments on the above loan. The Mexican government and Countries Bank have agreed to enter into a debt/equity swap. At the current exchange rate, 1 peso equals $.125; however, as a transaction fee, the exchange rate used for the swap is $.126. Therefore, Countries Bank receives 79,365,000 pesos in exchange for the $10 million of dollar-denominated debt (Countries Bank would have received 80 million pesos if the official exchange rate had been used; the difference is a transaction fee). Countries Bank will use these proceeds to purchase 50,000 shares of MexPower, a state-owned utility. MexPower is not publicly traded; however, a third party recently paid 140 million pesos for a 10% stake in MexPower (100,000 shares). The secondary market for the dollar-denominated debt issued by the Mexican government is thinly traded. Therefore, the fair value of this swap transaction will be measured by the fair value of the shares of MexPower received. Based on the recent cash transaction, the fair value of the MexPower shares received by Countries Bank is estimated to be 70 million pesos. In U.S. dollars, the fair value of Countries Bank's MexPower stake is $8.75 million (70 million pesos x .125). Therefore, Countries Bank will recognize a $1.25 million loss on this debt/equity swap ($10 million − $8.75 million).

Other Issues

With the exception of a discount from the official exchange rate imposed as a transaction fee, all other costs and expenses associated with the swap are to be charged to income as incurred. Any discount from the official exchange rate has the effect of reducing the fair value of the equity investment received by the lender; therefore, such a discount is considered in determining the amount of any loss recognized by the lender as a result of the swap.

Given the subjective nature of the valuation process, the fair value of the equity investment/net assets received might exceed the carrying amount of the loan. This apparent gain (or recovery of previous losses recognized on the loan) should not be recognized until the equity investment/net assets received are converted into unrestricted cash or cash equivalents.

A particular lender may have loans outstanding to a number of financially troubled countries. A loss recognized in a foreign debt/equity swap would be one piece of evidence suggesting that the allowance for loan losses, relating to loans outstanding to other financially distressed countries, should be increased.

CHAPTER 11
FOREIGN OPERATIONS AND EXCHANGE

CONTENTS

IMPRESS™ Cross-References	11.02
Overview	11.03
SOP 93-4 Foreign Currency Accounting and Financial Statement Presentation for Investment Companies	11.03
Background	11.03
Standards	11.04
Scope	11.04
General Conclusions	11.04
Investments—Purchased Interest	11.05
Illustration of the Accrual of Interest—Stable Exchange Rate	11.05
Investments—Marking to Market	11.06
Illustration of the Computation of Unrealized Gain	11.06
Investments—Sale	11.07
Investments—Sale of Interest	11.08
Income—Interest	11.08
Income—Accretion and Amortization	11.08
Illustration of the Computation of a Foreign Currency Gain—Bond Expiration	11.09
Dividends	11.09
Withholding Tax	11.09
Expenses	11.10
Receivables and Payables	11.10
Illustration of the Computation of a Foreign Currency Loss—Payables	11.10
Cash	11.11
Forward Exchange Contracts	11.11
Financial Statement Presentation	11.11
Other Issues	11.12

CROSS-REFERENCES

1999 MILLER GAAP GUIDE: Chapter 17, "Foreign Operations and Exchange"

1999 MILLER GAAP IMPLEMENTATION MANUAL: EITF: Chapter 12, "Foreign Currency Transactions"

1999 MILLER GAAP FOR NOT-FOR PROFIT ORGANIZATIONS: Chapter 2, "Overview of Current Pronouncements"; Chapter 11, "Display of Certain GAAP Transactions"

CHAPTER 11
FOREIGN OPERATIONS AND EXCHANGE

OVERVIEW

There are two major areas of foreign operations:

- Translation of foreign currency financial statements for purposes of consolidation, combination, or reporting on the equity method (one-line consolidation)
- Accounting and reporting of foreign currency transactions, including forward exchange contracts

GAAP for foreign operations and exchange are found in the following pronouncements that are included in the highest level of authority in the SAS-69 GAAP hierarchy:

FAS-52	Foreign Currency Translation
FIN-37	Accounting for Translation Adjustments upon Sale of Part of an Investment in a Foreign Entity

The following additional source of GAAP that is in a lower level of the SAS-69 GAAP hierarchy is discussed in this Manual:

SOP 93-4	Foreign Currency Accounting and Financial Statement Presentation for Investment Companies (Level B)

SOP 93-4: Foreign Currency Accounting and Financial Statement Presentation for Investment Companies

BACKGROUND

A number of U.S. investment companies offer closed-end single-country funds (e.g., the Germany Fund). These funds typically adopt the U.S. dollar as their functional currency, even though many of the transactions of the fund are denominated in a different currency (e.g., the mark for the Germany Fund). The U.S. dollar is typically adopted as the functional currency because sales, redemptions, and dividends are paid to shareholders in U.S. dollars.

SOP 93-4 is designed to provide guidance to investment companies in computing and reporting foreign currency gains and losses in two types of investment transactions: (1) transactions involving securities denominated in or expected to be settled in a currency other than the U.S. dollar and (2) investments in a currency other than the U.S. dollar. This Statement also provides guidance in handling other transactions (e.g., receivables and payables) denominated in currency other than the U.S. dollar.

STANDARDS

Scope

The provisions of SOP 93-4 apply to all investment companies subject to the provisions of the AICPA Audit and Accounting Guide titled *Audits of Investment Companies*. If the single-country fund invests in a country that is classified as "highly inflationary" (per FAS-52, par. 11), the measurement and disclosure guidelines in SOP 93-4 may not be appropriate.

General Conclusions

The following conditions can give rise to a foreign currency gain or loss:

1. The value of securities held, based on current exchange rates, differs from the securities cost.
2. The amount of a receivable or payable at the transaction date differs from the amount ultimately received or paid upon settlement, or differs from the amount receivable or payable at the reporting date based on current exchange rates.
3. The amount of interest, dividends, and withholding taxes at the transaction date differs from the amount ultimately received or paid, or differs from the amount receivable or payable at the reporting date based on current exchange rates.
4. Expenses accrued at the transaction date(s) differ from the amount ultimately paid, or differ from the amount payable at the reporting date based on current exchange rates.
5. Forward exchange contracts or foreign exchange futures contracts need to be marked to market.

All of these conditions result from changes in the exchange rate between the U.S. dollar and the foreign currency applicable to the fund. Before the settlement date of the transaction, a revaluation of securities, receivables, payables, etc., is classified as an unrealized gain or loss. When the transaction is settled (the cash flow occurs), the gain or loss is realized.

Differences between the amounts that were originally recorded and the amounts at which transactions are settled, or the amounts at which unsettled transactions are measured on the reporting date (based on the current exchange rate), are a function of two factors: (1) changes in the exchange rate and (2) changes in market prices. In recording the original transaction, the transaction at settlement, and the unsettled transaction at a reporting date, the reporting currency is used (i.e., typically the U.S. dollar).

The two components of gain/loss identified in the previous paragraph (changes in exchange rates and changes in market prices) must be separately identified, computed, and reported for all transactions other than for investments. Entities can choose to separately disclose the two components of gain/loss for investment transactions, or to combine these two elements.

Investments—Purchased Interest

Interest-bearing securities are often purchased between coupon dates. Accrued interest since the last coupon date is included in the purchase price of the security. The purchaser is to recognize this accrued interest as interest receivable, measured on the basis of the spot exchange rate on the transaction date. If a reporting date intervenes before the purchased interest is received, the interest receivable is measured at the reporting date on the basis of the spot exchange rate on that date. After the settlement date, interest is to be accrued on a daily basis using each day's spot exchange rate. If the exchange rate is relatively stable, however, interest can be accrued either weekly or monthly.

Illustration of the Accrual of Interest—Stable Exchange Rate

New Millennium Germany, a single-country closed-end fund, purchases an investment grade corporate bond for 1,000,000 marks on December 1, 19X8. The interest rate is 8%, and the investment is purchased at face value. The semiannual interest payment dates are September 1 and March 1. The exchange rate at December 1, 19X8, is $.58 per mark. This transaction would be recorded at December 1, 19X8 (in the fund's functional currency, the U.S. dollar), as follows:

Investment in Corporate Debt (1,000,000 x $.58)	$580,000	
Interest Receivable (1,000,000 x .08 x 4/12 x $.58)	15,467	
Cash		$595,467

The exchange rate is relatively stable during December. New Millennium will accrue interest at December 31, 19X8, using the average exchange rate for December ($.57 per mark). The appropriate journal entry is as follows:

Interest Receivable (1,000,000 x .08 x 1/12 x $.57)	$3,800	
Interest Income		$3,800

Investments—Marking to Market

As discussed previously, due to changes in both exchange rates and market values, the market value of a security at a valuation date (a reporting date) may differ from the amount at which the security was originally recorded on the transaction date. The two components of any unrealized gain or loss on securities *do not* have to be separately reported. However, SOP 93-4 indicates that in many cases such separate reporting would provide valuable information to users of the fund's financial statements.

The two components—changes in exchange rates and changes in market prices—of any unrealized gains or losses can be computed as follows:

Unrealized foreign currency gain or loss
 (Cost in foreign currency x Valuation date spot rate)
  – Cost in functional currency

Unrealized market value appreciation or depreciation
 (Market value in foreign currency
  – Original cost in foreign currency)
  x Valuation date spot rate

In the above computations, weekly or monthly average exchange rates can be used if daily fluctuations in exchange rates are not significant. Also, if an entity holds a short-term security that is being carried at amortized cost, amortized cost should be substituted for market value in the above formulas.

Illustration of the Computation of Unrealized Gain

The New Millennium Germany Fund purchases 1,000 shares of WMB Motors on December 1, 19X8, at a price of 40 marks per share. The exchange rate on December 1, 19X8, is $.58 per mark. On December 31, 19X8, the market price of WMB Motors is 41 marks per share, and the average exchange rate during December was $.57 (the exchange rate was relatively stable during the month). The two components of the unrealized gain recognized by New Millennium would be computed as follows:

Unrealized foreign currency gain or loss

$$(1{,}000 \text{ shares} \times 40 \text{ marks per share} \times \$.57)$$
$$- (1{,}000 \text{ shares} \times 40 \text{ marks per share} \times \$.58) = (\$400)$$

Unrealized market value appreciation or depreciation

$$[(1{,}000 \text{ shares} \times 41 \text{ marks per share})$$
$$- (1{,}000 \text{ shares} \times 40 \text{ marks per share})] \times \$.57 = \$570$$

PROOF:

$$(1{,}000 \text{ shares} \times 41 \text{ marks per share} \times \$.57)$$
$$- (1{,}000 \text{ shares} \times 40 \text{ marks per share} \times \$.58) = \$170$$

This proof is based on the following formula: (Market value in foreign currency x Valuation date spot rate) – (Cost in foreign currency x Transaction date spot rate)

Investments—Sale

A realized gain or loss on a security sale has two components: a realized exchange gain or loss and a realized market gain or loss. However, separately computing and displaying these two components is *optional*. If the entity chooses to report both pieces of the realized gain or loss, these amounts would be computed as follows:

Realized foreign currency gain or loss

(Cost in foreign currency x Sale date spot rate)
– Cost in functional currency

Realized market gain or loss

(Sale proceeds in foreign currency
– Original cost in foreign currency)
x Sale date spot rate

Upon the sale of securities, a receivable is recorded based on the exchange rate on the trade date. Any change in the exchange rate between the trade date and the settlement date will be recognized as a gain or loss when the trade is settled.

Investments—Sale of Interest

An entity may sell an interest-bearing security between coupon dates. The difference between the recorded interest receivable and the foreign currency received, translated into the functional currency at the current exchange rate, represents a realized gain or loss.

Income—Interest

Interest on a security denominated in a foreign currency is to be accrued daily. First the interest is measured in the foreign currency, and then it is converted into the functional currency using the daily spot exchange rate. If the exchange rate is relatively stable, this calculation can be based on the average weekly or monthly exchange rate.

Interest receivable, which includes both accrued interest and purchased interest, is initially measured in the foreign currency. At the valuation date (which may be daily), the receivable is converted into the functional currency using the current exchange rate. The difference between the interest receivable, converted at the spot exchange date on the valuation date, and interest accrued in the foreign currency is the unrealized foreign currency gain or loss.

Income—Accretion and Amortization

Bonds are often purchased at a premium or a discount. Any such premium or discount should initially be amortized daily on a foreign currency basis. At maturity, the carrying value of the bond in the foreign currency will equal the foreign currency proceeds received. However, in most cases there will be a realized foreign currency gain or loss.

The purchase price of the bond, at the trade date, is converted into the entity's functional currency using that day's exchange rate. Daily amortization of discount or premium, in the entity's foreign currency, is converted into functional currency using the daily exchange rate (again, if exchange rates are relatively constant, a weekly or monthly average rate can be used). The sum of the purchase price of the bond (converted into functional currency on the trade date) plus (minus) amortization of the discount (premium) over the life of the bond (converted into functional currency at periodic spot rates) will produce the carrying value of the bond in the entity's functional currency. The proceeds received upon the expiration of the bond, its face value in foreign currency, is to be converted into the entity's functional currency using the exchange rate in effect on the maturity date. In most cases, the proceeds in functional currency will differ from the carrying value of the bond in functional currency. This is what gives rise to a foreign currency gain or loss.

Illustration of the Computation of a Foreign Currency Gain—Bond Expiration

The New Millennium Germany Fund purchased a 25,000,000-mark bond on October 1, 19X8, at 97%. The exchange rate on this date was $.56 per mark. The carrying value of this bond in U.S. dollars, the functional currency, on October 1, 19X8, is $13,580,000 (25,000,000 marks x 97% x $.56). Over the remaining life of this bond, New Millennium must amortize the discount of 750,000 marks. Based on the spot rates in effect when this discount was amortized, the functional currency amount of the discount amortization was $412,500. The spot exchange rate is $.59 on the bond's due date. Therefore, on the bond's due date the New Millennium Germany Fund will receive 25,000,000 marks, which is convertible into $14,750,000 (25,000,000 marks x $.59). The carrying value of the bond in U.S. dollars is $13,992,500 ($13,580,000 + $412,500). Therefore, New Millennium would have a realized foreign currency gain of $757,500.

Dividends

Dividend income on securities denominated in a foreign currency is to be recognized on the ex-dividend date. The amount of the dividend in foreign currency is to be converted into functional currency using the exchange rate on that date (DR, Dividend Receivable; CR, Dividend Income). The related DR account is to be translated daily at the spot exchange rate; differences that arise as a result of this process are unrealized gains or losses. When the dividend is received, the unrealized gain or loss account is reclassified as realized gain or loss.

Withholding Tax

In some cases, taxes are withheld from investment and dividend income at the source. These withheld amounts may or may not be reclaimable by the fund. If the tax withheld is not reclaimable, it should be accrued on each income recognition date if the tax rate is fixed and known. If the tax withheld is reclaimable, it should be recorded as a receivable and not as an expense. If the tax rate is not known or estimable, the expense (when the tax is not reclaimable) or the receivable (when the tax is reclaimable) is recorded on the date the (net) investment income is received. When the net investment income is received, the realized foreign currency gain or loss is computed on the gross income receivable and the accrued tax expense.

Expenses

Expenses should be accrued as incurred and translated into the functional currency using the exchange rate on the day the expense is incurred. The difference between the expense accrued in the functional currency and the related foreign currency accrued expense balance (a liability) translated into the functional currency using the exchange rate on the valuation date is the unrealized foreign currency gain or loss. When the expense is paid, the unrealized foreign currency gain or loss is reclassified as a realized gain or loss.

Receivables and Payables

Receivables and payables typically arise to record items of income and expense and to record the purchase or sale of securities. At each valuation date, all receivables and payables should be translated into the functional currency using the exchange rate on the valuation date. In most cases, there will be a difference between the amount of the receivable or payable translated at the valuation date and the functional currency amount that was recorded at various spot rates for income or expense items (or for purchases and sales of securities on different dates). This difference is an unrealized gain or loss. When a receivable or payable is settled, the difference between the amount received or paid (in functional currency) and the functional currency amount that was recorded at various spot rates for income or expense items (or for purchases and sales of securities on different dates) is a realized gain or loss.

Illustration of the Computation of a Foreign Currency Loss—Payables

The New Millennium Germany Fund incurs the following expenses during December 19X8: 10,000 marks on 12/7; 11,000 marks on 12/14; 12,000 marks on 12/21; and 13,000 marks on 12/28. The spot exchange rates on these dates are $.55, $.59, $.57, and $.58, respectively. Therefore, the functional currency value of these expenses is $26,370 [(10,000 marks x $.55) + (11,000 marks x $.59) + (12,000 marks x $.57) + (13,000 marks x $.58)]. The exchange rate on December 31, 19X8, is $.58. Also, these expenses represent the December 31, 19X8, accrued expense balance. New Millennium's accrued expense balance, in its functional currency, is $26,680 at year-end. Therefore, New Millennium would have an unrealized (the liability is not yet settled) foreign currency loss of $310 ($26,680 − $26,370).

Cash

Receipts of foreign currency (cash) are to be treated as if a foreign-currency denominated security had been purchased. The foreign currency received is to be converted into the functional currency using the exchange rate on the day the cash is received. Every disbursement of foreign currency is to be treated as if a security had been sold. The functional equivalent of the foreign currency disbursed is to be credited (using specific identification, FIFO, or average cost to determine the amount of the functional currency to be released).

The acquisition of foreign currency does not result in a gain or loss. However, the disposition of foreign currency typically does result in a gain or loss. The gain or loss is measured as the difference between the functional currency equivalent on the date the foreign currency was acquired and the functional currency equivalent on the date the foreign currency is disbursed.

The functional currency equivalent of foreign currency held is to be computed on each valuation date. Any difference between this amount and the functional currency equivalent of the foreign currency on the date it was acquired is an unrealized gain or loss.

Forward Exchange Contracts

A *forward exchange contract* is an agreement between two parties to exchange two currencies at a specified rate on a specified date in the future. If a fund enters into a forward exchange contract, the contract is to be initially recorded at the forward rate and marked to market on a daily basis.

Unrealized gain or loss on these contracts are computed as follows: the foreign currency amount valued at the valuation date forward rate minus the amount to be received or paid at the settlement date. On the settlement date, the unrealized gain or loss is reclassified as realized gain or loss.

Financial Statement Presentation

A section of the Statement of Operations is titled "Realized and Unrealized Gain (Loss) from Investments and Foreign Currency." This section follows the presentation of investment income and investment expenses. All foreign currency gains and losses should be reported in this section. Gains or losses from non-investment transactions would have their own line item in the Statement: "Foreign currency transactions" (with separate line items for realized and unrealized gains and losses). If foreign currency gains and losses from investment transactions are computed separately, these amounts would be included in the line item "Foreign currency transactions" as well. If foreign currency gains and losses from investment transactions are not computed separately, they would be aggregated with market gains or losses from investment transactions and reported in the line item "Investments."

The Statement of Assets and Liabilities and the Statement of Changes in Net Assets should reflect the same unrealized and realized gain and loss components. It is permissible to combine (*a*) net realized gains and losses from investments with net realized gains and losses from foreign currency transactions and (*b*) net unrealized appreciation (depreciation) on investments with the net unrealized appreciation (depreciation) on the translation of assets and liabilities in foreign currencies.

The notes to the financial statements should disclose the entity's policy regarding the treatment of unrealized and realized gains or losses from investments. Otherwise these amounts do not have to be separately disclosed; however, such disclosure may provide useful information to financial statement users.

Certain taxes on foreign source income are not reclaimable. To the extent such taxes exist, the relevant amount should be deducted from the related amount of income. Either this reduction in the income amount is shown parenthetically on the face of the income statement or else a contra-account (to the income item) should be presented on the face of the income statement. Taxes that are based on the aggregate income or capital gains of the investment company are to be treated in a manner similar to income taxes.

Other Issues

Investing in foreign securities poses a number of risks. In addition to the foreign currency risks already discussed, risks related to liquidity, size, and valuation need to be monitored by management and considered for disclosure. Some foreign markets are illiquid. Therefore, quoted market prices may not necessarily be indicative of net realizable value. Some foreign markets are relatively small, and a fund may hold an investment that represents a sizable stake in the overall market. In these cases, quoted market prices may not be indicative of net realizable value. For the reasons previously discussed, determining the proper valuation of securities is sometimes subjective. The fund's board of directors has the ultimate responsibility for determining the fair values of securities.

CHAPTER 12
INCOME TAXES

CONTENTS

IMPRESS™ Cross-References	**12.02**
Overview	**12.03**
FIG-FAS 109: A Guide to Implementation of Statement 109 on Accounting for Income Taxes	**12.04**
Background	**12.04**
Standards	**12.04**
Scheduling	**12.04**
Recognition and Measurement	**12.06**
Change in Tax Status	**12.07**
Illustration of Change in Tax Status	**12.08**
Business Combinations	**12.08**
Disclosure	**12.10**
Allocation of Tax Expense	**12.10**
Transition	**12.10**
Tax-Planning Strategies	**12.12**
Illustration of Multiple Tax Planning Strategies	**12.13**

IMPRESS™

CROSS-REFERENCES

1999 MILLER GAAP GUIDE: Chapter 21, "Income Taxes"

1999 MILLER GAAP IMPLEMENTATION MANUAL: EITF: Chapter 14, "Income Taxes"

1999 MILLER GAAP FOR NOT-FOR-PROFIT ORGANIZATIONS: Chapter 13, "Tax Reporting Requirements"

CHAPTER 12
INCOME TAXES

OVERVIEW

The tax consequences of many transactions recognized in the financial statements are included in determining income taxes currently payable in the same accounting period. Sometimes, however, tax laws differ from the recognition and measurement requirements of financial reporting standards. Differences arise between the tax bases of assets or liabilities and their reported amounts in the financial statements. These differences are called *temporary differences* and they give rise to deferred tax assets and liabilities.

Temporary differences ordinarily reverse when the related asset is recovered or the related liability is settled. A *deferred tax liability* or *deferred tax asset* represents the increase or decrease in taxes payable or refundable in future years as a result of temporary differences and carryforwards at the end of the current year.

The objectives of accounting for income taxes are to recognize:

- The amount of taxes payable or refundable for the current year
- The deferred tax liabilities and assets that result from future tax consequences of events that have been recognized in the enterprise's financial statements or tax returns

GAAP for accounting for income taxes are in the following pronouncements that are included in the highest level of authority in the SAS-69 GAAP hierarchy:

APB-10	Paragraph 6, Tax Allocation Accounts—Discounting Paragraph 7, Offsetting Securities against Taxes Payable
APB-23	Accounting for Income Taxes—Special Areas
FAS-109	Accounting for Income Taxes
FIN-18	Accounting for Income Taxes in Interim Periods

The following additional source of GAAP that is in a lower level of the SAS-69 GAAP hierarchy is discussed in this Manual:

FIG-FAS 109	A Guide to Implementation of Statement 109 on Accounting for Income Taxes (Level D)

FIG-FAS 109: A Guide to Implementation of Statement 109 on Accounting for Income Taxes

BACKGROUND

FAS-109 (Accounting for Income Taxes) has resulted in many implementation issues. The FASB prepared an Implementation Guide to deal with several of the most frequently asked questions.

STANDARDS

Scheduling

Question 1: When is it necessary to schedule reversal patterns of existing temporary differences?

Answer: Scheduling individual years in terms of reversals of temporary differences is required under FAS-109 in the following circumstances:

- When deferred taxes that do not relate to a specific asset or liability are classified as current or noncurrent based on the timing of their reversal.
- When deferred tax assets are recognized without consideration of offsetting, after which an assessment is required concerning the need for a valuation allowance. The timing of reversal of temporary differences may be an important consideration in determining the need for and amount of a valuation allowance on deferred tax assets.
- When tax rate changes are phased in, which will often require scheduling.

Question 2: FAS-109 states that future originating temporary differences for existing depreciable assets and their subsequent reversals are a factor in assessing the likelihood of future realization of a tax benefit of deductible temporary differences and carryforwards. Should future originating and reversing temporary differences always be scheduled for purposes of determining the need for a valuation allowance for deferred tax assets related to existing deductible temporary differences and carryforwards?

Answer: Not necessarily. There are four possible sources of taxable income to support the realizability of deferred tax assets. When it can easily be demonstrated that future taxable income will be sufficient, scheduling is generally not necessary. However, if reversal of taxable temporary differences is the basis for a realization assumption for deferred tax assets, the timing of reversal is important and may require scheduling.

Question 3: Does FAS-109 require separate deferred tax computations for each state or local tax jurisdiction?

Answer: As a general rule, the answer is "yes," if there are significant differences between the tax laws of the different jurisdictions involved. In the United States, however, many state and local income taxes are based on U.S. federal income tax, and aggregate computations of deferred tax assets and liabilities may be appropriate.

Question 4: An enterprise may have a basis under the tax law for claiming certain deductions (e.g., repair expense) on its income tax return. It may have recognized a liability (including interest) for the probable disallowance of that deduction that, if disallowed, would be capitalized for tax purposes and deductible in future years. How should an item like this be considered in the scheduling of future taxable or deductible differences?

Answer: If expenses are disallowed, taxable income of that year is higher, which provides a source of taxable income for purposes of assessing the need for a valuation allowance for deductible temporary differences. Taxable income after the year of disallowance will be lower, because of annual deductions attributable to those capitalized amounts. A deductible amount for the accrued interest is scheduled for the future year in which that interest is expected to be deductible (i.e., when the underlying issues are expected to be settled with the tax authority).

Question 5: A change in tax law may require a change in accounting method for tax purposes (e.g., the uniform cost capitalization rules required by the Tax Reform Act of 1986). For calendar-year taxpayers, inventories on hand at the beginning of 1987 are revalued under the new rules, and the initial catch-up adjustment is deferred and taken into taxable income over not more than four years. Does the deferral of the initial catch-up adjustment for a change in accounting method for tax purposes give rise to a temporary difference?

Answer: Yes. The uniform cost capitalization rules initially resulted in two temporary differences—one related to the additional amounts initially capitalized into inventory for tax expense and one related to the deferred income for tax purposes that results from the initial catch-up adjustment.

Question 6: The Omnibus Budget Reconciliation Act of 1987 requires family-owned farming businesses to use the accrual method of accounting for tax purposes. The initial catch-up adjustment to change from the cash method to the accrual method is deferred and included in taxable income if the business ceases to be family-owned. It also is included in taxable income if gross receipts from farming activities in future years drop below certain 1987 levels. Does the deferral of the initial catch-up adjustment for that change in accounting method for tax purposes give rise to a temporary difference?

Answer: Yes. The entire amount of the catch-up adjustment is a temporary difference.

Question 7: State income taxes are deductible for U.S. federal income tax purposes. Does a deferred state income tax liability or asset give rise to a temporary difference for purposes of determining a deferred U.S. federal income tax liability or asset?

Answer: Yes. A deferred state income tax liability or asset gives rise to a temporary difference for purposes of determining deferred taxes for U.S. federal income tax purposes.

Recognition and Measurement

Question 8: The temporary difference for the "base-year tax reserve" of a savings and loan association is one of the exceptions to comprehensive recognition of deferred taxes under FAS-109. If a deferred tax liability is not recognized for that temporary difference, should a savings and loan association anticipate future percentage-of-taxable-income (PTI) bad-debt deductions in determining the deferred tax liability for other types of temporary differences?

Answer: No. Deferred tax assets and liabilities for temporary differences are measured based on enacted tax rates expected to apply to taxable income when the deferred tax asset or liability is expected to be realized or settled. For the same reason that other special deductions may not be anticipated, it is not permissible to reduce a deferred tax liability by anticipating future PTI bad-debt reductions.

Question 9: An enterprise charged losses directly to contributed capital in a quasi-reorganization. At that time, the deferred tax asset for the enterprise's deductible temporary differences and carryforwards was offset by a valuation allowance. Part of those deductible temporary differences were related to losses that were included in determining income in prior years, and the remainder were attributable to losses that were charged directly to contributed capital. When recognized by reducing or eliminating the valuation allowance, how should the tax benefit of such deductible temporary differences and carryforwards be reported?

Answer: All unrecognized tax benefits of deductible temporary differences and carryforwards that existed at the time of a quasi-reorganization (except as provided in FAS-109, par. 39) should be reported as a direct addition to contributed capital when recognized at a date after the quasi-reorganization. ARB-43, Chapter 7 (Capital Accounts), indicates that the benefit of an operating loss or tax credit carryforward that existed at the date of a quasi-reorganization should not be included in the determination of income of the "new" enterprise, regardless of whether they were charged to income before the quasi-reorganization or were charged directly to contributed capital as part of the quasi-reorganization. A charge to income is appropriate only if, subsequent to a quasi-reorganization, the enterprise determines that due to a change in circumstances it should recognize or increase a valuation allowance to reduce the tax benefits that were recognized in recording the quasi-reorganization.

Question 10: Some enterprises have credited a net gain directly to contributed capital at the date of a quasi-reorganization. Does the answer to Question 9 change for those enterprises?

Answer: No. The accounting for any subsequently recognized tax benefit of deductible temporary differences and carryforwards that exist at the time of a quasi-reorganization should not change based on whether gains were credited or losses charged directly to contributed capital.

Change in Tax Status

Question 11: What disclosure is required if a change in an enterprise's tax status becomes effective after year-end but before financial statements are issued?

Answer: This change should not be reflected in the financial statements of the previous year, but disclosure should include the change in the enterprise's tax status for the following year and the effects of that change, if material.

Question 12: Should an enterprise that changes from taxable C corporation status to nontaxable S corporation status eliminate its entire U.S. federal deferred tax liability?

Answer: The enterprise should continue to recognize a deferred tax liability to the extent that it would be subject to a corporate-level tax on net unrealized "built-in gains."

Illustration of Change in Tax Status

Company M's assets are as followed when its S corporation election becomes effective:

	Tax Basis	Reported Amount	Temporary Difference	Built-In Gain (Loss)
Marketable Securities	$100	$ 80	$(20)	$(8)
Inventory	50	100	50	20

If the enterprise has no tax loss or tax credit carryforwards available to offset the built-in gain and if marketable securities and inventory will both be sold in the same year, the $20 built-in gain on the inventory is offset by the $8 built-in loss on the marketable securities, and the $12 difference would be shown as a deferred tax liability.

Business Combinations

Question 13: FAS-109 requires the tax benefit of acquired deductible differences and carryforwards that are initially recognized in financial statements subsequent to the acquisition date to be applied, first, to reduce to zero any goodwill related to that acquisition; second, to reduce to zero other noncurrent intangible assets; and third, to reduce income tax expense. Does the requirement to adjust goodwill for subsequently recognized deductible temporary differences and carryforwards relate to negative goodwill as well as to positive goodwill?

Answer: No. The requirement to reduce goodwill for those tax benefits relates only to positive goodwill. Unallocated negative goodwill would not be increased by these tax benefits.

Question 14: Tax law permits an acquiring enterprise's deductible temporary differences and carryforwards to reduce future taxable income attributable to the acquired enterprise if consolidated tax returns are filed subsequent to acquisition. Accounting for the business combination should recognize reductions in the acquiring enterprise's existing valuation allowance for deferred tax assets as a result of an assessment of realization by the combined enterprise. If there is a valuation allowance for the acquiring enterprise's deferred tax assets at the acquisition date, how should tax benefits for the related deductible temporary differences and carryforwards be reported if and when they are recognized in subsequent years?

Answer: The tax benefit should be recognized as a reduction in income tax expense when recognized in financial statements in subsequent years. The reasoning is that the tax benefit does not result from utilizing the deductible temporary differences or carryforwards of the acquired enterprise.

Question 15: How should a deferred tax liability or asset be determined for a purchase business combination that results in negative goodwill?

Answer: Allocation of negative goodwill reduces the values otherwise assignable to the noncurrent assets acquired, other than long-term investments in marketable securities. That reduction, however, changes the temporary differences related to those assets—which in turn changes the amount of deferred tax asset or liability, which changes the amount of negative goodwill. Calculating the amount of deferred taxes and negative goodwill requires the simultaneous computation of the assigned value of those acquired assets and the amount of deferred tax asset or liability.

Question 16: FAS-109 states that deferred taxes shall not be provided for temporary differences related either to positive goodwill for which amortization is not deductible for tax purposes or to unallocated negative goodwill. Should temporary differences related to intangible assets such as customer lists and trademarks be treated the same way?

Answer: No. A deferred tax liability or asset should be recognized for temporary differences related to intangible assets other than goodwill. This includes customer lists and trademarks.

Question 17: In a taxable purchase business combination, an enterprise allocates for tax purposes the purchase price to the assets acquired and liabilities assumed in a manner that maximizes the potential income tax benefits from the combination. Although the enterprise has a basis under the tax law for the allocation claimed in initial filings with the tax authority, the enterprise believes that the tax authority will deny portions of the allocation and the amount assigned to goodwill will ultimately be greater. Should deferred income taxes recognized at the date of the business combination be based on the tax basis of acquired assets or liabilities claimed in the initial filings or on the best estimate of the tax basis that will ultimately be accepted by the tax authority? What is the appropriate accounting in later periods for changes in the purchase price allocation for tax purposes?

Answer: Deferred tax assets and liabilities at the date of a business combination should be based on management's best estimate of the tax basis of acquired assets and liabilities that will ultimately be accepted by the tax authority. At or before settlement with the tax authority, management may change its estimate of the tax basis of acquired assets. When the tax basis of the acquired assets and liabilities is settled, the amount of deferred tax assets and liabilities should be adjusted to reflect the revised tax basis and the amount of any settlement for prior-year income taxes. The effect of this adjustment increases or decreases the remaining balance of goodwill attributable to the transaction.

Disclosure

Question 18: FAS-109 requires disclosure of the significant components of income tax expense attributable to continuing operations. Should the total of the amounts disclosed for the components of tax expense equal the amount of income tax expense that is reported in the statement of earnings? Should the amounts for current and deferred tax expense be disclosed before or after reduction for the tax benefit of operating loss carryforwards and tax credits?

Answer: The total of the amounts disclosed for the components of tax expense should be the amount of tax expense reported in the statement of earnings for continuing operations. Separate disclosure is required of (*a*) the tax benefit of operating loss carryforwards and (*b*) tax credits and tax credit carryforwards that were recognized.

Allocation of Tax Expense

Question 19: How should income tax expense be allocated between pretax income from continuing operations and other items when the enterprise has temporary differences?

Answer: FAS-109 states that the amount of income tax expense or benefit allocated to continuing operations is the tax effect of pretax income or loss from continuing operations that occurred during the year (subject to certain adjustments). Income tax expense allocated between pretax income from continuing operations and other items should include deferred taxes.

Transition

Question 20: How and when should an enterprise that adopted FAS-109 before the issuance of FIG-FAS 109 account for the effect of initially complying with the subsequently issued implementation guidance?

Answer: In this circumstance, the effects of adopting this implementation guidance should be reported as a cumulative effect of a change in accounting principle in accordance with APB-20 (Accounting Changes).

Question 21: If FAS-109 is not adopted until the first fiscal year beginning after December 15, 1992, may it be applied initially in other than the first interim reporting period of that year with restatement of prior interim periods?

Answer: No. FAS-109 was effective as of the beginning of the first fiscal year beginning after December 15, 1992, and financial information for the first interim period of that year should conform to the standard.

Question 22: An enterprise adopts FAS-109 without restating the financial statements of prior years because to do so is impracticable, and it does not adjust any remaining amounts that were originally assigned on a net-of-tax basis as permitted by APB-16 (Business Combinations). Instead, the enterprise records deferred tax assets and liabilities for the difference between the tax bases and the remaining balances for financial reporting of the acquired assets and liabilities, including those assets and liabilities reported on a net-of-tax basis.

After an enterprise makes the transition to FAS-109, the future recovery or settlement of the pretax amounts of assets and liabilities that are reported on a net-of-tax basis will often result in an after-tax gain or loss. After the transition to FAS-109, should an asset or liability reported net-of-tax that is expected to result in an after-tax loss when it is recovered or settled in future years be remeasured (i.e., adjusted to a pretax amount rather than a net-of-tax amount and a corresponding tax asset recognized) or otherwise adjusted because the asset is considered to be impaired or the liability is considered to be understated?

Answer: No. Remeasurement or adjustment of certain purchased assets or liabilities when other assets or liabilities acquired in the same business combination are stated at net-of-tax amounts is impractical and is not permitted in the adoption of FAS-109.

Question 23: The tax benefit of acquired deductible temporary differences and carryforwards that are initially recognized at the date of transition is one of the effects referred to in FAS-109 for which part of the adjustment to the statement might have to be excluded from net income. Those tax benefits are excluded when initially recognized after the business combination, either at the transition date or in subsequent periods, until first goodwill and then other noncurrent intangible assets related to that acquisition are reduced to zero. If a purchase business combination occurred in a prior year that is not restated when FAS-109 is initially applied, the remaining balances of any assets and liabilities recognized in that business combination are adjusted to pretax amounts unless to do so is impracticable. In either case, how should an enterprise determine the amount of acquired deductible temporary differences and operating loss or tax credit carryforwards from a prior purchase business combination for which any subsequently recognized tax benefits first should be applied to reduce to zero any goodwill and other noncurrent intangible assets related to that business combination?

Answer: At the date of the purchase business combination, the amount of acquired deductible temporary differences and carryforwards for which any subsequently recognized tax benefit first should be applied to reduce goodwill and other intangible assets is the total of (*a*) any operating loss or tax credit carryforward for which a tax benefit was not recognized and (*b*) any excess of the tax basis over the pretax fair value of the net assets acquired for which a tax benefit was not reflected in assigning values to those assets. The remaining acquired deductible temporary differences and carryforwards, if any, are the amount for which any tax benefits that are recognized either at the transition date or in subsequent periods are excluded from net income until goodwill and other noncurrent intangible assets related to the acquisition are reduced to zero.

Question 24: Information about a prior business combination may be unavailable or the cost to develop such information may be excessive (e.g., the amount of acquired deductible temporary differences and carryforwards for which subsequently recognized tax benefits are excluded from net income until goodwill and other noncurrent intangible assets related to that acquisition are reduced to zero). How much, if any, of those tax benefits should be excluded from net income at the transition date and in subsequent periods?

Answer: No portion of the transition adjustment is allocated to reduce goodwill and other noncurrent intangible assets. Immediately after the transition date, however, the amount of any deductible temporary differences and carryforwards for which a tax benefit was not recognized is presumed to have been acquired in the prior business combination. That presumption may be overcome to the extent that some or all of the deductible temporary differences and carryforwards can be attributed to events that occurred after the date of the business combination. The tax benefits that are not clearly attributable to events occurring after the combination date should be applied to reduce to zero any goodwill and noncurrent intangible assets from the acquisition. Any additional tax benefits recognized should reduce income tax expense.

Tax-Planning Strategies

Question 25: FAS-109 indicates that tax-planning strategies include elections for tax purposes. What are some examples of those elections?

Answer: Examples are as follows:

- Election to file a consolidated tax return
- Election to claim either a deduction or a tax credit for foreign taxes paid
- Election to forego carrying an operating loss back and only carry that loss forward

Question 26: An enterprise might identify several qualifying tax-planning strategies that would either reduce or eliminate the need for a valuation allowance for its deferred tax assets. May the enterprise recognize the effect of one strategy in the current year and postpone recognition of the effect of the other strategies to a later year?

Answer: No. The enterprise should recognize the effect of all tax-planning strategies that meet the criteria of FAS-109 in the current year.

Illustration of Multiple Tax Planning Strategies

Amber Co. has determined that its allowance on deferred tax assets should be $60,000, without regard to tax-planning strategies. The company has identified two income tax–planning strategies that would reduce its allowance on deferred tax assets by $10,000 (Strategy 1) and by $15,000 (Strategy 2), respectively. Both qualify as tax-planning strategies under FAS-109. Amber cannot recognize the effect of only Strategy 1 or only Strategy 2 but, rather, must recognize the impact of both and report an allowance on deferred tax assets of $35,000 [$60,000 – ($10,000 + $15,000)].

Question 27: Because the effects of known qualifying tax strategies must be recognized, is management required to make an extensive effort to identify all tax-planning strategies that meet the criteria for tax-planning strategies?

Answer: Management is required to make a reasonable effort to identify significant tax-planning strategies. If evidence indicates that other sources of taxable income will be adequate to eliminate the need for a valuation allowance, consideration of tax-planning strategies is not required.

Question 28: Under current U.S. federal income tax law, approval of a change from taxable C corporation status to nontaxable S status is automatic if the enterprise meets the criteria for S corporation status. If an enterprise meets those criteria but has not changed to S corporation status, would a strategy to change to nontaxable S corporation status be a qualifying tax-planning strategy that would permit an enterprise to not recognize deferred taxes?

Answer: No. The effect of a change in tax status should be recognized on the date when the change in tax status occurs.

CHAPTER 13
INTANGIBLE ASSETS

CONTENTS

IMPRESS™ Cross-References	**13.02**
Overview	**13.03**
AIN-APB 17: Intangible Assets: Unofficial Accounting Interpretations of APB Opinion No. 17	**13.03**
Background	**13.03**
Standards	**13.04**
Internally Developed Intangibles	**13.04**
Goodwill in a Step Transaction	**13.04**

CROSS-REFERENCES

1999 MILLER GAAP IMPLEMENTATION MANUAL: Chapter 5, "Business Combinations"

1999 MILLER GAAP GUIDE: Chapter 23, "Intangible Assets"

1999 MILLER GAAP IMPLEMENTATION MANUAL: EITF: Chapter 15, "Intangible Assets"

1999 MILLER GAAP FOR NOT-FOR-PROFIT ORGANIZATIONS: Chapter 2, "Overview of Current Pronouncements"

CHAPTER 13
INTANGIBLE ASSETS

OVERVIEW

Intangible assets are long-lived assets used in the production of goods and services. They are similar to property, plant, and equipment except for their lack of physical properties. Examples of intangible assets include copyrights, patents, trademarks, and goodwill. They generally are subject to amortization over their estimated useful lives, subject to certain limitations for intangibles acquired on or before October 31, 1970.

The following pronouncements contain GAAP for intangible assets that are included in the highest level of authority in the SAS-69 GAAP hierarchy:

APB-16	Business Combinations
APB-17	Intangible Assets
FAS-44	Accounting for Intangible Assets of Motor Carriers
FAS-72	Accounting for Certain Acquisitions of Banking or Thrift Institutions
FIN-9	Applying APB Opinions No. 16 and 17 When a Savings and Loan Association or a Similar Institution Is Acquired in a Business Combination Accounted for by the Purchase Method

The following additional source of GAAP that is in a lower level of the SAS-69 GAAP hierarchy is discussed in this Manual:

AIN-APB 17   Intangible Assets: Unofficial Accounting Interpretations of APB Opinion No. 17 (Level D)

AIN-APB 17: Intangible Assets: Unofficial Accounting Interpretations of APB Opinion No. 17

BACKGROUND

AIN-APB 17 answers two questions about the application of APB-17 (Intangible Assets), one concerning the potential capitalization of internally developed intangible assets and the other concerning goodwill in a step acquisition.

STANDARDS

Internally Developed Intangibles

Question 1: Does APB-17 encourage the capitalization of identifiable internally developed intangible assets that were previously charged to expense?

Answer: No. APB-17 does not change accounting for intangibles other than to require the amortization of intangible assets acquired after October 31, 1970. It does not specifically address the issue of capitalization of internally developed intangible assets.

Goodwill in a Step Transaction

Question 2: APB-17 requires amortization of intangible assets acquired after October 31, 1970. When a company purchases two or more blocks of voting common stock of another company at various dates before and after November 1, 1970, eventually obtaining control or the ability to exercise significant influence, how should the investing company account for any goodwill related to the investment?

Answer: Goodwill should be separately identified with each step in the acquisition. Goodwill assigned to purchases before November 1, 1970, is not required to be amortized, although APB-17 encourages amortization if evidence suggests that the goodwill has a limited life. Goodwill assigned to purchases after October 31, 1970, must be amortized in accordance with APB-17.

CHAPTER 14
INTEREST ON RECEIVABLES AND PAYABLES

CONTENTS

IMPRESS™ Cross-References	**14.02**
Overview	**14.03**
AIN-APB 21: Interest on Receivables and Payables: Accounting Interpretations of APB Opinion No. 21	**14.03**
Background	**14.03**
Standards	**14.04**

IMPRESS™

CROSS-REFERENCES

1999 MILLER GAAP GUIDE: Chapter 25, "Interest on Receivables and Payables"

1999 MILLER GAAP IMPLEMENTATION MANUAL: EITF: Chapter 16, "Interest on Receivables and Payables"

1999 MILLER GAAP FOR NOT-FOR-PROFIT ORGANIZATIONS: Chapter 2, "Overview of Current Pronouncements"

CHAPTER 14
INTEREST ON RECEIVABLES AND PAYABLES

OVERVIEW

Business transactions often involve the exchange of cash or other assets for a note or other instrument. When the interest rate on the instrument is consistent with the market rate at the time of the transaction, the face amount of the instrument is assumed to be equal to the value of the other asset(s) exchanged. An interest rate that is different from the prevailing market rate, however, implies that the face amount of the instrument may not equal the value of the other asset(s) exchanged. In this case, it may be necessary to impute interest that is not stated as part of the instrument, or to recognize interest at a rate other than that stated in the instrument.

Promulgated GAAP in the area of recognizing interest on receivables and payables are found in the following pronouncement that is included in the highest level of authority in the SAS-69 GAAP hierarchy:

    APB-21   Interest on Receivables and Payables

The following additional source of GAAP that is in a lower level of the SAS-69 GAAP hierarchy is discussed in this Manual:

    AIN-APB 21   Interest on Receivables and Payables: Accounting Interpretations of APB Opinion No. 21 (Level D)

AIN-APB 21: Interest on Receivables and Payables: Accounting Interpretations of APB Opinion No. 21

BACKGROUND

AIN-APB 21 provides implementation guidance for APB-21.

STANDARDS

Question: APB-21 requires interest to be imputed for some rights to receive or to pay money on fixed or determinable dates. For example, a pipeline company may make an advance payment to encourage exploration. The intent is for this advance payment to be satisfied by the delivery of future production. However, if future production is not sufficient to discharge the amount of the advance payment, there is an obligation to pay cash to settle the obligation. Does APB-21 apply to such advances?

Answer: No. APB-21 applies not to amounts that will not be repaid in the future, but rather to amounts that will be applied to the purchase price of property, goods, or services. The advance described above fits this definition even though there is an obligation to pay cash if future production is not sufficient to settle the liability.

CHAPTER 15
INTERIM FINANCIAL REPORTING

CONTENTS

IMPRESS™ Cross-References	**15.02**
Overview	**15.03**
FTB 79-9: Accounting in Interim Periods for Changes in Income Tax Rates	**15.03**
Background	**15.03**
Standards	**15.03**

CROSS-REFERENCES

1999 MILLER GAAP GUIDE: Chapter 26, "Interim Financial Reporting"

1999 MILLER GAAP IMPLEMENTATION MANUAL: EITF: Chapter 17, "Interim Financial Reporting"

1999 MILLER GAAS GUIDE: Chapter 13, "Interim Reviews, Condensed Financials, Filings Under Federal Securities Statutes, and Letters to Underwriters"

CHAPTER 15
INTERIM FINANCIAL REPORTING

OVERVIEW

Interim financial reports may be issued quarterly, monthly, or at other intervals, and may include complete financial statements or summarized data. In addition, they usually include the current interim period and a cumulative year-to-date period, or last 12 months to date, with comparative reports on the corresponding periods of the immediately preceding fiscal year.

GAAP for interim financial statements are found primarily in the following pronouncement that is included in the highest level of authority in the SAS-69 GAAP hierarchy:

APB-28   Interim Financial Reporting

The following additional source of GAAP that is in a lower level of the SAS-69 GAAP hierarchy is discussed in this Manual:

FTB 79-9   Accounting in Interim Periods for Changes in Income Tax Rates (Level B)

FTB 79-9: Accounting in Interim Periods for Changes in Income Tax Rates

BACKGROUND

Federal tax rates may change, raising questions about how a company with a fiscal year other than the calendar year should account for the change in interim periods.

STANDARDS

Question: How should a company with a fiscal year other than a calendar year account during interim periods for the reduction in the corporate tax rate resulting from the Revenue Act of 1978?

Answer: FIN-18 (Accounting for Income Taxes in Interim Periods), paragraph 24, requires that the effects of a tax rate change be reflected in a revised annual effective tax rate calculation in the same way that the change will be applied to the company's taxable income for the year. The revised annual tax rate would then be applied to pretax income for the year-to-date at the end of the current interim period.

CHAPTER 16
INVENTORY PRICING AND METHODS

CONTENTS

IMPRESS™ Cross-References	**16.02**
Overview	**16.03**
PB-2: Elimination of Profits Resulting from Intercompany Transfers of LIFO Inventories	**16.03**
Background	**16.03**
Standards	**16.04**

IMPRESS™

CROSS-REFERENCES

1999 Miller GAAP Guide: Chapter 27, "Inventory Pricing and Methods"

1999 Miller GAAP Implementation Manual: EITF: Chapter 18, "Inventory"

1999 Miller Governmental GAAP Guide: Chapter 13, "Assets"

1999 Miller GAAS Guide: Chapter 8, "Evidence"

CHAPTER 16
INVENTORY PRICING AND METHODS

OVERVIEW

The preparation of financial statements requires careful determination of an appropriate dollar amount of inventory. Usually, that amount is presented as a current asset in the balance sheet and is a direct determinant of cost of goods sold in the income statement; as such, it has a significant impact on the amount of net income. When the matching principle is applied in determining net income, the valuation of inventories is of primary importance.

GAAP for the measurement of inventories are found in the following pronouncements and are included in the highest level of authority in the SAS-69 GAAP hierarchy:

APB-28	Interim Financial Reporting
ARB-43	Chapter 4, Inventory Pricing
FAS-2	Accounting for Research and Development Costs
FIN-1	Accounting Changes Related to the Cost of Inventory

The following additional source of GAAP that is in a lower level of the SAS-69 GAAP hierarchy is discussed in this Manual:

PB-2	Elimination of Profits Resulting from Intercompany Transfers of LIFO Inventories (Level C)

PB-2: Elimination of Profits Resulting from Intercompany Transfers of LIFO Inventories

BACKGROUND

The AcSEC issued PB-2 as a reminder concerning inventory transfers between or from LIFO pools, either within a company or between subsidiaries or divisions of a reporting entity. A LIFO liquidation or decrement occurs when the number of units (or total base year cost if the dollar-value LIFO method is used) in a LIFO pool is less at the end of the year than at the beginning of the year, causing prior-year costs, rather than current-year costs, to be charged to current-year income.

STANDARDS

ARB-51 (Consolidated Financial Statements) states that the purpose of consolidated financial statements is to present the results of operations and the financial position of the parent company and its subsidiaries as if the group were a single company. Intercompany profits on assets remaining within the group should be eliminated in the preparation of consolidated financial statements so that the results of operations and financial position are not affected by inventory transfers within the reporting entity. Inventory transferred between or from LIFO pools may cause LIFO inventory liquidations that could affect the amount of intercompany profit to be eliminated.

Different approaches are used to eliminate such profit in the preparation of consolidated financial statements. The AcSEC believes that each reporting entity should adopt an approach that, if consistently applied, defers reporting intercompany profits from transfers within a reporting entity until those profits are realized by the reporting entity through sales outside the consolidated group of entities. The approach selected should be one that is suited to the circumstances of the reporting entity.

CHAPTER 17
INVESTMENT TAX CREDIT

CONTENTS

IMPRESS™ Cross-References	**17.02**
Overview	**17.03**
AIN-APB 4: Accounting for the Investment Tax Credit: Accounting Interpretations of APB Opinion No. 4	**17.03**
Background	**17.03**
Standards	**17.04**

CROSS-REFERENCES

1999 MILLER GAAP GUIDE: Chapter 28, "Investment Tax Credit"

1999 MILLER GOVERNMENTAL GAAP GUIDE: Chapter 13, "Assets"

CHAPTER 17
INVESTMENT TAX CREDIT

OVERVIEW

The investment tax credit (ITC) was a selective reduction in income taxes based on the reporting entity's investment in qualifying property. GAAP permit two methods of accounting for the ITC: (1) the *deferral method*, in which the benefit of the ITC is amortized over the period that the qualifying property is used, and (2) the *flow-through method*, in which the benefit is recognized entirely in the year in which the qualifying property is acquired. The Accounting Principles Board (APB) first stated a preference for the deferral method, because the philosophy at that time emphasized income reporting via matching, which led to the conclusion that the ITC was effectively a reduction of the cost of the qualifying asset. The APB later indicated that both methods are acceptable. The flow-through method has been more widely used in practice.

Promulgated GAAP for ITCs are found in the following pronouncements that are included in the highest level of authority in the SAS-69 GAAP hierarchy:

APB-2	Accounting for the "Investment Credit"
APB-4	Accounting for the "Investment Credit"
FAS-109	Accounting for Income Taxes

The following additional source of GAAP that is in a lower level of the SAS-69 GAAP hierarchy is discussed in this Manual:

AIN-APB 4	Accounting for the Investment Tax Credit: Accounting Interpretations of APB Opinion No. 4 (Level D)

AIN-APB 4: Accounting for the Investment Tax Credit: Accounting Interpretations of APB Opinion No. 4

BACKGROUND

AIN-APB 4 provides guidance on two implementation issues associated with APB-4: (1) required disclosures associated with the ITC

17.04 Investment Tax Credit

and (2) allowable methods of accounting for the ITC under the Revenue Act of 1971.

STANDARDS

Questions 1 and 2: What disclosure is required in relation to accounting for the investment tax credit?

Answer: Disclose the method of accounting for the investment tax credit, regardless of whether the amount of the ITC is material. If an entity uses one method for "old" credits (e.g., deferral method) and another method for "new" credits (e.g., flow-through method), both methods are to be disclosed. Disclose the amount of the ITC, if it is material. Materiality is to be evaluated using the income tax provision, net income, and the trend in earnings. ITC amounts are to be disclosed unless they are clearly insignificant.

Question 3: What methods may be used to account for ITCs allowable under the Revenue Act of 1971?

Answer: The only acceptable methods of accounting for the ITC are the deferral method and the flow-through method. Under the deferral method, it is not acceptable to amortize the ITC over the period the asset must be held to avoid recapture of the ITC. This recapture period does not mirror the asset's estimated useful life.

Financing institutions will often lease assets to other parties. The ITC received by the financier is to be included as part of the proceeds received for the leased asset. As such, the ITC would be included in determining the loan's yield. The loan's yield is recognized in income over the term of the lease.

In some cases, the ITC is passed along to the lessee. The lessee is to account for the ITC in accordance with its policy for purchased property (i.e., use either the deferral method or the flow-through method). If the deferral method is used and the lease does not meet the FAS-13 (Accounting for Leases) criteria for lease capitalization, the ITC is to be amortized over the term of the lease. For this purpose, the term of the lease includes any renewal periods that are likely to be exercised.

CHAPTER 18
INVESTMENTS IN DEBT AND EQUITY SECURITIES

CONTENTS

IMPRESS™ Cross-References	18.02
Overview	18.03
SOP 90-3: Definition of the Term *Substantially the Same for Holders of Debt Instruments,* as Used in Certain Audit Guides and a Statement of Position	18.04
Background	18.04
Standards	18.05
Scope	18.05
Conclusions	18.05
Illustration of Applying Criteria	18.06
FIG-FAS 115: A Guide to Implementation of Statement 115 on Accounting for Certain Investments in Debt and Equity Securities	18.07
Background	18.07
Standards	18.07
Illustration of Sale of Available-for-Sale Securities	18.16
Illustration of Transferring a Security from Available-for-Sale to Held-to-Maturity	18.18
Illustration of Disclosing Unrealized Gains and Losses	18.21

CROSS-REFERENCES

1999 MILLER GAAP GUIDE: Chapter 29, "Investments in Debt and Equity Securities"

1999 MILLER GAAP IMPLEMENTATION MANUAL: EITF: Chapter 19, "Investments in Debt and Equity Securities"

1999 MILLER GOVERNMENTAL GAAP GUIDE: Chapter 13, "Assets"; Chapter 14, "Accounting and Financial Reporting for Certain Investments and External Investment Pools"; Chapter 15, "Deposit and Investment Portfolio Disclosures and Reverse Repurchase Agreements"

1999 MILLER GAAP FOR NOT-FOR-PROFIT ORGANIZATIONS: Chapter 2, "Overview of Current Pronouncements"; Chapter 5, "Assets"; Chapter 9, "Note Disclosures"

1999 MILLER GAAS GUIDE: Chapter 8, "Evidence"

CHAPTER 18
INVESTMENTS IN DEBT AND EQUITY SECURITIES

OVERVIEW

The primary issue in accounting and reporting for debt and equity investments is the appropriate use of market value. GAAP for many investments are included in the following pronouncement that is included in the highest level of authority in the SAS-69 GAAP hierarchy:

FAS-115   Accounting for Certain Investments in Debt and Equity Securities

FAS-115 addresses accounting and reporting for (*a*) investments in equity securities that have readily determinable fair values and (*b*) all investments in debt securities. It requires that these securities be classified in three categories and given specific accounting treatments, as follows:

Classification	*Accounting Treatment*
Held-to-maturity Debt securities with the intent and ability to hold to maturity	Amortized cost
Trading securities Debt and equity securities bought and held primarily for sale in the near term	Fair value, with unrealized holding gains and losses included in earnings
Available-for-sale Debt and equity securities not classified as held-to-maturity or trading	Fair value, with unrealized holding gains and losses excluded from earnings and reported as a separate component of shareholders' equity

The following additional sources of GAAP that are in lower levels of the SAS-69 GAAP hierarchy are discussed in this Manual:

SOP 90-3   Definition of the Term *Substantially the Same for Holders of Debt Instruments*, as Used in Certain Audit Guides and a Statement of Position (Level B)

FIG-FAS 115   A Guide to Implementation of Statement 115 on Accounting for Certain Investments in Debt and Equity Securities (Level D)

SOP 90-3: Definition of the Term *Substantially the Same for Holders of Debt Instruments,* as Used in Certain Audit Guides and a Statement of Position

BACKGROUND

Banks, and other financial institutions, will sometimes sell investment securities with the intent to reacquire either the same or similar securities. These actions are often tax-motivated. The accounting issue is whether these transactions are a sale or a borrowing. The AICPA's *Bank Audit Guide* provides that no sale has occurred when the proceeds from the sale of a debt security are immediately reinvested in identical or similar securities. If a period of time elapses between the sale and subsequent investment, the critical factor is whether the bank was at risk for a reasonable period of time to warrant recognition as a sale. What constitutes a reasonable period of time for sale recognition depends on the nature of the underlying security; securities that are sold and then subsequently repurchased within a short period of time might still qualify for sale treatment if the price of the underlying debt instrument is volatile.

SOP 90-3 addresses whether two debt instruments are substantially the same. This guidance is designed to help classify various types of repurchase agreements as a sale or as a financing. For example, an entity may sell a debt instrument with an agreement to repurchase another debt instrument. If the debt instrument to be repurchased is substantially the same as the debt instrument that was sold, the transaction would be treated as a financing. Otherwise, the transaction would be treated as a sale.

STANDARDS

Scope

SOP 90-3 pertains to the sale and purchase, or the exchange, of debt instruments between two entities that both hold the debt instrument as an asset. The term *debt instrument* is defined broadly, including those instruments traditionally viewed as securities and those not classified as such. The debt instruments encompassed by SOP 90-3 include notes, bonds, debentures, money market instruments, certificates of deposit, mortgage loans, commercial loans, commercial paper, and mortgage-backed certificates. SOP 90-3 does not apply in circumstances where an entity originates or acquires a whole loan mortgage and then exchanges the loan for a participation certificate issued by a government-sponsored enterprise or agency (e.g., FHLMC, FNMA, or GNMA). However, exchanges of participation certificates are included within the purview of SOP 90-3.

Since SOP 90-3 was issued before March 15, 1992 (the effective date of SAS-69), entities that were using a different approach for determining whether two debt instruments were substantially the same prior to the release of SOP 90-3 need not change the approach they were using. This provision is referred to as the grandfather clause of SAS-69.

Conclusions

For debt instruments to be classified as substantially the same, all of six criteria must be met. This has the practical effect of making it quite difficult for two debt instruments to be viewed as substantially the same. The six criteria that must be met in order for two debt instruments to be classified as substantially the same are as follows:

1. The debt instruments must have the same primary obligor. However, if the debt instrument is guaranteed by a sovereign government, a central bank, or a government-sponsored enterprise or agency thereof, the debt must be guaranteed by the same party. Also, the terms of the guarantee must be identical.
2. Each debt instrument must be identical in form and type so that all provide the same risks and rights to their holders. For example, the following types of exchanges would not meet this criterion: (*a*) GNMA I securities for GNMA II securities, (*b*) loans to foreign debtors that are otherwise the same except for different U.S. foreign tax credits, and (*c*) commercial paper for redeemable preferred stock.

3. Each debt instrument must carry the same contractual interest rate.

4. In general, the debt instruments must have the same maturity. In the case of mortgage-backed pass-through and pay-through securities, the mortgages underlying the securities must have similar remaining weighted average maturities that result in approximately the same market yield. For example, an exchange of GNMA securities that have a high prepayment record for GNMA securities with a low prepayment record would not meet this criterion.

5. Mortgage-backed pass-through or pay-through securities must be collateralized by a similar pool of mortgages, such as single-family residential mortgages.

6. In general, each debt instrument must have the same unpaid principal amount. In the case of mortgage-backed pass-through or pay-through securities, the aggregate principal amounts of the mortgage-backed securities given up and the mortgage-backed securities reacquired must be within the accepted "good delivery" standard for the type of mortgage-backed security involved. These specific standards are promulgated by the Public Securities Association and are discussed in *Uniform Practices for the Clearance and Settlement of Mortgage-Backed Securities and Other Related Securities*.

Illustration of Applying Criteria

First Interstate Bank of Texas transfers a portfolio of mortgage-backed pass-through securities to First Virginia Bank. At issue is whether this transfer of debt instruments would represent the transfer of instruments that are substantially the same.

Criteria 2–4 and 6 are met. Criterion 5 also is met—both sets of mortgage-backed securities are collateralized by a similar pool of mortgages: single-family residential mortgages. However, criterion 1, which requires the debt instruments to have the same primary obligor, is not met; there is a different set of primary obligors on First Interstate's loans than on First Virginia's loans. Therefore, this transfer does not represent the transfer of debt instruments that are substantially the same.

FIG-FAS 115: A Guide to Implementation of Statement 115 on Accounting for Certain Investments in Debt and Equity Securities

BACKGROUND

FIG-FAS 115, reported on in this section, includes responses to 61 specific questions regarding the application of FAS-115.

STANDARDS

Question 1: Does FAS-115 apply to a loan that has been insured, such as a loan insured by the Federal Housing Administration, or to a conforming mortgage loan?

Answer: No. FAS-115 applies only to debt securities, including debt instruments that have been securitized. A loan is not a debt security until it has been securitized.

Question 2: For a loan that was restructured in a troubled debt restructuring involving a modification of terms, does FAS-115 apply to the accounting by the creditor (i.e., investor) if the restructured loan meets the definition of a *security* in FAS-115?

Answer: Yes, FAS-115 applies to all debt securities. See FAS-125 (Accounting for Transfers and Servicing of Financial Assets and Extinguishments of Liabilities); FTB 94-1 (Application of Statement 115 to Debt Securities Restructured in a Troubled Debt Restructuring); and EITF Issue No. 94-8, "Accounting for Conversion of a Loan into a Debt Security in a Debt Restructuring," for further guidance on this general topic.

Question 3: Are options on securities covered by FAS-115?

Answer: In some cases. An investment in an option on an equity interest is covered by FAS-115 if the option has a fair value that is "currently available on a securities exchange." An equity interest includes any security that gives the holder the right to acquire (e.g., warrants, rights, calls) or to sell (e.g., puts) an ownership interest in an enterprise at a fixed or determinable price. FAS-115 does not cover written options, cash-settled options on equity securities, options on equity-based indexes, or options on debt securities.

Question 4: What accounting literature addresses the accounting for equity securities that do not have readily determinable fair values?

Answer: APB-18 (The Equity Method of Accounting for Investments in Common Stock) provides guidance in accounting for equity securities that do not have readily determinable fair values. If the investment does not qualify for treatment under the equity method (i.e., typically less than a 20% ownership stake), the investment is accounted for using the cost method. Investments accounted for using the cost method are to be adjusted to reflect other-than-temporary declines in fair value. (There is an exception to this general requirement for investments made by insurance companies—see FAS-60 (Accounting and Reporting by Insurance Enterprises)). There is currently no authoritative guidance as to the accounting for options and warrants in the absence of a readily determinable fair value.

Question 5: An entity invests in a limited partnership interest (or a venture capital company) that meets the definition of an *equity security* but does not have a readily determinable fair value. That is, it does not have a fair value per unit that is "currently available on a securities exchange" under paragraph 3(a) or a "fair value per share (unit) [that] is determined and published and is the basis for current transactions" under paragraph 3(c). However, substantially all of the partnership's assets consist of investments in debt securities or equity securities that have readily determinable fair values. Is it appropriate to "look through" the form of an investment to determine whether FAS-115 applies?

Answer: No, an entity should not "look through" its investment to the nature of the securities held by an investee. Therefore, given the lack of a readily determinable market value in this case, FAS-115 would not apply. Guidance in accounting for limited partnership investments can be found in EITF Topic No. D-46, "Accounting for Limited Partnership Investments."

Question 6: Does FAS-115 apply to certificates of deposit (CDs) or guaranteed investment contracts (GICs)?

Answer: It depends on whether the CD or GIC meets the definition of a *security*. The definition of a *security* in FAS-115 was modeled after the Uniform Commercial Code definition. Most CDs and GICs would not be classified as securities under this definition; however, certain jumbo CDs and GICs might qualify as securities.

Question 7: Are short sales of securities (sales of securities that the seller does not own at the time of the sale) covered by FAS-115?

Answer: No. A short sale gives rise to an obligation to deliver securities. Short sales are not investments and therefore do not fall under the FAS-115 purview. Various AICPA Industry Audit Guides require obligations due to short sales to be periodically adjusted to market value. Changes in the underlying obligation are reflected in earnings as they occur.

Question 8: If, subsequent to the purchase of equity securities, an investor enters into an arrangement that limits its ability to sell the securities, would the shares be considered "restricted" under footnote 2 to paragraph 3?

Answer: No. Restrictions on the sale of stock, as contemplated by FAS-115, refer to governmental or contractual restrictions. Presumably these types of restrictions would exist at the time the security was purchased.

Question 9: Does FAS-115 apply to preferred stock that is convertible into marketable common stock?

Answer: If the convertible preferred stock is redeemable (either on a fixed date or at the option of the holder), it would be classified as a debt security. Therefore, FAS-115 would apply even if the preferred stock did not have a readily determinable fair value. A convertible preferred stock that is not redeemable would be subject to the provisions of FAS-115 only if the preferred stock (now treated as an equity security) has a readily determinable fair value.

Question 10: Does FAS-115 apply to financial statements issued by a trust?

Answer: It depends. FAS-115 applies if the trust does not report all of its investments at fair value. Some trusts record all investments at fair or market value, with any resulting changes reflected in income or in the change in net assets. FAS-115 does not apply in such cases.

Question 11: Paragraph 6 states, "At each reporting date, the appropriateness of the [security's] classification shall be reassessed." If paragraph 6 requires an enterprise to reassess its classification of securities, why do transfers or sales of held-to-maturity securities for reasons other than those specified in paragraphs 8 and 11 call into question ("taint") an enterprise's intent to hold other debt securities to maturity in the future?

Answer: The point of paragraph 6 is primarily to require a periodic evaluation of an entity's ability to hold a security to maturity. An enterprise's intent to hold a security to maturity should not change; however, the ability of the enterprise to hold the security to maturity may change. Also, while an entity may initially classify a debt security as available-for-sale, subsequent developments may indicate that the entity has the ability to hold the securities to maturity. Assuming management intends to hold the debt securities to maturity, the investment would be reclassified from the available-for-sale portfolio to the held-to-maturity portfolio.

Question 12: What are the consequences of a sale or transfer of held-to-maturity securities for a reason other than those specified in paragraphs 8 and 11? In other words, what does it mean to "call into question [the entity's] intent to hold other debt securities to maturity in the future"?

Answer: It means to question the appropriateness of continuing to classify any debt securities as held-to-maturity. If the sale represents a material contradiction of the entity's stated intent to hold securities to maturity, any remaining securities classified as held-to-maturity would need to be reclassified as available-for-sale. Also, if a pattern of sales of held-to-maturity securities has occurred, any remaining securities classified as held-to-maturity would need to be reclassified. The reclassification would occur in the reporting period in which the sale occurred.

Question 13: If a sale or transfer of a security classified as held-to-maturity occurs for a reason other than those specified in paragraphs 8 and 11, does the sale or transfer call into question ("taint") the enterprise's intent about only the same type of securities (e.g., municipal bonds) that were sold or transferred, or about all securities that remain in the held-to-maturity category?

Answer: All securities that remain in the held-to-maturity category would be tainted.

Question 14: If held-to-maturity securities are reclassified to available-for-sale because sales occurred for reasons other than those specified in paragraphs 8 and 11, what amount of time must pass before the enterprise can again classify securities as held-to-maturity?

Answer: This is a matter of judgment. The key issue is whether circumstances have changed sufficiently for management to assert with a greater degree of credibility that it has the intent and ability to hold the debt securities to maturity.

Question 15: Is it consistent with FAS-115 to have a documented policy to initially classify all debt securities as held-to-maturity but then automatically transfer every security to available-for-sale when it reaches a predetermined point before maturity (e.g., every held-to-maturity security will be transferred to available-for-sale 24 months before its stated maturity) so that an entity has the flexibility to sell securities?

Answer: No. Such a policy would suggest that the entity does not have the intent and ability to hold the security to maturity.

Question 16: May securities classified as held-to-maturity be pledged as collateral?

Answer: Yes. However, the entity must believe that it will be able to satisfy the liability and thereby recover unrestricted access to the debt security that is serving as collateral for the borrowing.

Question 17: May held-to-maturity securities be subject to a repurchase agreement (or a securities lending agreement)?

Answer: Yes, if the repurchase agreement is accounted for as a secured borrowing. The entity must intend and expect to repay the borrowing and thereby recover unrestricted access to the debt security that is serving as collateral for the borrowing. In some cases (e.g., the securities underlying the repurchase agreement are not substantially the same), repurchase agreements are treated as sales.

Question 18: May convertible debt securities be classified as held-to-maturity?

Answer: Although such treatment is not specifically prohibited, classifying convertible debt securities as held-to-maturity generally would be inappropriate. Convertible debt securities generally carry a lower interest rate than standard debt securities. However, the holder of a debt security stands to profit from the conversion feature if the common stock of the entity issuing the convertible security rises in value. It is implausible to suggest that an entity would not avail itself of such a profit opportunity because it characterized securities as held-to-maturity. If an entity exercises a conversion feature on a security being treated as held-to-maturity, it will call into question the appropriateness of classifying any other securities as held-to-maturity.

Question 19: May a callable debt security be classified as held-to-maturity?

Answer: Yes. The debt instrument's maturity date is viewed as being accelerated if an issuer exercises its call provision. The issuer's exercise of a call feature in no way invalidates the holder's treatment of the security as held-to-maturity.

Question 20: May a puttable debt security be classified as held-to-maturity?

Answer: Yes, if the entity has the intent and ability to hold the puttable debt security to maturity. If the entity exercises the put feature, it will call into question the appropriateness of classifying any other debt securities as held-to-maturity.

Question 21: The Federal Financial Institutions Examination Council (FFIEC) Policy Statement, "Supervisory Policy Statement on Securities Activities," issued in December 1991 and adopted by the

18.12 *Investments in Debt and Equity Securities*

respective regulators, identifies criteria for determining when a mortgage derivative product should be considered a "high-risk mortgage security." In certain situations, regulators can direct institutions to sell high-risk mortgage securities. If a mortgage derivative product (held by a regulated institution) is not a high-risk mortgage security at purchase but could later become a high-risk mortgage security before maturity due to a change in market interest rates and the related change in the security's prepayment risk, can it be classified at acquisition as a held-to-maturity security under FAS-115?

Answer: The entity should consider the divestiture policy of its particular regulator in deciding whether it can support classifying this type of debt instrument as held-to-maturity. Additional guidance is provided in EITF Topic No. D-39, "Questions Related to the Implementation of FASB Statement No. 115."

Question 22: May a mortgage-backed interest-only certificate be classified as held-to-maturity?

Answer: In most cases, no. The risk and volatility of this type of instrument makes active management more likely. See EITF Issue No. 94-4, "Classification of an Investment in a Mortgage-Backed Interest-Only Certificate as Held-to-Maturity" for additional details.

Question 23: If an enterprise holds a debt security classified as held-to-maturity, and that security is downgraded by a rating agency, would a sale or transfer of that security call into question the entity's intent to hold other debt securities to maturity in the future?

Answer: No. A downgrade by a rating agency is an example of a significant deterioration in the issuer's creditworthiness. A sale or transfer that results from such a deterioration does not "taint" the remaining held-to-maturity portfolio (see FAS-115, par. 8a).

Question 24: What constitutes a "major" business combination or a "major" disposition under paragraph 8(c)?

Answer: Paragraph 8(c) of FAS-115 permits the sale or transfer of held-to-maturity securities as part of a "major" business combination or "major" disposition if necessary to maintain the enterprise's existing interest rate risk position or credit risk policy. However, FAS-115 does not define what constitutes a "major" business combination or disposition. The Statement does state that the sale of a segment qualifies as a major disposition. The purchase or sale of a large pool of financial assets or liabilities would not constitute a major business combination or disposition. In addition, the sale of held-to-maturity securities to fund a business combination is not permitted.

Question 25: Is it consistent with FAS-115 to reassess the classification of held-to-maturity securities concurrent with or shortly after a major business combination accounted for as a purchase?

Answer: Yes, provided that a sale or transfer of held-to-maturity securities is necessary to maintain the enterprise's existing interest rate risk position or credit risk policy. Some of the acquiring enterprise's held-to-maturity securities may need to be transferred or sold because of the nature of the liabilities assumed.

Question 26: May securities classified as held-to-maturity be sold under the exception provided in paragraph 8(c) in anticipation of or otherwise prior to a major business combination or disposition without calling into question the enterprise's intent to hold other debt securities to maturity in the future?

Answer: No. Any such transfers or sales should occur at the same time as or after the business combination or disposition.

Question 27: Paragraph 74 states that "... necessary transfers or sales should occur concurrent with or shortly after the business combination or disposition." How long is *shortly*?

Answer: FAS-115 does not define *shortly*. However, as time elapses it becomes increasingly difficult to justify that any sale or transfer of held-to-maturity securities was necessitated by the combination or disposition, and not by other events and circumstances.

Question 28: If a regulator directs a particular institution (rather than all institutions supervised by that regulator) to sell or transfer held-to-maturity securities (e.g., to increase liquid assets), are those sales or transfers consistent with paragraph 8(d)?

Answer: No. The exception provided in paragraph 8(d) pertains only to a change in regulations affecting all entities affected by the legislation or regulator. However, this type of sale does not necessarily "taint" the remainder of the held-to-maturity portfolio. A forced sale by a regulator *may* qualify as an event that is isolated, nonrecurring, and unusual, and that could not have been reasonably anticipated (see FAS-115, par. 8, and Question 32).

Question 29: Is a sale of held-to-maturity securities in response to an unsolicited tender offer from the issuer consistent with paragraph 8?

Answer: No. Such a sale does not fall under one of the specific exceptions outlined in paragraphs 8(a)–8(f). It also does not qualify as an event that is isolated, nonrecurring, and unusual, and that could not have been reasonably anticipated. Therefore, if held-to-maturity securities are sold in response to the tender offer, the remaining held-to-maturity portfolio is tainted.

Question 30: Is it consistent with FAS-115 for an insurance company or other regulated enterprise to classify securities as held-to-maturity and also indicate to regulators that those securities could be sold to meet liquidity needs in a defined interest rate scenario whose likelihood of occurrence is reasonably possible but not probable?

Answer: No. Stating that held-to-maturity securities could be sold if a particular interest-rate environment developed is inconsistent with management's intent and ability to hold these securities to maturity.

Question 31: Is it ever appropriate to apply the exceptions in paragraphs 8(a)–8(f) to situations that are similar, but not the same?

Answer: No. The exceptions outlined in paragraphs 8(a)–8(f) are quite specific by design. They should not be extended to similar fact patterns. Paragraph 8 does permit a general exception to the requirement for holding held-to-maturity securities to maturity. That is, held-to-maturity securities can be sold in response to an event that is isolated, nonrecurring, and unusual, and that could not have been reasonably anticipated.

Question 32: What constitutes an event that is "isolated, nonrecurring, and unusual...that could not have been reasonably anticipated" as described in paragraph 8?

Answer: This general exception provision involves four elements. Three of these elements are as follows: (1) Was the event isolated?, (2) Was the event nonrecurring?, and (3) Was the event unusual? The fourth element pertains to the extent to which the event could have been reasonably anticipated. Very few events will meet all four of these conditions. In general, the types of events that would qualify are extremely remote disaster scenarios. For example, a run on a bank or on an insurance company would qualify.

Question 33: Paragraph 11(b) allows a sale of a held-to-maturity security to be considered a maturity when the enterprise has collected a substantial portion (at least 85%) of the principal outstanding at acquisition due to scheduled payments on a debt security payable in equal installments (that comprise both principal and interest) over its term. What types of securities would typically qualify or not qualify for this exception?

Answer: This exception applies to (*a*) debt securities that are payable in equal installments, comprising both principal and interest, and (*b*) variable rate debt securities that would be payable in equal installments if there were no change in interest rates. It does not apply to debt securities for which the principal payment is level and the interest amount is based on the outstanding principal balance.

Investments in Debt and Equity Securities   18.15

Question 34: How often must sales occur for an activity to be considered "trading"?

Answer: FAS-115 describes trading securities as securities that will be held for only a short period of time or that will be sold in the near term. Securities that management intends to hold for only hours or days must be classified as trading securities. However, securities that will be held for a longer period of time are not precluded from being classified as trading securities.

Question 35: If an enterprise acquires a security without intending to sell it in the near term, may the enterprise classify the security in the trading category?

Answer: Yes. In general, securities classified as trading will be held for a short period of time or will be sold in the near term. This general requirement is not an absolute. However, the decision to classify a security as trading is to be made at the time the security is acquired. Transfers of securities into or out of the trading category should be rare.

Question 36: If an enterprise decides to sell a security that has been classified as available-for-sale, should the security be transferred to trading?

Answer: No. Securities that will mature within one year or that management intends to sell within one year should not automatically be transferred into the trading category. Similarly, if an entity decides to sell a held-to-maturity security (in response to one of the conditions outlined in paragraph 8 of FAS-115), such security should not be reclassified as available-for-sale or trading. Refer to paragraphs 21 and 22 of FAS-115 for mandated disclosures relating to the sale.

Question 37: What should be the initial carrying amount under FAS-115 of a previously nonmarketable equity security that becomes marketable (i.e., due to a change in circumstances, it now has a fair value that is readily determinable)?

Answer: In general, the basis for applying the provisions of FAS-115 should be the security's cost. However, if the change in marketability provides evidence that an other-than-temporary impairment has occurred, the impairment loss should be recognized and the writedown recorded prior to applying FAS-115. (This treatment assumes that the nonmarketable security had not been accounted for using the equity method.)

Question 38: What should be the initial carrying amount under FAS-115 of a marketable equity security that should no longer be

18.16 *Investments in Debt and Equity Securities*

accounted for under the equity method (e.g., due to a decrease in the level of ownership)?

Answer: The initial carrying amount of the security should be the previous carrying amount of the investment.

Question 39: How is a sale of an available-for-sale security recorded?

Answer: In general, cash or a receivable account should be debited for the amount of the proceeds, and the investment account should be credited for its fair value (i.e., its selling price). Any unrealized gain or loss relating to the investment being sold (recorded in stockholders' equity) is reversed into earnings. Deferred tax accounts that relate to any unrealized gain or loss are also adjusted. This general procedure needs to be modified if the entity has not yet recorded all changes in the value of the security being sold (some entities record these changes only at reporting dates), or if a write-down for an other-than-temporary impairment has already been recorded.

Illustration of Sale of Available-for-Sale Securities

Pluto Enterprises purchases 1000 shares of Venus, Inc., common stock for $10 per share on April 1, 19X7. Pluto accounts for these securities as available-for-sale securities. The fair value of Venus' stock at December 31, 19X7, is $12 per share. Therefore, in Pluto's December 31, 19X7, balance sheet, its investment in the Venus securities would be recorded at $12,000. A $2,000 unrealized gain would be recorded in the stockholders' equity section of Pluto. Pluto's effective tax rate is 34%. Pluto sells these shares on June 30, 19X8, at $7 per share. Pluto adjusts the carrying value of securities only at year-end. The journal entry to record the sale would be as follows:

Cash (1,000 shares x $7 per share)	$7,000	
Unrealized gain	2,000	
Deferred tax liability ($2000 x 34%)	680	
Loss on sale of securities	3,000	
Available-for-sale securities		$12,000
Income tax expense		680

Question 40: How is a sale of a trading security recorded?

Answer: For trading securities, changes in fair value are recorded as they occur. Therefore, in most cases, the entry is to debit cash (or a receivables account) for the proceeds received, and to credit the trading securities account for the fair value of the securities sold (i.e., the selling price of the securities). This procedure must be modified if, for example, changes in the fair value of securities are recorded at the end of the day. Also, for those entities not taxed on a marked-to-market basis, the deferred tax accounts would be adjusted.

Question 41: If a derivative instrument is used to hedge a security classified as available-for-sale, may changes in the fair value of the derivative instrument also be recorded in the separate component of shareholders' equity?

Answer: Yes. FAS-115 does not change the accounting for derivative instruments used to hedge a security. Generally, while the hedge contract is open, changes in the value of the contract are recorded in a separate component of shareholders' equity. Subsequently, but no later than when the derivative contract is closed, any resulting gain or loss is treated as an adjustment to the cost basis of the security. In the case of a debt security, any such gain or loss is amortized over the remaining life of the debt security as an adjustment to its yield.

Question 42: If an interest rate swap is used to change the interest rate characteristics of an available-for-sale security from a fixed rate to a floating rate or vice versa (described in EITF Issue No. 84-36, "Interest Rate Swap Transactions," as being like a hedge), may the accounting described in paragraph 115 be applied?

Answer: Yes. The phrase "used to hedge" encompasses the above transaction.

Question 43: When securities are transferred from available-for-sale to held-to-maturity or vice versa, is the subsequent amortization of a premium or discount based on the amortized cost of the security or on its fair value at the date of transfer?

Answer: The answer to this question depends on whether the transfer is from the available-for-sale category to the held-to-maturity category, or vice versa.

- *Transfer from Available-for-Sale to Held-to-Maturity*—The difference between the par value of the debt security that is transferred and its fair value on the date of transfer is accounted for as a yield adjustment in accordance with the provisions of FAS-91 (Accounting for Nonrefundable Fees and Costs Associated with Originating or Acquiring Loans and Initial Direct Costs of Leases). The fair value of the debt security on the date of transfer, adjusted for subsequent amortization, serves as the security's amortized cost basis for required disclosures.

- *Transfer from Held-to-Maturity to Available-for-Sale*—In this case, the amortized cost of the security in the held-to-maturity portfolio is transferred to the available-for-sale portfolio for purposes of determining future amortization. In addition, the amortized cost of the security is used for comparing the cost of the security with its fair value (for the purpose of computing unrealized gain or loss) and for disclosure purposes.

Question 44: Paragraph 15 indicates that for transfers involving the trading category, the unrealized holding gain or loss should be recognized in earnings. How should the gain or loss be classified on the income statement?

Answer: Unrealized gains or losses that have accumulated before the transfer date should be recognized in the income statement when securities are transferred into the trading category. Such gains or losses are recognized in a manner consistent with how realized gains and losses for the category from which the security being transferred are treated.

Question 45: How is a transfer from available-for-sale to held-to-maturity accounted for?

Answer: The following are some of the salient points in transferring a security from available-for-sale to held-to-maturity:

a. Any unrealized holding gain or loss is combined with any unamortized premium or discount. This aggregate figure serves as the "adjusted" discount or premium, which is the amount that is amortized against income in the future. The net effect is to state the security at its fair value on the date of transfer.

b. The adjusted discount or premium is amortized to income over the remaining life of the debt security.

c. Any unrealized holding gain or loss (reflected in stockholders' equity) on the transfer date is amortized to income over the remaining life of the debt security.

d. The net effect of steps b and c is that only the unamortized discount or premium (on the transfer date) from the original par value of the debt security is reflected in income over the remaining life of the debt security.

e. Future changes in the fair value of the debt security are ignored, because the security is now classified as held-to-maturity.

Illustration of Transferring a Security from Available-for-Sale to Held-to-Maturity

Sonic, Inc., has a $1,000 par value bond that it acquired at $1,100 on January 1, 19X7. The bond has a 10-year life. During 19X7, $10 of the bond premium would be amortized. The bond is originally accounted for as available-for-sale. On December 31, 19X7, the fair value of the bond is $1,180. Therefore, at December 31, 19X7, Sonic would have $90 of unrealized gain in stockholders' equity. The $90 of unrealized gain plus the $90 of unamortized premium has the effect of stating the bond at its fair value, $1,180.

On January 1, 19X8, Sonic transfers this debt security into its held-to-maturity category. On the date of transfer, the adjusted bond premium is $180 ($90 of original unamortized premium and the $90 unrealized gain). The remaining life of the debt security is 9 years. Each year for the next 9 years, Sonic will amortize $20 of the bond investment premium. This has the effect of reducing income. Sonic also will amortize the unrealized gain that existed on the date of transfer at the rate of $10 per year ($90/9 years). This has the effect of increasing income. The net effect of both amortization entries is a reduction in Sonic's income of $10 per year for the next 9 years (the remaining life of the bond). This amount, $10, is equal to what would be amortized based on the original unamortized bond premium.

Question 46: Paragraph 16 provides an example of when a decline in the fair value of a debt security is other than temporary. What other factors indicate that impairment is other than temporary? How is an equity security evaluated for other-than-temporary impairment?

Answer: Paragraph 16 specifically mentions a decline in the issuer's creditworthiness as an indication of an other-than-temporary impairment. In addition, an impairment may need to be recognized if a debt security will be disposed of before its maturity date and if its value has declined due to an increase in interest rates or a change in foreign exchange rates. Additional guidance can be found in SEC Staff Accounting Bulletin No. 59 (Accounting for Noncurrent Marketable Equity Securities) and AU Section 332 (Long-Term Investments).

Question 47: Should an enterprise recognize an other-than-temporary impairment when it decides to sell a specific available-for-sale debt security at a loss shortly after the balance sheet date?

Answer: In most cases, yes. A loss should be recognized if the enterprise does not expect the fair value of the security to recover before the planned sale date. The loss resulting from an other-than-temporary impairment is to be recorded in the period in which the decision to sell the security was made, not in the period when the actual sale occurs. Refer to EITF Topic No. D-44 (Recognition of Other-Than-Temporary Impairment upon the Planned Sale of a Security Whose Cost Exceeds Fair Value), SEC Staff Accounting Bulletin No. 59 (Accounting for Noncurrent Marketable Equity Securities), and AU Section 332 (Long-Term Investments) for additional guidance.

Question 48: May a valuation allowance be used to recognize impairment on securities subject to FAS-115?

Answer: No. A general allowance for unidentified impairments in an overall portfolio is inappropriate. Other-than-temporary impairments are to be evaluated on a security-by-security basis. When such an impairment is identified, the related security is to be written down to this reduced value, which serves as the security's cost basis going forward. Such a write-down is recognized in earnings when it occurs.

Question 49: After an other-than-temporary impairment has been recognized on an available-for-sale security, how should subsequent recoveries be accounted for?

Answer: After an other-than-temporary impairment in value is recognized, a security's new cost basis is not to be changed due to subsequent recoveries in the fair value of the security. Unrealized gains or losses are computed by a comparison of the security's new cost basis and the fair value of the security. However, a recovery in the fair value of the security is not to be recognized in earnings until the security is sold.

Question 50: EITF Issue No. 89-4, "Accounting for a Purchased Investment in a Collateralized Mortgage Obligation Instrument or in a Mortgage-Backed Interest-Only Certificate," provides guidance on recognizing impairment for certain types of securities. Does FAS-115 supersede that guidance?

Answer: Yes. EITF Issue No. 89-4 measured impairment by referring to undiscounted cash flows. The focus of FAS-115 in measuring impairment is on fair value. Refer to EITF Issue No. 93-18, "Recognition of Impairment for an Investment in a Collateralized Mortgage Obligation Instrument or in a Mortgage-Backed Interest-Only Certificate," for additional information.

Question 51: Must the statement of cash flows show purchases, sales, and maturities of securities reported as cash equivalents?

Answer: No. FAS-115 does not change the portion of FAS-95 (Statement of Cash Flows) that permits cash equivalents to be shown as a net change within the statement of cash flows. However, FAS-115 does require the disclosure of the amortized cost and fair values of cash equivalents, shown separately by major security type. In addition, a note should explain what portion of each category of securities is shown as cash equivalents in the statement of financial position and the statement of cash flows.

Question 52: Must the disclosures required in paragraphs 19–22 of FAS-115 be included in interim financial statements?

Answer: Only if a complete set of financial statements is presented at an interim-period date. If the interim financial statements are limited to summary financial information, per the requirements of

APB-28 (Interim Financial Reporting), the above-mentioned disclosure requirements of FAS-115 are not required.

Question 53: Paragraph 21(e) requires disclosure of the change in the net unrealized holding gain or loss on trading securities that has been included in earnings during the period. How is that amount calculated?

Answer: Paragraph 21(e) requires the disclosure of gains or losses recognized in income during the period that resulted from trading securities still held at the end of the period.

Illustration of Disclosing Unrealized Gains and Losses

Rutledge, Inc., reports $100,000 of net gains and losses from trading securities in its 19X7 income statement. Of this amount, $80,000 resulted from securities that were sold during 19X7. Therefore, to satisfy the disclosure requirement of paragraph 21(e), Rutledge would disclose that $20,000 of gains recognized during 19X7 pertain to trading securities still held at December 31, 19X7.

Question 54: If an enterprise recognizes a deferred tax asset relating only to a net unrealized loss on available-for-sale securities and at the same time concludes that it is more likely than not that some or all of that deferred tax asset will not be realized, is the offsetting entry to the valuation allowance reported in the component of shareholders' equity related to the unrealized loss under FAS-115 or as an item in determining income from continuing operations?

Answer: The offsetting entry to the valuation allowance would be reported as a component of shareholders' equity. This is because the valuation allowance is directly related to the unrealized loss on the available-for-sale securities.

Question 55: An enterprise has recognized a deferred tax asset relating to other deductible temporary differences in a previous fiscal year and at the same time has concluded that no valuation allowance was warranted. If in the current year the enterprise recognizes a deferred tax asset relating to a net unrealized loss on available-for-sale securities that arose in the current year and at the same time concludes that a valuation allowance is warranted, is the offsetting entry reported in the FAS-115 component of shareholders' equity or as an item in determining income from continuing operations?

Answer: Management needs to determine the extent to which the valuation allowance directly pertains to the unrealized loss on avail-

18.22 *Investments in Debt and Equity Securities*

able-for-sale securities. The offsetting entry is reported in the FAS-115 component of shareholders' equity only to the extent that the valuation allowance pertains to the available-for-sale securities.

Question 56: If an enterprise does not need to recognize a valuation allowance at the same time that it establishes a deferred tax asset relating to a net unrealized loss on available-for-sale securities, but in a subsequent fiscal year concludes that it is more likely than not that some or all of that deferred tax asset will not be realized, is the offsetting entry to the valuation allowance reported in the FAS-115 component of shareholders' equity or as an item in determining income from continuing operations?

Answer: The offsetting entry should be included as an item in determining income from continuing operations.

Question 57: An enterprise recognizes a deferred tax asset relating to a net unrealized loss on available-for-sale securities and at the same time concludes that a valuation allowance is warranted. In a subsequent fiscal year the enterprise makes a change in judgment about the level of future years' taxable income such that all or a portion of that valuation allowance is no longer warranted. Is the offsetting entry reported in the FAS-115 component of shareholders' equity or as an item in determining income from continuing operations?

Answer: The entry to record the reversal in the valuation allowance account should be recorded as an item in determining income from continuing operations. This is the case even though the original entry was to the FAS-115 component of shareholders' equity. However, if the entity generates taxable income in the current year that can utilize the benefit of the deferred tax asset (rather than a change in judgment about future years' taxable income), the reduction of the valuation allowance account is allocated to that taxable income. See paragraphs 26 and 35–38 of FAS-109 (Accounting for Income Taxes) for additional information.

Question 58: If a company has a significant investment in a particular security and believes that an attempt to sell the entire investment at one time would significantly affect the security's market price, should the size of the investment be considered in determining the fair value of the security?

Answer: No. If a quoted market price is available, fair value is determined by multiplying the number of shares held by the market price per share.

Question 59: How should an enterprise determine the fair value of a debt security when quoted market prices are not available?

Answer: In the absence of market prices, estimates of fair value should consider existing prices for similar debt instruments and the results of various valuation techniques. Valuation techniques include (*a*) discounting cash flows from the debt security using a discount rate commensurate with the risks involved, (*b*) option-pricing models, (*c*) matrix pricing, (*d*) option-adjusted spread models, and (*e*) fundamental analysis. See paragraph 111 of FAS-115 for additional guidance.

Question 60: Does the planned sale of securities following a major business combination preclude accounting for the combination as a pooling of interests?

Answer: The sale of held-to-maturity securities as a result of a "major" business combination (FAS-115, par. 8c) would not preclude use of the pooling-of-interests method. A planned sale of available-for-sale securities also would not run afoul of the pooling rules. See EITF Topic No. D-40, "Planned Sale of Securities following a Business Combination Expected to Be Accounted for as a Pooling of Interests," for additional details.

Question 61: How should an enterprise that adopted FAS-115 before the issuance of FIG-FAS 115 account for the effects (other than a correction of an error), if any, of initially complying with FIG-FAS 115?

Answer: Previously issued financial statements that have adopted FAS-115 are not permitted to be restated as a result of FIG-FAS 115. If an enterprise needs to reclassify certain securities as the result of the issuance of FIG-FAS 115, the securities should be accounted for in accordance with paragraphs 15 and 22 of FAS-115. Other changes that result from applying the provisions of FIG-FAS 115 are to be applied prospectively. In addition, concurrent with adopting the provisions of FIG-FAS 115, but no later than December 31, 1995, entities can reassess the classification of investment securities. Any transfers that result are to be recorded at fair value and accounted for in accordance with paragraph 15 of FAS-115. Any reclassifications of held-to-maturity securities do not "taint" the remainder of the held-to-maturity portfolio; this provision represents a one-time opportunity to reassess the appropriateness of classifying certain debt securities as held to maturity.

CHAPTER 19
LEASES

CONTENTS

IMPRESS™ Cross-References	19.02
Overview	19.03
FTB 79-10: Fiscal Funding Clauses in Lease Agreements	19.05
Background	19.05
Standards	19.05
FTB 79-12: Interest Rate Used in Calculating the Present Value of Minimum Lease Payments	19.06
Background	19.06
Standards	19.06
FTB 79-14: Upward Adjustment of Guaranteed Residual Values	19.06
Background	19.06
Standards	19.06
FTB 79-15: Accounting for Loss on a Sublease Not Involving the Disposal of a Segment	19.07
Background	19.07
Standards	19.07
FTB 79-16 (R): Effect of a Change in Income Tax Rate on the Accounting for Leveraged Leases	19.07
Background	19.07
Standards	19.08
FTB 79-17: Reporting Cumulative Effect Adjustment from Retroactive Application of FASB Statement No. 13	19.08
Background	19.08
Standards	19.08
FTB 79-18: Transition Requirement of Certain FASB Amendments and Interpretations of FASB Statement No. 13	19.09
Background	19.09
Standards	19.09
FTB 85-3: Accounting for Operating Leases with Scheduled Rent Increases	19.10

Background	19.10
Standards	19.10
FTB 86-2: Accounting for an Interest in the Residual Value of a Leased Asset	19.11
Background	19.11
Standards	19.11
FTB 88-1: Issues Relating to Accounting for Leases	19.12
Background	19.12
Standards	19.12

CROSS-REFERENCES

1999 MILLER GAAP GUIDE: Chapter 30, "Leases"

1999 MILLER GAAP IMPLEMENTATION MANUAL: EITF: Chapter 20, "Leases"

1999 MILLER GOVERNMENTAL GAAP GUIDE: Chapter 19, "Leases"; Chapter 29, "General Long-Term Debt Account Group"; Chapter 30, "General Fixed Assets Account Group"

CHAPTER 19
LEASES

OVERVIEW

A *lease* is an agreement that conveys the right to use property, usually for a specified period. Leases typically involve two parties: the owner of the property (lessor) and the party contracting to use the property (lessee). Because of certain tax, cash flow, and other advantages, leases have become an important alternative to the outright purchase of property by which companies (lessees) acquire the resources needed to operate.

Leases include agreements that, while not nominally referred to as leases, have the characteristic of transferring the right to use property (e.g., heat supply contracts), and agreements that transfer the right to use property even though the contractor may be required to provide substantial services in connection with the operation or maintenance of the assets.

The term *lease*, as used in promulgated GAAP, does *not* include the following:

- Agreements that are contracts for services that do not transfer the right to use property from one contracting party to another
- Agreements that concern the right to explore for or exploit natural resources such as oil, gas, minerals, and timber
- Agreements that represent licensing agreements for items such as motion picture films, plays, manuscripts, patents, and copyrights

A central accounting issue associated with leases is the identification of those leases that are treated appropriately as sales of the property by lessors and as purchases of the property by lessees (*capital leases*). Those leases that are not identified as capital leases are called *operating leases* and are not treated as sales by lessors and as purchases by lessees. Rather, they are treated on a prospective basis as a series of cash flows from the lessee to the lessor.

GAAP for leases include the largest number of authoritative accounting pronouncements of any single subject in accounting literature. Pronouncements that follow FAS-13 explain, interpret, or amend that pronouncement in a variety of ways; many of them arose as a result of attempts to implement FAS-13. Following are pronouncements that collectively establish promulgated GAAP for lease accounting that are included in the highest level of authority in the SAS-69 GAAP hierarchy:

FAS-13	Accounting for Leases
FAS-22	Changes in the Provisions of Lease Agreements Resulting from Refundings of Tax-Exempt Debt
FAS-23	Inception of the Lease
FAS-27	Classification of Renewals or Extensions of Existing Sales-Type or Direct Financing Leases
FAS-28	Accounting for Sales with Leasebacks
FAS-29	Determining Contingent Rentals
FAS-91	Accounting for Nonrefundable Fees and Costs Associated with Originating or Acquiring Loans and Initial Direct Costs of Leases
FAS-98	Accounting for Leases: • Sale-Leaseback Transactions Involving Real Estate • Sales-Type Leases of Real Estate • Definition of the Lease Term • Initial Direct Costs of Direct Financing Leases
FIN-19	Lessee Guarantee of the Residual Value of Leased Property
FIN-21	Accounting for Leases in a Business Combination
FIN-23	Leases of Certain Property Owned by a Governmental Unit or Authority
FIN-24	Leases Involving Only Part of a Building
FIN-26	Accounting for Purchase of a Leased Asset by the Lessee during the Term of the Lease
FIN-27	Accounting for a Loss on a Sublease

The following additional sources of GAAP that are in lower levels of the SAS-69 GAAP hierarchy are discussed in this Manual:

FTB 79-10	Fiscal Funding Clauses in Lease Agreements (Level B)
FTB 79-12	Interest Rate Used in Calculating the Present Value of Minimum Lease Payments (Level B)
FTB 79-14	Upward Adjustment of Guaranteed Residual Values (Level B)
FTB 79-15	Accounting for Loss on a Sublease Not Involving the Disposal of a Segment (Level B)

FTB 79-16 (R)   Effect of a Change in Income Tax Rate on the Accounting for Leveraged Leases (Level B)

FTB 79-17   Reporting Cumulative Effect Adjustment from Retroactive Application of FASB Statement No. 13 (Level B)

FTB 79-18   Transition Requirement of Certain FASB Amendments and Interpretations of FASB Statement No. 13 (Level B)

FTB 85-3   Accounting for Operating Leases with Scheduled Rent Increases (Level B)

FTB 86-2   Accounting for an Interest in the Residual Value of a Leased Asset (Level B)

FTB 88-1   Issues Relating to Accounting for Leases (Level B)

FTB 79-10: Fiscal Funding Clauses in Lease Agreements

BACKGROUND

Fiscal funding clauses are frequently found in lease agreements in which the lessee is a governmental entity. The clause generally provides for the lease to be cancelable if the legislature or other funding authority does not appropriate the funds necessary for the governmental unit to fulfill its obligations under the lease agreement.

STANDARDS

Question: What effect, if any, does the existence of a fiscal funding clause in a lease agreement have on the classification of the lease in accordance with FAS-13 (Accounting for Leases)?

Answer: The existence of a fiscal funding agreement in a lease necessitates an assessment of the probability that the lease will be canceled through the existence of the fiscal funding agreement. If the likelihood of this occurring is assessed as being remote, the lease is considered noncancelable. If the probability is considered other than remote, the lease is considered cancelable and, therefore, is classified as an operating lease. The term *remote* is used in FTB 79-10 in the same manner as in FAS-5 (Accounting for Contingencies) (i.e., the chance of the future event or events occurring is slight).

FTB 79-12: Interest Rate Used in Calculating the Present Value of Minimum Lease Payments

BACKGROUND

FAS-13 requires the lessee to use its incremental borrowing rate (or the lessor's implicit interest rate in certain circumstances) in calculating the minimum lease payments. The *incremental borrowing rate* is defined as the rate the lessee would have incurred to borrow over a similar term the funds necessary to purchase the leased asset.

STANDARDS

Question: May a lessee use its secured borrowing rate in calculating the present value of minimum lease payments in accordance with FAS-13?

Answer: FAS-13, paragraph 30, does not preclude the lessee from using its secured borrowing rate as its incremental borrowing rate if that rate is determinable, reasonable, and consistent with the financing that would have been used in the circumstances surrounding the lease.

FTB 79-14: Upward Adjustment of Guaranteed Residual Values

BACKGROUND

FAS-13 requires the lessor to periodically review the estimated residual value of sales-type, direct-financing, and leveraged leases. FAS-13 also prohibits an upward adjustment in residual values.

STANDARDS

Question: Does the prohibition of upward adjustments of estimated residual values in FAS-13 also apply to upward adjustments that result from renegotiations of the guaranteed portions of residual values?

Answer: The FAS-13 prohibitions against upward adjustments of residual values of leased assets are equally applicable to the guaranteed portion of the residual values. If a lease initially transferred substantially all of the risks and rewards of ownership of the leased property to the lessee, it is not reasonable that the lessor could subsequently increase the benefits that were accounted for as having been retained initially.

FTB 79-15: Accounting for Loss on a Sublease Not Involving the Disposal of a Segment

BACKGROUND

The general principle of recognizing loss on transactions is well established, and extends to contracts that are expected to result in a loss. FAS-13, however, does not specifically refer to the recognition of a loss on a lease contract.

STANDARDS

Question: Should a loss on a sublease not involving a disposal of a segment be recognized, and how is that loss determined?

Answer: If costs expected to be incurred on an operating sublease exceed anticipated revenue on the sublease, the sublessor should recognize a loss. Similarly, a loss should be recognized on a direct financing sublease if the carrying amount of the investment in the sublease exceeds (1) the total of rentals expected to be received and (2) the property's estimated residual value. An exception to this requirement exists if the lessor's tax benefits from the transactions are sufficient to offset that loss.

FTB 79-16 (R): Effect of a Change in Income Tax Rate on the Accounting for Leveraged Leases

BACKGROUND

When an important assumption changes, FAS-13 requires a recalculation of the rate of return and allocation of income from the inception of the lease. The change in the recalculated balances of net investment is recognized as a gain or loss in the year in which the assumption is changed.

STANDARDS

Question: What effect, if any, does a change in income tax rate have on accounting for leveraged leases under FAS-13?

Answer: The lessor's income tax rate is an important assumption in accounting for a leveraged lease. Accordingly, the effect of a change in income tax rate should be recognized in the first accounting period ending on or after the date on which the legislation affecting the change becomes law. If such a change results in a significant variation in the normal relationship between income tax expense and pretax accounting income, the reasons for that variation should be disclosed if they are not otherwise apparent.

FTB 79-17: Reporting Cumulative Effect Adjustment from Retroactive Application of FASB Statement No. 13

BACKGROUND

Retroactive application of the provisions of FAS-13 are required in financial statements for fiscal years beginning after December 31, 1980. Financial statements of prior years are to be restated. The cumulative effect on retained earnings at the beginning of the earliest period restated shall be included in determining net income of that period.

STANDARDS

Question: If a company presents in its annual report five annual income statements that were retroactively restated to apply the provisions of FAS-13, must the cumulative effect of applying those provisions be included in any year's income statement?

Answer: The cumulative effect would not be included in net income of any period presented unless the year prior to the earliest year presented could not be restated.

FTB 79-18: Transition Requirement of Certain FASB Amendments and Interpretations of FASB Statement No. 13

BACKGROUND

FAS-13 has been amended and interpreted many times. The transition requirements of FAS-13 amendments and interpretations state that the amendment or interpretation should be applied retroactively at the same time—and in the same manner—that an enterprise applies the provisions of FAS-13 retroactively. Enterprises may have already applied FAS-13 retroactively and published annual financial statements based on retroactively adjusted accounts before the effective date of a particular amendment or interpretation. In this instance, the enterprise may, but is not required to, apply the provisions of the amendment or interpretation retroactively.

STANDARDS

Question: In applying the transition requirement of amendments and interpretations of FAS-13, what does the phrase "have published annual financial statements" mean and what disclosure is required to indicate that FAS-13 has been applied retroactively without restatement of the prior years' financial statements due to immateriality?

Answer: The phrase "have published annual financial statements" refers to those financial statements that a company normally includes in its annual report to shareholders for its established 12-month reporting period. The word *published* is intended to identify those financial statements that are distributed to all shareholders. When the retroactive application of FAS-13 does not require restatement of prior years' financial statements due to immateriality, notes to the financial statement should disclose that the enterprise has applied FAS-13 retroactively and that prior years' financial statements were not restated because the impact was immaterial. The absence of such disclosure would indicate that FAS-13 had not been applied retroactively.

FTB 85-3: Accounting for Operating Leases with Scheduled Rent Increases

BACKGROUND

FAS-13 specifies that rent income generally should be recognized by lessors and lessees as it becomes receivable or payable. If the rental payments vary from a straight-line pattern, the income or expense should be recognized on a straight-line basis unless another systematic and rational method is more representative of the time pattern in which the benefit from use of the asset was diminished (lessor) or received (lessee). It has been suggested that, under certain circumstances, rentals should be recognized on a basis that is neither straight-line nor representative of the time pattern of the physical use of the asset. Examples of situations in which another pattern of recognition might be appropriate are (*a*) rent reductions in the early periods to induce the lessee to sign the lease and (*b*) scheduled rent increases that anticipate inflation.

STANDARDS

Question: If an operating lease includes a scheduled rent increase, is it ever appropriate for lessees and lessors to recognize rent expense or income on a basis other than straight-line?

Answer: The effects of scheduled rent increases, which are included in the calculation of the minimum lease payments, should be recognized in a straight-line basis over the lease term, unless some other systematic and rational allocation basis is more representative of the time pattern in which the leased property is used. Factors such as the time value of money, anticipated inflation, and expected future revenues to allocate scheduled rent increases are inappropriate, because they do not relate to the time pattern of the physical use of the leased asset. These factors may affect the amount of rent, however, if they affect the amount of contingent rentals that are not part of the minimum lease payment amount.

FTB 86-2: Accounting for an Interest in the Residual Value of a Leased Asset

BACKGROUND

FTB 86-2 responds to five questions related to accounting for the residual value of a leased asset.

STANDARDS

Question 1: How should an enterprise account for the acquisition from a lessor of the unconditional right to own and possess, at the end of the least term, an asset subject to the lease? How should an enterprise account for the acquisition of the right to receive all or a portion of the proceeds from the sale of a leased asset at the end of the lease?

Answer: At the date the rights are acquired, both transactions involve a right to receive, at the end of the lease term, all or a portion of the future benefit included in the leased asset. This right should be accounted for as the acquisition of an asset.

Question 2: How should an enterprise acquiring an interest in the residual value of a leased asset determine the cost at acquisition?

Answer: The cost is the amount of cash disbursed, the fair value of other consideration given (which could include noncash assets or services rendered), and the present value of liabilities assumed. The fair value of the interest in the residual value at the date of the agreement should be used to measure the cost of the interest if that fair value is more clearly evident than the fair value of the assets surrendered, services rendered, or liabilities assumed.

Question 3: How does an enterprise that acquires an interest in the residual value of a leased asset account for that asset during the lease term?

Answer: An enterprise that acquires an interest in the residual value of a leased asset should not recognize increases in the asset's estimated value over the remaining term of the lease. The asset should be reported at no more than its acquisition cost until sale or disposition. If the value of the asset declines below its carrying amount and that decline is considered other than temporary, the asset should be written down to fair value and the amount of the write-down should be recognized as a loss. Subsequent increases in fair value before sale or disposition should not be recorded.

19.12 Leases

Question 4: Do the provisions indicated in the answer to Question 3 apply to lease brokers?

Answer: Yes.

Question 5: If a lessor sells substantially all of the minimum rental payments associated with a sales-type, direct financing, or leveraged lease and retains an interest in the residual value of the leased asset, how should the lessor account for that asset over the remaining lease term?

Answer: The lessor should not recognize increases in the leased asset's residual value over the remaining lease term. If the fair value of the residual declines, however, that decline should be recognized as a loss if the decline is considered other than temporary. Subsequent recoveries in fair value should not be recorded.

FTB 88-1: Issues Relating to Accounting for Leases

BACKGROUND

FTB 88-1 responds to five questions with regard to lease accounting in the following areas:

- Time pattern of the physical use of the property in an operating lease
- Lease incentives in an operating lease
- Applicability of leveraged lease accounting to existing assets of the lessor
- Money-over-money lease transactions
- Wrap lease transactions

STANDARDS

Question 1: For operating leases that include scheduled rent increases designated to accommodate the lessee's projected physical use of the property, how should the rental payment obligation be recognized by the lessee and the lessor in accordance with FAS-13?

Answer: Both the lessee and the lessor should recognize the lease payments as follows:

1. If rent escalates in contemplation of the lessee's physical use of the leased property, but the lessee takes possession of or controls the physical use of the property at the beginning of the lease term, all rent payments (including the escalated payments) should be recognized as rental expense (by the lessee) or revenue (by the lessor) on a straight-line basis.
2. If rent escalates under a master leasing agreement because the lessee gains access to and control over additional leased property at the time of the escalation, the escalated rents should be considered rental expense (by the lessee) or revenue (by the lessor) attributed to the additional leased property and should be recognized in proportion to the relative fair value of the additional property.

Question 2: For operating leases that include an incentive for the lessee to sign (e.g., up-front cash payment to the lessee), should the lessee or lessor ever recognize rental expense or revenue other than on a straight-line basis?

Answer: Incentive payments to the lessee represent reductions in rent expense by the lessee and rental revenue to the lessor. They should be recognized on a straight-line basis over the lease term.

Question 3: For a lease to be classified as direct financing, the cost or carrying amount, if different, and the fair value of the asset must be the same at the inception of the lease. For a lease to qualify for leveraged lease accounting, it must be a direct financing lease. How does the lessor apply these requirements to leasing an asset that the lessor has owned and previously placed in service?

Answer: The carrying amount of an asset previously placed in service may not be significantly different from its fair value, but the two are not likely to be the same. Therefore, leveraged lease accounting is not appropriate, other than when an asset to be leased is acquired by the lessor. Any write-down to the existing asset's fair value in contemplation of leasing the asset precludes the transaction from being accounted for as a leveraged lease.

Question 4: An enterprise manufactures or purchases an asset, leases the asset to a lessee, and obtains nonrecourse financing in excess of the asset's cost using the leased asset and the future lease rentals as collateral (referred to as a money-over-money lease transaction). Should the enterprise ever recognize any of the amount by which the cash received plus the present value of any estimated residual retained exceeds the carrying amount of the leased asset as profit on the transaction at the beginning of the lease term? If not, how should the lessor account for the transaction?

Answer: Other than recognizing manufacturer's or dealer's profit in a sales-type lease, an enterprise should never recognize as income the proceeds from the borrowing in a money-over-money lease at the beginning of the lease term. The enterprise should account for the transaction as (1) the manufacture or purchase of an asset; (2) the leasing of the asset under an operating, direct financing, or sales-type lease; and (3) the borrowing of funds. The asset and the liability for the nonrecourse financing should not be offset in the statement of financial position unless a legal right of setoff exists.

Question 5: A lessor purchases an asset, leases it to a lessee, obtains nonrecourse financing using the lease rentals or the lease rentals and the asset as collateral, sells the asset and the nonrecourse debt to a third-party investor, and leases the asset back while remaining the principal lessor under the original lease (referred to as a wrap-lease transaction). How should the enterprise account for this transaction?

Answer: If the leased asset is real estate, FAS-98 applies to the sale-leaseback transaction. If the property is not real estate, the enterprise should account for the transaction as a sale-leaseback transaction in accordance with FAS-13.

CHAPTER 20
LONG-TERM CONSTRUCTION CONTRACTS

CONTENTS

IMPRESS™ Cross-References	20.02
Overview	20.03
SOP 81-1: Accounting for Performance of Construction-Type and Certain Production-Type Contracts	20.03
Background	20.03
Standards	20.05
Basic Accounting Policy	20.06
Profit Center	20.06
Measuring Progress on Accounts	20.07
Income Determination—Revenue Elements	20.07
Basic Contract Price	20.08
Contract Options and Additions	20.08
Change Orders	20.08
Claims	20.08
Income Determination—Cost Elements	20.09
Revised Estimates	20.10
Provisions for Anticipated Losses	20.10

IMPRESS™

CROSS-REFERENCES

1999 MILLER GAAP GUIDE: Chapter 31, "Long-Term Construction Contracts"

1999 MILLER GOVERNMENTAL GAAP GUIDE: Chapter 24, "Capital Projects Funds"

1999 MILLER GAAS GUIDE: Chapter 8, "Evidence"; Chapter 18, "Audits of Construction Contractors"

CHAPTER 20
LONG-TERM CONSTRUCTION CONTRACTS

OVERVIEW

Long-term construction contracts present a difficult financial reporting problem primarily because of their large dollar amounts and their relatively long duration (i.e., they span more than one accounting period, sometimes beginning and ending several years apart). GAAP in the area of revenue recognition for long-term construction contracts deal with this situation by permitting two methods—the *percentage-of-completion method* and the *completed-contract method*. The percentage-of-completion method is appropriate in situations in which reliable estimates of the degree of completion are possible, in which case a pro rata portion of the income from the contract is recognized in each accounting period covered by the contract. If reliable estimates are not available, the completed-contract method is used, in which income is deferred until the end of the contract period.

The following pronouncement is the source of GAAP for long-term construction contracts that is included in the highest level of authority in the SAS-69 hierarchy:

ARB-45   Long-Term Construction-Type Contracts

The following additional source of GAAP that is in a lower level of the SAS-69 GAAP hierarchy is discussed in this Manual:

SOP 81-1   Accounting for Performance of Construction-Type and Certain Production-Type Contracts (Level B)

SOP 81-1: Accounting for Performance of Construction-Type and Certain Production-Type Contracts

BACKGROUND

SOP 81-1 provides guidance on the application of GAAP in accounting for the performance of contracts for which the customer provides specifications for any of the following:

- Construction of facilities
- Production of goods
- Provision of related services

In the present business environment, there are many types of contracts, ranging from relatively simple to highly complex and from short-term to long-term. These contracts are used in many industries for construction, production, and provision of a broad range of goods and services. At the time SOP 81-1 was written, existing GAAP for these types of contracts were not stated in sufficient detail for the scope of activities to which they were applied. SOP 81-1 was intended to provide the needed guidance.

The basic accounting issue for contract accounting is the point(s) at which revenue should be recognized as earned and costs should be recognized as expenses. This may involve the allocation of revenues and expenses of relatively long-term events over relatively short-term accounting periods. This allocation process often requires estimates to deal with the uncertainties inherent in the performance of contracts.

ARB-45 describes two generally accepted methods of accounting for long-term construction contracts:

1. *Percentage-of-completion*—Recognizes income as work progresses on the contract
2. *Completed-contract*—Recognizes income only when the contract is completed

The units-of-delivery method, which is a modification of the percentage-of-completion method, recognizes revenue on a contract as deliverable products are completed.

The following three key estimates are required to account for long-term construction contracts:

1. The extent of progress toward completion
2. Contract revenues
3. Contract costs

The Committee on Accounting Procedures indicates that when estimates of costs to complete the contract and the extent of progress toward completion are reasonably dependable, the percentage-of-completion method is preferable. When these estimates are unreliable, the completed-contract method is required. The two methods are not considered alternatives for the same circumstances.

STANDARDS

SOP 81-1 applies to accounting for performance of contracts. It is not limited to long-term contracts, nor is it limited to construction contracts. Contracts covered are binding agreements between a buyer and a seller in which the seller agrees, for compensation, to perform a service to the buyer's specifications. These contracts are legally enforceable agreements. Performance often will extend over long periods, and the seller's right to receive payment depends on performance in accordance with the agreement. Contracts that are covered by SOP 81-1 include the following:

- Construction industry contracts (e.g., general building and heavy earthmoving)
- Contracts to design and build ships and transport vessels
- Contracts to design, develop, manufacture, or modify complex aerospace or electronic equipment
- Contracts for construction consulting services
- Contracts for services performed by architects, engineers, or architectural or engineering design firms

Contracts covered by SOP 81-1 may be classified into four broad types based on the method of pricing:

1. *Fixed-price or lump-sum*—An agreement to perform all acts under the contract for a stated price
2. *Cost-type (including cost-plus)*—An agreement to perform under a contract for a price to be determined on the basis of a defined relationship to the costs to be incurred
3. *Time-and-material*—An agreement to perform all acts required under the contract for a price based on fixed hourly rates for some measure of the labor hours required
4. *Unit-price*—An agreement to perform all acts required under the contract for a specified price for each unit of output

The term *contractor* refers to a person or entity that enters into a contract to construct facilities, produce goods, or render services to the specifications of a buyer as a general or prime contractor, as a subcontractor, or as a construction manager. The term *profit center* refers to the unit for the accumulation of revenues and costs and the measurement of income. Revenues, costs, and income are usually determined for a single contract, but under specified circumstances they may be determined for a combination of two or more contracts, a segment of a contract, or a group of combined contracts.

Basic Accounting Policy

The percentage-of-completion method and the completed-contract method constitute the basic accounting policy decision within GAAP. As stated previously, the determination of which is preferable depends on a careful evaluation of circumstances, and the two methods are not alternatives for the same situation. The basic policy followed should be disclosed in a note to the financial statements.

The use of the percentage-of-completion method depends on the ability to make reasonably dependable estimates of the extent of completion, contract revenues, and contract costs. The percentage-of-completion method is preferable as an accounting policy in circumstances where these estimates can reasonably be made. Entities with significant contracting operations generally have the ability to produce reasonably reliable estimates and, accordingly, the percentage-of-completion method is preferable in most circumstances. In some circumstances, estimating the final outcome of a contract may be impractical except to assure that no loss will be incurred. In this case, the contractor should use a zero estimate of profit, and equal amounts of revenues and costs should be recognized until results can be estimated more precisely.

The completed-contract method recognizes income only when the contract is completed or substantially completed. During the period of performance, billings and costs are accumulated on the balance sheet as inventory, but no profit or income is recorded until the contract is complete or substantially complete. The completed-contract method is appropriate when reasonably dependable estimates of the extent of completion, contract revenues, and/or contract costs cannot be made, or when the contractor's financial position and results of operations would not vary materially from those resulting from the use of the percentage-of-completion method. When there is assurance that no loss will be incurred on a contract, the percentage-of-completion method based on a zero profit margin is preferable until more precise estimates can be made.

Profit Center

The basic assumption is that each contract is a profit center for revenue recognition, cost accumulation, and income measurement. A group of contracts may be so closely related, however, that they are effectively parts of a single project with an overall profit margin. In these circumstances, consideration should be given to combining the contracts for purposes of profit recognition.

Contracts may be combined for accounting purposes when the following criteria are met:

- They are negotiated as a package in the same economic environment with an overall profit margin.
- They constitute in essence an agreement to do a single project.
- They require closely interrelated construction activities with common costs.
- They constitute in substance an agreement with a single customer.

A single contract or a group of contracts that otherwise meet the test for combining may include several elements or phases, each of which was negotiated separately without regard to the performance of the others. A contract may be segmented for accounting purposes if the following steps were taken and are documented and verifiable:

- The contractor submitted bona fide proposals on the separate components of the project and on the entire project.
- The customer had the right to accept the proposals either on the separate components of the project or on the entire project.
- The aggregate amount of the proposal on the separate components approximated the amount of the proposal on the entire project.

Measuring Progress on Accounts

Some methods used in practice measure progress toward completion in terms of costs, others in terms of units of work, and others in terms of value added. All are acceptable in appropriate circumstances. The method or methods selected should be applied consistently.

Several approaches can be described as based on input measures. These methods are based on costs and on other efforts expended. An example is the efforts-expended approach, in which a measure of work, such as labor-hours, machine-hours, or materials quantities, is used as a measurement of the extent of progress. Output methods, on the other hand, measure progress in terms of results achieved. Estimating the extent of progress toward completion based on units completed is an example of an output method.

Income Determination—Revenue Elements

The major factors that must be considered in determining total estimated revenues are the basic contract price, contract options and additions, change orders, and claims.

Basic Contract Price

The estimated revenue from a contract is the total amount that a contractor expects to realize from the contract. It is determined primarily by the terms of the contract. The contract may be relatively fixed or highly variable and, as a result, subject to a great deal of uncertainty. One problem peculiar to cost-type contracts is the determination of reimbursable costs that should be reflected as revenue.

Contract Options and Additions

An option or an addition to an existing contract is treated as a separate contract in any of the following circumstances:

- The product or service to be provided differs significantly from the product or service provided under the original contract.
- The price of the new product or service is negotiated without regard to the original contract and involves different economic judgments.
- The product or service to be provided under the exercise option or amendment is similar to that under the original contract, but the contract price and anticipated contract cost relationship are significantly different.

If none of these circumstances is present, the option or addition may be combined with the original contract for purposes of revenue recognition.

Change Orders

Change orders are modifications of an original contract that effectively change the provisions of the contract without adding new provisions. Change orders may have a significant impact on the amount of contract revenue to be recognized.

Claims

Claims are amounts in excess of the agreed contract price that a contractor seeks to collect from customers or others as a result of customer-caused delays, errors in specifications and designs, contract terminations, change orders in dispute, and other similar causes. Recognition of such claims is appropriate only if it is probable that the claim will result in additional contract revenue and if the amounts can be reliably estimated.

Income Determination—Cost Elements

At any point in the contract, estimated contract costs consist of two components: costs incurred to date and estimated costs to complete the contract. Costs incurred to date generally can be determined with reasonable certainty, depending on the adequacy and effectiveness of the cost accounting system. Estimating the costs to complete the contract generally involves greater uncertainty.

Contract costs are accumulated in the same manner as inventory and are charged to operations as the related revenue from the contract is recognized. General principles for accounting for production costs are as follows:

1. All direct costs (e.g., materials, labor, subcontracting costs) are included in contract costs.
2. Indirect costs allocable to all contracts, such as indirect labor, contract supervision, tools and equipment, and supplies, may be allocated to contracts as indirect costs if otherwise allowable under GAAP.
3. General and administrative costs ordinarily should be charged to expense, but may be included as contract costs under certain circumstances.
4. Selling costs are generally excluded from contract costs.
5. Costs under cost-type contracts are charged to contract costs in conformity with GAAP in the same manner as costs under other types of contracts.
6. In computing estimated gross profit or in providing for losses on contracts, estimates of costs to complete should reflect all the types of costs included in contract costs.
7. Inventoriable costs should not be carried at amounts that, when added to the estimated costs to complete, are greater than the estimated realizable value of the contract.

Estimating the costs to complete a contract should result from the following:

1. Systematic and consistent procedures that are correlated with the cost accounting system to provide a basis for periodically comparing actual and estimated amounts
2. Quantities and prices of all significant elements of costs
3. Estimation procedures that include the same elements of cost that are included in actual accumulated costs
4. The effects of future wage and price escalations
5. Periodic review and revision, as appropriate, to reflect new information

Revised Estimates

Adjustments to the original estimates of the total contract revenue, total contract cost, and extent of progress toward completion may be required as work progresses under the contract and as experience is gained. Such revisions should be accounted for by the cumulative catch-up method in accordance with APB-20 (Accounting Changes).

Provisions for Anticipated Losses

When current estimates indicate that the total contract revenues and costs will result in a loss, a provision of the entire loss on the contract should be made. This is true for both the percentage-of-completion method and the completed-contract method. A provision for loss should be made in the accounting period in which it becomes evident.

A provision for a loss on a contract should be shown separately as a liability on the balance sheet—unless related costs are accumulated in the balance sheet, in which case the loss provision may be offset against the related accumulated costs. In a classified balance sheet, a provision shown as a liability should be classified as a current liability.

CHAPTER 21
NONMONETARY TRANSACTIONS

CONTENTS

IMPRESS™ Cross-References	21.02
Overview	21.03
FTB 85-1: Accounting for the Receipt of Federal Home Loan Mortgage Corporation Participating Preferred Stock	21.03
Background	21.03
Standards	21.04

CROSS-REFERENCES

1999 MILLER GAAP GUIDE: Chapter 33, "Nonmonetary Transactions"

1999 MILLER GAAP IMPLEMENTATION MANUAL: EITF: Chapter 21, "Nonmonetary Transactions"

1999 MILLER GAAP FOR NOT-FOR-PROFIT ORGANIZATIONS: Chapter 2, "Overview of Current Pronouncements"; Chapter 10, "Cash Flows"; Chapter 14, "Payroll and Miscellaneous Requirements"

CHAPTER 21
NONMONETARY TRANSACTIONS

OVERVIEW

As a general rule, GAAP require that exchanges be recorded based on the fair value inherent in the transaction. This applies to both monetary and nonmonetary transactions. Certain exceptions exist, however, for nonmonetary transactions. Different accounting bases may be required for these transactions, depending on the unique characteristics of the exchange transaction.

The following pronouncements are the sources of GAAP for nonmonetary transactions that are included in the highest level of authority in the SAS-69 hierarchy:

APB-29	Accounting for Nonmonetary Transactions
FIN-30	Accounting for Involuntary Conversions of Nonmonetary Assets to Monetary Assets

The following additional source of GAAP that is in a lower level of the SAS-69 GAAP hierarchy is discussed in this Manual:

FTB 85-1	Accounting for the Receipt of Federal Home Loan Mortgage Corporation Participating Preferred Stock (Level B)

FTB 85-1: Accounting for the Receipt of Federal Home Loan Mortgage Corporation Participating Preferred Stock

BACKGROUND

On December 6, 1984, the Federal Home Loan Mortgage Corporation (FHLMC) created a new class of participating preferred stock and distributed that stock to the 12 district banks of the Federal Home Loan Banking System. The system banks then distributed the stock to their member institutions that owned stock in the district banks as of December 31, 1984. Before that time, the FHLMC had one

21.04 *Nonmonetary Transactions*

class of stock outstanding that was callable at par value and was owned by the 12 district banks.

STANDARDS

Question: How should the members of the Federal Home Loan Banking System account for the receipt of the preferred stock?

Answer: The preferred stock is a nonmonetary asset that should be recognized by member institutions at its fair value on December 31, 1984, in accordance with APB-29 (Accounting for Nonmonetary Transactions). The resulting income should be presented as an extraordinary item.

CHAPTER 22
PENSION PLANS—EMPLOYERS

CONTENTS

IMPRESS™ Cross-References	22.02
Overview	22.03
PB-12: Reporting Separate Investment Fund Option Information of Defined-Contribution Pension Plans	22.04
Background	22.04
Standards	22.04
FIG-FAS 87: A Guide to Implementation of Statement 87 on Employers' Accounting for Pensions	22.05
Background	22.05
Standards	22.05
Exceptions to the General Rule	22.06
Illustration of Return on Asset Component of Net Periodic Pension Cost	22.08
Illustration of Overfunded Plan When FAS-87 Is Adopted	22.16
Illustration of Attribution with Multiple Formulas	22.19
Illustration of Attribution of the Projected Benefit Obligation to a Qualified Pension Plan and an Excess Benefit Pension Plan	22.21
Illustration of Combining Two Plans	22.30

IMPRESS™

CROSS-REFERENCES

1999 MILLER GAAP IMPLEMENTATION MANUAL: Chapter 23, "Pension Plans—Settlements and Curtailments"; Chapter 25, "Postemployment and Postretirement Benefits Other Than Pensions"

1999 MILLER GAAP GUIDE: Chapter 34, "Pension Plans—Employers"

1999 MILLER GAAP IMPLEMENTATION MANUAL: EITF: Chapter 23, "Pension Accounting"

1999 MILLER GOVERNMENTAL GAAP GUIDE: Chapter 21, "Pension Obligation"; Chapter 28, "Pension Trust Funds"

1999 MILLER GAAP FOR NOT-FOR-PROFIT ORGANIZATIONS: Chapter 16, "Cost Accounting Standards"

1999 MILLER GAAS GUIDE: Chapter 8, "Evidence"; Chapter 20, "Audits of Employee Benefit Plans"

CHAPTER 22
PENSION PLANS—EMPLOYERS

OVERVIEW

GAAP for employers' accounting for pension plans center on the determination of annual pension expense (identified as net periodic pension cost) and the presentation of an appropriate amount of pension liability in the statement of financial position. Net periodic pension cost has often been viewed as a single homogeneous amount, but it is actually made up of several components that reflect different aspects of the employer's financial arrangements, as well as the cost of benefits earned by employees.

In applying principles of accrual accounting for pension plans, the FASB emphasizes three fundamental features:

1. *Delayed recognition*—Changes in the pension obligation and changes in the value of pension assets are recognized not as they occur, but systematically and gradually over subsequent periods.

2. *Net cost*—The recognized consequences of events and transactions affecting a pension plan are reported as a single net amount in the employer's financial statements. This approach results in the aggregation of items that would be presented separately for any other part of the employer's operations: the compensation cost of benefits, the interest cost resulting from deferred payment of those benefits, and the results of investing pension assets.

3. *Offsetting*—Pension assets and liabilities are shown net in the employer's statement of financial position, even though the liability has not been settled. The assets may still be controlled and substantial risks and rewards associated with both are clearly borne by the employer.

The following pronouncement is the source of GAAP for pension plans—employers that is included in the highest level of authority in the SAS-69 hierarchy.

FAS-87   Employers' Accounting for Pensions

The following additional sources of GAAP that are in lower levels of the SAS-69 GAAP hierarchy are discussed in this Manual:

PB-12   Reporting Separate Investment Fund Option Information of Defined-Contribution Pension Plans (Level C)

FIG-FAS 87 A Guide to Implementation of Statement 87 on Employers' Accounting for Pensions (Level D)

PB-12: Reporting Separate Investment Fund Option Information of Defined-Contribution Pension Plans

BACKGROUND

The AICPA Audit and Accounting Guide titled *Audits of Employee Benefit Plans* is unclear with regard to the reporting of separate investment fund option information of defined-contribution pension plans. This has resulted in a divergence in practice.

A plan provides for participant-directed investment programs if it allows participants to choose among various investment alternatives.

STANDARDS

The plan should disclose information about the net assets and significant components of the changes in net assets for each investment fund option. If the investment fund option contains both participant-directed and nonparticipant-directed investments, the participant-directed and nonparticipant-directed portions should be disclosed separately.

Aggregation of investment fund options with similar investment objectives is not appropriate, except that any individual investment fund option that has net assets of less than 5% of the plan's total assets may be combined with funds that have similar investment objectives. If investment options are aggregated in this way, that fact should be disclosed. If the plan provides for self-directed investing whereby each participant selects his or her own specific investments (e.g., individual stocks or bonds), changes in these investments may be aggregated and presented in one column as one fund option.

Information about the net assets and the significant components of the changes in net assets for each investment fund option is required as part of the basic financial statements. This information may be presented in any of the following ways:

- In a multicolumnar format on the face of the financial statements
- As notes to the financial statements
- As a separate financial statement for each investment fund option

Single line item presentation of the net assets available for benefits may be appropriate, unless an individual investment fund option has a material asset or liability other than investments that requires disclosure.

FIG-FAS 87: A Guide to Implementation of Statement 87 on Employers' Accounting for Pensions

BACKGROUND

FIG-FAS 87, reported on in this section, includes responses to 107 specific questions regarding the application of FAS-87.

STANDARDS

Question 1: Does FAS-87 apply to employers that are (*a*) state and local governmental units and (*b*) federal executive agencies?

Answer: No. GASB Statement No. 4 (Applicability of FASB Statement No. 87, "Employers' Accounting for Pensions," to State and Local Governmental Employers) indicates that state and local governmental employers are not to change their accounting for pension plans in response to FAS-87. The General Accounting Office (GAO) has the statutory authority to establish accounting standards for federal agencies. The GAO guidelines do not mention FAS-87 in accounting for pensions in federal agencies.

Question 2: Does FAS-87 apply to a non–U.S. pension plan that provides death and disability benefits that are greater than the incidental death and disability benefits allowed in U.S. tax-qualified pension plans?

Answer: Yes, if the non–U.S. pension plan is in substance similar to a U.S. plan.

Question 3: Does FAS-87 amend or supersede paragraphs 6–8 of APB-12 (regarding deferred compensation contracts)?

22.06 Pension Plans—Employers

Answer: No. APB-12 addresses the accounting for deferred compensation contracts with individual employees. These deferred compensation contracts do not, in the aggregate, constitute a pension plan.

Question 4: How should an employer with regulated operations account for the effects of applying FAS-87 for financial reporting purposes if another method of accounting for pensions is used for determining allowable pension cost for rate-making purposes?

Answer: FAS-87 applies to an employer with regulated operations. However, FAS-71 (Accounting for the Effects of Certain Types of Regulation) may require that an asset or liability be recorded for the difference between net periodic pension cost recognized under FAS-87 and pension cost allowed for rate-making purposes. If the entity is subject to the provisions of FAS-71, an asset is recognized if the provisions of paragraph 9 of that Statement are met. A liability is recorded if the conditions of paragraph 11(b) of FAS-71 are met. A detailed illustration of the these provisions is provided in FIG-FAS 87.

Exceptions to the General Rule

For entities subject to FAS-71, an asset is generally recognized when net periodic pension cost per FAS-87 exceeds pension cost allowable for rate-making purposes (FAS-71, par. 9). However, the criteria of paragraph 9 would not be met if (1) it is probable that the regulator will soon adopt FAS-87 for rate-making purposes and (2) it is *not* probable that the regulator will permit the entity to recover the difference between FAS-87 pension costs and pension costs allowable by the regulator, before the regulator adopts the FAS-87 approach.

For entities subject to FAS-71, a liability generally is recognized when net periodic pension cost per FAS-87 is less than pension cost allowable for rate-making purposes (FAS-71, par. 11b). However, the criteria of paragraph 11(b) would not be met if (1) it is probable that the regulator will soon adopt FAS-87 for rate-making purposes, (2) the regulator will not hold the employer responsible for the costs that were intended to be recovered by the current rates and that have been deferred by the change in method, *and* (3) the regulator will provide revenue to cover these same costs when they are ultimately recognized under the provisions of FAS-87.

Question 5: If an employer has a pension plan that also provides postemployment health care benefits, should FAS-87 apply to those benefits?

Answer: No. FAS-106 (Employers' Accounting for Postretirement Benefits Other Than Pensions) provides guidance in accounting for postemployment health care benefits.

Question 6: Does footnote 4 of FAS-87 (which states that "the interest cost component of net periodic pension cost shall not be considered to be interest for purposes of applying FASB Statement No. 34, *Capitalization of Interest Cost*") proscribe the capitalization of the interest cost component of net periodic pension cost when employee compensation is capitalized as part of the cost of inventory or other assets?

Answer: No. Net periodic pension cost, including the interest element included in that amount, is viewed as an element of employee compensation. If it is appropriate to capitalize employee compensation as part of the cost of inventory or as part of a self-constructed asset, the entire amount of net periodic pension cost is included in making this computation.

Question 7: May an employer have net periodic pension cost that is a net credit (i.e., net periodic pension income)?

Answer: Yes. The computation of net periodic pension cost involves the combination of elements that are both expenses/losses and revenues/gains. The revenues/gains components (e.g., return on plan assets, amortization of a transition asset) of the pension cost computation may exceed the expense/loss portion of the computation of net periodic pension cost.

Question 8: If an employer has net periodic pension cost that is a net credit (i.e., net periodic pension income), how should that be treated if employee compensation is capitalized as part of the cost of inventory or other assets?

Answer: The portion of net periodic pension income that is capitalized as part of the cost of an asset would serve to reduce the applicable asset's cost.

Question 9: If an employer sponsoring a pension plan that is overfunded has net periodic pension cost that is a net credit (i.e., net periodic pension income) and the employer makes no contribution to the pension plan because it cannot currently deduct the amount for tax purposes, is the difference between net periodic pension income and the tax-deductible amount a timing difference as discussed in paragraphs 15–17 of APB-11? If it is a timing difference, when and how will it reverse?

Answer: Although APB-11 has been superseded by FAS-109 (Accounting for Income Taxes), it would appear that this question is still relevant. FAS-109 refers to temporary differences not timing differences. A difference between the net periodic pension income and the tax-deductible expense would create a temporary difference (i.e., the financial reporting basis of the pension liability or asset would differ from its tax basis). The temporary difference may reverse in the future when net periodic pension cost exceeds amounts funded (the pension plan may not be overfunded indefinitely). Alternatively, if the pension plan continues to be overfunded for an extended period of time, the employer may terminate the plan and capture the excess assets. In this case, the gain for accounting purposes would be less than the taxable amount.

Question 10: If transferable securities issued by the employer are included in plan assets, should the measurement of plan assets also include the interest accrued but not yet received on those securities?

Answer: Yes. Amounts accrued by the employer but not yet paid to the plan (which are to be excluded per paragraph 19) differ from interest accrued but not yet received on securities.

Question 11: If an employer has a nonqualified pension plan (for tax purposes) that is funded with life insurance policies owned by the employer, should the cash surrender value of those policies be considered plan assets for purposes of applying FAS-87?

Answer: Not if the employer is the owner or beneficiary of the life insurance policies. The applicable accounting treatment is specified in FTB 85-4 (Accounting for Purchases of Life Insurance).

Question 12: If the actual return on plan assets for a period is a component of net periodic pension cost, how does the expected return on plan assets affect the determination of net periodic pension cost?

Answer: When the current year's net periodic pension cost is computed, both the actual return on plan assets and any difference between this actual return and the expected return are considered. The net result of this treatment is that the expected return on plan assets, not the actual return, is included in the computation of the current year's net periodic pension cost. Also, the difference between the actual return on plan assets and the expected return on assets is deferred to future years (unrecognized net gain or loss).

Illustration of Return on Asset Component of Net Periodic Pension Cost

As of January 1, 19X8, GAF, Inc., has pension plan assets of $500,000. The expected return on plan assets for 19X8 is 10%. Contributions and benefit payments during the year were both $100,000. At December 31, 19X8, plan assets are $600,000. Service cost is $100,000 and interest cost is $80,000. GAF has no other components of net periodic pension cost. GAF would compute net periodic pension cost as follows:

Service cost	$100,000
Interest cost	80,000
Actual return on plan assets	(100,000)
Unrecognized gain on plan assets	50,000
Net periodic pension cost	$130,000

The net effect of the above treatment is that only the expected return on plan assets, $50,000 ($500,000 x 10%), is ultimately considered when net periodic pension cost is computed. Recognition of the difference between the actual return of $100,000 and the expected return of $50,000 is deferred to a future period (i.e., $50,000 is recorded as an unrecognized net gain).

Question 13: If an employer has a substantive commitment to have a formula greater than the pension plan's written formula, how should the difference between the effects of a retroactive plan amendment that was anticipated as part of that substantive commitment and the effects of the actual retroactive plan amendment be accounted for?

Answer: The accounting depends on whether the difference results from an intended modification of the formula for which there is a substantive commitment. If it does, then the accounting should follow paragraphs 24–28 of FAS-87. If it does not, the difference is a gain or loss and should be accounted for in accordance with the provisions of paragraphs 29–34 of FAS-87.

Question 14: Once a schedule of amortization of unrecognized prior service cost from a specific retroactive plan amendment has been established, should that schedule remain the same or is it subject to revision on a periodic basis?

Answer: An amortization schedule of unrecognized prior service cost should be revised only if one of three conditions occur: (1) the pension plan is curtailed, (2) events indicate that the period for which the employer will receive benefits from a retroactive plan benefit is shorter than initially estimated, or (3) the future economic benefits have been impaired. The amortization schedule should not be revised because of variances in the expected service lives of employees. Finally, FAS-87 specifically proscribes reducing the length of such an amortization schedule (i.e., under no circumstances can unrecognized prior service cost be recognized more slowly than originally planned).

Question 15: In a business combination that is accounted for by the purchase method under APB-16, if the acquiring employer includes the employees of the acquired employer in its pension plan and grants them credit for prior service (the acquired employer did not have a pension plan), should the credit granted for prior service be treated as unrecognized prior service cost or as part of the cost of the acquisition?

Answer: It depends. If the selling entity requires that prior service credit be granted as a condition of the acquisition, the prior service credit granted would be treated as part of the cost of the acquisition; the offsetting debit is to goodwill. In all other cases, the granting of prior service credit is treated as a retroactive plan amendment; the offsetting debit is to unrecognized prior service cost.

Question 16: In determining the periods for (*a*) amortization of unrecognized prior service cost, (*b*) minimum amortization of unrecognized net gain or loss, or (*c*) amortization of the unrecognized net asset or net obligation existing at the date of initial application of FAS-87, is it necessary to include the service periods of employees who are expected to receive only a return of their contributions (plus interest, if applicable) to a contributory defined benefit pension plan in determining the future service periods of employees who are expected to receive benefits under that pension plan?

Answer: No. Only the expected future service periods of employees who are expected to receive a benefit provided by the employer need to be included.

Question 17: Are the service periods of employees who are expected to terminate before their benefits are vested included in the determination of the average remaining service period of employees who are expected to receive benefits under the pension plan?

Answer: No. Only the expected service periods of employees who are expected to receive benefits under the pension plan need to be included.

Question 18: Is there a specific threshold for determining if a pension plan has "almost all" inactive participants for purposes of selecting the amortization period for certain components of net periodic pension cost?

Answer: No. Judgment is required for determining whether "almost all" of a pension plan's participants are inactive.

Question 19: May an employer adopt an accounting policy to immediately recognize the cost of all plan amendments that grant increased benefits for services rendered in prior periods (prior service cost)?

Answer: No. The cost of a retroactive plan amendment may be charged to expense immediately only if it is determined, after a case-by-case review of the facts, that the employer will not receive any future economic benefits from the plan amendment. Although FAS-87 allows alternatives to the amortization method discussed in paragraph 25, there is the expectation that such alternative amortization methods would relate to the average remaining service period of employees who are active on the date of the plan amendment (or, in some cases, to the remaining life expectancy of inactive employees). In no case can amortization expense under an alternative method be less than what would be required if the method discussed in paragraph 25 were employed.

Question 20: If an employer has a history of granting retroactive plan amendments every three years, should the resulting unrecognized prior service costs be amortized over a three-year period?

Answer: This decision needs to be made on a case-by-case basis after the applicable facts and circumstances are considered. If it is determined that future economic benefits that result from a plan amendment will last only three years, the unrecognized prior service cost should be charged to expense over this time period. For example, if employees become accustomed to a retroactive increase in plan benefits every three years, the expected future economic benefits may not continue if this pattern is broken.

Question 21: If an employer grants a retroactive plan amendment that reduces the projected benefit obligation (a negative retroactive plan amendment), what method should be used to reduce any existing unrecognized prior service cost when several prior retroactive plan amendments in the aggregate have resulted in unrecognized prior service costs that exceed the effects of the negative retroactive plan amendment?

Answer: If a negative retroactive plan amendment can be specifically related to a prior positive retroactive plan amendment, the negative plan amendment would be charged against the prior positive plan amendment. In most cases, however, this type of specific matching will not be possible. In these cases, the negative plan amendment can be charged against prior positive plan amendments using any reasonable systematic and rational method (e.g., last-in, first-out; first-in, first-out; pro rata). Whatever method is selected needs to be applied in a consistent manner.

Question 22: If an employer amends a pension plan to delete a provision that a percentage of the employee's accumulated benefits be paid to the employee's spouse if the employee dies before reaching a specified age, should the reduction in benefits be accounted for as a retroactive plan amendment?

Answer: Yes. This is an example of a negative retroactive plan amendment.

Question 23: If an employer initially applies FAS-87 on January 1, 1987, but during 1987 changes its final-pay pension plan to a career-average-pay pension plan effective January 1, 1987, should the employer adjust the pension plan's unrecognized net asset or net obligation existing at the date of initial application of FAS-87 to reflect the reduction in the projected benefit obligation?

Answer: No. The reduction in pension benefits should be treated the same as any other negative retroactive plan amendment.

Question 24: Should the amount and timing of pension plan contributions and benefit payments expected to be made during the year be considered in determining the expected return on plan assets for that year?

Answer: Yes. The expected return on plan assets should consider the asset amounts that will be available for investment purposes during the year, including new contributions made.

Question 25: May the market-related value of plan assets at the date of initial application of FAS-87 be other than the fair value of those assets for purposes of determining the expected return on plan assets?

Answer: Yes. However, there are practical and theoretical reasons why the fair value of plan assets (rather than a market-related value) should be used to compute the expected return on plan assets at the initial adoption of FAS-87. From a practical standpoint, use of the fair value of plan assets is simpler. If the market-related value of plan assets is used, there is a risk that the difference between the fair value of plan assets and the market-related value may be counted twice. The difference between fair value and market-related value is part of the net transition asset or liability. If the entity is not careful, that same difference between fair value and market-related value might be included erroneously as an actuarial gain or as a return on plan assets. From a theoretical perspective, use of the fair value of plan assets to compute expected return in the year FAS-87 is adopted is preferred. The initial adoption of FAS-87 represents a "fresh start" to pension accounting. All previous unrecognized net gains and losses and unrecognized prior service cost amounts are reflected within the net pension asset or liability at transition.

Question 26: May an employer that has several pension plans with similar plan assets use different asset valuation methods to determine the market-related value of those plan assets?

Answer: Ordinarily not, especially since one objective of FAS-87 is to enhance the comparability of pension plan information. However, different asset valuation methods may be appropriate if they reflect underlying differences in the pension plans' inherent facts and circumstances.

Question 27: Is there a limitation on the number of classes into which plan assets may be divided for purposes of selecting asset valuation methods for determining the market-related value of plan assets?

Answer: No. However, the method selected for each asset class should be appropriate for recognizing changes in the fair value of assets in a systematic and rational manner over a period not to exceed five years. Asset valuation methods adopted should be applied consistently within each class, and the method used to divide assets into different classes should be applied consistently.

Question 28: Is the following an acceptable asset valuation method for determining the market-related value of plan assets? The market-related value of plan assets is determined with a total return-on-plan asset component consisting of three layers:

a. An expected return-on-plan asset component based on the beginning-of-year market-related value of plan assets, cash flow during the year, and the expected long-term rate of return on plan assets

b. An amount equal to the change in the accumulated benefit obligation that resulted from any change during the year in the assumed discount rates used to determine the accumulated benefit obligation (The amount is reduced pro rata if plan assets are less than the accumulated benefit obligation.)

c. A variance component equal to a percentage (e.g., 20% if a five-year-averaging period is used) of the difference between the actual return on plan assets based on the fair values of those plan assets and the expected return on plan assets derived from components (a) and (b).

Answer: No. Factor (b), the change in the accumulated benefit obligation resulting from changes in the assumed discount rate, is unrelated to changes in the fair value of plan assets. Only changes in the fair value of plan assets between various dates can be considered in computing the market-related value of plan assets.

Question 29: How does the use of a market-related value of plan assets affect the determination of net periodic pension cost?

Answer: The use of a market-related value of plan assets affects the determination of net periodic pension cost in two ways. First, the expected return on plan assets is based on the market-related value of plan assets (not based on the fair value of plan assets). Second, unrecognized net gains and losses based on the fair value of plan assets may not yet be reflected in calculating the market-related value of assets. To the extent this is true, such amounts are excluded from the unrecognized net gain or loss subject to amortization in the following period.

Question 30: If an employer uses a market-related value of plan assets in determining net periodic pension cost, is the determination of an additional minimum liability also based on that value of plan assets?

Answer: No. The minimum pension liability, if any, is equal to the shortfall of plan assets, measured at fair value, from the accumulated benefit obligation.

Question 31: If all or almost all of a pension plan's participants are inactive due to a temporary suspension of the pension plan (i.e., for a limited period of time, employees will not earn additional defined benefits), should the minimum amortization of an unrecognized net gain or loss be determined based on the average remaining life expectancy of the temporarily inactive participants?

Answer: No. The amortization period should be based on the average remaining service period of temporarily inactive participants who are expected to receive benefits under the pension plan.

Question 32: If all employees covered by a pension plan are terminated but not retired, should the minimum amortization of an unrecognized net gain or loss be determined based on the average remaining life expectancy of the inactive participants?

Answer: Yes.

Question 33: May an employer immediately recognize gains and losses instead of delaying their recognition?

Answer: Yes. However, the following three conditions must be met if the entity plans to immediately recognize gains and losses: (1) the method must be used consistently, (2) the method must be applied to all gains and losses (on both plan assets and pension plan obligations), and (3) the entity's policy to immediately recognize gains and losses must be disclosed.

Question 34: If an employer recognized an additional minimum liability at its prior fiscal year-end, what balance sheet pension account(s) should be affected during subsequent interim periods for the accrual of net periodic pension cost or for contributions made to the pension plan?

Answer: The offsetting credit (debit) to the recognition of net periodic pension cost (pension plan contributions) is to unfunded accrued pension cost (prepaid pension cost). Any balance in the unfunded accrued or prepaid pension cost account is to be combined with the additional minimum liability for presentation in the interim statement of financial position.

Question 35: May an employer recognize an additional pension asset for an overfunded pension plan beyond that which results from (*a*) funding more than the amount of net periodic pension cost or (*b*) recognizing net periodic pension income?

Answer: No. Although theoretically an entity has an asset to the extent that the fair value of plan assets exceeds the projected benefit obligation (PBO), this asset cannot be recognized immediately. However, an asset due to an excess of fair value of plan assets over the PBO is recognized immediately in a purchase business combination.

Question 36: If a pension plan has fixed-income investments (such as guaranteed investment contracts or bonds) that it intends to hold until they mature, should the determination of the additional minimum liability be based on the amortized cost of those fixed-income investments or on their fair value?

Answer: The fair value of the fixed-income investments should be used to compute any additional minimum liability. The intent of the minimum liability calculation in FAS-87 is to compare the current fair value of plan assets with the current projected benefit obligation (using the discount rate at which that liability could be effectively settled).

Question 37: If an employer has a financial report date of December 31 and a measurement date of September 30, how should the employer determine whether an additional minimum liability is required?

Answer: The unfunded accrued or prepaid pension cost is to be measured as of December 31. The funded status of the pension plan (the fair value of plan assets minus the projected benefit obligation) should be measured as of September 30 and adjusted to reflect amounts received from or paid to the employer during the fourth quarter. The unfunded accrued or prepaid pension cost amount is combined with the funded status of the pension plan to determine whether the entity must present an additional minimum pension liability.

Question 38: When an employer determines the unrecognized net asset or net obligation and the additional minimum liability of its pension plan existing at the date of initial application of FAS-87, is it

22.16 *Pension Plans—Employers*

necessary to make adjustments for amounts the employer contributed to the pension plan during the period between the beginning measurement date and the beginning of the financial reporting year if those dates are different?

Answer: Yes. See the example below for an illustration of this procedure when the pension plan is overfunded upon the adoption of FAS-87. An additional illustration in which the pension plan is underfunded upon the adoption of FAS-87 is included in FIG-FAS 87.

Illustration of Overfunded Plan When FAS-87 Is Adopted

Aerodynamics, Inc., has a December 31 fiscal year-end and a September 30 measurement date. Aerodynamics plans to adopt FAS-87 for its December 31, 1986, financial statements. As of September 30, 1985, there is no unfunded accrued or prepaid pension cost. The fair value of plan assets and of the projected benefit obligation are as follows on September 30, 1985, and December 31, 1985:

	September 30	December 31
Projected benefit obligation	$(350,000)	$(375,000)
Plan assets at fair value	400,000	410,000
Overfunded obligation	$ 50,000	$ 35,000

During the fourth quarter, Aerodynamics contributes $20,000 to the pension plan and recognizes $6,500 of net periodic pension cost. Therefore, at December 31, 1985, Aerodynamics has a prepaid pension cost amount of $13,500. Aerodynamics' unrecognized net asset at the initial application of FAS-87 (December 31, 1985) is as follows:

Plan assets in excess of projected benefit obligation at September 30, 1985	$50,000
Plus fourth quarter contributions	20,000
	$70,000
Less prepaid pension cost at December 31, 1985	13,500
Unrecognized net asset	$56,500

Question 39: In determining whether an additional minimum liability is required, may an employer compare the fair value of plan assets to a measure of the pension obligation greater than the accumulated benefit obligation (such as the projected benefit obligation)?

Answer: No. The only exception to this is a business combination accounted for as a purchase. In that case, the fair value of plan assets is compared with the projected benefit obligation.

Pension Plans—Employers **22.17**

Question 40: If an acquiring employer has accounted for a business combination by the purchase method under APB-16, should that employer's determination of any additional minimum liability consider the remaining portion of (*a*) the net-of-tax pension asset or pension liability or (*b*) the gross pension asset or pension liability determined at the date of the acquisition?

Answer: The determination of any additional minimum liability should be based on the gross pension asset or pension liability.

Question 41: If an employer recognizes an additional minimum liability and recognizes an equal amount as an intangible asset, should those amounts be classified as current or as noncurrent in the statement of financial position?

Answer: The intangible asset should be classified as noncurrent, because it is being amortized over future years. Any portion of the additional minimum liability that is expected to be funded over the next year should be classified as a current liability. The remaining balance of the additional minimum liability is noncurrent.

Question 42: If an employer recognizes an additional minimum liability and recognizes an equal amount as an intangible asset, is the intangible asset subject to separate amortization over a specified period?

Answer: No. The intangible asset results either from unrecognized prior service cost or from an unrecognized net obligation (existing at the date of initial adoption of FAS-87). FAS-87 specifies how unrecognized prior service cost and an unrecognized net obligation are to be amortized. Therefore, the intangible asset is effectively amortized through the amortization of these amounts.

Question 43: For the year 1988 in Illustration 5, Case 2, of FAS-87 (pp. 108–111), shouldn't an intangible asset have been recognized for the entire amount of the additional minimum liability ($128,000), rather than an intangible asset of $92,000 and a charge to equity of $36,000, since a portion of the unrecognized net obligation existing at the date of initial application of FAS-87 remains as of December 31, 1988?

Answer: Yes. There was an error in Illustration 5, Case 2, as originally issued by the FASB. Editions of *Current Text* and *Original Pronouncements* for 1986–87 and later have been corrected.

Question 44: If a career-average-pay pension plan has a formula that provides pension benefits equal to 1% of each year's salary for that year's service and if prospective (flat-benefit) plan amendments are granted every three years as part of union negotiations (e.g., a negotiated increase may provide that additional benefits of $360 per year are earned for each of the following three years of service), should the projected unit credit method be used for both the career-average-pay and the flat-benefit portions of the pension benefits provided under the pension plan?

Answer: No. The projected unit credit method should be used to apportion the career-average-pay portion of the plan to the expected service period of active employees. The unit credit method should be used for the flat-benefit portion of the plan.

Question 45: If an employer has a pension plan that provides a pension benefit of 1% of final pay for each year of service up to a maximum of 20 years of service and final pay is frozen at year 20, should the employer attribute the total projected benefits under the pension plan for an employee over the employee's expected service period even if that service period is anticipated to exceed the 20-year limitation?

Answer: No. If a pension plan attributes all of its prospective benefits over a 20-year time period, the service cost component should be recognized over this time period even if the employee is expected to work beyond 20 years. Note, however, that interest cost would continue to accrue on the projected benefit obligation beyond 20 years.

Question 46: Would the answer to Question 45 be different if the pension plan's formula provided a pension benefit of 1% of final pay for each year of service up to a maximum of 20 years of service and final pay was not frozen at year 20?

Answer: No. The only difference is that a liability gain or loss will exist beyond year 20 if future experience regarding employee pay levels differs from that which was assumed.

Question 47: How should an employer determine the accumulated and projected benefit obligations if a pension plan has more than one formula and an employee's pension benefits are determined based on the formula that provides the greatest pension benefit at the time the employee terminates or retires? (For example, if the employee terminates in year 10, the pension plan's flat-benefit formula provides a greater pension benefit than does the pension plan's pay-related formula; however, if the employee terminates in year 11, the pension plan provides that same employee with a greater benefit under its pay-related formula than under its flat-benefit formula.)

Answer: A pension plan that uses more than one formula may not assign the same benefit for each year of service. Therefore, the employer may need to use an attribution approach that does not assign the same level of benefits for each year of service. In calculating the accumulated benefit obligation, the employer should choose the formula that produces the greatest liability amount based on service rendered to date. Since the accumulated benefit obligation (ABO) cannot exceed the projected benefit obligation (PBO), the calculated PBO for service already rendered must equal or exceed the ABO. For service not yet rendered, the PBO should be calculated using the formula that results in the largest measure of the liability. A number of illustrations of these concepts are included in FIG-FAS 87. One illustration adapted from FIG-FAS 87 appears below.

Illustration of Attribution with Multiple Formulas

FRW, Inc., has a pension plan that uses two benefit formulas. The plan benefit that participants will receive is the larger of the amounts computed by each of the two formulas. Formula A provides a flat benefit of $900 for each of the first 20 years of an employee's service, with no pension benefits earned for service beyond 20 years. Formula B provides a benefit equal to 1% of final pay for each year of service.

A employee starts at a salary of $21,000 in year 1 and receives a $2,000 increase in salary for each year of service. (For purposes of simplicity, the accumulated and projected benefit obligations are expressed in terms of the annual pension benefits that begin when the employee retires.) This employee of FRW is expected to retire at the end of year 30 with a final salary of $79,000. Formula A would provide an annual pension benefit of $18,000 for 30 years of service ($900 in each of the first 20 years of service and no additional benefits for any service beyond 20 years). Formula B would provide a pension benefit of $23,700 for 30 years of service (30 x 1% x $79,000, or $790 for each year of service). Under Formula A, $900 of service cost is attributed to each of the first 20 years of service; no service cost is attributed to employee service beyond 20 years. Under Formula B, $790 of service cost is attributed to each of the 30 expected years of employee service.

At the end of year 20, the ABO and the PBO under Formula A, both $18,000, exceed the comparable amounts computed under Formula B. For example, the PBO under Formula A at the end of 20 years is $15,800 (20 x 1% x $79,000). Therefore, at the end of year 20, both the ABO and the PBO are measured using Formula A. However, by the end of year 30, the benefit under Formula B, $23,700, will exceed the benefit under Formula A, still $18,000 because no benefits are earned under Formula A after 20 years. Therefore, additional pension benefits of $570 [($23,700 − $18,000) / 10] are attributed to years 21–30.

The accumulated and projected benefit obligations for years 1–30 are as follows:

22.20 Pension Plans—Employers

Year	ABO	PBO
1–19	—(a)	—(a)
20	$18,000(a)	$18,000(a)
21	18,000(a)	18,570(b)
22	18,000(a)	19,140(b)
23	18,000(a)	19,710(b)
24	18,000(a)	20,280(b)
25	18,000(a)	20,850(b)
26	18,460(c)	21,420(b)
27	19,710(c)	21,990(b)
28	21,000(c)	22,560(b)
29	22,330(c)	23,130(b)
30	23,700(b)	23,700(b)

(a)$900 x years of service, not to exceed 20 years (Formula A)

(b)Formula A benefits earned through year 20 plus attribution of additional projected benefits under Formula B (for years 21–30 of employee service) in proportion to the number of completed years of service compared to the number of years of service that are expected to be completed for the period during which Formula B is applied. Although no additional pension benefits are "earned" in years 21 and 22, because the PBO in those years is less than $18,000 ($16,590 at end of year 21 and $17,380 at end of year 22), $570 of pension benefits is attributed to each of those years of service based on the total incremental pension benefits for years 21–30 ($5,700 / 10 years).

(c)Computed as 1% of the end-of-year salary times the number of years worked. For example, in year 29, 1% of $77,000 times 29 years is $22,330; in year 30, 1% of $79,000 times 30 years is $23,700.

Question 48: Can a pension plan have an accumulated benefit obligation that exceeds the projected benefit obligation?

Answer: No. The projected benefit obligation must always equal or exceed the accumulated benefit obligation.

Question 49: How is the projected benefit obligation attributed to a qualified pension plan (for tax purposes) and an excess benefit (top-hat) pension plan during an employee's service period if the employee is expected to receive a pension benefit under the excess benefit pension plan (i.e., the employee's pension benefit at retirement is expected to exceed the Section 415 limitations of the U.S. Internal Revenue Code)?

Answer: The projected benefit obligation should be attributed to the qualified pension plan (for tax purposes) until the Section 415 limitations are reached. Thereafter, any incremental pension benefits are attributed to the excess benefit plan. The following example illustrates this computation.

Illustration of Attribution of the Projected Benefit Obligation to a Qualified Pension Plan and an Excess Benefit Pension Plan

The pension plan formula of SBS, Inc., provides for an annual pension benefit of 1.5% of final salary for each year of service. Employee Jones has a beginning salary of $400,000, receives increases of $30,000 per year, and retires at the end of 21 years at a salary of $1,000,000. Section 415 will permit annual pension benefit payments of $200,000 for all the years Jones will receive benefit payments.

Attribution of the accumulated and projected benefit obligations is shown in the following table. Rather than being calculated, the actuarial present value of the accumulated and projected benefit obligations are expressed in terms of the benefit that Jones is expected to receive upon retirement.

Year of Service	Salary	Total ABO	Pension PBO	Qualified Plan ABO	Plan ABO	Excess Plan ABO	Plan PBO
1	$400,000	$ 6,000	$15,000	$ 6,000	$15,000		
2	430,000	12,900	30,000	12,900	30,000		
3	460,000	20,700	45,000	20,700	45,000		
4	490,000	29,400	60,000	29,400	60,000		
5	520,000	39,000	75,000	39,000	75,000		
6	550,000	49,500	90,000	49,500	90,000		
7	580,000	60,900	105,000	60,900	105,000		
8	610,000	73,200	120,000	73,200	120,000		
9	640,000	86,400	135,000	86,400	135,000		
10	670,000	100,500	150,000	100,500	150,000		
11	700,000	115,500	165,000	115,500	165,000		
12	730,000	131,400	180,000	131,400	180,000		
13	760,000	148,200	195,000	148,200	195,000		
14	790,000	165,900	210,000	165,900	200,000		$10,000
15	820,000	184,500	225,000	184,500	200,000		25,000
16	850,000	204,000	240,000	200,000	200,000	$ 4,000	40,000
17	880,000	224,400	255,000	200,000	200,000	24,400	55,000
18	910,000	245,700	270,000	200,000	200,000	45,700	70,000
19	940,000	267,900	285,000	200,000	200,000	67,900	85,000
20	970,000	291,000	300,000	200,000	200,000	91,000	100,000
21	1,000,000	315,000	315,000	200,000	200,000	115,000	115,000

Question 50: If a pension plan's formula provides an annual pension benefit equal to 1% of each year's salary (i.e., the formula does not base pension benefits for the current year on any future salary level), should the projected unit credit method be used to attribute

the service cost component of net periodic pension cost over employees' service periods?

Answer: Yes. This pension plan benefit is based on the level of employee pay. As such, it is in essence a career-average-pay pension plan. FAS-87 requires the use of the projected unit credit method for pay-related pension plans.

Question 51: What is intended by the fourth sentence of paragraph 143 of FAS-87, which states the following: "The Board perceives a difference between an employer's promise to pay a benefit of 1 percent of an employee's final pay and a promise to pay an employee a fixed amount that happens to equal 1 percent of the employee's current pay"? Is the Board referring to a career-average-pay pension plan in the latter part of the sentence?

Answer: No. The intended distinction is between a final-pay pension plan (discussed in the first half of the sentence) and a flat-benefit pension plan (discussed in the latter half of the sentence).

Question 52: What constitutes a substantive commitment requiring recognition of pension benefits beyond those defined in the pension plan's written formula?

Answer: FAS-87, paragraph 41, states, "[I]n some situations a history of regular increases in non-pay-related benefits or benefits under a career-average-pay plan and other evidence may indicate that an employer has a present commitment to make future amendments and that the substance of the plan is to provide benefits attributable to prior service that are greater than the benefits defined by the written terms of the plan." In the determination of whether such a "substantive commitment" exists, all the facts and circumstances surrounding the pension plan should be carefully considered. Actions of the employer, including communications to employees, should be considered. A history of regular plan amendments is not enough, by itself, to demonstrate a substantive commitment. However, if the employer has a history of regular plan amendments, prior service cost should be amortized more quickly than might normally be the case (see paragraph 27 of FAS-87).

Question 53: Should an employer's accounting for its pension plan anticipate a retroactive plan amendment that is not part of a series of retroactive plan amendments necessary to effect a substantive commitment to have a formula greater than its written form?

Answer: No.

Question 54: Is it always necessary for assumed compensation levels to change each time assumed discount rates (and expectations of future inflation rates inherently contained in the assumed discount rates) change?

Answer: No. FAS-87 requires that assumed discount rates and compensation levels consider the same future economic conditions. However, it does not suggest that these future economic conditions—for example, inflation—will affect discount rates and compensation levels in exactly the same way, or to the same extent.

Question 55: May an employer determine a range of discount rates each year based, for example, on the Pension Benefit Guaranty Corporation's interest rates and high-quality bond rates and continue to use the prior year's assumed discount rates as long as those rates fall within the range?

Answer: No. On a yearly basis the employer should make its best estimate of what discount rate most closely approximates the rate inherent in the price at which the pension benefit obligation could be effectively settled. For example, this rate might be the interest rate inherent in annuity contracts or the interest rate on high-quality bonds.

Question 56: May an employer determine a range of discount rates as described in Question 55 and then arbitrarily select the assumed discount rates from within that range?

Answer: No. The employer should make its best estimate of the discount rate consistent with effectively settling the pension benefit obligation. This process should be performed yearly.

Question 57: If an employer changes its basis of estimating assumed discount rates, for example, by using high-quality bond rates for one year and annuity rates for the following year, is that a change in method of applying an accounting principle?

Answer: No. This type of change would be viewed as a change in estimate. The decision to use a particular methodology in one year (e.g., the interest rate on high-quality bonds versus the interest rate inherent in annuity contracts) does not obligate the entity to continue using that approach in future years. The objective is to use a method that produces a discount rate that most closely approximates the rate inherent in the price at which the pension obligation could be effectively settled. However, if the facts and circumstances have not changed from the prior year, it generally would be inappropriate to change the method of selecting the discount rate. For example, an entity may historically have determined the discount rate by reference to the high-quality bond rate. Absent a change in circumstances that suggests this method does not produce the most appropriate measure of the discount rate at which the pension benefit obligation could be effectively settled, it should be used consistently from one year to the next.

Question 58: If a pension plan has a bond portfolio that was dedicated at a yield significantly higher or lower than current interest rates, may the historical rates of return as of the dedication date be used in discounting the projected and accumulated benefit obligations to their present value?

Answer: No. It would be acceptable to consider current rates of return on high-quality fixed-income investments. The use of historical rates of return is not permitted.

Question 59: May the assumed discount rates used to discount the vested, accumulated, and projected benefit obligations be different?

Answer: Yes, if the circumstances justify different discount rates. For example, different discount rates may be appropriate for active and retired employees because of differences in the maturity and duration of expected pension benefits. However, the discount rate used to value pension benefits maturing in any particular year should not differ, regardless of whether the obligation is presently classified as vested, accumulated, or projected.

Question 60: What assumed discount rates and expected long-term rate of return on plan assets should be used to determine (*a*) the unrecognized net asset or net obligation at the date of initial application of FAS-87 and (*b*) net periodic pension cost, if an employer with a September 30, 1986, fiscal year-end elects in its fourth quarter to apply FAS-87 early and restate its prior interim reports?

Answer: The assumptions that would be appropriate as of the beginning measurement date for the fiscal year should be used.

Question 61: Because a current settlement of the portion of the projected benefit obligation that relates to future compensation levels is unlikely, may an employer use those interest rates implicit in current prices of annuity contracts to determine the accumulated benefit obligation, and use interest rates expected to be implicit in future prices of annuity contracts to determine the pension obligation in excess of the accumulated benefit obligation?

Answer: No. FAS-87 requires the selection of a discount rate consistent with the rate inherent in the price at which the pension obligation could be effectively settled currently. An employer would not purchase an annuity contract to cover pension benefits based on future compensation levels, and an insurance company would not write such a contract without charging for the additional risk it would be assuming. However, this fact is irrelevant for selecting the appropriate discount rate. When FAS-87 discusses interest rates on annuity contracts, it is presenting one approach for determining the appropriate discount rate for valuing the pension plan benefit obligation. (Another approach is the interest rate on high-quality fixed-income investments.) The objective is *not* to determine the price an insurance company would charge for assuming the employer's obligation. Rather, the rates implicit in the current prices of annuity contracts might serve as a useful measure of the appropriate discount rate for valuing the pension plan obligation.

Question 62: Should the expected return on future years' contributions to a pension plan be considered in determining the expected long-term rate of return on plan assets?

Answer: No. The expected long-term rate of return on plan assets should be limited to the return expected on existing plan assets and on contributions received during the current year.

Question 63: Should changes under existing law in benefit limitations (such as those currently imposed by Section 415 of the U.S. Internal Revenue Code) that would affect benefits provided by a pension plan be anticipated in measuring the service cost component of net periodic pension cost and the projected benefit obligation?

Answer: Yes. Changes in existing pension law that would affect benefits provided should be considered in measuring service cost and the projected benefit obligation if such changes in laws have already been enacted. Possible changes to law should not be anticipated.

Question 64: If Section 415 of the U.S. Internal Revenue Code is incorporated by reference into a pension plan's formula, thereby limiting certain participants' accumulated benefits, should determination of the pension plan's accumulated benefit obligation reflect the current limitation if (*a*) the pension plan's formula requires automatic increases in accumulated benefits as each change in the limitation under existing law occurs and (*b*) future service is not a prerequisite for participants to receive those increases?

Answer: No. The calculation of the accumulated benefit obligation should reflect those increases in the limitation under existing law that would be consistent with the pension plan's other assumptions. This result presupposes that the employee does not have to render any additional service to be eligible for these benefits. However, if an employee would not automatically receive these benefit increases upon retiring or terminating his or her service, the accumulated benefit obligation should be calculated based on the Section 415 limitation as it currently exists.

Question 65: If an actuarial valuation is made as of a pension plan's year-end and that date precedes the employer's measurement date for the pension plan, is it always necessary to have another actuarial valuation made as of the measurement date?

Answer: No. FAS-87 does require that the projected benefit obligation reflect the actuarial present value of benefits attributed to employee service rendered before the measurement date. Actuarial assumptions for turnover, mortality, discount rates, etc., should be appropriate as of the measurement date. However, it may be possible to measure the projected benefit obligation at the measurement date with a sufficient degree of reliability based on rolling forward the earlier actuarial valuation of the PBO. In such a case, a new actuarial valuation is not required. This situation is analogous to taking a physical inventory before year-end and rolling the inventory balance forward to the financial statement date.

Question 66: How should net periodic pension cost for the year be determined if it is necessary to have an actuarial valuation as of the measurement date (e.g., December 31) in addition to the actuarial valuation as of the pension plan's preceding year-end (e.g., June 30)?

Answer: Measurement of net periodic pension cost should be based on the most recent measurements of plan assets and obligations. If two actuarial measurements are completed during the year, net periodic pension cost should be the sum of two separate six-month periods (in the case above, January 1–June 30 and July 1–December 31). Net periodic pension cost for the first six months (latter six months) would be determined as of the preceding December 31 (the preceding June 30).

Question 67: If an employer that has a December 31 financial report date and uses a December 31 measurement date measures its plan assets and obligations as of an interim date during its fiscal year (e.g., because of a significant retroactive plan amendment), should net periodic pension cost for the subsequent interim periods be based on those measurements?

Answer: Yes. Net periodic pension cost should be based on the most recent measurement of plan assets and obligations that is available. Paragraph 53 of FAS-87 states, "[M]easurements of net periodic pension cost for both interim and annual financial statements shall be based on the assumptions used for the previous year-end measurements unless more recent measurements of both plan assets and obligations are available...."

Question 68: Under the circumstances described in Question 67, should net periodic pension cost for the preceding interim periods be adjusted?

Answer: No.

Question 69: If an employer uses a measurement date of September 30 but does not complete the actual measurements until some time later in the year—for example, in December—should the determination of the pension obligations be based on the assumed discount rates and other actuarial assumptions as of December?

Answer: No. The employer should use the actuarial assumptions that were appropriate as of the measurement date (September 30).

Question 70: If an employer has several pension plans with varying measurement dates, should the pension disclosures be segregated by measurement date?

Answer: No. The use of different measurement dates for different pension plans does not, in itself, necessitate the separate presentation of pension plans by each measurement date. However, the entity must disclose the different measurement dates used.

Question 71: Should an employer that uses a measurement date that is 3 months earlier than its financial report date have 12 months of net periodic pension cost in the first year of initial application of FAS-87?

Answer: Yes. For example, if a company with a December 31 year-end and a September 30 measurement date initially applies FAS-87 in 1986, its net periodic pension cost would be measured from September 30, 1985, through September 30, 1986.

Question 72: What are examples of "nonbenefit liabilities" that should be disclosed in accordance with paragraph 54 (a) of FAS-87, if significant?

Answer: Some examples of "nonbenefit liabilities" include (*a*) unsettled security purchases, (*b*) unsecured borrowings, and (*c*) borrowings secured by investments in real estate.

Question 73: If an employer has (*a*) a qualified pension plan (for tax purposes) and (*b*) a nonqualified pension plan (which pays pension benefits in excess of the maximum allowed for the qualified pension plan by Section 415 of the U.S. Internal Revenue Code—an excess benefit [top-hat] pension plan) and the plans cover the same employees, may those pension plans be considered in substance a single pension plan under FAS-87?

Answer: No. In most cases a qualified pension plan (for tax purposes) is legally prohibited from using its assets to pay benefits of an excess benefit pension plan. Therefore, in the situation described above, each plan would be accounted for separately. The fact that the employer could (a) contribute less to the qualified plan and use any savings to pay benefits under the excess benefit plan or (b) terminate the qualified plan and use the assets that revert to it to pay benefits under the excess plan does not, in itself, indicate that the two pension plans should be combined.

Question 74: The pension asset or pension liability recognized by the acquiring employer in a business combination accounted for by the purchase method under APB-16 may reflect estimates of future tax effects. Does this affect the reconciliation required by paragraph 54(c) of FAS-87?

Answer: Yes. The tax valuation adjustment will become another line item in the reconciliation of the funded status of the plan to the accrued (prepaid) pension liability (asset) reported in the employer's statement of financial position.

Question 75: May an employer restate certain pension disclosures for the prior year to make them comparable with disclosures for the initial year of application of FAS-87?

Answer: Yes. Restating certain pension disclosures for the prior year to make them comparable with disclosures for the initial year of application of FAS-87 is permitted; it is not required. For example, an employer with a year-end of December 31 initially applies FAS-87 in 1986. In its December 31, 1986, financial statements, the employer has two options with regard to 1985 pension plan information. The employer can present the actuarial present value of the pension plan liability at December 31, 1985 (vested, accumulated, and projected), the fair value of plan assets, the weighted-average discount rate, and any assumptions about increases in future compensation costs. Alternatively, the employer can present the FAS-36 pension plan disclosures for 1985. In either case, pension cost for 1985 is computed in accordance with the provisions of APB-8.

Question 76: For annual and interim reports for the year of initial application of FAS-87, should an employer follow paragraph 19(c) of APB-20, which requires disclosure of "the effect of adopting the new accounting principle on income before extraordinary items and on net income (and on the related per share amounts) of the period of the change"?

Answer: Yes.

Question 77: For annual and interim reports for the year of initial application of FAS-87, should an employer follow paragraph 19(d) of APB-20, which requires that "income before extraordinary items and net income computed on a pro forma basis should be shown on the face of the income statements for all periods presented as if the newly adopted accounting principle had been applied during all periods affected"?

Answer: No. FAS-87 is to be applied prospectively in computing net periodic pension cost. Since net periodic pension cost is considered in determining income, pro forma income amounts do not have to be computed.

Question 78: If an employer elects to delay recognition of an additional minimum liability (FAS-87, pars. 36–38) until 1989, to which balance sheet account should the funded status of the plan be reconciled in the periods prior to 1989?

Answer: The funded status of the plan should be reconciled to the unfunded accrued or prepaid pension cost account.

Question 79: Should the assumptions disclosed for the year that FAS-87 is initially applied be as of the beginning or ending measurement date?

Answer: The assumptions for the weighted-average discount rate and compensation cost increase, if applicable, affect the determination of the projected benefit obligation. As such, these assumptions should be as of the ending measurement date. In most cases, the assumption as to the weighted-average long-term rate of return on plan assets is as of the beginning of the year. This is because the expected return on plan assets is used in computing net periodic pension cost for the upcoming year. If the expected return on plan assets changes during the year due to an interim actuarial valuation, both the expected return on plan assets at the beginning of the year and the new expected return should be disclosed (alternatively, an appropriately blended expected rate of return on plan assets can be disclosed). In years subsequent to the initial application of FAS-87, all of these assumptions are available at both the beginning and the ending measurement dates.

Question 80: If an employer combines several of its pension plans after initial application of FAS-87 and the assets of each predecessor pension plan are available to satisfy the previously existing obligations of the other, how should the combined pension plan be accounted for?

Answer: The fair value of pension plan assets and the actuarial present value of pension plan obligations (vested, accumulated, and projected) should be combined and reported as a single amount. Similarly, the determination of any required additional minimum liability is computed on a combined basis. Unrecognized net gain or loss, unrecognized transition assets and liabilities, and unrecognized prior service cost are treated as follows:

Item	Combination Treatment	Amortization Treatment
Unrecognized net gain/loss	Aggregate amounts from previously separate pension plans	Amortize using the average remaining service period of the combined employee group
Unrecognized transition asset/ liability	Aggregate amounts from previously separate pension plans	Amortize using a weighted average of the remaining amortization periods previously used be the separate pension plans
Unrecognized prior service cost	Aggregate amounts from previously separate pension plans	Amortize separately, as previously determined, based on specific employee groups covered

Illustration of Combining Two Plans

TELWIN, Inc., has two separate pension plans, Plan A and Plan B, that it plans to combine into one plan on December 31, 1990. TELWIN adopted the provisions of FAS-87 for the year ended December 31, 1986. Relevant details about each separate pension plan and about how the combination would be effected follow.

Prior to Combination of Plan A and Plan B

	Plan A	Plan B
Assumptions:		
Weighted-average discount rate	11%	10.5%
Expected long-term rate of return on plan assets	12%	12%
Average remaining service period	20 years	13 years
Average remaining service period at date of initial application of FAS-87	20 years	13 years
Number of employees as of December 31, 1990, expected to receive benefits under the pension plan	400	550

Pension Plans—Employers 22.31

Amortization Method:		
Unrecognized prior service cost	Straight-line amortization over average remaining service period of employees expected to receive benefits (20 years)	Straight-line amortization over average remaining service period of employees expected to receive benefits (13 years)
Unrecognized net gain or loss	Minimum amortization specified in paragraph 32 of FAS-87	Minimum amortization specified in paragraph 32 of FAS-87
Unrecognized net asset or net obligation existing at date of initial application of FAS-87	Straight-line amortization over average remaining service period of employees expected to receive benefits (20 years)	Straight-line amortization over 15 years
Actuarial present value of benefit obligations:		
Vested benefit obligation	$ (596)	$ (726)
Accumulated benefit obligation	$ (678)	$ (854)
Projected benefit obligation	$(1,004)	$(1280)
Plan assets at fair value	1,608	410
Projected benefit obligation (in excess of) less than plan assets	$ 604	$ (870)
Remaining unrecognized net (asset) obligation existing at date of initial application	(40)	500
Unrecognized net (gain) loss	(228)	82
Unrecognized prior service cost	240	642
Prepaid pension cost	$ 576	$ 354

After Combination of Plan A and Plan B

	Combined Plan AB
Assumptions:	
Weighted-average discount rate	10.6%[a]
Expected long-term rate of return on plan assets	12%[b]
Average remaining service period	15.95 years[c]
Number of employees as of December 31, 1990, expected to receive benefits under the pension plan	950

22.32 *Pension Plans—Employers*

Amortization method:

Unrecognized prior service cost	The existing unrecognized prior service costs of Plan A and Plan B continue to be amortized separately. The amortization bases used prior to the combination continue to apply.
Unrecognized net gain or loss	Minimum amortization specified in paragraph 32 (average remaining service period is 15.95 years[c])
Remaining unrecognized net obligation existing at date of initial application of FAS-87	Straight-line amortization over 10.4 years[d]

---

[a] The weighted-average assumed discount rate reflects the rate at which the pension obligation could be effectively settled. (This illustration assumes that 10.6% is the appropriate discount rate. The discount rate is calculated without reference to either of the discount rates on the previously separate plans.)

[b] There is no change in the expected long-term rate of return on plan assets, because both Plan A and Plan B assume the same rate of return.

[c] The average remaining service period of employees who are expected to receive benefits under the pension plan is weighted by the number of covered employees from each group. This calculation is performed as follows: (20 years x 400/950) + (13 years x 550/950) = 15.95 years.

[d] The amortization period for the remaining unrecognized net obligation existing at the date of initial application of FAS-87 is determined by weighting (1) the average *remaining* amortization period for each plan and (2) the *absolute value* of the remaining unrecognized net asset or net obligation existing at the date FAS-87 was adopted. In this example, the calculation is as follows: [(20 years − 5 years) x 40/540] + [(15 years − 5 years) x 500/540] = 10.4 years (rounded).

	Combined Plan AB
Actuarial present value of benefit obligations:	
Vested benefit obligation	$(1,322)
Accumulated benefit obligation	$(1,532)
Projected benefit obligation	$(2,284)
Plan assets at fair value	$ 2,018
Projected benefit obligation in excess of plan assets	$ (266)
Remaining unrecognized net obligation existing at date of initial application	460
Unrecognized net gain	(146)
Unrecognized prior service cost	882
Prepaid pension cost	$ 930

Question 81: If an employer divides a pension plan into two or more separate pension plans after the date of initial application of FAS-87, how should (*a*) the remaining unrecognized net asset or net obligation existing at the date of initial application of FAS-87, (*b*) the unrecognized net gain or loss arising subsequent to initial application, and (*c*) any unrecognized prior service cost be allocated to each of the separate plans?

Answer: Any remaining unrecognized net asset or obligation and any unrecognized net gain or loss are to be allocated to the respective pension plans based on the beginning balance of the projected benefit obligation in each of the separate plans. Unrecognized prior service costs should be allocated to the new pension plans based on the average remaining service lives of the employees expected to receive benefits under each of the respective plans. FIG-FAS 87 contains a detailed example of this computation.

Question 82: Are annuity contracts defined differently in FAS-87 and FAS-88? If so, how are the definitions different, and why?

Answer: Yes. Settlement accounting does not apply if annuity contracts are purchased from an enterprise that is controlled by the employer (FAS-88). Therefore, if an employer purchases annuity contracts from an enterprise that is controlled by the employer, no settlement gain or loss is recognized on the transaction. Under FAS-87, pension benefits covered by annuity contracts purchased from a captive insurer are to be excluded from the projected benefit obligation and from plan assets. The net effect of the above is that no settlement gain or loss is recognized if annuity contracts are purchased from an entity controlled by the employer; however, unless these annuity contracts are purchased from a captive insurer, the pension benefits covered by the contracts are excluded from the PBO and from plan assets.

Question 83: Is a guaranteed investment contract (GIC) an annuity contract?

Answer: No. All a GIC does is transfer investment risk to the insurer. In an annuity contract, the insurer assumes an unconditional legal obligation to provide specified pension benefits to specific individuals.

Question 84: If a GIC is not considered an annuity contract, how should an employer value the contract if it has a specified maturity date and there is no intent to liquidate the contract before that date?

Answer: The GIC should still be valued at its fair value on a yearly basis even if the employer has no intent to liquidate the contract before its maturity date. The employer may estimate the fair value of the GIC by looking to current interest rates on similar debt securities of comparable risk and duration.

Question 85: Should the market value adjustment in an immediate participation GIC be considered in determining its fair value?

Answer: Yes. The contract value adjusted for any such market value adjustment represents the contract's cash surrender value. In some cases an immediate participation GIC can be converted into an annuity contract. In these cases the conversion value of the contract is relevant in estimating the contract's fair value.

Question 86: A not-for-profit organization has a defined benefit pension plan that covers employees at the national level and in all local chapters. If (*a*) each chapter is required to contribute to the pension plan based on a predetermined formula (e.g., on a percentage-of-salary basis), (*b*) plan assets are not segregated or restricted on a chapter-by-chapter basis, and (*c*) the pension obligations for a chapter's employees are retained by the pension plan if a chapter withdraws from the pension plan, as opposed to being allocated to the withdrawing chapter, should that arrangement be accounted for as a single-employer pension plan or as a multiemployer pension plan?

Answer: The not-for-profit organization should account for the pension plan as a single-employer plan in its consolidated financial statements. However, each of the separate chapters should account for the plan as a multiemployer plan in its individual financial statements. Each chapter should recognize its required yearly contribution, whether fully funded or not, as net periodic pension cost. If the yearly contribution is not fully funded, the local chapter would need to record a liability. Each local chapter must make the disclosures of paragraph 69 of FAS-87 and the required related-party disclosures of FAS-57 (if applicable).

Question 87: Does the answer to the previous question also apply to a similar parent–subsidiary arrangement if each subsidiary issues separate financial statements?

Answer: Yes. The parent would account for the pension plan as a single-employer plan in the consolidated financial statements. Each subsidiary would account for the plan as a multiemployer plan in its individual financial statements.

Questions 88–94 pertain to pension plan issues when a business combination accounted for as a purchase under the provisions of APB-16 is consummated. The acquired enterprise sponsors a single-employer defined benefit pension plan on the date of acquisition.

Question 88: Should the pension asset or pension liability recognized by the acquiring employer be separately amortized to income in periods subsequent to the acquisition?

Answer: No. Any such pension asset or liability should not be separately amortized. However, a pension asset or liability recognized by the acquiring employer will be affected by the accounting for the pension plan in future periods. A pension plan asset that exists at the date of acquisition will be reduced in each year in which (*a*) the employer's funding is less than net periodic pension cost or (*b*) an asset reversion occurs. A pension plan liability that exists at the date of acquisition will be reduced in each year in which (*a*) the employer's funding exceeds net periodic pension cost or (*b*) a pension plan settlement or curtailment results in net periodic pension income.

Question 89: Should the pension asset or pension liability recognized by the acquiring employer reflect estimates of future tax effects?

Answer: Yes. The pension asset or liability recognized by the acquiring employer should reflect future tax effects if recovery of the pension asset or settlement of the pension liability would give rise to taxable or tax-deductible amounts.

Question 90: How should the acquiring employer record a purchase if it has elected to apply FAS-87 early but the acquired employer has not?

Answer: The acquiring employer should apply FAS-87 to the purchase and to the acquired pension plans.

Question 91: Is the acquiring employer required to apply FAS-87 early for all of its domestic pension plans if, before the acquisition, the acquired employer elected to apply FAS-87 early for its domestic pension plans?

Answer: No. However, the acquiring employer is encouraged to apply FAS-87 early for all of its domestic pension plans.

Question 92: If the acquiring employer is *not* required to apply FAS-87 early in the circumstances described in the preceding question:

a. Must the accounting for the acquired pension plans revert to the accounting under APB-8?

b. If accounting for the acquired pension plans is permitted to remain under FAS-87 while accounting for the other domestic pension plans continues to follow APB-8, is that considered piecemeal early application of FAS-87?

c. How should the acquiring employer record the purchase?

Answer: The answers to the three questions posed above are as follows:

a. No. It is not necessary, nor is it desirable, for the acquired pension plans to revert to APB-8. However, the acquired pension plans are not precluded from reverting to APB-8.

b. No. The fact that some of the entity's pension plans follow FAS-87 (the plans of the acquired entity) and some of the pension plans follow APB-8 (the acquiror's plans) reflects a business combination. This result is not due to the piecemeal adoption of FAS-87.

c. If the acquired pension plans continue to follow FAS-87, the assignment of purchase price to the pension plan's assets and liabilities should follow paragraph 74 of FAS-87. If the acquired pension plans revert to APB-8, allocation of the purchase price to the pension plan's assets and liabilities should follow APB-16 (before its amendment by FAS-87).

Question 93: Should the acquiring employer's determination of the unrecognized net asset or net obligation at the date of initial application of FAS-87 consider the remaining portion of (a) the net-of-tax pension asset or pension liability or (b) the gross pension asset or pension liability determined at the date of an acquisition?

Answer: The acquiring employer's determination of the unrecognized net asset or net obligation at the date of initial application of FAS-87 should be based on the gross pension asset or pension liability.

Question 94: Would the answers to Questions 88–93 change if either the acquiring employer or the acquired employer were a foreign enterprise?

Answer: No.

Question 95: Is it acceptable to apply the net periodic pension cost and disclosure requirements of FAS-87 early but wait until 1989 to apply the balance sheet requirements of paragraphs 36–38 of FAS-87?

Answer: Yes.

Question 96: Can an employer elect to apply FAS-87 early for some but not all of its U.S. pension plans? Can an employer elect to apply FAS-87 early for some but not all of its non–U.S. pension plans?

Answer: If FAS-87 is adopted early for some U.S. pension plans, it needs to be adopted early for all U.S. pension plans. FAS-87 can be adopted early on a country-by-country basis for non–U.S. pension plans. However, FAS-87 should be adopted early for all pension plans within a particular foreign country if one such pension plan chooses early adoption.

Question 97: If an employer that has not elected to apply FAS-87 early establishes a new pension plan, can that pension plan be accounted for in accordance with FAS-87 if the employer continues to apply APB-8 in accounting for its previously existing pension plans located in the same country?

Answer: No. However, APB-8 would allow the employer to select pension plan assumptions and an attribution method that are consistent with the FAS-87 methodology.

Question 98: If FAS-87 is not applied for U.S. pension plans until the fiscal year beginning after December 15, 1986, may FAS-87 be applied initially in later interim reporting periods of that fiscal year with restatement of prior interim reports?

Answer: No. FAS-87 is effective for U.S. pension plans as of the beginning of the fiscal year immediately subsequent to December 15. Therefore, reporting for the first interim period in the first fiscal year following December 15, 1986, should be in conformity with the requirements of FAS-87.

Question 99: If FAS-87 is not applied for non–U.S. pension plans or for nonpublic enterprises that sponsor no defined benefit plans with more than 100 participants until the fiscal year beginning after December 15, 1988, may FAS-87 be applied initially in later interim reporting periods of that fiscal year with restatement of prior interim reports?

Answer: No. See the answer to the previous question for further details.

Question 100: If an employer disposes of a segment of a business including a related pension plan in the year of initial application of FAS-87, does FAS-87 apply to that pension plan for the interim period prior to its disposal?

Answer: Yes.

Question 101: Do pension plans in Puerto Rico and other U.S. territories qualify as non–U.S. pension plans or as domestic pension plans?

Answer: Based on an analogy to FTB 79-4, Puerto Rican pension plans, and pension plans in other U.S. territories, are considered domestic pension plans.

Question 102: If an employer has several pension plans and the average remaining service period of employees who are expected to receive benefits under each pension plan is less than 15 years, may the employer elect to use (*a*) a 15-year period to amortize the unrecognized net obligations of its underfunded pension plans existing at the date of initial application of FAS-87 and (*b*) the average remaining service period to amortize the unrecognized net assets of its overfunded pension plans existing at that date?

Answer: In general, no. Different amortization periods should not be used for different employee groups that are essentially the same. The burden of proof is on the employer to justify the different amortization periods.

Question 103: In determining the unrecognized net asset or net obligation existing at the date of initial application of FAS-87, which pension items are included in the unfunded accrued or prepaid pension cost balance recognized in the employer's statement of financial position?

Answer: All items related to the pension plan and included in the employer's statement of financial position are considered in determining the previously recognized unfunded accrued or prepaid pension cost balance. These items include the following:

a. Any difference between the cumulative funding and the cumulative expense under APB-8

b. The remaining *gross* pension asset or pension liability as a result of a purchase business combination

c. Any unamortized credit resulting from an asset reversion transaction

d. Any remaining portion of a liability for special termination benefits pursuant to FAS-74

e. Any remaining portion of a pension liability recognized as part of the disposal of a business segment

Question 104: If an employer has no unfunded accrued or prepaid pension cost recognized in its statement of financial position at the date of initial application of FAS-87, may it recognize a pension asset if plan assets exceed the projected benefit obligation?

Answer: No. Any unrecognized net asset that exists at transition will be amortized in the future as a reduction of net periodic pension cost.

Question 105: If the average remaining service period of employees who are expected to receive benefits under the pension plan is more than 15 years at the date of initial application of FAS-87, can the unrecognized net asset or net obligation be amortized over a 15-year period?

Answer: No. A 15-year period is available only if the average remaining service period is less than 15 years.

Question 106: Does the alternative 15-year period noted in paragraph 77 of FAS-87 apply to a pension plan that has all or almost all inactive participants whose average remaining life expectancy is less than 15 years?

Answer: No.

Question 107: If a pension plan curtailment occurs that causes almost all of the pension plan's participants to become inactive, should the employer continue to amortize any remaining portion of the unrecognized net asset or net obligation existing at the date of initial application of FAS-87 using the same amortization period determined at that date?

Answer: Yes. The remaining unrecognized net asset or net obligation is the amount that remains after the employer recognizes the effect of the pension plan curtailment (see FAS-88, pars. 12 and 13).

CHAPTER 23
PENSION PLANS—SETTLEMENTS AND CURTAILMENTS

CONTENTS

IMPRESS™ Cross-References	23.02
Overview	23.03
FIG-FAS 88: A Guide to Implementation of Statement 88 on Employers' Accounting for Settlements and Curtailments of Defined Benefit Pension Plans and for Termination Benefits	23.04
Background	23.04
Standards	23.04
Illustration of Substituting New Plan for Existing Plan	23.11
Illustration of Accounting for Net Assets at Transition When a Settlement Gain Is Recognized	23.16
Illustration of Incorporation and Subsequent Spin-Off of a Pension Plan	23.18
Illustration of Pension Plan Curtailment: Remaining Unrecognized Net Asset at Transition Is Less Than Unrecognized Net Loss Subsequent to Transition	23.24
Illustration of Pension Plan Curtailment: Remaining Unrecognized Net Asset at Transition Exceeds Unrecognized Net Loss Subsequent to Transition	23.25
Illustration of Curtailment: Termination Benefits Offered to Employees	23.27

CROSS-REFERENCES

1999 MILLER GAAP IMPLEMENTATION MANUAL: Chapter 22, "Pension Plans—Employers"; Chapter 25, "Postemployment and Postretirement Benefits Other Than Pensions"

1999 MILLER GAAP GUIDE: Chapter 35, "Pension Plans—Settlements and Curtailments"

1999 MILLER GAAP IMPLEMENTATION MANUAL: EITF: Chapter 23, "Pension Accounting"

1999 MILLER GOVERNMENTAL GAAP GUIDE: Chapter 17, "Claims, Judgements, and Special Termination Benefits"

CHAPTER 23
PENSION PLANS—SETTLEMENTS AND CURTAILMENTS

OVERVIEW

A *settlement of a pension plan* is an irrevocable action that relieves the employer (or the plan) of primary responsibility for an obligation and eliminates significant risks related to the obligation and the assets used to effect the settlement. Examples of transactions that constitute a settlement include (*a*) making lump-sum cash payments to plan participants in exchange for their rights to receive specified pension benefits and (*b*) purchasing nonparticipating annuity contracts to cover vested benefits.

A *curtailment* is a significant reduction in, or an elimination of, defined benefit accruals for present employees' future services. Examples of curtailments are (*a*) termination of employees' services earlier than expected, which may or may not involve closing a facility or discontinuing a segment of a business, and (*b*) termination or suspension of a plan so that employees do not earn additional defined benefits for future services.

The following pronouncement is the source of GAAP for pension plans—settlements and curtailments that is included in the highest level of authority in the SAS-69 hierarchy:

FAS-88   Employers' Accounting for Settlements and Curtailments of Defined Benefit Pension Plans and for Termination Benefits

The following additional source of GAAP that is in a lower level of the SAS-69 GAAP hierarchy is discussed in this Manual:

FIG-FAS 88   A Guide to Implementation of Statement 88 on Employers' Accounting for Settlements and Curtailments of Defined Benefit Pension Plans and for Termination Benefits (Level D)

FIG-FAS 88: A Guide to Implementation of Statement 88 on Employers' Accounting for Settlements and Curtailments of Defined Benefit Pension Plans and for Termination Benefits

BACKGROUND

FIG-FAS 88, reported on in this section, includes responses to 70 specific questions regarding the application of FAS-88.

STANDARDS

Question 1: Should an employer recognize a settlement gain or loss in the period in which all of the following occur: (a) the employer decides to terminate a defined benefit pension plan and establish a successor pension plan, (b) a nonparticipating annuity contract for the vested benefits of all plan participants is purchased but can be rescinded if certain regulatory approvals for the termination of the pension plan are not obtained, and (c) it is determined that the regulatory approvals are probable?

Answer: No. FAS-88 specifies three criteria that define when a pension plan settlement has occurred. A *settlement* is defined as a transaction that (1) is irrevocable, (2) relieves the employer (or the pension plan) of the primary responsibility for a pension plan obligation, and (3) eliminates significant risks related to the pension plan obligation and plan assets used to effect the settlement. In the situation described above, an irrevocable transaction has not occurred. The probability that an irrevocable action will be completed is not relevant.

Question 2: If an employer decides in 1991 to terminate its pension plan, withdraw excess plan assets, and establish a successor pension plan but is unable to effect the transactions (which include the settlement of the vested benefit obligation) until regulatory approval is obtained, does the purchase of nonparticipating annuity contracts in January 1992 (after regulatory approval has been obtained and before issuance of the 1991 financial statements) require adjustment of the 1991 financial statements?

Answer: No. As discussed in the answer to Question 1, a *settlement* is defined as a transaction that (1) is irrevocable, (2) relieves the employer (or the pension plan) of the primary responsibility for a pension plan obligation, and (3) eliminates significant risks related to the pension plan obligation and plan assets used to effect the settlement. All three of these criteria are not met until January 1992. However, the employer would need to disclose its plans to terminate the pension plan and its receipt of the required regulatory approvals in January 1992.

Question 3: If plan participants have agreed to accept lump-sum cash payments in exchange for their rights to receive specified pension benefits and the amounts of the payments have been fixed, may a settlement gain or loss be recognized before the cash payments are made to plan participants?

Answer: It depends. If the cash payments have yet to be made, the agreement itself may be revocable. Moreover, if the pension plan assets have not been used to effect the settlement, the employer may still be subject to risks related to these assets. Either of these conditions would preclude the employer from recognizing a settlement gain or loss.

Question 4: If an employer withdraws excess plan assets (cash) from a pension plan but is not required to settle a pension benefit obligation as part of the asset reversion transaction, should any of the previously unrecognized net gain or loss be immediately recognized?

Answer: No. The above facts are not consistent with a pension plan settlement. Therefore, any previously unrecognized net gain or loss should not be recognized.

Question 5: What is the accounting for the transaction described in Question 4?

Answer: The employer's withdrawal of cash is considered a negative plan contribution. The employer should debit cash and should credit accrued (prepaid) pension cost.

Question 6: If individual nonparticipating annuity contracts are to be used to settle a pension benefit obligation, may a settlement gain or loss be recognized if the individual annuity contracts have not been issued?

Answer: It depends. The issuance of individual annuity contracts is not the critical event in determining whether a settlement gain or loss can be recognized. However, the failure to issue individual contracts, along with other evidence, may indicate that the pension benefit obligation has not been effectively settled. In order for a settlement gain or loss to be recognized, an irrevocable transaction that relieves the employer (or the pension plan) from primary responsibility for the pension benefit obligation and that eliminates significant risks associated with the pension obligation and pension

23.06 *Pension Plans—Settlements and Curtailments*

assets must have occurred. A commitment to purchase annuity contracts is not sufficient for a settlement gain or loss to be recognized.

Question 7: If individual nonparticipating annuity contracts are to be used to settle a pension benefit obligation, may a settlement gain or loss be recognized if the premium for the purchase of the individual annuity contracts has not been paid?

Answer: It depends. As discussed previously, for a settlement gain or loss to be recognized, an irrevocable transaction that relieves the employer (or the pension plan) of primary responsibility for the pension benefit obligation and that eliminates significant risks associated with the pension obligation and pension assets must have occurred. The failure to pay the insurance premium may indicate that the transaction is revocable. In addition, if pension plan assets have not been transferred to effect the settlement, they may still be at risk. In order for a settlement gain or loss to be recognized, the insurance company must have unconditionally assumed the legal obligation to provide the promised pension benefits.

Question 8: If a contract is entered into that requires an insurance company to pay only a portion of specific participants' pension benefits—for example, payments due retirees for the next five years—has a settlement occurred?

Answer: No. A contract to provide pension benefits for a specified period of time is a limited-term annuity. As such, it does not eliminate the risks associated with the pension benefit obligation. For example, the risk related to employee life expectancy (i.e., the duration of the pension benefits) remains. For an annuity contract with a life insurance company to qualify for settlement accounting, the contract needs to be a life annuity and not a limited-term annuity.

Question 9: Does the following constitute a settlement?

    a. An employer (or the pension plan) irrevocably purchases an insurance contract that guarantees payment of those pension benefits vested as of the date of the purchase.

    b. The purchase price of the insurance contract significantly exceeds the purchase price of a nonparticipating annuity contract covering the same pension benefits.

    c. As compensation for the risk of guaranteeing those pension benefits, the insurance company receives an annual fee based on a percentage of the actuarial present value of the covered pension benefits.

    d. If a specified ratio of assets to the covered pension benefit obligation is maintained, the employer (or the pension plan) continues to manage the assets used to effect the purchase; however, the insurance contract requires that a certain percentage of the assets be invested in high-quality bonds or a dedicated bond portfolio, depending on the ratio of assets to the covered pension benefit obligation.

e. Upon final satisfaction of all of the pension benefit obligation covered by the insurance contract and payment of all of the contract's administrative fees due to the insurance company, the insurance company will remit to the employer (or the pension plan) any amounts remaining in the insurance contract's account balance. The employer (or the pension plan) is also permitted to make interim withdrawals from the account with prior notification of the insurance company, unless a withdrawal causes the ratio of assets to the covered pension benefit obligation to drop below a specified percentage.

Answer: No. The employer has not effectively transferred the risks and rewards associated with the pension plan assets and obligations. The type of annuity contract described in this question is a participating annuity contract. Since the employer is still subject to the pension plan's risks and rewards, the FAS-88 criteria for settlement accounting have not been met.

Question 10: What is the rationale for requiring settlement accounting for only certain participating annuity contracts?

Answer: The FASB had two basic reasons for requiring settlement accounting for only certain participating annuity contracts. First, some contacts that are essentially nonparticipating annuity contracts could be structured as participating contracts by requiring the payment of a small additional premium for a *de minimis* participation feature. Employers might have attempted to structure the purchase of an annuity contract in this manner to avoid having to recognize a pension plan settlement. Therefore, settlement plan accounting is applied to a participating annuity contract if the contract is essentially equivalent to a nonparticipating contract. Second, in some cases it might make economic sense for the employer to purchase a participating contract. Assuming that the requisite risks and rewards are transferred under the terms of the participating contract, settlement accounting is required. However, if the employer's exposure to pension plan gains and losses is substantially the same both before and after the employer enters into the participating annuity contract, settlement accounting would not be permitted.

Question 11: Are there quantitative criteria that can be used to determine whether the purchase of a participating annuity contract qualifies for settlement accounting?

Answer: No. Whether the purchase of a participating annuity contract qualifies for settlement accounting depends on the facts and circumstances of the particular case.

23.08 Pension Plans—Settlements and Curtailments

Question 12: If a parent company's wholly owned subsidiaries, Subsidiaries A and B, have separate pension plans, and Subsidiary B purchases nonparticipating annuity contracts from Subsidiary A (which is an insurance company) to provide the vested benefits under Subsidiary B's pension plan, does that purchase constitute a settlement in the parent company's consolidated financial statements? Does the transaction constitute a settlement in the separately issued financial statements of Subsidiary B?

Answer: The above transaction does not constitute a settlement in the parent company's consolidated financial statements. FAS-88 specifically precludes settlement accounting if an annuity contract is purchased from an insurance company controlled by the employer. In this case, the parent company is still subject to the risks associated with the pension benefit obligation and plan assets (all that has happened is that they have been transferred within the consolidated group, from Subsidiary B to Subsidiary A). The settlement would be recognized in Subsidiary B's separate financial statements, assuming the other criteria for settlement accounting have been met. The related-party nature of the pension settlement must be disclosed in the notes to the financial statements.

Question 13: Is the relative cost of the participation right (10%) used in Illustration 2, Example 2C, of FAS-88 (pp. 29–31) intended to be an indication of a criterion that could be used to determine whether the purchase of a participating annuity contract qualifies for settlement accounting?

Answer: No. The facts assumed in that example were chosen solely to illustrate the application of paragraphs 9 and 10 of FAS-88.

Question 14: If an employer terminates its pension plan, settles a pension benefit obligation, withdraws excess plan assets, and establishes a successor pension plan that has the same pension benefit formula, have both a settlement and a curtailment occurred?

Answer: No. A settlement has occurred but not a curtailment. Although employees will no longer earn benefits for future service under the old plan, they will earn credit under the new plan. For accounting purposes, the old and new pension plans are viewed as essentially one plan. The settlement of the pension benefit obligation and the withdrawal of excess plan assets are recognized (i.e., the settlement). If the new pension plan provides increased (reduced) pension benefits for future service, a pension plan amendment (negative amendment) has occurred.

Question 15: If as part of the sale of a segment or a portion of a line of business (refer to Question 37) there is a transfer of a pension benefit obligation to the purchaser (i.e., the purchaser assumes the pension benefit obligation for specific employees), have both a settlement and a curtailment occurred?

Answer: It depends. A settlement has occurred if the criteria in paragraph 3 of FAS-88 are met. However, if there is a reasonable chance that the purchaser may not provide the promised pension benefits and if the employer remains contingently liable for such benefits, a settlement has not occurred. A curtailment has occurred if the sale significantly reduces the expected future years of employee service of present employees covered by the employer's pension plan.

Question 16: Are *annuity contracts* defined differently in FAS-87 and FAS-88? If so, how are the definitions different, and why?

Answer: Yes. Per FAS-88, annuity contracts purchased from an entity that is controlled by the employer are not eligible for settlement accounting. The FASB's rationale for this requirement is that pension plan risks are merely being shifted from one part of the entity to another part of the same entity. Per FAS-87, pension benefits covered by annuity contracts are excluded from the measurement of the projected benefit obligation and from plan assets. However, if the annuity contract is purchased from a captive insurer (a more limited definition than an insurer controlled by the employer), the projected benefit obligation is not reduced and the annuity contract purchased from the captive insurer is included among plan assets. This treatment is largely justified on the basis of practical expediency.

Question 17: If nonparticipating annuity contracts are purchased from a less-than-majority-owned investee that is not controlled by the employer and the criteria for a settlement are satisfied, is the resulting settlement gain or loss subject to partial recognition (i.e., should it be reduced to reflect the employer's ownership)?

Answer: No. The entire settlement gain or loss should be recognized. This treatment represents a departure from the normal practice of eliminating the applicable portion (based on ownership) of gains or losses from intercompany transactions. However, this treatment does not establish a new precedent for the treatment of nonpension intercompany transactions.

Question 18: Is there a specific threshold for determining if an event results in (*a*) a *significant* reduction of expected years of future service of present employees covered by a pension plan or (*b*) an elimination of the accrual of pension benefits for some or all of the future services of a *significant* number of employees covered by a pension plan?

Answer: No. Judgment should be exercised based on the facts and circumstances that are unique to each case.

Question 19: If an employer has a pension plan covering employees in several divisions and the employer terminates employees in one of those divisions, does a curtailment occur if the expected years of future service of present employees in that division are reduced significantly but the reduction is not significant in relation to the expected years of future service of all employees covered by the pension plan?

Answer: No. FAS-88 is to be applied on an overall basis for each individual pension plan. In the above example, the reduction in the expected years of future service is not significant for the pension plan as a whole. The above example would give rise to a pension plan gain or loss (see FAS-87, pars. 29, 32, and 33, for additional details).

Question 20: Can a curtailment occur if an employer either (*a*) temporarily lays off a significant number of present employees covered by a pension plan or (*b*) temporarily suspends a pension plan so that employees covered by the pension plan do not earn additional pension benefits for some or all of their future services?

Answer: Yes. A curtailment occurs if there is a significant reduction in pension benefits for some or all of the future services of employees covered by the pension plan. This result holds regardless of whether the cause is a temporary employee layoff or a temporary suspension of the pension plan.

Question 21: If unrelated, individually insignificant reductions of expected years of future service of employees covered by a pension plan accumulate to a significant reduction over a single year or more than one year, does that constitute a curtailment?

Answer: No. Each of these reductions leads to a pension plan gain or loss (see FAS-87, pars. 29, 32, and 33, for additional details).

Question 22: If individually insignificant reductions of expected years of future service of employees covered by a pension plan are (*a*) caused by one event, such as a strike, or (*b*) related to a single plan of reorganization and those reductions accumulate to a significant reduction during more than one fiscal year, does a curtailment occur?

Answer: Yes. The fact that the significant reduction occurs over a period of time does not change the fact that an event giving rise to curtailment accounting has occurred.

Question 23: Does a curtailment occur if an employer terminates a pension plan and establishes a successor pension plan that provides additional but reduced pension benefits for all years of employees' future service?

Answer: No. In this case the pension plan continues to provide benefits for future employee service, albeit at a reduced level. Per FAS-88, a curtailment involves the elimination, for a significant number of employees, of pension credit for some or all of their expected future service. This example represents a reduction of future benefits, not an elimination of such benefits. FAS-87 requires that a reduction in future pension benefits be treated as a negative plan amendment.

Question 24: Can a curtailment occur if a pension plan is terminated and replaced by a successor pension plan?

Answer: Yes. A curtailment involves the elimination, for a significant number of employees, of the accrual of defined pension benefits for some or all of their expected future service. The substitution of a new pension plan for an existing pension plan would represent a curtailment if (*a*) a significant number of employees covered under the old pension plan are not covered under the new pension plan or (*b*) a significant number of years of future employee service do not result in the accrual of defined pension benefits.

Illustration of Substituting New Plan for Existing Plan

Rorer Industries offers a pension plan that provides employees a flat pension benefit of $1,000 for each year of service. At December 31, 1998, Rorer terminates this plan and replaces it with a new pension plan. Under the new plan, employees will be provided with a pension benefit of $500 for each year of service. At December 31, 1998, Employee A had worked for Rorer for five years. The typical Rorer employee has five years of service.

Given the above facts, Rorer needs to account for the substitution of a new pension plan for its existing plan as a curtailment. At December 31, 1998, the accumulated pension benefit obligation for Employee A was $5,000. Given the terms of the new pension plan, Employee A will not earn additional defined pension benefits under the new plan until the year 2004 (the accumulated pension benefit obligation for Employee A under the new plan will not reach $5,000 until December 31, 2003). Therefore, Employee A will provide five years of future service without accruing any additional defined pension benefits. Since Employee A is a typical Rorer employee, these facts are consistent with a significant reduction in the accrual of additional pension benefits for future years of employee service.

Question 25: If an employer disposes of a segment or a portion of a line of business (refer to Question 37) that results in a termination of some employees' services earlier than expected but does not significantly reduce the expected years of future service of present employees covered by the pension plan, should the effects that reducing the pension plan has on the workforce be measured in the same manner

23.12 *Pension Plans—Settlements and Curtailments*

as a curtailment (FAS-88, pars. 12 and 13) to determine the gain or loss on the disposal pursuant to paragraphs 15–17 of APB-30 (Reporting the Results of Operations—Reporting the Effects of Disposal of a Segment of a Business, and Extraordinary, Unusual, and Infrequently Occurring Events and Transactions)?

Answer: Yes. The above facts do not represent a curtailment, since the expected years of future service of present employees covered by the pension plan have not been significantly reduced. However, the effects of the reduction in the workforce should be treated in the same manner as a curtailment for the purpose of calculating the gain or loss on disposal.

Question 26: What is considered a successor pension plan for purposes of applying FAS-88?

Answer: This question is relevant because if a pension obligation is settled and the pension plan is terminated without being replaced by a successor plan, a pension plan termination and curtailment have both occurred.

An employer that terminates a pension plan may establish a new plan, or it may amend one or more existing pension plans. The new plan or the amended plan may provide for the accrual of defined pension benefits for the future services of present employees who were covered by the previous (terminated) pension plan. In these cases, a successor plan would exist unless (*a*) the defined pension benefits provided by the new plan are significantly fewer than the pension benefits provided by the old plan or (*b*) the present employees covered by the new plan are significantly fewer than the employees covered by the old plan.

FAS-88 does not apply to an employer's withdrawal from a multiemployer pension plan. If an employer withdraws from a multiemployer plan and establishes a new pension plan for its employees, the new plan is not considered a successor plan. In some cases the employer may be responsible for a portion of the plan's unfunded pension obligation. If the requirements of FAS-5 (Accounting for Contingencies) are met, the employer should accrue a liability for its share of the unfunded obligation.

Question 27: If settlement of the pension benefit obligation as part of a pension plan termination occurs (and there is no successor pension plan) in a financial reporting period that differs from the period in which the effects of the curtailment resulting from the pension plan termination ordinarily would be recognized, should the effects of both the settlement and the curtailment be recognized in the same financial reporting period?

Answer: Generally not. The effects of a settlement should be recognized in accordance with paragraph 9 of FAS-88; the effects of a curtailment should be recognized in accordance with paragraph 14 of FAS-88. This may result in the effects of the settlement and the curtailment being recognized in different financial reporting periods. However, there are a few exceptions to this general requirement:

a. The pension plan termination results from the disposal of a segment of the business (refer to APB-30).

b. The pension plan termination results from other events qualifying for special recognition (see APB-30, pars. 13–17).

c. If the gain or loss from the pension plan's termination occurs after the measurement date but before the employer's fiscal year-end, the effects of both the settlement and the curtailment should be recognized in the current year.

FIG-FAS 88 presents an example of where the effects of a pension plan settlement and curtailment are recognized in different reporting periods. The effects of the pension plan curtailment are recognized on the date of the pension plan amendment. The effects of the settlement are recognized when the employer is relieved of its obligation for providing the pension plan benefits (in the example presented, this was the date that nonparticipating annuity contracts were purchased).

Question 28: If a gain or loss from a settlement occurs after the pension plan's measurement date but before the employer's fiscal year-end, should the employer include that gain or loss in determining that fiscal year's results of operations?

Answer: Generally, no. The gain or loss from the settlement generally would be recognized during the ensuing fiscal year. However, there are two exceptions to this general rule:

1. If the gain or loss results from a pension plan termination and the employer does not begin a successor plan, the effects of the pension plan curtailment and settlement should both be recognized during the current fiscal year.

2. If the gain or loss is directly related to an event occurring in the current fiscal year that is within the scope of paragraph 16 of FAS-88 (primarily a gain or loss on a curtailment or settlement that is directly related to a disposal of a business segment), the gain or loss should be recognized in the current year.

If the gain or loss is not recognized currently, and if recognizing the gain or loss currently would have been material to either the results of operations or the financial position, the following items should be disclosed: (*a*) the nature of the event giving rise to the pension plan gain or loss, (*b*) the consequences of the event, and (*c*) when the gain or loss will be recognized in the financial statements.

23.14 *Pension Plans—Settlements and Curtailments*

Question 29: If in terminating its pension plan (old assets) an employer settles the pension benefit obligation and withdraws excess plan assets and then contributes and allocates those assets to participants' accounts in a new defined contribution pension plan, may the employer combine any net gain or loss from the settlement and curtailment of the old plan with the net periodic pension cost from the contribution to the defined contribution pension plan and thereby report both on a net basis for purposes of classification in the income statement or disclosure in accompanying footnotes?

Answer: No. In the facts at hand, both a pension plan termination and a contribution to a defined contribution plan have taken place. These are two separate events and they need to be recognized as such. As a result of the pension plan termination, all previously unrecognized pension plan amounts are now recognized. Net periodic pension cost is recognized for the amount contributed to the defined contribution pension plan.

Question 30: If a market-related value of plan assets other than fair value is used for purposes of determining the expected return on plan assets, is that basis also to be used in determining the maximum gain or loss subject to pro rata recognition in earnings when a pension benefit obligation is settled?

Answer: No. The fair value of the plan assets on the date of settlement is to be used.

Question 31: As of what date should plan assets and the projected benefit obligation be measured in determining the accounting for a settlement?

Answer: Plan assets and the projected benefit obligation should be measured as of the date of the settlement, which is the date on which the FAS-88 criteria for settlement accounting have been met. The appropriate date for measuring plan assets and the projected benefit obligation is important because these amounts determine (*a*) the maximum gain or loss subject to pro rata recognition in earnings (e.g., if 100% of the projected benefit obligation is settled, then 100% of the maximum gain or loss is recognized in earnings) and (*b*) the percentage reduction in the projected benefit obligation.

Question 32: If the interest rates implicit in the purchase price of nonparticipating annuity contracts used to effect a settlement are different from the assumed discount rates used to determine net periodic pension cost, should the employer measure the portion of the projected benefit obligation being settled (and the remaining portion, if appropriate) using the implicit annuity interest rates and include any resulting gain or loss in the maximum gain or loss subject to pro rata recognition in earnings?

Answer: Yes. As discussed in the answer to Question 31, plan assets and the projected benefit obligation are measured as of the settlement date. In measuring the portion of the projected benefit obligation being settled, the employer should use the purchase price of the nonparticipating annuity contracts. Any gain or loss resulting from remeasuring the plan assets and the projected benefit obligation as of the settlement date are included in computing the maximum gain or loss subject to pro rata recognition in earnings.

Question 33: If a settlement occurs in the circumstances described in Question 32 and the interest rates implicit in the purchase price of nonparticipating annuity contracts used to effect the settlement are different from the assumed discount rates used to determine net periodic pension cost, is it appropriate to measure the unsettled portion of the projected benefit obligation using the implicit annuity interest rates?

Answer: Maybe. The employer should consider measuring the projected benefit obligation for the unsettled portion of the pension obligation using the interest rate implicit in the annuity contract under the following circumstances:

1. If the demographics of the participants for whom the PBO was settled are similar to the demographics of participants for whom the PBO was *not* settled (in particular, the length of time until pension payments will be made should be similar for each group)
2. If the interest rates implicit in the annuity contracts represent the best estimate of the interest rates at which the unsettled portion of the PBO could be effectively settled

Question 34: If an employer settles a pension benefit obligation and withdraws excess plan assets as part of terminating its pension plan, should the settlement gain or loss determined pursuant to paragraph 9 of FAS-88 be adjusted to eliminate any unrealized gains or losses relating to securities issued by the employer if those securities are included in the plan assets withdrawn?

Answer: No. It is the settlement of the pension plan, not the withdrawal of plan assets, that precipitates the recognition of any previously unrecognized net gain or loss. The withdrawal of plan assets does not affect the recognition of the settlement gain or loss. In addition, the nature of the plan assets that are withdrawn does not affect the recognition of the settlement gain or loss.

Question 35: If the remaining unrecognized net asset at transition is reduced when a settlement gain is recognized, how is any remaining balance of the unrecognized net asset at transition amortized in future periods?

23.16 Pension Plans—Settlements and Curtailments

Answer: Any remaining balance of the unrecognized net transition asset is amortized on a straight-line basis over the remainder of the amortization period established at transition.

Illustration of Accounting for Net Assets at Transition When a Settlement Gain Is Recognized

Before a pension plan settlement (December 31, 1988), Ranalli's Lawn America, Inc., had a projected benefit obligation of $4,000,000 and plan assets of $4,200,000. Ranalli's had an unrecognized transition net asset of $400,000 and an unrecognized net gain of $600,000. Ranalli's unrecognized net asset at transition (January 1, 1985) was $667,000. The amortization period was initially established at ten years. As a result of the settlement, Ranalli's PBO was reduced by $2,600,000. The settlement was effected through the purchase of nonparticipating annuity contracts. The purchase price was $1,600,000. The company wants to determine the effects of this pension plan settlement.

The maximum gain that could be recognized as a result of this settlement is $1,000,000 (the difference between the reduction in the PBO, $2,600,000, and the cost of purchasing the annuity contracts, $1,600,000). However, only 65% of this maximum gain can be recognized (65% equals the percentage reduction in the PBO, $2,600,000/$4,000,000). The $650,000 gain is recognized by reducing the unrecognized transition net asset and the unrecognized net gain on a proportional basis. Therefore, the unrecognized transition net asset is reduced by $260,000 [($400,000/$1,000,000) x $650,000] and the unrecognized net gain is reduced by $390,000 [($600,000/$1,000,000) x $650,000]. The remaining unrecognized transition net asset is $140,000 ($400,000 − $260,000). This remaining amount is amortized over six years (the original amortization period of ten years less the four years that have already lapsed). The yearly amortization of the transition asset for the next six years is $23,300 per year.

Question 36: If a negative pension plan amendment adopted shortly before the date of initial application of FAS-87 is the reason an unrecognized net asset exists at transition, should any portion of the unrecognized net asset at transition that remains as of the date of a settlement be included in the maximum gain or loss subject to pro rata recognition in earnings?

Answer: Yes. Any unrecognized net asset at transition that remains at the time of a settlement is included in determining the maximum gain or loss subject to pro rata recognition in earnings. The source of the unrecognized net asset at transition is irrelevant for this purpose.

Question 37: If an employer sells a portion of a line of business that is not a segment of a business as defined in paragraph 13 of APB-30 and the employer settles a pension benefit obligation related to the employees affected by the sale, should the settlement gain or loss be recognized pursuant to (*a*) paragraphs 9–11 of FAS-88 or (*b*) paragraphs 15–17 of APB-30 as required by Interpretation 1 of APB-30?

Answer: It depends. If the settlement is directly caused (e.g., it may be necessary to effect the sale) by the sale of some portion of a line of business, the settlement gain or loss should be recognized in accordance with paragraphs 15–17 of APB-30. If the pension plan settlement is not directly caused by the sale of a portion of a line of business, the settlement gain or loss is recognized pursuant to paragraphs 9–11 of FAS-88.

Question 38: If in the last interim period of its fiscal year an employer decides to apply FAS-87 early, does paragraph 20 of FAS-88 apply to an asset reversion transaction that included settlement of a significant portion of the projected benefit obligation if that transaction occurred in a previous interim period of that fiscal year?

Answer: No. Paragraph 20 of FAS-88 applies only to asset reversion transactions that occur in fiscal years after the first fiscal year in which FAS-87 is applied. If an employer initially adopts FAS-87 in a quarter other than its first, it is required to restate its previously issued quarterly statements to conform with FAS-87. In restating these previously issued quarterly statements, the employer would account for the pension plan settlement in accordance with the provisions of paragraphs 9–11 of FAS-88.

Question 39: How should an employer determine and report a gain or loss from a settlement or curtailment that occurs as a direct result of a disposal of a segment or a portion of a line of business?

Answer: A gain or loss from a settlement or curtailment that occurs as a direct result of a disposal of a segment or a portion of a line of business should be included as part of the gain or loss on the disposal. The settlement should be accounted for in conformity with paragraphs 9 and 10 of FAS-88, and the accounting for the curtailment should follow the guidance in paragraphs 12 and 13 of FAS-88. FIG-FAS 88 contains a detailed numerical example of the required accounting treatment.

Question 40: If an employer incorporates a division of its operations and subsequently spins it off to owners of the enterprise and also transfers to the new entity's pension plan either (*a*) a pension benefit obligation related to the employees transferred as part of the spinoff or (*b*) plan assets, how should the employer and the new entity account for the transaction?

Answer: APB-29 (Accounting for Nonmonetary Transactions) precludes the recognition of a gain or loss on the distribution of nonmonetary assets to owners of the enterprise. In a similar fashion, the recognition of a gain or loss resulting from the transfer of pension assets or of the pension plan obligation in a spinoff is prohibited. The allocation between the existing employer and the spinoff entity of any (*a*) unrecognized (transition) net asset or obligation, (*b*) unrecognized net gain or loss subsequent to transition, and (*c*) unrecognized prior service cost is handled in one of two ways. Any unrecognized (transition) net asset or obligation or unrecognized net gain or loss is allocated between the employer's existing pension plan and the pension plan of the new (spinoff) entity in proportion to the projected benefit obligation of each plan. Any unrecognized prior service cost is allocated between the two pension plans based on an analysis of the individual employees covered by each pension plan. The following example illustrates the accounting when both plan assets and a pension benefit obligation are transferred to the pension plan of a new (spinoff) entity.

Illustration of Incorporation and Subsequent Spin-Off of a Pension Plan

XYZ, Inc., incorporated one of its divisions, ABC, Inc. ABC is later spun off to XYZ's shareholders. ABC assumes XYZ's pension obligation that relates to ABC's employees. The accumulated benefit obligation assumed by ABC (all of which is vested) is $60,000. ABC's projected benefit obligation is $12,000 higher than this amount based on the expected future salary levels of these employees. In addition, XYZ transfers to ABC $56,000 in plan assets. The appropriate accounting treatment for XYZ, Inc., and ABC, Inc., is illustrated below.

	Old Plan Before Spinoff	Old Plan After Spinoff
Assets and obligations:		
Accumulated benefit obligation	$(144,000)	$(84,000)
Effects of future compensation levels	(36,000)	(24,000)
Projected benefit obligation	(180,000)	(108,000)
Plan assets at fair value	320,000	264,000
Items not yet recognized in earnings:		
Remaining unrecognized net asset at transition	(80,000)	(48,000)
Unrecognized prior service cost	50,000	35,000
Unrecognized net gain subsequent to transition	(110,000)	(66,000)
(Accrued) prepaid pension cost	$ —	$ 77,000

Spreadsheet Notes

1. The allocation of the $180,000 projected benefit obligation between the two plans was based on an analysis of the individual employees covered by each plan.

2. The allocation of the $320,000 of plan assets between the two plans was chosen by XYZ's management (we assume that no regulatory requirements apply).

3. The allocation of the unrecognized transition asset and the unrecognized net gain between the two plans was based on the percentage of the total projected benefit obligation assumed by each plan (60% for the old plan, 40% for the new plan).

4. The allocation of unrecognized prior service cost between the two plans was based on an analysis of the individual employees covered by each plan (for illustrative purposes we have assumed that this allocation differs from the PBO assumed by each plan).

Journal Entries

XYZ, Inc.

Prepaid Pension Cost	$77,000	
Stockholders' Equity		$77,000

[To record the transfer of plan assets, a pension benefit obligation, and net deferred amounts from XYZ, Inc., to ABC, Inc. Note that the credit to stockholders' equity represents the net of all assets and liabilities transferred from XYZ to ABC.]

ABC, Inc.

Stockholders' Equity	$77,000	
Accrued Pension Cost		$77,000

[To record the receipt of plan assets, a pension benefit obligation, and net deferred amounts from XYZ, Inc., to ABC, Inc. Note that the debit to stockholders' equity represents the net of all assets and liabilities received from XYZ.]

Question 41: What is the proper sequence of events to follow in measuring the effects of a settlement and a curtailment that are to be recognized at the same time?

Answer: Although the method selected may affect the determination of the aggregate gain or loss recognized, management decides whether the effects of the settlement are recognized first or the effects of the curtailment. Once management has selected a method, however, that method must be followed in future years when a settlement and a curtailment occur simultaneously.

Question 42: Because the amount of the vested benefit obligation settled and the amount of plan assets used to purchase nonparticipating annuity contracts are equal in Illustrations 1 and 2 of FAS-88, is it appropriate to conclude that no gains and losses occurred when the projected benefit obligation and the plan assets were measured as of the date of the settlement?

Answer: No. The "Before" columns in these illustrations reflect the measurement of the plan assets and the projected benefit obligation as of the settlement date. Any gains and losses arising from measuring these two accounts at the settlement date have already been recognized. See Question 31 for additional discussion.

Question 43: Is the method in Illustration 2, Examples 2B and 2C, of FAS-88 that allocates an amount equal to the settlement gain on a pro rata basis to the remaining unrecognized net asset at transition and the unrecognized net gain subsequent to transition the only method of allocation permitted under those circumstances by FAS-88?

Answer: No. An amount equal to the settlement gain could first be applied against any remaining unrecognized transition net asset. If any settlement gain remained, it would be applied against the unrecognized net gain arising after transition. If this method is selected, it must be applied consistently across years. Although this alternative method is acceptable, allocating the settlement gain based on the projected benefit obligation is preferable because it is a more unbiased method.

Question 44: Is the method in Illustration 2, Example 2C, of FAS-88 that determines the maximum gain subject to pro rata recognition in earnings by first reducing the unrecognized net gain subsequent to transition by the cost of the participation right the only method of allocation permitted under those circumstances by FAS-88?

Answer: No. In the determination of the maximum gain subject to pro rata recognition in earnings, the cost of the participation right could be allocated as follows:

1. To the remaining unrecognized net asset at transition
2. To the unrecognized net gain subsequent to transition
3. On a pro rata basis between these two amounts based on their relative amounts

Any one of these three methods is acceptable, and the method illustrated in Example 2C of Illustration 2 allocates the cost of the participation right to the unrecognized net gain subsequent to transition. However, the preferred method is to allocate the cost of the participation right on a pro rata basis between the remaining unrecognized net asset at transition and the unrecognized net gain. Whichever method is selected must be applied on a consistent basis.

Question 45: May an employer adopt an accounting policy that requires recognition of gains and losses from all settlements during the year for a pension plan if the cost of those settlements exceeds the service cost component of net periodic pension cost for that pension plan for the year?

Answer: Yes. Recognition of gains and losses from pension plan settlements is required if the cost of those settlements exceeds the sum of the service cost and interest cost components for the year in question. However, recognition of settlement gains and losses is permitted, but not required, if the aggregate settlement cost is below the sum of service cost and interest cost. The policy adopted must be applied on a consistent basis across years.

Question 46: If an employer's accounting policy is not to recognize a gain or loss from a settlement if the cost of all settlements during the year does not exceed the sum of the service cost and interest cost components of net periodic pension cost for the pension plan for the year, how should the employer account for the following situation: (*a*) It is estimated at the beginning of the year that the cost of all settlements during the year will not exceed the threshold amount described above; (*b*) a pension benefit obligation is settled during the first quarter and a settlement gain or loss is not recognized; and (*c*) in the second quarter and subsequent to the issuance of the first quarter's interim report, it is determined that the cost of all settlements during the year will exceed the threshold amount?

Answer: In this case, the change in handling settlement gains and losses should be treated as a change in accounting estimate. The settlement gain or loss would be recognized in the second quarter.

Question 47: How should an employer determine the amount of unrecognized prior service cost that should be recognized in the event of a curtailment if the employer amortizes unrecognized prior service cost on a straight-line basis over the average remaining service period of employees expected to receive the related pension benefits?

Answer: FAS-88 requires that the unrecognized prior service cost associated with future years of employee service that is no longer expected to be rendered should be recognized as part of a curtailment. This basic approach applies even if the employer amortizes unrecognized prior service cost on a straight-line basis over employees' average remaining service period. However, if the employer amortizes unrecognized prior service cost using this alternate approach, the determination of the unrecognized prior service cost associated with the curtailment may be less precise. As a practical matter, the unrecognized prior service cost associated with the curtailment may have to be determined by referring to the reduction in the (remaining) expected future years of service. For example, as of January 1, 1999, the remaining expected future years of service that pertain to unrecognized prior service costs is ten years. As the result of a curtailment during 1999, the remaining expected years of future service is five years. In this case, 50% of the unrecognized prior service cost is associated with the curtailment.

Question 48: If a curtailment occurs because an employer terminates or suspends a pension plan (so that employees do not earn additional pension benefits for future service) but the employees continue to work for the employer, should any unrecognized prior service cost that is associated with the employees who are affected by the pension plan termination or suspension be included in determining the net gain or loss that is to be recognized for the curtailment?

Answer: Yes. One reason why the cost of a retroactive pension plan amendment is deferred is the likelihood that the employer will receive future benefits as a result of the plan amendment. These future benefits are associated with future employee service for those employees active at the date of the plan amendment who are expected to receive benefits under the plan. Any future economic benefits the employer was expecting to receive as a result of the retroactive plan amendment are in all likelihood dissipated by the suspension or termination of the pension plan. As such, some, or all, of the unrecognized prior service cost should no longer be deferred. Further, if the pension plan is terminated, all unrecognized prior service cost must be recognized.

Question 49: If a curtailment results from a pension plan suspension that may be only temporary (e.g., the pension plan suspension will end as soon as the employer's financial condition sufficiently improves), how is the net gain or loss from the curtailment determined?

Answer: The curtailment gain or loss should be determined based on the probable duration of the pension plan suspension. [The term *probable* is defined in accordance with FAS-5 (Accounting for Contingencies).] In some cases, it may be possible to determine only a range for the likely duration of the pension plan suspension. If no length of time estimated within that range is more likely than any other length of time, the expected duration of the pension plan suspension is to be calculated to produce minimum curtailment gain or loss.

Question 50: If the remaining unrecognized net asset or net obligation at transition is reduced as part of the accounting for a curtailment, how is any remaining balance of the unrecognized net asset or net obligation at transition amortized in future periods?

Answer: Any remaining unrecognized transition net asset or net obligation is to be amortized on a straight-line basis over what remains of the amortization period determined at the time FAS-87 was adopted. See Question 35 for additional discussion.

Question 51: If a curtailment occurs that causes almost all of the pension plan's participants to become permanently inactive, should the employer continue to amortize any remaining balance of the unrecognized net asset or net obligation at transition using the amortization period determined at transition?

Answer: Yes. Given the type of curtailment described, it is reasonable to expect that some portion of the unrecognized transition net asset or net obligation would be recognized. However, a portion of the transition net asset or net obligation may remain. Any remaining transition net asset or net obligation should continue to be amortized over what remains of the amortization period determined at transition. See Question 35 for additional discussion.

Question 52: If both a remaining unrecognized net asset at transition and a larger (smaller) unrecognized net loss subsequent to transition exist at the date of a curtailment that decreases (increases) the projected benefit obligation, how should the effects of the curtailment be applied to those previously unrecognized pension amounts?

Answer: The appropriate accounting treatment is as follows:

1. Any reduction in the projected benefit obligation that is not recognized as a curtailment gain should be offset against the unrecognized net loss subsequent to transition.

2. Any increase in the projected benefit obligation that is not recognized as a curtailment loss should be offset against the remaining unrecognized net asset at transition.

No further offsetting of amounts is permitted. More specifically, the following accounting treatments are specifically proscribed:

1. Offsetting an unrecognized net loss subsequent to transition against any remaining unrecognized net asset at transition

2. Increasing an unrecognized net loss subsequent to transition

The first illustration below presents the appropriate accounting treatment when the remaining unrecognized net asset at transition is less than the unrecognized net loss subsequent to transition. The second illustration presents the appropriate accounting treatment when the remaining unrecognized net asset at transition exceeds the unrecognized net loss subsequent to transition.

Illustration of Pension Plan Curtailment: Remaining Unrecognized Net Asset at Transition Is Less Than Unrecognized Net Loss Subsequent to Transition

Herring's Haberdashery sponsors a defined benefit pension plan. Herring's terminates a significant number of employees in an attempt to lower manufacturing costs. Herring's management makes the termination decision on September 30, 1997, and the effects of the terminations are reasonably estimable at that time. The termination date is November 30, 1997. Herring's had an unrecognized net asset at the time it adopted FAS-87. As a result of the plan curtailment, Herring's escapes a pension liability for those employees whose benefits are not yet vested, and its pension obligation is reduced to the extent that future compensation levels are no longer relevant for the terminated employees. Herring's projected benefit obligation is reduced by $220,000 ($180,000 from the elimination of future compensation levels on pension benefits to be received and $40,000 from the elimination of nonvested accumulated benefits). The appropriate accounting for this curtailment is as follows:

Since the projected benefit obligation is reduced, Herring's will recognize a net gain on the curtailment. Per FAS-88, when the effect of a curtailment is the recognition of a net gain, the gain is recorded on the date the employees terminate (November 30, 1997). In the following schedule, plan assets and the projected benefit obligation are also measured as of that date.

	11/30/97		
	Before Curtailment	Effects of Curtailment	After Curtailment
Assets and obligations:			
Vested benefit obligation	$(3,100,000)		$(3,100,000)
Nonvested benefits	(500,000)	$ 40,000	(460,000)
Accumulated benefit obligation	(3,600,000)	40,000	(3,560,000)
Effects of future compensation levels	(800,000)	180,000	(620,000)
Projected benefit obligation	(4,400,000)	220,000	(4,180,000)
Plan assets at fair value	4,200,000		4,200,000
Items not yet recognized in earnings:			
Remaining unrecognized net asset at transition	(400,000)		(400,000)
Unrecognized net loss subsequent to transition	600,000	(200,000)	400,000
Prepaid pension cost	$ -0-	$ 20,000	$ 20,000

Spreadsheet Notes

1. FAS-88 requires that the potential curtailment gain—the $220,000 decrease in the projected benefit obligation—first be offset against any existing unrecognized net loss. In this case, there is an unrecognized net loss of $200,000 (a $600,000 unrecognized net loss subsequent to transition, net of the $400,000 remaining unrecognized net asset at transition). Therefore, the curtailment gain recorded by Herring's Haberdashery is $20,000.

Journal Entry

Prepaid Pension Cost	$20,000	
Gain from Curtailment		$20,000

Illustration of Pension Plan Curtailment: Remaining Unrecognized Net Asset at Transition Exceeds Unrecognized Net Loss Subsequent to Transition

The facts are the same as in the previous illustration except for the following:

1. Herring's supplements the retirement benefits of those employees who are terminated. This increases the projected benefit obligation by $440,000.
2. The unrecognized net loss subsequent to transition is $200,000.

Since the projected benefit obligation is increased, Herring's will recognize a net loss on the curtailment. Per FAS-88, when the effect of a curtailment is the recognition of a net loss, the loss is recorded when it is probable that the curtailment will occur and the effects are estimable (September 30, 1997). In the following schedule, plan assets and the projected benefit obligation are also measured as of that date.

	9/30/97 Before Curtailment	Effects of Curtailment	After Curtailment
Assets and obligations:			
Vested benefit obligation	$(3,100,000)	$(440,000)	$(3,540,000)
Nonvested benefits	(500,000)	40,000	(460,000)
Accumulated benefit obligation	(3,600,000)	(400,000)	(4,000,000)
Effects of future compensation levels	(800,000)	180,000	(620,000)
Projected benefit obligation	(4,400,000)	(220,000)	(4,620,000)
Plan assets at fair value	4,200,000		4,200,000

23.26 Pension Plans—Settlements and Curtailments

Items not yet recognized in earnings:
Remaining unrecognized net
   asset at transition (400,000) 200,000 (200,000)
Unrecognized net loss
   subsequent to transition 200,000 200,000

Prepaid pension cost $ (400,000) $ (20,000) $ (420,000)

Spreadsheet Notes

1. FAS-88 requires that the potential curtailment loss—the $220,000 increase in the projected benefit obligation—first be offset against any existing unrecognized net gain. In this case, there is an unrecognized net gain of $200,000 ($400,000 remaining unrecognized net asset at transition, net of the $200,000 of unrecognized net loss subsequent to transition). Therefore, the curtailment loss recorded by Herring's Haberdashery is $20,000.

Journal Entry

Loss from Curtailment $20,000
   Accrued Pension Cost $20,000

Question 53: If both a remaining unrecognized net asset at transition and an unrecognized net gain subsequent to transition exist at the date of a curtailment that increases the projected benefit obligation, should the effects of the curtailment be offset (a) initially against the remaining unrecognized net asset at transition, (b) initially against the unrecognized net gain subsequent to transition, or (c) against both on a pro rata basis?

Answer: Any one of these approaches is acceptable, as long as the approach selected is applied on a consistent basis. However, the preferable approach is to apply the curtailment loss against both the remaining unrecognized net asset at transition and the unrecognized net gain subsequent to transition on a pro rata basis. See Question 43 for additional discussion.

Question 54: How should (a) the liability and the loss from employees' acceptance of an offer of special termination benefits and (b) the change in the projected benefit obligation due to the related curtailment be determined?

Answer: The liability and the loss from employees' acceptance of an offer of special termination benefits are computed as the difference between:

1. The actuarial present value of the accumulated benefit obligation for those employees receiving special termination benefits

before consideration of the effects on the accumulated benefit obligation of those benefits *and*

2. The actuarial present value of the accumulated benefit obligation for those employees receiving special termination benefits after consideration of the effects on the accumulated benefit obligation of those benefits.

These amounts are determined as of the date the employees accept the offer of special termination benefits.

The change in the projected benefit obligation due to the related curtailment is determined as the difference between:

1. The projected benefit obligation for the affected employees before their acceptance of the special termination benefits *and*

2. The projected benefit obligation for the affected employees determined by applying the normal pension plan formula and assuming no future service due to the termination.

The following illustration presents the applicable accounting treatment for this circumstance.

Illustration of Curtailment: Termination Benefits Offered to Employees

On July 1, 1999, AHB, Inc., offers its employees special pension benefits in connection with their voluntary termination of employment. Employees who accept this offer will receive an additional ten years of credited service, and employees can retire at age 50 instead of at age 55. Employees must elect to receive these special benefits, in exchange for their voluntary termination of employment, by November 1, 1999.

On November 1, 1999, employees representing 20% of AHB's workforce accept the special termination benefits. The actuarial present value of the accumulated benefit obligation for these employees, before consideration of the special termination benefits, as of November 1, 1999, is $1,050,000. After consideration of the special termination benefits, the actuarial present value of the accumulated benefit obligation is $1,250,000.

Future compensation levels are no longer relevant for the 20% of AHB's workforce who accept the special termination benefits and who voluntarily leave AHB's employ. This has the effect of reducing AHB's projected benefit obligation by $160,000.

At the time the special termination benefits are accepted, the remaining unrecognized net obligation at transition was $1,600,000. Of this amount, $300,000 was assigned to the future years of service of the 20% of employees who accepted AHB's special termination offer. The appropriate accounting is as follows:

On November 1, 1999, AHB will recognize a loss of $340,000 (this includes the loss from issuing the special termination benefits and the loss on the curtailment). Note that the loss is recorded on November 1, 1999, because it is not until this date that the number of employees accepting the special termination benefits is known. The following schedule analyzes the effects of the special termination benefits on the applicable pension-related accounts.

	11/1/99		
	Before Employee Terminations	Effects of Terminations	After Employee Terminations
Assets and obligations:			
Vested benefit obligation			
Employees accepting offer	$(1,050,000)	$ (200,000)	$(1,250,000)
Other employees	(1,550,000)		(1,550,000)
Nonvested benefits	(400,000)		(400,000)
Accumulated benefit obligation	(3,000,000)	(200,000)	(3,200,000)
Effects of future compensation levels	(1,000,000)	160,000	(840,000)
Projected benefit obligation	(4,000,000)	(40,000)	(4,040,000)
Plan assets at fair value	2,800,000		2,800,000
Items not yet recognized in earnings:			
Remaining unrecognized net obligation at transition	1,600,000	(300,000)	1,300,000
Unrecognized net gain subsequent to transition	(600,000)		(600,000)
Accrued pension cost	$ (200,000)	$ (340,000)	$ (540,000)

Spreadsheet Notes

1. The loss from the issuance of the special termination benefits is $200,000 ($1,250,000 – $1,050,000).

2. The $160,000 decrease in the projected benefit obligation is a potential gain. FAS-88 requires that this amount first be offset against any remaining unrecognized net loss subsequent to transition. AHB does not have an unrecognized net loss subsequent to transition; it has an unrecognized net gain. Therefore, the entire potential gain of $160,000 is recognized (this amount represents a curtailment gain).

3. FAS-88 requires that the remaining unrecognized net obligation at transition is treated as unrecognized prior service cost. The reduction in unrecognized prior service cost associated with the years of future service the terminated employees are expected to work is $300,000. This amount represents a curtailment loss.

4. The total loss is $340,000 (the $200,000 loss from issuing the special termination benefits, the $160,000 gain from the reduction in the projected benefit obligation, and a $300,000 loss from the immediate recognition of a portion of the unrecognized net obligation at transition).

Journal Entry

Loss on Employee Terminations	$340,000	
Accrued Pension Cost		$340,000

Question 55: If (*a*) an employer adopts a plan to terminate employees that will significantly reduce the expected years of future service of present employees covered by a pension plan and (*b*) the sum of the effects of the resulting curtailment identified in paragraphs 12 and 13 of FAS-88 is expected to be a net gain, should that gain be recognized in earnings when the related employees terminate or when the plan is adopted?

Answer: The curtailment gain should be measured and recognized when the employees terminate.

Question 56: If (*a*) an employer amends its pension plan to provide for the plan's termination (or suspension) and thereby eliminates for a significant number of employees the accrual of all (or some) of the pension benefits for their future services after a subsequent date (i.e., the effective date of the pension plan termination or suspension is subsequent to the amendment date) and (*b*) the sum of the effects of the resulting curtailment identified in paragraphs 12 and 13 of FAS-88 is a net gain, should that gain be recognized in earnings when the employer amends its pension plan or when the pension plan termination (or suspension) is effective?

Answer: The curtailment gain should be measured and recognized when the pension plan is amended.

Question 57: If an employer's offer of special termination benefits results in a curtailment, is it possible that the offer of termination benefits could be recognized in a reporting period different from the period in which the curtailment is recognized?

Answer: Yes. These two events may be recorded in different reporting periods. A loss from a curtailment is recognized when the curtailment is probable and its effects are reasonably estimable. The costs of termination benefits are recorded when the employees elect to receive the special termination benefits and the cost of these benefits is reasonably estimable.

Question 58: When should the effects of an offer of special termination benefits and a related curtailment be recognized if (*a*) an employer offers special termination benefits before the year of initial application of FAS-87 and (b) employees accept the offer in the year FAS-87 is initially applied?

Answer: The liability and the loss for the special termination benefits should be recognized in the period in which employees accept the offer of special termination benefits and the amount can be reasonably estimated. The net pension obligation or asset at transition should be based on the employer's best estimate of the projected benefit obligation after consideration of the effect of the curtailment, but not the effect of the special termination benefits. See FIG-FAS 88 for an illustration of the appropriate accounting treatment.

Question 59: If an employer sponsors a pension plan that provides supplemental early retirement benefits, should those pension benefits be accounted for as contractual termination benefits?

Answer: No. The provision of supplemental early retirement benefits should be included in the computation of net periodic pension cost. Contractual termination benefits arise from the occurrence of a specific event that results in involuntary employee termination.

Question 60: Should termination indemnities that are associated with preretirement termination of employment be accounted for as contractual termination benefits?

Answer: *Termination indemnities,* which are more common outside the United States, are amounts payable to employees, often as a lump sum, upon termination of employment. The payment of termination indemnities should be accounted for as contractual termination benefits if they are paid only as the result of a specific event that results in involuntary termination. In these cases, a liability and a loss should be accrued when it is probable that employees will receive this benefit and the amount can be reasonably estimated. If virtually all employees who terminate their employment receive these benefits, the payments are in substance a pension plan and they should be accounted for under the provisions of FAS-87.

Question 61: If an employer offers for a short period of time special termination benefits to employees, may the employer recognize a loss at the date the offer is made based on the estimated acceptance rate?

Answer: No. Before the employer can recognize a liability and a loss, employees must accept the offer and the amount of the special termination benefits must be reasonably estimable. However, if the offer of special termination benefits is directly related to the disposal of a segment or a portion of a line of business, these benefits should be accounted for in accordance with APB-30 (including Interpretation 1 of APB-30).

Question 62: How should an employer account for an offer of special termination benefits if some employees accept the offer in the year before initial application of FAS-87 and other employees accept the offer in the year of initial application of FAS-87?

Answer: Any special termination benefits accepted in the year before initial application of FAS-87 should be accounted for in accordance with the provisions of FAS-74 (Accounting for Special Termination Benefits Paid to Employees). Special termination benefits accepted in the year of initial application of FAS-87 should be accounted for in accordance with the provisions of FAS-88. Any remaining liability determined under the provisions of FAS-74 is to be included in determining the net asset or obligation upon initial adoption of FAS-87.

Question 63: Would a gain or loss from a settlement or curtailment or the cost of termination benefits normally be classified as an extraordinary item?

Answer: Not unless the requirements of APB-30 for classification as an extraordinary item—i.e., unusual in nature and infrequent in occurrence—are met. In most cases, a pension plan settlement, curtailment, or offer of special termination benefits would not meet the requirements for classification as an extraordinary item.

Question 64: Do any of the following meet the "unusual nature and infrequency of occurrence criteria" of APB-30, thereby causing any resulting gain or loss to be classified as extraordinary?

a. An employer terminates its only pension plan and does not establish a successor pension plan.

b. An employer terminates its only pension plan, withdraws excess plan assets, and establishes a successor pension plan, but because of current regulatory guidelines is not permitted to effect the same series of transactions again for 15 years.

c. An employer terminates one of its foreign pension plans, withdraws excess plan assets, and establishes a successor pension plan. The employer has never effected this series of transactions in the past and has no intention of repeating these actions in the future.

d. An employer terminates its underfunded pension plan, and a regulatory agency takes over the pension plan and initiates a lien against 30% of the employer's net worth.

Answer: No. The basic problem with (a)–(d) above is that although they may be infrequent in occurrence, they are not unusual in nature. Terminating a pension plan is a normal occurrence in the current business environment.

Question 65: If, after the initial interim period of its fiscal year, an employer elects early application of FAS-87, should the first interim period of that fiscal year be restated to reflect any gain for an asset reversion transaction that occurred in a prior fiscal year that is to be recognized (as the cumulative effect of a change in accounting principle) pursuant to paragraph 20 of FAS-88?

Answer: Yes. FAS-88 applies as of the first interim period during the year in which FAS-87 is initially adopted.

Question 66: If an employer withdraws excess plan assets from its pension plan and is subject to an excise tax, is the excise tax an expense in the period of the withdrawal or should it be accounted for under FAS-109 as an income tax and deferred if related gains (such as a settlement gain) will be recognized for financial reporting purposes in subsequent periods?

Answer: An excise tax due to an employer's withdrawal of excess plan assets does not constitute an income tax. This excise tax follows a particular transaction, and the presence of taxable income is not a prerequisite for its imposition. Therefore, the excise tax should be recognized in the period the excess assets are withdrawn, and it should not be displayed as part of income tax expense on the income statement.

Question 67: Does paragraph 20 of FAS-88 apply to a prior asset reversion transaction that did not include a settlement of a pension benefit obligation?

Answer: An asset reversion transaction without a settlement could occur (*a*) if the employer's purchase of an insurance contract does not meet the criteria for a settlement or (*b*) if plan assets are removed from a non–U.S.-based plan without settlement of the obligation. In either case, paragraph 20 of FAS-88 does not apply, because the asset reversion transaction does not result in a settlement.

Question 68: Does the limitation imposed by the last sentence of paragraph 20 of FAS-88 apply if an unrecognized net obligation exists at transition?

Answer: Yes. No gain can be recognized when an unrecognized net obligation exists at transition.

Question 69: If the limitation imposed by the last sentence of paragraph 20 of FAS-88 applies, what is the accounting for any remaining unamortized amount related to a prior asset reversion transaction?

Answer: Any remaining unamortized amount related to a prior asset reversion transaction is to be included in determining the prepaid or accrued pension cost balance. Any resulting credit balance should not be amortized to income. Rather, the remaining credit balance will be eliminated in future years when net periodic pension cost is less than the employer's contribution to the pension plan. See FIG-FAS 88 for an illustration of this accounting treatment.

Question 70: An employer encounters the following situation: (a) Pursuant to paragraph 20 of FAS-88, the employer recognizes a gain as the cumulative effect of a change in accounting principle for a prior asset reversion transaction, and (b) at the date of initial application of FAS-87, the employer has a net operating loss carryforward both for tax purposes and for financial reporting. Under FAS-109, may the employer recognize a tax benefit for the current period's operating loss and offset tax expense attributable to the cumulative effect?

Answer: No. There is no tax benefit attributable to the current period's operating loss. Given the facts above, if the employer has a $200 operating loss and a $200 cumulative effect gain (paragraph 20), the employer's income statement would appear as follows:

Operating loss	$(200)
Cumulative effect	200
Net income	$ 0

CHAPTER 24
PERSONAL FINANCIAL STATEMENTS

CONTENTS

Overview	24.03
SOP 82-1: Accounting and Financial Reporting for Personal Financial Statements	24.03
Background	24.03
Standards	24.04
Form of the Statements	24.04
Methods of Presentation	24.04
Guidelines for Determining Current Values and Amounts	24.05
Receivables	24.05
Marketable Securities	24.05
Options	24.05
Investments in Life Insurance	24.05
Investments in Closely Held Businesses	24.06
Real Estate	24.06
Intangible Assets	24.06
Future Interests and Similar Assets	24.07
Payables and Other Liabilities	24.07
Noncancelable Commitments	24.07
Income Taxes Payable	24.07
Estimated Income Taxes on the Difference between the Estimated Current Values of Assets and the Current Amounts of Liabilities and Their Tax Bases	24.08
Financial Statement Disclosure	24.08

CHAPTER 24
PERSONAL FINANCIAL STATEMENTS

OVERVIEW

Standards for the preparation of financial statements that have been issued by the FASB and other standard-setting bodies are generally intended for business enterprises. As a general rule, these standards are not intended for use in preparing financial statements for individuals. No standards concerning the preparation of personal financial statements are included in Level A of the SAS-69 GAAP hierarchy.

The following pronouncement establishes standards for the preparation of personal financial statements:

SOP 82-1   Accounting and Financial Reporting for Personal Financial Statements (Level B)

This pronouncement includes requirements for the form and content of financial statements and related disclosures. A primary difference between these requirements and those for business enterprises is the use of fair value for all assets.

SOP 82-1: Accounting and Financial Reporting for Personal Financial Statements

BACKGROUND

SOP 82-1 deals with the preparation and presentation of personal financial statements for individuals or groups of related individuals (e.g., a husband and wife, a family).

The primary focus of personal financial statements is a person's assets and liabilities. The users of these statements normally consider estimated current value information to be more relevant to their decision-making than historical cost information. SOP 82-1 explains how the estimated current amounts of assets and liabilities should be determined and applied in the presentation of personal financial statements.

STANDARDS

Form of the Statements

Personal financial statements consist of the following:

Statement of financial condition—Presents the estimated current values of assets, estimated current amounts of liabilities, estimated income taxes on the differences between the estimated current values of assets and the estimated current amounts of liabilities and their tax bases, and net worth as of a specified date.

The term *net worth* is used to designate the difference between total assets and total liabilities, after deduction of estimated income taxes on the differences between the current amounts of these items and their tax bases.

Statement of changes in net worth—Presents the major sources of increases and decreases in net worth (e.g., income (loss), changes in the estimated current values of assets, changes in the estimated amounts of liabilities, changes in the estimated income tax on the differences between the estimated current value of assets and the estimated current amount of liabilities and their related tax bases.)

Comparative financial statements—Presents information about the current period and one or more prior periods (optional).

Methods of Presentation

Assets and liabilities should be recognized on the accrual basis rather than on the cash basis. The most useful presentation of assets and liabilities is in their order of liquidity and maturity, respectively, without classification as current and noncurrent.

In personal financial statements for one of a group of joint owners of assets, the statements should include only the person's interest as a beneficial owner. Business interests that constitute a large part of a person's total assets should be shown separately from other investments. The estimated current value of an investment in a separate entity should be shown in one amount as an investment if the entity is marketable as a going concern. Assets and liabilities of the separate entity should not be combined with similar personal items.

The estimated current values of assets and the estimated current amounts of liabilities of limited business activities not conducted in a separate business entity (e.g., investment in real estate and a related mortgage) should be presented in separate amounts, particularly if a large portion of the liabilities may be satisfied with funds from sources unrelated to the investment.

Guidelines for Determining Current Values and Amounts

The estimated current value of an asset in personal financial statements is the amount at which the item could be exchanged between a buyer and a seller, each of whom is well informed and willing, and neither of whom is compelled to buy or sell. Costs of disposal should be considered in estimating current values. Recent transactions involving similar assets and liabilities in similar circumstances ordinarily provide a reasonable basis for determining the current value of an asset and the estimated current amount of a liability. In the absence of recent similar transactions, adjustments of historical cost for changes in a specific price index, appraisals, and discounted amounts of projected cash receipts and payments may be appropriate.

Receivables

Receivables should be presented at amounts of cash the person estimates will be collected, using appropriate interest rates at the date of the financial statements.

Marketable Securities

Marketable securities should be based on quoted market prices, if available, based on the closing price on the date of the financial statements if the securities were traded on that date. Bid-and-ask quotations may be used to estimate the current value. An adjustment to market price may be required if the investor owns sufficient amounts of securities that his or her sale of the securities would influence the market price.

Options

If published prices of options are unavailable, the current value of options should be determined on the basis of the values of the assets subject to option, taking into consideration such factors as the exercise prices and length of the option period.

Investments in Life Insurance

The estimated current value of life insurance is the cash value of the policy less the amount of any loans against it. The face value of the policy should be disclosed.

Investments in Closely Held Businesses

There is no one generally accepted procedure for determining the estimated current value of an investment in a closely held business. Alternative valuation procedures include the following:

- Multiple of earnings
- Liquidation value
- Reproduction value
- Appraisal
- Discounted amounts of projected cash receipts and payments
- Adjustments of book value or cost of the person's share of equity

The objective should be to approximate the amount at which the investment could be exchanged between a buyer and a seller, each of whom is well informed and willing, and neither of whom is compelled to buy or sell.

Real Estate

Investments in real estate, including leaseholds, should be presented at current value, with consideration given to information such as the following:

- Sales of similar property in similar circumstances
- The discounted amount of projected receipts and payments relating to the property or the net realizable value of the property, based on planned courses of action
- Appraisals based on estimates of selling prices and costs
- Appraisals used to obtain financing
- Assessed value for property taxes

Intangible Assets

Investments in intangible assets should be based on discounted amounts of projected cash receipts and payments arising from the planned use or sale of the assets. The cost of a purchased intangible asset may be used if no other information is available.

Future Interests and Similar Assets

Nonforfeitable rights to receive future sums should be presented as assets at their discounted amounts if those rights have all of the following characteristics:

- The rights are for fixed or determinable amounts.
- The rights are not contingent on the holder's life expectancy or the occurrence of a particular event, such as disability or death.
- The rights do not require future performance of service by the holder.

Examples of rights that may have these characteristics are guaranteed minimum portions of pensions, deferred compensation contracts, and beneficial interests in trusts.

Payables and Other Liabilities

Payables and other liabilities should be presented at their discounted amounts of cash to be paid. The discount rate should be the rate implicit in the transaction in which the debt was incurred—unless the debtor is able to discharge the debt currently at a lower amount, in which case the debt should be presented at the lower amount.

Noncancelable Commitments

Noncancelable commitments to pay future sums should be presented as liabilities at their discounted amounts if those commitments have all of the following characteristics:

- The commitments are for fixed or determinable amounts.
- The commitments are not contingent on others' life expectancies or on the occurrence of a particular event, such as disability or death.
- The commitments do not require future performance of services by others.

Income Taxes Payable

The liability for income taxes should include unpaid income taxes for completed tax years and an estimate of the amount of income taxes accrued for the elapsed portion of the current year of the financial statements.

Estimated Income Taxes on the Difference between the Estimated Current Values of Assets and the Current Amounts of Liabilities and Their Tax Bases

A provision should be made for estimated income taxes on the difference between the estimated current values of assets and the estimated current amounts of liabilities and their tax bases. This estimate should include consideration of negative tax bases of tax shelters, if any. This amount should be presented between liabilities and net worth in the statement of financial condition. Methods and assumptions used to estimate the income taxes should be disclosed.

Financial Statement Disclosure

Personal financial statements should include information to make the statements adequately informative. The following list indicates the nature and type of information that should be disclosed. It is not all-inclusive.

1. The name(s) of individual(s) covered by the financial statements
2. A statement that assets are presented at their estimated current values and liabilities at their estimated current amounts
3. The method used to estimate current values of assets and current amounts of liabilities
4. If assets are held jointly by the person and others, the nature of the joint ownership
5. If the person's investment portfolio is material in relation to other assets and is concentrated in one or a few companies, the names of the companies or industries and the current values of their securities
6. If the person has a material investment in a closely held business:
    - The name of the company and the person's percentage ownership
    - The nature of the business
    - Summarized financial information about the assets, liabilities and results of operations of the business
7. Descriptions of intangible assets and their estimated useful lives
8. Amount of life insurance
9. Nonforfeitable rights (that do not have the characteristics described above)

10. Tax information as follows:
    - The methods and assumptions used to compute the estimated income taxes on the difference between the estimated current values of assets and the estimated current amounts of liabilities and their tax bases
    - Unused operating losses and capital loss carryforwards
    - Other unused deductions and credits and their expiration dates
    - The difference between the estimated current values of major assets and the estimated current amounts of liabilities or categories of assets and liabilities and their tax bases
11. Maturities, interest rates, collateral, and other details related to receivables and debt
12. Noncancelable commitments (that do not have the characteristics described above)

Generally accepted accounting principles other than those described in SOP 82-1 may be applicable to personal financial statements. For example, FAS-5 (Accounting for Contingencies) and FAS-57 (Related Party Disclosures) may provide useful guidance in the preparation of personal financial statements.

CHAPTER 25
POSTEMPLOYMENT AND POSTRETIREMENT BENEFITS OTHER THAN PENSIONS

CONTENTS

IMPRESS™ Cross-References	**25.02**
Overview	**25.03**
FIG-FAS 106: A Guide to Implementation of Statement 106 on Employers' Accounting for Postretirement Benefits Other Than Pensions	**25.04**
Background	**25.04**
Standards	**25.04**
Illustration of a Frontloaded Plan	**25.09**
Illustration of a Negative Plan Amendment and a Curtailment That Reduces the APBO	**25.12**
Illustration of Negative Plan Amendment—Curtailment Gain	**25.13**
Illustration of Negative Plan Amendment—Curtailment Loss	**25.15**
Illustration of Immediate Termination of Plan	**25.21**

CROSS-REFERENCES

1999 MILLER GAAP IMPLEMENTATION MANUAL: Chapter 22, "Pension Plans—Employers"; Chapter 23, "Pension Plans—Settlements and Curtailments"

1999 MILLER GAAP GUIDE: Chapter 36, "Postemployment and Postretirement Benefits Other Than Pensions"

1999 MILLER GAAP IMPLEMENTATION MANUAL: EITF: Chapter 24, "Postemployment and Postretirement Benefits Other Than Pensions"

1999 MILLER GOVERNMENTAL GAAP GUIDE: Chapter 22, "Certain Postemployment Benefits"

1999 MILLER GAAS GUIDE: Chapter 8, "Evidence"; Chapter 20, "Audits of Employee Benefit Plans"

CHAPTER 25
POSTEMPLOYMENT AND POSTRETIREMENT BENEFITS OTHER THAN PENSIONS

OVERVIEW

FAS-106 requires the accrual of postretirement benefits in a manner similar to the recognition of net periodic pension cost under FAS-87 (Employers' Accounting for Pensions). The provisions of FAS-106 are similar in most respects to those of FAS-87 and differ only where there are compelling reasons for different treatments.

Similar to FAS-87, FAS-106 incorporates the following features in the required accounting for postretirement benefits:

1. *Delayed recognition*—Certain changes in the obligation for postretirement benefits and in the value of plan assets are not required to be recognized as they occur. Rather, they can be recognized systematically over future periods.

2. *Net cost*—The recognized consequences of events and transactions affecting a postretirement benefit plan are reported as a single amount in the employers' financial statements. That amount includes at least three types of events or transactions that might otherwise be reported separately—exchanging a promise of deferred compensation for current employee services, the interest cost arising from the passage of time until those benefits are paid, and the returns from the investment in plan assets if the plan is funded.

3. *Offsetting*—Plan assets (assets that have been segregated and restricted for the payment of postretirement benefits) offset the accumulated postretirement benefit obligation in determining amounts in the employer's statement of financial position. Also, the return on plan assets reduces postretirement benefit cost in the employer's statement of income. That reduction is reflected, even though the obligation has not been settled and the investment in the assets may be largely controlled by the employer, and substantial risks and rewards associated with both the obligation and the assets are borne by the employer.

The FASB has also established accounting standards for employers that provide benefits for former or inactive employees after employment, but before retirement (*postemployment benefits*). FAS-112 requires employers to recognize the obligation to provide postemployment benefits in accordance with FAS-43 (Accounting for Compensated Absences) if the criteria for accrual established in that pronouncement are met. If the FAS-43 criteria are not met, the employer should account for postemployment benefits when it is probable that a liability has been incurred and the amount of that liability can be reasonably estimated, in accordance with FAS-5 (Accounting for Contingencies).

The following pronouncements are the sources of GAAP for postemployment and postretirement benefits other than pensions that are included in the highest level of authority in the SAS-69 hierarchy:

APB-12	Omnibus Opinion—1967
FAS-106	Employers' Accounting for Postretirement Benefits Other Than Pensions
FAS-112	Employers' Accounting for Postemployment Benefits

The following additional source of GAAP that is in a lower level of the SAS-69 GAAP hierarchy is discussed in this Manual:

FIG-FAS 106	A Guide to Implementation of Statement 106 on Employers' Accounting for Postretirement Benefits Other Than Pensions (Level D)

FIG-FAS 106: A Guide to Implementation of Statement 106 on Employers' Accounting for Postretirement Benefits Other Than Pensions

BACKGROUND

FIG-FAS 106, reported on in this section, includes responses to 64 specific questions regarding the application of FAS-106.

STANDARDS

Question 1: Does FAS-106 apply to long-term disability benefits paid to former employees on disability retirement under an employer's postretirement benefit plan?

Answer: Yes, as long as the benefits provided are postretirement benefits. Disability benefits paid to former or inactive employees who are not on disability retirement should be accounted for in accordance with FAS-112 (Employers' Accounting for Postemployment Benefits). Similarly, if disability income benefits are paid pursuant to a pension plan, the applicable accounting guidance is found in FAS-87 (Employers' Accounting for Pensions).

Question 2: If some employees, upon their retirement, voluntarily elect under the provisions of the Consolidated Omnibus Budget Reconciliation Act of 1985 (COBRA), as amended, to continue their health care coverage provided through the active employee health care plan and the cost to the employer of their continuing coverage exceeds the retirees' contributions, should the employer account for that cost under FAS-106?

Answer: No. The right to continue health care coverage under COBRA is not based on employee retirement. This right generally is available to any terminated employee. Therefore, employers should follow FAS-112 when the cost of continuing health care coverage under COBRA exceeds the former employees' contributions.

Question 3: A collectively bargained defined benefit postretirement health care plan of a single employer may stipulate that benefits will be provided for the duration of the collective-bargaining agreement, or the plan may imply or explicitly state that benefits are subject to renegotiation upon the expiration of the current collective-bargaining agreement. Past negotiations have resulted in the continuation of the plan, although the plan has been amended at various times. Should the accumulated postretirement benefit obligation (APBO) be measured based only on benefits expected to be paid during the period in which the current agreement will be in force?

Answer: No. The APBO should be measured assuming that the defined benefit postretirement health care plan will continue after the expiration of the existing collective-bargaining agreement. Unless there is evidence to the contrary, a postretirement benefit plan that currently exists is expected to continue in the future.

Question 4: How should an employer account for a deferred compensation contract that does not provide a vested benefit for the employee's prior service at the date the contract is entered into? For example, an employee must render 30 years of service to receive benefits under a deferred compensation contract and has rendered 16 years of service at the date of entering into the contract. Credit is granted for that prior service in determining eligibility for the benefit to be provided. Should the total obligation be accrued over the remaining 14 years of service, or should the employer immediately recognize the portion related to the 16 years of service already rendered?

Answer: The total obligation under the deferred compensation contract should be accrued over the remaining 14 years of service. An obligation related to the prior service would be accrued only if the employee was entitled to part of the benefit without regard to future service (i.e., if the credit for prior service results in a vested benefit).

Question 5: An employee becomes fully eligible for benefits under a deferred compensation contract five years after entering into the contract. The contract states, however, that if the employee dies or becomes disabled, benefits will be payable immediately. The contract is not one of a group of contracts that possess the characteristics of a pension plan. What is the attribution period?

Answer: If the employee is expected to provide service over the five-year period, the obligation should be accrued over this time period. If the employee dies or becomes disabled before the five-year period expires, any remaining unrecognized cost would be recognized in the period in which the death or disability occurred. No accrual is required if the employee is not expected to work for the employer for the next five years.

Question 6: Can future amendments to a written postretirement health care plan that change the amount of a defined dollar cap be anticipated as part of the substantive plan?

Answer: Yes, if the employer's past practices indicate that plan amendments are a common occurrence. For example, the employer may have a history of regularly increasing (or decreasing) the defined dollar cap under a postretirement health care plan.

Question 7: Is a postretirement health care plan with a defined dollar cap considered to be a plan that provides benefits defined in terms of monetary amounts as discussed in paragraph 26?

Answer: No. In this scenario, the benefit is reimbursement of specified eligible medical claims. The fact that the employer's reimbursement of these claims is limited to a specific dollar amount (i.e., the dollar cap) does not indicate that the benefits are defined in monetary amounts.

Question 8: Should the assumed discount rates used to measure an employer's postretirement benefit obligation be the same rates used to measure its pension obligation under FAS-87?

Answer: Not necessarily. As in FAS-87, the discount rate chosen to measure the liability for postretirement benefit obligations should reflect the interest rate on high-quality debt instruments of a duration comparable to that of the benefit obligation. However, a different discount rate may be appropriate, because the timing of expected payments under the postretirement benefit plan may differ from the expected timing of pension payments.

Question 9: An employer sponsors a health care plan that provides benefits to both active employees and retirees under age 65. The plan requires active employees and retirees to contribute to the plan. Can the contributions of active employees ever be used to reduce the employer's cost of providing benefits to retirees?

Answer: Yes, but only if contributions by active employees exceed the cost of providing health care benefits for this group over its working life and the employer has no obligation to refund the excess contributions. The cost of providing health care coverage for active employees should be measured on the assumption they are the only group covered by the plan (i.e., retirees would be excluded in this computation).

Question 10: An employer has a contributory health care plan covering active employees and retirees under which retirees pay 100% of the average cost of benefits determined based on the combined experience of active employees and retirees. The employer pays all of the remaining cost. The active employees do not contribute to the plan. Under this arrangement, does the employer have an obligation under FAS-106?

Answer: Yes, if the actual cost of providing health care benefits to retirees exceeds their contributions. If this is the case, the employer is subsidizing the retirees' health care benefits. The employer has an obligation for the difference between the expected cost of the retirees' benefits and the expected contribution amounts.

Question 11: Are there any circumstances under which an employer may measure its postretirement health care benefit obligation by projecting the cost of premiums for purchased health care insurance?

Answer: Yes, if the postretirement benefit plan provides that the benefit to be received by retirees is a payment of their future health care insurance premiums.

Question 12: If an employer has measured its postretirement health care benefit obligation by projecting the cost of premiums for purchased health care insurance, does that reduce or eliminate the applicability of any provisions of FAS-106, for example, the calculation and disclosure of service and interest cost?

Answer: No. All of the FAS-106 provisions, including the disclosure of service and interest cost, still apply.

Question 13: Should employers assume a trend of decreasing (or increasing) Medicare reimbursement rates if Medicare has consistently reduced (or increased) the portion of benefits it will cover? For example, certain health care costs may have increased by 15% last year but Medicare may have covered only a smaller increase, which increased the employer's or retirees' share of the cost of benefits. When determining its postretirement benefit obligation, should an employer assume that such a reduction in Medicare coverage would continue?

Answer: Generally not. Changes in Medicare coverage should be projected only if they result from currently enacted legislation or regulations. Future changes in Medicare legislation or regulations should not be anticipated even if past experience indicates that such changes are likely.

Question 14: An employer modifies the eligibility requirements under its postretirement benefit plan by changing the plan's credited service period from "25 years of service after age 40" to "15 years of service after both (*a*) reaching age 50 and (*b*) rendering 10 years of service." What is the beginning of the attribution period?

Answer: The credited service period for this pension plan is undefined. Therefore, the attribution period begins on the date of hire. The net effect of the above change is to lengthen the attribution period for employees under age 40.

Question 15: An employer provides retiree health care and life insurance benefits under one plan. Employees are eligible for health care and death benefits upon attaining age 55 and having rendered 20 years of service; however, the life insurance benefits are based on final pay. Does basing the life insurance benefits on final pay extend the full eligibility date to a plan participant's expected retirement date? For example, if an employee is expected to fulfill the 20-year service requirement before age 55 and is expected to retire at age 62 with salary increases in all years of service, is the employee's full eligibility date the date he or she reaches age 62?

Answer: Yes, assuming the additional life insurance benefits earned between age 55 and the employee's expected retirement date are not trivial in relation to the total benefit to be received. This postretirement benefit plan has an indefinite credited service period. Therefore, the attribution period begins on the date of hire and ends on the full eligibility date. The full eligibility date is the date on which an employee has earned all of the benefits that he or she will receive under the postretirement benefit plan. In this case, the full amount of life insurance benefits to be received will not be known until the employee retires.

Question 16: Would the answer to Question 15 be different if the benefits were provided and accounted for under two separate plans, one providing life insurance benefits and the other providing health care benefits?

Answer: Yes. If health care and life insurance benefits are provided under separate plans, the full eligibility date would be determined separately for each plan.

Question 17: If the terms of the plan in Question 15 specified which 20-year service period constituted the credited service period—for example, the first 20 years after date of hire, or the first 20 years of service after age 35—would basing life insurance benefits on final pay still extend the full eligibility date to the expected date of retirement?

Answer: Yes, assuming the additional life insurance benefits earned between age 55 and the employee's expected retirement date are not trivial in relation to the total benefit to be received.

Question 18: Under what conditions would a plan be considered a frontloaded plan?

Answer: A plan is considered frontloaded if all, or a disproportionate portion of, expected benefits to be received under the plan are attributed to employees' early years of service. If a plan is frontloaded, the expected postretirement benefit obligation (EPBO) should not be attributed ratably to each year of credited service in the credited service period but should be attributed in accordance with the plan benefit formula. The employee group as a whole is evaluated in determining whether the plan is frontloaded.

Illustration of a Frontloaded Plan

TWR, Inc., offers a postretirement benefit plan that provides both health care and life insurance benefits. Employees are eligible for health care and death benefits upon attaining age 55 and after having completed 20 years of service. Life insurance benefits are based on final pay, and employees are expected to receive annual pay raises between age 55 and their expected retirement age, 62. An employee named Jane Doe is hired at age 20 at a starting salary of $30,000. TWR assumes annual pay increases of 4%, a life expectancy of 75 years, and a discount rate of 7%.

The EPBO for Jane Doe at age 40 is $43,091 ($28,500 for health care benefits and $14,591 for life insurance benefits). A ratable allocation of the EPBO over her expected working life, 42 years, would result in an accumulated postretirement benefit obligation (APBO) of $20,519 at the end of year 20 ($13,571 for health care benefits and $6,948 for life insurance benefits; both of these amounts are 20/42 of the applicable EPBO). Based on the

25.10 *Postemployment and Postretirement Benefits Other Than Pensions*

respective benefit formulas, the APBO at the end of 20 years would be $28,500 for health care benefits and $6,157 for life insurance benefits. Since the APBO based on the benefit formulas, $34,657, is significantly greater than a ratable allocation of the EPBO, $20,519, the postretirement plan is considered to be frontloaded. For frontloaded benefit plans, benefits should be attributed using the respective benefit formulas. Therefore, TWR would report an APBO of $34,657 for Jane Doe at the end of year 20.

Question 19: An employer has a retiree health care plan that bases benefits on length of service; to be eligible for any benefits under it, employees must render a minimum of 10 years of service after they reach age 45. However, upon attaining age 45, employees receive credit for 3% of the maximum benefit for each year of service before age 45. For example, at age 45 an employee hired at age 25 receives credit for 60% (3% x 20 years) of the plan's postretirement health care benefits. When does the credited service period begin?

Answer: The credited service period begins at the date of hire. The total benefits to be received are a function of the total years of service, including service before age 45.

Question 20: An employer requires that, in order to be eligible to participate in its retiree health care plan, an employee must participate in its contributory active health care plan. An employee can join the active plan at any time before retirement but must have worked 10 years and attained age 55 while in service to be eligible for benefits under the retiree plan. When does the attribution period begin?

Answer: At the date of hire if the employee is expected to participate in the active health care plan. This is because the plan does not specify which 10 years of service must be worked in order to qualify for benefits under the plan. If an employee is not expected to participate in the active health care plan, the employee would not be considered a plan participant for purposes of the postretirement benefit plan.

Question 21: Should an employer's annual accrual for the service cost component of net periodic postretirement benefit cost relate to only those employees who are in their credited service periods?

Answer: In most cases, yes. However, in some cases a plan will establish a nominal service period in relation to the employee's expected total years of service. For example, an employee is hired at age 25 and is expected to work until age 62. The plan may specify that the credited service period begins at age 55 and runs until retirement. In this case, the credited service period according to the plan would be nominal in relation to the total expected years of service. In such instances, the attribution period, and the recognition of service cost, would begin at the date of hire.

Question 22: In determining the attribution period, what is considered a nominal credited service period?

Answer: Judgment is required in determining what qualifies as a nominal credited service period. Generally the service period would be considered nominal if it is very short in relation to the total expected years of employee service before full eligibility for benefits.

Question 23: An employer's previous accounting for postretirement benefits has considered the written plan to be the substantive plan. On July 1, 1996, its Board of Directors approves a negative plan amendment (i.e., an amendment that reduces benefits attributable to prior service) that will be effective on January 1, 1998. The employer intends to announce the negative plan amendment to plan participants on July 1, 1997. When should the effects of the negative plan amendment be considered for accounting purposes?

Answer: July 1, 1997, the date on which the negative plan amendment is communicated to employees. It would have been appropriate to account for the effects of the negative plan amendment on July 1, 1996, the date the amendment was approved by the Board, if the amendment had been communicated to employees at that time or within a reasonable period of time thereafter. A reasonable period of time would be the time it would normally take to prepare information about the amendment and to distribute it to employees and retirees. A one-year period is excessive for this purpose.

Question 24: Is it important to distinguish between a reduction in the accumulated postretirement benefit obligation (APBO) caused by a negative plan amendment and a reduction caused by a curtailment?

Answer: Yes. A reduction in the APBO caused by a curtailment is potentially recognizable as a current component of income. Conversely, a reduction in the APBO caused by a negative plan amendment that exceeds any unrecognized prior service cost or unrecognized transition obligation is *not* immediately recognized as a reduction of current postretirement benefit costs.

Question 25: What is the difference between a negative plan amendment and a curtailment that reduces the APBO?

Answer: A negative plan amendment is a change in the terms of the plan that reduces or eliminates benefits for employee services already rendered. A curtailment reduces the APBO by reducing the number of employees covered under the plan and/or by eliminating the benefits attributable to future service for some or all plan participants.

Illustration of a Negative Plan Amendment and a Curtailment That Reduces the APBO

Company A sponsors a postretirement health care plan that previously was noncontributory. A plan amendment requiring current and future retirees to contribute $200 per month toward the cost of benefits provided would be a negative plan amendment because this change serves to reduce the APBO for employee service already rendered.

Company B sponsors a postretirement life insurance plan. Life insurance benefits previously were defined based on final pay. Company B changes this plan on December 31, 1997, to fix the life insurance benefits payable based on salaries in effect on that date. This change qualifies as a curtailment because the accrual of additional death benefits based on future employee service has been eliminated.

Question 26: Company B sponsors a postretirement life insurance plan. Life insurance benefits previously were defined based on final pay. Company B changes this plan on December 31, 1997, to fix the life insurance benefits payable based on salaries in effect on that date. Before this change, the APBO at December 31, 1997, included an amount—$400,000—based on projected future employee pay levels. Thus, the APBO at December 31, 1997, decreases by $400,000 as a result of the plan amendment because increases in employees' future pay levels will no longer increase their death benefits under the plan. Why is the $400,000 a "potentially" currently recognizable curtailment gain?

Answer: Whether some or all of the $400,000 curtailment gain is to be recognized in income depends on the existence and amount of a previously unrecognized net loss, unrecognized prior service cost, and an unrecognized transition obligation.

Question 27: Should the accounting for a curtailment always consider any unrecognized prior service cost or unrecognized transition obligation?

Answer: Yes. The theoretical reason for not immediately recognizing prior service cost as a current component of postretirement benefit cost is that amendments of the postretirement benefit plan will result in a positive future economic benefit (e.g., a more motivated and committed workforce). A curtailment raises doubt about the existence of these future economic benefits. Therefore, FAS-106 requires recognition of any unrecognized prior service cost. In the case of a curtailment, the treatment of unrecognized transition obligation is similar to the treatment of unrecognized prior service cost.

Question 28: Does a curtailment result only from events that occur outside a postretirement benefit plan?

Answer: No. Although many curtailments result from events that occur outside the postretirement benefit plan—for example, (*a*) closing a plant, (*b*) selling a division or subsidiary, or (*c*) laying off a number of employees—a curtailment can also result from events that occur inside—for example, from a negative plan amendment that has the effect of eliminating the accrual of some or all of the future benefits for a significant number of plan participants.

Question 29: Does a gain result if, at the time of a curtailment, there exists unrecognized negative prior service cost due to a previous plan amendment that reduced benefits under the plan?

Answer: Yes. In accounting for a curtailment, unrecognized (negative) prior service cost that results from a reduction in benefits (a negative plan amendment) is treated the same as unrecognized prior service cost that results from an increase in benefits. Therefore, any unrecognized negative prior service cost associated with future years of service that are affected by the curtailment is a gain. To the extent that this gain is not offset by any other curtailment losses, it is recognized currently as a component of income.

Question 30: What are examples of the accounting for a negative plan amendment that results in a curtailment?

Answer: The first illustration that follows is an example of a negative plan amendment that results in a curtailment gain. The second illustration is an example of a negative plan amendment that results in a curtailment loss.

Illustration of Negative Plan Amendment— Curtailment Gain

X^4, Inc., sponsors a defined benefit postretirement benefit plan. The only benefit provided under the plan is a life insurance benefit. The amount of life insurance provided under the plan is based on final pay levels. On December 31, 1998, X^4 eliminates this benefit for those employees who are not age 45 or older. This group constitutes a significant portion of X^4's workforce. This change in the postretirement benefit plan results in two separate reductions in the APBO. First, benefits earned by employees under age 45, based on past pay levels, are eliminated (resulting in a $300,000 reduction in the APBO). Second, the APBO had been calculated based on assumptions about future pay levels. Since employees under age 45 will no longer be plan participants, the future pay levels of these employees, which were consid-

25.14 Postemployment and Postretirement Benefits Other Than Pensions

ered in calculating the APBO, are no longer relevant (resulting in a $500,000 reduction in the APBO). This change in the postretirement benefit plan results in the elimination of future benefit accruals for this group of employees. As such, the $500,000 reduction in the APBO is potentially recognizable as a current curtailment gain. This curtailment would be accounted for in the following manner:

	December 31, 1998				
	Before Negative Plan Amendment	Negative Plan Amendment	After Negative Plan Amendment	Curtailment	After Curtailment
APBO	$(1,500,000)	$ 300,000	$(1,200,000)	$ 500,000	$(700,000)
Items not yet recognized in earnings:					
Unrecognized prior service cost	100,000	(100,000)	- 0 -		
Unrecognized transition obligation	140,000	(140,000)	- 0 -		
Unrecognized net loss	200,000		200,000	(200,000)	
Negative prior service cost		(60,000)	(60,000)		(60,000)
	$ 440,000	$(300,000)	$ 140,000	$(200,000)	$ (60,000)
Accrued postretirement benefit cost	$(1,060,000)	$ - 0 -	$(1,060,000)	$ 300,000	$(760,000)

The journal entry to record the curtailment gain is as follows:

Accrued postretirement benefit cost	$300,000	
Curtailment gain		$300,000

The following facts should be noted about the above accounting:

1. Any decrease in the APBO as a result of a negative plan amendment is used first to reduce any existing unrecognized prior service cost and then to reduce any remaining unrecognized transition obligation. Any amount that remains from the negative plan amendment is treated as "negative prior service cost." The negative prior

service cost, $60,000, is recognized by being amortized over future periods beginning January 1, 1999. The negative prior service cost is amortized by assigning an equal amount to each remaining year of service up to the full eligibility date for each plan participant who was active at the date of the amendment but was not yet fully eligible for benefits at that date. Only participants who are over age 45 and who do not yet qualify for plan benefits qualify under this definition.

2. The decrease in the APBO as a result of the curtailment is used first to reduce any unrecognized net loss existing on the curtailment date. Any remaining curtailment amount is recognized currently in income. The curtailment gain currently recognized is *not* a component of net periodic postretirement benefit cost, and the gain should be disclosed separately.

Illustration of Negative Plan Amendment— Curtailment Loss

Crown Color, Inc., sponsors an unfunded postretirement health care plan covering employees at three locations. On December 1, 1998, Crown Color amends its benefit plan. Any employee of its Butte, Montana, plant who does not retire by December 31, 1998, is not entitled to receive benefits under the plan. Employees of the Butte plant who retire by December 31, 1998, will receive benefits under the terms of the postretirement health care plan. Crown Color's employees at its other two locations are not affected by this change in the postretirement benefit plan.

As a result of the above, Crown Color's accumulated postretirement benefit obligation is reduced by $200,000. This reflects an elimination of benefits attributed to years of service already rendered by employees who are not yet eligible to retire and to service rendered by those employees who choose not to retire (this reduction represents the results of the negative plan amendment). As a result of the early retirement of other (eligible) employees at the Butte plant, Crown Color's APBO increases by $100,000 (this represents a curtailment).

Before these changes, Crown Color's unrecognized transition obligation was $400,000. At the date of transition to FAS-106, the remaining expected years of service of employees at the Butte location represented 35% of the total remaining expected years of service of all of Crown Color's employees. This will be accounted for in the following manner:

25.16 *Postemployment and Postretirement Benefits Other Than Pensions*

	December 31, 1998				
	Before Negative Plan Amendment	Negative Plan Amendment	After Negative Plan Amendment	Curtailment	After Curtailment
APBO	$(475,000)	$ 200,000	$(275,000)	$(100,000)	$(375,000)
Items not yet recognized in earnings:					
Unrecognized prior service cost	50,000	(50,000)	- 0 -		
Unrecognized transition obligation	400,000	(150,000)	250,000	(87,500)	162,500
Unrecognized net gain	(75,000)		(75,000)	75,000	
	$ 375,000	$(200,000)	$ 175,000	$ (12,500)	$ 162,500
Accrued postretirement benefit cost	$(100,000)	$ - 0 -	$(100,000)	$(112,500)	$(212,500)

The journal entry to record the curtailment loss is as follows:

Curtailment loss	$112,500	
Accrued postretirement benefit cost		$112,500

The following facts should be noted about the above accounting:

1. The increase in the APBO as a result of the curtailment is used first to reduce any unrecognized net gain at the date of the curtailment.
2. As a result of the plan amendment, 35% of the total expected remaining years of service, for all of Crown Color's locations, have been eliminated. Therefore, Crown Color should accelerate the recognition of 35% of the unrecognized transition obligation that remains *after* the negative plan amendment is recorded (i.e., 35% of $250,000, the remaining unrecognized transition obligation after the negative plan amendment becomes effective, is immediately recognized).
3. The curtailment loss is not a component of net periodic postretirement benefit cost and therefore should be disclosed separately.

Question 31: An employer adopts an amendment to its postretirement health care plan that has the dual effect of expanding the plan's coverage and increasing the deductible. Should the increase in the deductible be measured and recognized separately from the benefit improvement?

Answer: No. It is not unusual for numerous plan changes to be made at the same time. Some of the changes may increase benefits; other changes may decrease benefits. All of the changes should be considered together to determine whether there has been a net increase in benefits (a positive plan amendment) or a net decrease in benefits (a negative plan amendment).

Question 32: In applying the provisions of paragraphs 59 and 60 of FAS-106 for the recognition of gains and losses, is it appropriate for an employer to elect annually a new method of amortization of unrecognized gains and losses?

Answer: No. The employer should choose a method of amortizing gains and losses and follow the chosen method consistently from period to period. Any change in the method of recognizing gains and losses would fall within the scope of APB-20 (Accounting Changes) and would need to meet the preferability requirement of APB-20. Although the employer has some discretion in choosing how to recognize gains and losses, the amortization of these items must equal or exceed the minimum amortization as set forth in paragraph 59 of FAS-106.

Question 33: An employer sponsors a contributory postretirement health care plan that has an annual limitation on the dollar amount of the employer's share of the cost of benefits (a defined dollar capped plan). The cap on the employer's share of annual costs and the retirees' contribution rates are increased 5% annually. Any amount by which incurred claims costs exceed the combined employer and retiree contributions is initially borne by the employer but is passed back to retirees in the subsequent year through supplemental retiree contributions for that year. In 1995, incurred claims costs exceed the combined employer and retiree contributions, requiring a supplemental retiree contribution in 1996. If the employer decides in 1996 to absorb the excess that arose in 1995 rather than pass it on to the retirees, when should the employer recognize the loss due to that temporary deviation from the substantive plan?

Answer: The loss should be recognized at the time the employer makes the decision to deviate from the substantive plan. In this case, the loss would be recognized in 1996.

Question 34: If an employer previously projected that health care costs under a defined dollar capped plan would exceed the cap in 199X, but actual claims in that year do not exceed the cap, should a gain be recognized immediately in 199X in accordance with paragraph 61?

Answer: No. The above situation represents a situation where the experience of the benefit plan is better than expected. This situation gives rise to an unrealized gain. Under the provisions of FAS-106, paragraph 56, this type of gain is not recognized currently in income but rather is deferred and, in some cases, amortized against income in future periods (see par. 59). A gain is recognized immediately only when the employer deviates, on a temporary basis, from the provisions of the substantive plan and, as a result, there is a reduction in the APBO.

Question 35: What situation would result in a gain that would be recognized immediately in accordance with paragraph 61?

Answer: A gain would occur if plan participants agreed to make a one-time contribution to the plan that exceeds the amount called for under the terms of the substantive plan. Future contributions by plan participants are expected to revert to the level specified by the substantive plan.

Question 36: May an employer include in plan assets the assets of a "rabbi trust" (so named because the first grantor trust to receive a favorable ruling from the Internal Revenue Service was one formed for a rabbi)?

Answer: No. Plan assets held in a rabbi trust are *explicitly* available to the employer's creditors in the event of bankruptcy. Under FAS-106, assets must be segregated and restricted (typically in a trust) to qualify as plan assets. EITF Issue No. 93-3, "Plan Assets under FASB Statement No. 106," states that a trust does not have to be "bankruptcy-proof" for the trust assets to qualify as plan assets under FAS-106. However, the EITF states that trust assets would *not* qualify as plan assets if such assets were *explicitly* available to the employer's general creditors in the event of bankruptcy. (See *1999 Miller GAAP Implementation Manual: EITF* for a further discussion of EITF Issue No. 93-3.)

Question 37: An insurance contract (see FAS-106 for a formal definition) with a captive insurance company does not qualify as a plan asset. However, can an investment contract with a captive insurance company qualify as a plan asset if it meets the criteria in paragraph 63?

Answer: Yes, assuming the investment contract with the captive insurance company is segregated and restricted for the payment of plan benefits (see pars. 7 and 8 of FAS-97 (Accounting and Reporting by Insurance Enterprises for Certain Long-Duration Contracts and for Realized Gains and Losses from the Sale of Investments) for a definition of *investment contract*). An investment contract with a captive insurance company represents an obligation of the employer to pay cash to the benefit plan to be used for the purpose of providing postretirement benefits. Since an accrued liability of the employer to pay cash is not considered a plan asset, the investment contract is to be considered a debt security of the employer. This debt security must be currently transferable to be included in plan assets.

Question 38: If an employer issues its own debt or equity securities directly to its postretirement benefit trust, may those securities be included in plan assets under FAS-106?

Answer: Yes, provided there are no restrictions on the transfer of these assets. The plan trustee must have the unilateral right to unconditionally sell, transfer, or otherwise dispose of the securities. Assets that are not currently transferable but that can be converted into transferable assets should not be considered plan assets. For example, nontransferable convertible preferred stock does not qualify as a plan asset even if it can be converted into transferable common stock.

Question 39: Before adopting FAS-106, what disclosures about its postretirement benefit plans should an employer provide in its financial statements?

Answer: Before adopting FAS-106, the provisions of FAS-81 (Disclosure of Postretirement Health Care and Life Insurance Benefits) continue to apply. Also, public companies may be required to make additional disclosures according to the provisions of Staff Accounting Bulletin No. 74.

Question 40: Should an employer's disclosure of the weighted average of the assumed discount rates for its postretirement benefit obligation be the same as its disclosure for its pension benefit obligation?

Answer: Not necessarily (see the answer to Question 8 for additional discussion). Even if the discount rates are the same, the weighted average of those rates may differ between the timing and pattern of benefits to be provided and may be different for a postretirement benefit plan than for a pension plan. A pension plan typically provides a fixed yearly benefit, which is not expected to change over time. However, a postretirement health care plan is likely to pay more of its benefits as retirees age (since health typically deteriorates with age).

Question 41: An employer has two legally separate postretirement benefit plans. Both plans are unfunded (defined benefit) plans covering the same employees. One plan provides postretirement medical care and the other provides postretirement dental care. May the employer account for the two plans as one plan?

Answer: Yes. FAS-106, paragraph 76, allows the employer to combine unfunded (defined benefit) postretirement healthcare plans if either (a) different benefits are provided to the same group of employees or (b) the same benefits are provided to different groups of employees. However, if either of these plans were funded (i.e., if they held plan assets), they could not be combined but must be measured separately.

Question 42: When is it appropriate for the employer in Question 41 to change from one-plan accounting to two-plan accounting—that is, to accounting for each plan separately?

Answer: The employer must move to two-plan accounting if the provisions of paragraph 76 of FAS-106 are no longer met. For example, two-plan accounting would become mandatory if either (a) different benefits were provided to different groups of employees or (b) one or both of the plans became funded (i.e., held plan assets). If the conditions of paragraph 76 continue to be met, the employer would have to meet the preferability requirement of APB-20 (Accounting Changes) in order to support a voluntary change from one-plan accounting to two-plan accounting.

Question 43: An employer that has a single-employer postretirement benefit plan decides to provide health care benefits to its retirees by participating with several unrelated employers in a group postretirement health care benefit arrangement that does not result from collective bargaining. The arrangement is administered by an independent board of trustees and provides a uniform level of benefits to all retirees by utilizing group medical insurance contracts. Each participating employer is assessed an annual contribution for its share of insurance premiums, plus administrative costs. Employers may require their respective retirees to pay a portion of the annual assessment. Retirees whose former employer stops paying the annual assessment have the right to continue participation if they assume the cost of the annual premiums needed to maintain their existing benefits. Should the employer account for this arrangement as a multiemployer plan?

Answer: No. The key factor is that in a multiemployer plan the obligation to retirees does not depend on the former employer's continued participation. This feature is lacking from the above example.

Question 44: May a multiemployer plan be considered a substantially equivalent replacement plan (a successor plan) for an employer that terminates its single-employer defined benefit postretirement plan in such a way that acceleration of the recognition of unrecognized prior service cost is not required?

Answer: No. Multiemployer plans and single-employer plans are sufficiently different from each other that either one is precluded from being a successor plan for the other. In a multiemployer plan, the employer promises to make a defined contribution. A single-employer plan that gives rise to prior service cost is a defined benefit plan. The nature of the employer's promise—to make a defined contribution or to provide defined benefits—is fundamentally different between these two types of plans.

Question 45: Before adopting FAS-106, an employer recognizes a postretirement benefit liability as part of the purchase price allocation of an entity acquired in a purchase business combination. Must the employer (the acquiring entity) recognize postretirement benefit expense for the acquired entity's plan in accordance with FAS-106 in years after the purchase but before adopting that Statement?

Answer: No. Allocating a portion of the purchase price of another entity to the postretirement benefit obligation does not require the acquiring entity to adopt FAS-106 before its effective date. See EITF Issue No. 86-20, "Accounting for Other Postemployment Benefits of an Acquired Company," in *1999 Miller GAAP Implementation Manual: EITF* for a further discussion of this issue.

Question 46: An employer that immediately recognized its transition obligation upon adopting FAS-106 subsequently amends its plan to eliminate its obligation for postretirement benefits and partially compensates affected participants by increasing their pension benefits. How should those events be accounted for?

Answer: In this case, the employer has terminated its postretirement benefit plan and has effectively settled its postretirement benefit obligation by increasing the pension benefits that it will provide. The cost to the employer in providing enhanced pension benefits is the cost of settling the postretirement benefit plan. This increase in pension benefits results in an increase in "accrued pension cost" (or a decrease in "prepaid pension cost"). The existing obligation for the postretirement benefit plan should be eliminated. The difference between the reduction in the postretirement benefit liability and the increase in the liability for pension benefits equals the gain on the plan termination.

Illustration of Immediate Termination of Plan

GPP, Inc., sponsors a postretirement benefit plan and a pension plan. On December 31, 1999, GPP terminates its postretirement benefit plan. As partial compensation to the employees who are affected, GPP amends its pension plan so that current and future retirees will receive a pension benefit equal to 2% of final salary for each year of employment (GPP's previous pension benefit formula was 2% of an employee's salary over the employee's last five years of service). GPP's accrued postretirement benefit obligation at December 30, 1999, is $4,400,000; the projected benefit obligation on that date is $7,800,000. As a result of the change in the pension plan formula, GPP's pension liability increases by $750,000. GPP is interested in determining the gain on the plan termination.

The gain on the plan termination is the difference between the reduction in the accumulated postretirement benefit obligation and the increase in the projected benefit obligation. Therefore, GPP would recognize a gain of $3,650,000 ($4,400,000 − $750,000).

Question 47: What is the intent of paragraph 102 of FAS-106 on special termination benefits?

Answer: This paragraph provides guidance for the employer in accounting for the special termination benefits offered to employees in exchange for early retirement.

Question 48: How should an employer measure the postretirement benefit incentive that employees are to receive in exchange for their early termination of employment?

Answer: The termination incentive typically is measured as the difference between (1) the actuarial present value of the accumulated benefits for the terminating employees considering the enhanced benefits (It is assumed that the employees retire immediately.) *and* (2) the actuarial present value, based on benefits attributable to prior service, of the accumulated benefits for the terminating employees without the enhanced benefits. (It is assumed that the employees retire at the earliest date on which they would be eligible for postretirement benefits.)

FIG-FAS 106 contains a couple of detailed examples that illustrate this accounting treatment.

Question 49: An employer has two legally separate postretirement benefit plans: a defined benefit plan and a defined contribution plan. The terms of the defined benefit plan specify that the employer's obligation under that plan is reduced to the extent that a participant's account balance in the defined contribution plan will be used to pay incurred health care costs covered by the defined benefit plan. For purposes of applying FAS-106, should those plans be considered a single plan or two plans?

Answer: Two plans. The nature of the promises under each plan, the manner in which those promises are satisfied, the availability of plan assets to pay benefits, and the respective accounting for each type of plan are all so dissimilar as to preclude accounting for a defined benefit and a defined contribution plan as a single plan for FAS-106 purposes.

Question 50: If any assets of the defined contribution plan described in Question 49 have not yet been allocated to participants' individual accounts, do they reduce the accumulated postretirement benefit obligation of the defined benefit plan?

Answer: No. The employer's intent to allocate these assets to the accounts of individual employees in the future is not sufficient to reduce the employer's present obligation under the defined benefit plan. Under such an arrangement, the assets of individual employees in the defined contribution plan would be used to pay health care costs incurred in the future (the employer's obligation under the defined benefit plan is limited to covering health care costs in excess of amounts held in individual defined contribution accounts). When unallocated assets are assigned to the accounts of individual employees, the employer's obligation under the defined benefit plan is reduced. This reduction is recognized immediately as a component of net periodic postretirement benefit cost.

Question 51: Company A has a minority investment in Company B, which it accounts for using the equity method. Company A has a September 30 year-end, and Company B has a December 31 year-end. Company B is required to adopt FAS-106 on January 1, 1993. Company A is not required to adopt FAS-106 until October 1, 1993.

  a. May Company A adjust Company B's earnings to eliminate the effects of adopting FAS-106 when it includes Company B's results in its financial statements for the year ending September 30, 1993?

  b. Must Company A adopt FAS-106 early (i.e., in its fiscal year beginning October 1, 1992) so that its accounting method for postretirement benefits is the same as its investee's accounting method?

  c. May Company A and Company B adopt FAS-106 using different methods of recognizing the transition obligation?

Answer:

  a. No. Making this adjustment would involve changing the investee's accounting method from one that is consistent with GAAP (per FAS-106) to one that, for the investee, would not be consistent with GAAP (presumably the cash basis of accounting). There are also practical problems with this approach.

  b. No. The fact that an equity-method investee has adopted FAS-106 does not mean that the investor must also adopt FAS-106.

  c. Yes. The investor and investee can use different methods in recognizing the transition obligation. It may be desirable to have them handle the respective transition obligations in the same manner; however, it is not required.

Question 52: If a calendar-year nonpublic employer with a postretirement benefit plan has 500 or fewer plan participants on December 31, 1992, but more than 500 participants before the 1995 delayed effective date, must the employer adopt FAS-106 in the year of the increase or may it wait until 1995?

Answer: The employer can wait until 1995. If the employer does not meet the criteria for required adoption in 1993, future changes in the number of employees does not accelerate the required adoption date from 1995.

Question 53: If the nonpublic employer in Question 52 goes public in 1993 or 1994, may that employer still wait until 1995 to adopt FAS-106?

Answer: No. If an entity that has delayed adopting FAS-106 because of its nonpublic status goes public, it must adopt FAS-106 in the year it goes public.

Question 54: May an employer adopt FAS-106 early for some but not all of its postretirement benefit plans? For example, may an employer that is required to adopt FAS-106 in 1995 adopt the Statement in 1994 for its postretirement life insurance plan and wait until 1995 to adopt FAS-106 for its postretirement health care plan?

Answer: No. If an employer adopts FAS-106 earlier than its required effective date for any domestic postretirement benefit plan, the employer must apply FAS-106 to all its domestic postretirement benefit plans at the same time.

Question 55: How and when should an employer that adopted FAS-106 before the issuance of FIG-FAS 106 account for the effects (other than a correction of an error), if any, of initially complying with the subsequently issued implementation guidance?

Answer: The answer to Question 55 depends on whether the employer recognized the transition obligation (asset) immediately or deferred the recognition of the transition obligation or asset.

- *Transition obligation or asset was immediately recognized*—An employer that immediately recognized the FAS-106 transition obligation or asset before FIG-FAS 106 was issued is permitted, but is not required, to restate previously issued financial statements to reflect the guidance in FIG-FAS 106. The employer is *not* permitted to change either the method of initially recognizing the transition obligation or asset or the year FAS-106 is first applied.

If the employer chooses not to restate prior-year financial statements, the employer is required to treat the effects of applying FIG-FAS 106 as a cumulative-effect-type accounting change.

- *Recognition of the transition obligation or asset was deferred*—The guidance in FIG-FAS 106 may affect the determination of the transition obligation or asset. Any such adjustment to the transition obligation (asset) is to be treated as a cumulative-effect-type accounting change, and it should be amortized over the remaining amortization period.

Question 55 also addresses the treatment of negative plan amendments or curtailments, items accounted for under the delayed recognition provisions of FAS-106, other items, and how soon after issuance FIG-FAS 106 should be applied.

- *Negative plan amendments or curtailments*—Guidance in FIG-FAS 106 that affects negative plan amendments or curtailments is to be applied to future events or transactions. However, the employer may restate prior-year financial statements containing a negative plan amendment or curtailment to reflect the guidance in FIG-FAS 106.
- *Items accounted for under delayed recognition provisions of FAS-106*—Some of the recommendations in FIG-FAS 106 may affect items accounted for under FAS-106's delayed recognition provisions (e.g., amortization of an unrecognized gain or loss). These effects should be accounted for over future periods in a manner consistent with the FAS-106 guidance.
- *Other items*—Any other changes in accounting to reflect the guidance in FIG-FAS 106 is to be treated as a cumulative-effect-type accounting change.
- *Effective date of FIG-FAS 106*—The guidance in FIG-FAS 106 is to be applied as soon as reasonably practicable.

Question 56: A parent company has a postretirement benefit plan covering employees at some of its subsidiaries, and one subsidiary has its own separate postretirement benefit plan. The parent elects to adopt FAS-106 early and immediately recognize the transition obligation. May the transition obligation of the subsidiary with its own plan be recognized on a delayed basis in the consolidated financial statements of the parent and its subsidiaries?

Answer: No. The parent company is considered the employer, and its election as to how to treat the transition obligation applies to all benefit plans included within the consolidated financial statements. The subsidiary may choose delayed recognition in its separate financial statements.

Question 57: An employer adopts a negative plan amendment during the year and subsequently decides to adopt FAS-106 in that year, which is before its required adoption date. Should the transition obligation at the beginning of the year reflect the effect of the negative plan amendment?

Answer: Not unless the employer and the employee groups have a mutual understanding as to the nature, timing, and extent of the forthcoming negative plan amendment. If such a mutual understanding did not exist, the transition obligation at the beginning of the year of FAS-106's adoption should not reflect the effects of the negative plan amendment.

Question 58: May an employer change from delayed recognition to immediate recognition of the transition obligation after adopting FAS-106?

Answer: No. FAS-106 requires the employer to choose a single method of handling the transition process for all defined benefit and defined contribution plans. This method cannot be changed once it is selected.

Question 59: May an employer divide its transition obligation and recognize one portion immediately and the other portion on a delayed basis? For example, may the portion of the transition obligation relating to retirees be recognized immediately and the portion relating to active employees be recognized on a delayed basis?

Answer: No. The employer cannot unbundle the transition obligation. Even if FAS-106 permitted unbundling of the transition obligation, it would be a moot point. As stated above, FAS-106 requires the employer to choose a single method of handling the transition process for all defined benefit and defined contribution plans (and components thereof).

Question 60: May an employer immediately recognize the portion of its transition obligation that relates to either a previously discontinued operation or an operation that is discontinued in the year FAS-106 is adopted and amortize the remainder of its transition obligation over future service periods?

Answer: No. Employers are required to adopt a single method of handling the transition obligation when they initially adopt FAS-106.

Question 61: In its income statement, as part of discontinued operations, may an employer separately present the portion of its transition obligation immediately recognized that relates to previously discontinued operations, rather than include it as part of the cumulative-effect adjustment?

Answer: No. The immediate recognition of the transition obligation is to be presented on the face of the income statement as a cumulative-effect-type accounting change, net of the related income tax effect. However, within the "cumulative effect" portion of the income statement, the portion of the transition obligation pertaining to continuing and discontinued operations can be presented separately.

Question 62: An employer adopted FAS-106 on January 1, 1993, for its U.S. plans and immediately recognized its transition obligation. Must the employer use the same method of recognizing the transition obligation when it adopts FAS-106 for its plans outside the United States?

Answer: Yes. Employers are required to adopt a single method of handling the transition obligation when FAS-106 is initially adopted (see par. 110). This requirement applies to *all* defined benefit and defined contribution postretirement benefit plans, whether such plans are foreign or domestic.

Question 63: If an employer that immediately recognizes its transition obligation retroactively adjusts its purchase price allocation at the date of adopting FAS-106 to record a postretirement benefit obligation that it assumed in a purchase business combination consummated after December 21, 1990, may the corresponding debit to goodwill be written off as part of the adjustment to record the cumulative effect of adopting FAS-106?

Answer: Generally, no. If a purchase price allocation is adjusted retroactively to reflect a postretirement benefit obligation assumed in a purchase business combination, the offsetting debit to goodwill typically is combined with any other goodwill resulting from the acquisition. Cumulative goodwill amortization will be understated as a result of retroactively recognizing a postretirement benefit obligation as part of the purchase price allocation. The increased amortization of goodwill (from the acquisition date to the date of FAS-106 adoption) is recognized as part of the cumulative-effect-type accounting change required to adopt FAS-106. However, there may be rare instances where one event or a series of events, occurring between the acquisition date and the FAS-106 adoption date, indicate that goodwill has been impaired. If so, the impaired portion of the goodwill should be written off. Any goodwill write-off included as part of the cumulative-effect adjustment is to be disclosed.

Question 64: If the average remaining service period of active plan participants is longer than 20 years, may an employer elect to use a transition period that is shorter than the average remaining service period?

Answer: No. If the average remaining service period is longer than 20 years, this longer period must be used to amortize the transition obligation. However, the employer may choose a 20-year amortization period if the average remaining service period is shorter than 20 years.

CHAPTER 26
RESEARCH AND DEVELOPMENT COSTS

CONTENTS

IMPRESS™ Cross-References	**26.02**
Overview	**26.03**
FTB 84-1: Accounting for Stock Issued to Acquire the Results of a Research and Development Arrangement	**26.04**
Background	**26.04**
Standards	**26.04**

CROSS-REFERENCES

1999 MILLER GAAP GUIDE: Chapter 41, "Research and Development Costs"

CHAPTER 26
RESEARCH AND DEVELOPMENT COSTS

OVERVIEW

Research and development (R&D) cost is carefully defined in the authoritative accounting literature. Once R&D costs are appropriately identified, GAAP require that they be expensed in the period incurred. Some costs related to R&D activities, however, are appropriately capitalized and carried forward as assets if they have alternative future uses. R&D-related assets typically include items of property, plant, and equipment and intangible assets used in the ongoing R&D effort of the enterprise.

The following pronouncements are the sources of GAAP for research and development costs that are included in the highest level of authority in the SAS-69 hierarchy:

FAS-2	Accounting for Research and Development Costs
FAS-68	Research and Development Arrangements
FAS-86	Accounting for the Costs of Computer Software to Be Sold, Leased, or Otherwise Marketed
FIN-4	Applicability of FASB Statement No. 2 to Business Combinations Accounted for by the Purchase Method
FIN-6	Applicability of FASB Statement No. 2 to Computer Software

The following additional source of GAAP that is in a lower level of the SAS-69 GAAP hierarchy is discussed in this Manual:

FTB 84-1	Accounting for Stock Issued to Acquire the Results of a Research and Development Arrangement (Level B)

FTB 84-1: Accounting for Stock Issued to Acquire the Results of a Research and Development Arrangement

BACKGROUND

When an enterprise that is a party to an R&D arrangement acquires the results of that arrangement in exchange for cash, common stock, or other consideration, the transaction is a purchase of tangible or intangible assets. Accounting questions have been raised about the appropriate accounting for those assets.

STANDARDS

Question: How should an enterprise account for stock issued to acquire the results of an R&D arrangement?

Answer: When an enterprise acquires the results of an R&D arrangement by issuing stock, the enterprise should record the stock at its fair value, or at the fair value of the consideration received, whichever is more readily determinable. This accounting is required whether the enterprise exchanges stock for the results of the research and development arrangement, for rights to use the results, or for ownership interests in the arrangement or a successor arrangement. The fair value should be determined at the date the enterprise exercises its option to acquire the results of the R&D arrangement.

CHAPTER 27
RESULTS OF OPERATIONS

CONTENTS

IMPRESS™ Cross-References	27.02
Overview	27.03
SOP 98-5: Reporting on the Costs of Start-Up Activities	27.04
Background	27.04
Standards	27.05
AIN-APB 9: Reporting the Results of Operations: Unofficial Accounting Interpretations of APB Opinion No. 9	27.05
Background	27.05
Standards	27.06
AIN-APB 30: Reporting the Results of Operations: Accounting Interpretations of APB Opinion No. 30	27.06
Background	27.06
Standards	27.06

CROSS-REFERENCES

1999 MILLER GAAP GUIDE: Chapter 42, "Results of Operations"

1999 MILLER GAAP IMPLEMENTATION MANUAL: EITF: Chapter 25, "Results of Operations"

1999 MILLER GOVERNMENTAL GAAP GUIDE: Chapter 5, "Governmental Financial Reporting"

1999 MILLER GAAP FOR NOT-FOR-PROFIT ORGANIZATIONS: Chapter 2, "Overview of Current Pronouncements"; Chapter 11, "Display of Certain GAAP Transactions"

CHAPTER 27
RESULTS OF OPERATIONS

OVERVIEW

Reporting the results of operations, primarily determining and presenting net income and comprehensive income, is one of the most important aspects of financial reporting. GAAP provide specific guidance concerning how certain items should be presented in the income statement.

The following pronouncements are the sources of GAAP for reporting the results of operations that are included in the highest level of authority in the SAS-69 hierarchy:

APB-9	Reporting the Results of Operations
APB-20	Accounting Changes
APB-30	Reporting the Results of Operations—Reporting the Effects of Disposal of a Segment of a Business, and Extraordinary, Unusual, and Infrequently Occurring Events and Transactions
FAS-16	Prior Period Adjustments
FAS-130	Reporting Comprehensive Income (effective for fiscal years beginning after December 15, 1997)
FIN-27	Accounting for a Loss on a Sublease

The following additional sources of GAAP that are in lower levels of the SAS-69 GAAP hierarchy are discussed in this Manual:

SOP 98-5	Reporting the Costs of Start-Up Activities (Level B)
AIN-APB 9	Reporting the Results of Operations: Unofficial Accounting Interpretations of APB Opinion No. 9 (Level D)
AIN-APB 30	Reporting the Results of Operations: Accounting Interpretations of APB Opinion No. 30 (Level D)

SOP 98-5: Reporting on the Costs of Start-Up Activities

BACKGROUND

SOP 98-5 is the second in a series of projects by the AcSEC to consider reporting the costs of activities that are undertaken to create future economic benefits. The first project led to SOP 93-7 (Reporting on Advertising Costs).

Start-up activities are defined broadly as those one-time activities related to all of the following:

- Opening a new facility
- Introducing a new product or service
- Conducting business in a new territory
- Conducting business with a new class of customer or beneficiary
- Initiating a new process in an existing facility
- Commencing some new operation
- Organizing a new entity (i.e., organization costs)

In practice, start-up costs are referred to in different ways, including preoperating costs and organization costs. In SOP 98-5, they are referred to as start-up costs.

Certain costs are not considered start-up costs and should be accounted for in accordance with existing authoritative accounting pronouncements. They include the following:

- Costs of acquiring or constructing long-lived assets and getting them ready for their intended use
- Costs of acquiring or producing inventory
- Costs of acquiring intangible assets
- Costs related to internally developed assets
- Costs that are covered by FAS-2 (Accounting for Research and Development Costs)
- Costs of fund-raising incurred by not-for-profit organizations
- Costs of raising capital
- Costs of advertising
- Costs incurred in connection with existing contracts in accordance with SOP 81-1 (Accounting for Performance of Construction-Type and Certain Production-Type Contracts)

STANDARDS

According to SOP 98-5, costs of start-up activities, including organization costs, are to be expensed as incurred.

The following pronouncements are amended by SOP 98-5 to incorporate the conclusion that costs of start-up activities should be expensed as incurred:

- SOP 81-1 (Accounting for Performance of Construction-Type and Certain Production-Type Contracts)
- SOP 88-1 (Accounting for Developmental and Preoperating Costs, Purchases and Exchanges of Take-off and Landing Slots, and Airframe Modifications)
- SOP 93-4 (Foreign Currency Accounting and Financial Statement Presentation for Investment Companies)
- Audit and Accounting Guide, *Audits of Casinos*
- Audit and Accounting Guide, *Construction Contractors*
- Audit and Accounting Guide, *Audits of Federal Government Contractors*
- Audit and Accounting Guide, *Audits of Investment Companies*
- Audit and Accounting Guide, *Guide for Prospective Financial Information*
- Industry Audit Guide, *Audits of Airlines*

SOP 98-5 is effective for financial statements for fiscal years beginning after December 15, 1998, with earlier application encouraged. Restatement of previously issued financial statements is not permitted.

AIN-APB 9: Reporting the Results of Operations: Unofficial Accounting Interpretations of APB Opinion No. 9

BACKGROUND

AIN-APB 9 addresses whether a regulatory-agency requirement to recognize a particular write-off as an extraordinary loss is applicable in reports to shareholders.

STANDARDS

Question: The Interstate Commerce Commission has ruled that railroads must write off certain receivables from other railroads as extraordinary losses. Is this accounting treatment appropriate for annual reports to shareholders and for annual reports of entities other than railroads?

Answer: No. Regulatory authorities often rule on the accounting treatment of companies under their jurisdiction. Despite the appropriateness of this practice for regulatory reporting purposes, APB-9, as amended by APB-30, specifies that, regardless of size, losses from receivables do not constitute extraordinary losses. Treatment of uncollectible receivables as an extraordinary item in the financial statements should result in a qualified audit opinion.

AIN-APB 30: Reporting the Results of Operations: Accounting Interpretations of APB Opinion No. 30

BACKGROUND

AIN-APB 30 presents three issues that pertain to the application of APB-30.

STANDARDS

Question 1: What factors should be considered in determining whether a particular event or transaction (*a*) is an extraordinary item or (*b*) should otherwise be set forth in the income statement? How are these factors applied in practice?

Answer: The first question that should be asked is whether the transaction involves the sale, abandonment, or other disposal of a segment of a business. These transactions should be presented separately, but not as extraordinary items. In this context, a segment is a separate major line of business or class of customer. AIN-APB 30 presents four examples of transactions that qualify for presentation as the disposal of a segment. For example, the sale by a diversified company of a major division that represents the company's only activities in the electronics industry would be presented as the disposal of a segment if the division's assets and results of operations are separately identified for internal reporting purposes. AIN-APB 30 also provides four examples of transactions that are not segment disposals under APB-30. For example, a petrochemical company's sale of a 25% interest in a petrochemical plant that is accounted for as a corporate joint venture would not be a segment disposal if the remaining activities of the company are in the same line of business.

If it is determined that the transaction is not a segment disposal, the second question that should be asked is whether the criteria for extraordinary classification (i.e., unusual in nature and infrequent in occurrence) are met? AIN-APB 30 presents four examples each of transactions that do and do not meet the APB-30 criteria. For example, if a large portion of a tobacco manufacturer's crops are destroyed by a hail storm in a locality where hail storms are rare, the criterion for extraordinary classification would be met. On the other hand, if a citrus grower's Florida crop is damaged by frost and experience indicates that frost damage occurs every three or four years, the criterion of infrequent occurrence is not met and the loss would not be presented as extraordinary.

Question 2: APB-30 states that events and transactions that were reported as extraordinary items in statements of income for fiscal years ending before October 1, 1973, should not be restated, except that a statement of income including operations of discontinued segments of a business may be reclassified in comparative statements to conform to APB-30. If a gain or loss on such a disposal in a prior year was classified as an extraordinary item, but not computed in accordance with APB-30, should the prior-year income statement be reclassified and the gain or loss adjusted to comply with APB-30?

Answer: No. Reclassification as described in Question 2 is optional. There should not be a redetermination of net income using the measurement principles of APB-30. The method of computing the gain or loss on disposals of a segment should not be retroactively applied if it results in a change in net income of a prior year.

Question 3: If a company sells a portion of a business that does not meet the definition of a *segment* under APB-30, should the gain or loss be calculated using the measurement principles for determining the gain or loss on disposal of a segment in APB-30?

Answer: Yes. The gain or loss on the sale of a portion of a line of business that does not qualify as a segment under APB-30 should be calculated using the same measurement principles that would be used if it were a segment of a business. Such gains and losses are not extraordinary items, but they may require separate disclosure in a manner that keeps them from being confused with discontinued operations or extraordinary items. Revenues, costs, and expenses of that part of the business should not be segregated on the face of the income statement but may be disclosed in notes to the financial statements.

CHAPTER 28
REVENUE RECOGNITION

CONTENTS

IMPRESS™ Cross-References	28.02
Overview	28.03
FTB 90-1: Accounting for Separately Priced Extended Warranty and Product Maintenance Contracts	28.03
Background	28.03
Standards	28.04

CROSS-REFERENCES

1999 Miller GAAP Implementation Manual: Chapter 20, "Long-Term Construction Contracts"

1999 Miller GAAP Guide: Chapter 31, "Long-Term Construction Contracts"; Chapter 43, "Revenue Recognition"

1999 Miller GAAP Implementation Manual: EITF: Chapter 26, "Revenue Recognition"

1999 Miller Governmental GAAP Guide: Chapter 9, "Revenues"

1999 Miller GAAP for Not-for-Profit Organizations: Chapter 2, "Overview of Current Pronouncements"; Chapter 3, "Revenues"; Chapter 9, "Note Disclosures"

CHAPTER 28
REVENUE RECOGNITION

OVERVIEW

GAAP, as well as recognized industry practices, generally call for revenue recognition at the point of sale. One aspect of a sale that complicates this generally simple rule is a right of return on the part of the buyer. Revenue from sales in which a right of return exists is recognized at the time of sale only if certain specified conditions are met. If those conditions are met, sales revenue and cost of sales are reduced to reflect estimated returns and costs of those returns. If they are not met, revenue recognition is postponed.

The following pronouncement, which is the source of GAAP for revenue recognition when the right of return exists, is included in the highest level of authority in the SAS-69 hierarchy:

FAS-48   Revenue Recognition When Right of Return Exists

The following additional source of GAAP that is in a lower level of the SAS-69 GAAP hierarchy is discussed in this Manual:

FTB 90-1   Accounting for Separately Priced Extended Warranty and Product Maintenance Contracts (Level B)

FTB 90-1: Accounting for Separately Priced Extended Warranty and Product Maintenance Contracts

BACKGROUND

An *extended warranty* is an agreement to provide warranty protection in addition to that covered in the manufacturer's original warranty, if any, or to extend the period of coverage beyond that provided by the manufacturer's warranty. A *product maintenance contract* is an agreement to perform certain agreed-upon services to maintain a product for a specified period. Some contracts cover both an extended warranty and product maintenance. A *separately priced contract* is one in which the customer has the option to purchase the services provided under the contract for a stated amount that is separate from the price of the product.

STANDARDS

Question: How should revenue and costs from a separately priced extended warranty or a product maintenance contract be recognized?

Answer: Revenue should be deferred and recognized over the contract period on a straight-line basis, except when sufficient historical evidence indicates that the costs of performing under the contract are incurred in a pattern other than straight-line. In those circumstances, revenue should be recognized over the contract period in proportion to the costs expected to be incurred in performing the services required under the contract.

Costs that are directly related to the acquisition of the contract and that would not have been incurred if the contract had not existed should be deferred and charged to expense in proportion to the revenue recognized. All other costs should be charged to expense as incurred.

A loss exists if the total of the expected costs of providing services under the contract and unamortized acquisition costs exceeds the related unearned revenue. A loss is recognized by first charging any unamortized acquisition costs to expense and then by recognizing a liability for the excess.

CHAPTER 29
SEGMENT REPORTING

CONTENTS

IMPRESS™ Cross-References	29.02
Overview	29.03
FTB 79-4: Segment Reporting of Puerto Rican Operations	29.04
Background	29.04
Standards	29.04
FTB 79-5: Meaning of the Term "Customer" as It Applies to Health Care Facilities under FASB Statement No. 14	29.04
Background	29.04
Standards	29.04
FTB 79-8: Applicability of FASB Statements 21 and 33 to Certain Brokers and Dealers in Securities	29.05
Background	29.05
Standards	29.05

CROSS-REFERENCES

1999 MILLER GAAP GUIDE: Chapter 44, "Segment Reporting"

1999 MILLER GOVERNMENTAL GAAP GUIDE: Chapter 26, "Proprietary Funds"

1999 MILLER GAAP FOR NOT-FOR-PROFIT ORGANIZATIONS: Chapter 7, "Organizational Issues"; Chapter 11, "Display of Certain GAAP Transactions"

CHAPTER 29
SEGMENT REPORTING

OVERVIEW

The term *segment reporting* refers to the presentation of information about certain parts of an enterprise, in contrast to information about the entire enterprise. The need for segment information became increasingly apparent in the 1960s and 1970s as enterprises diversified their activities into different industries and product lines, as well as into different geographic areas. Financial analysts and other groups of financial statement users insisted on the importance of disaggregated information—in order for them to assess risk and perform other types of analyses. These needs resulted in the issuance of FAS-14 (Financial Reporting for Segments of a Business Enterprise) and several other pronouncements that amended FAS-14, which together provide the authoritative literature in effect through 1997. Beginning in 1998, the following pronouncement is the source of GAAP for segment reporting that is included in the highest level of authority in the SAS-69 hierarchy:

FAS-131   Disclosures about Segments of an Enterprise and Related Information (effective for financial statements for periods beginning after December 15, 1997)

The following additional sources of GAAP that are in lower levels of the SAS-69 GAAP hierarchy are discussed in this Manual:

FTB 79-4   Segment Reporting of Puerto Rican Operations (Level B)

FTB 79-5   Meaning of the Term "Customer" as It Applies to Health Care Facilities under FASB Statement No. 14 (Level B)

FTB 79-8   Applicability of FASB Statements 21 and 33 to Certain Brokers and Dealers in Securities (Level B)

FTB 79-4: Segment Reporting of Puerto Rican Operations

BACKGROUND

FAS-14 requires disclosure of certain information about an enterprise's foreign operations and export sales. The Statement further indicates that foreign operations include those revenue-producing operations that are located outside the enterprise's home country (e.g., the United States for U.S. enterprises).

STANDARDS

Question: Are Puerto Rican operations and operations in other areas under U.S. sovereignty or jurisdiction (e.g., Virgin Islands, American Samoa) considered foreign for purposes of applying FAS-14?

Answer: Puerto Rican operations, as well as those in other non-self-governing U.S. territories, should be considered domestic operations. Factors such as proximity, economic affinity, and similarities of business environments indicate this classification for these operations.

FTB 79-5: Meaning of the Term "Customer" as It Applies to Health Care Facilities under FASB Statement No. 14

BACKGROUND

FAS-14 requires disclosure when 10% or more of an enterprise's revenue is derived from sales to any single customer. The disclosures should state that fact and should give the amount of revenue derived from each customer. A group of customers under common control is considered a single customer.

STANDARDS

Question: Is an insuring entity (e.g., Blue Cross) considered a "customer" of a health care facility?

Answer: An insuring entity should not be considered a customer of a health care facility as the term *customer* is used in FAS-14. The fact that the insuring entity is a paying agent for the patient does not make the insuring entity the customer of the health care facility. The paying entity does not decide which services to purchase and from whom those services will be purchased.

FTB 79-8: Applicability of FASB Statements 21 and 33 to Certain Brokers and Dealers in Securities

BACKGROUND

FAS-21 (Suspension of the Reporting of Earnings per Share and Segment Information by Nonpublic Enterprises) suspends the requirement of FAS-14 for nonpublic entities. To be considered a nonpublic entity, an enterprise must not be required to file financial statements with the Securities and Exchange Commission (SEC).

STANDARDS

Question: Should closely held brokers and dealers in securities that file financial statements with the SEC be considered nonpublic for purposes of applying FAS-21?

Answer: The fact that a broker or a dealer must file financial statements with the SEC does not make an otherwise nonpublic enterprise a public enterprise for purposes of FAS-21.

CHAPTER 30
STOCKHOLDERS' EQUITY

CONTENTS

IMPRESS™ Cross-References	**30.02**
Overview	**30.03**
FTB 85-6: Accounting for a Purchase of Treasury Shares at a Price Significantly in Excess of the Current Market Price of the Shares and the Income Statement Classification of Costs Incurred in Defending against a Takeover Attempt	**30.04**
Background	**30.04**
Standards	**30.04**
Purchase Price in Excess of Market Price	**30.04**
Agreements with a Shareholder or Former Shareholder Not to Purchase Additional Shares	**30.04**
Costs of Defense and "Standstill" Agreement in a Takeover Attempt	**30.05**
PB-14: Accounting and Reporting by Limited Liability Companies and Limited Liability Partnerships	**30.05**
Background	**30.05**
Standards	**30.06**
Recognition of Assets and Liabilities	**30.06**
Financial Statement Display	**30.06**
Disclosures	**30.07**

30.02 *Stockholders' Equity*

IMPRESS™

CROSS-REFERENCES

1999 MILLER GAAP IMPLEMENTATION MANUAL: Chapter 31, "Stock Issued to Employees"

1999 MILLER GAAP GUIDE: Chapter 45, "Stockholders' Equity"

1999 MILLER GAAP IMPLEMENTATION MANUAL: EITF: Chapter 27, "Stockholders' Equity"

CHAPTER 30
STOCKHOLDERS' EQUITY

OVERVIEW

The various elements constituting stockholders' equity in the statement of financial position are classified according to source. Stockholders' equity may be classified broadly into four categories: (1) legal capital, (2) additional paid-in capital, (3) minority interests, and (4) retained earnings. Detailed information is presented in the body of the statement, in related notes, or in some combination thereof.

The following pronouncements are the sources of GAAP for stockholders' equity that are included in the highest level of authority in the SAS-69 hierarchy:

ARB-43	Chapter 1, Prior Opinions
	A. Rules Adopted by Membership
	B. Opinions Issued by Predecessor Committee
APB-6	Status of Accounting Research Bulletins, Paragraph 12, Treasury Stock
APB-12	Omnibus Opinion—1967, Paragraphs 9 and 10, Capital Changes
APB-14	Paragraph 16, Debt with Stock Purchase Warrants
FAS-129	Disclosure of Information about Capital Structure (Effective for financial statements for periods ending after December 15, 1997)

The following additional sources of GAAP that are in lower levels of the SAS-69 GAAP hierarchy are discussed in this Manual:

FTB 85-6	Accounting for a Purchase of Treasury Shares at a Price Significantly in Excess of the Current Market Price of the Shares and the Income Statement Classification of Costs Incurred in Defending against a Takeover Attempt (Level B)
PB-14	Accounting and Reporting by Limited Liability Companies and Limited Liability Partnerships (Level C)

ity

FTB 85-6: Accounting for a Purchase of Treasury Shares at a Price Significantly in Excess of the Current Market Price of the Shares and the Income Statement Classification of Costs Incurred in Defending against a Takeover Attempt

BACKGROUND

Most treasury stock transactions engaged in by an enterprise are solely capital transactions and do not involve recognition of revenue and expense. In some cases, however, treasury stock transactions may involve the receipt or payment of consideration in exchange for rights or privileges, which may require recognition of revenue or expense. FTB 85-6 was issued to clarify this and other issues that may arise in a takeover attempt.

STANDARDS

Purchase Price in Excess of Market Price

Question 1: How should a company account for a purchase of treasury shares at a price that is significantly in excess of the current market price of the shares?

Answer: This situation creates an assumption that the purchase price includes amounts attributable to items other than the shares purchased. The price paid in excess of the current market price of the shares should be attributed to the other elements in the transaction. If the fair value of those other elements is more clearly evident than the market value of the stock, the former amount should be assigned to those elements and the difference should be recorded as the cost of the treasury shares. If no stated or unstated consideration in addition to the capital stock can be identified, the entire purchase price should be assigned to the treasury stock.

Agreements with a Shareholder or Former Shareholder Not to Purchase Additional Shares

Question 2: Should amounts an enterprise pays to a shareholder (or former shareholder) that are attributed to an agreement precluding that shareholder (or former shareholder) from purchasing additional shares be capitalized as assets and amortized over the period of the agreement?

Answer: No, such payments should be expensed as incurred.

Costs of Defense and "Standstill" Agreement in a Takeover Attempt

Question 3: Should the costs a company incurs to defend itself in a takeover attempt or the costs of a "standstill" agreement be classified as extraordinary?

Answer: No. Neither meets the criteria for an *extraordinary* item as defined in APB-30 (Reporting the Results of Operations—Reporting the Effects of Disposal of a Segment of a Business, and Extraordinary, Unusual, and Infrequently Occurring Events and Transactions).

PB-14: Accounting and Reporting by Limited Liability Companies and Limited Liability Partnerships

BACKGROUND

Limited liability companies and limited liability partnerships (referred to hereafter as LLCs) are formed under the laws of individual states and therefore have characteristics that are not uniform. Generally, however, they have the following characteristics:

- They are unincorporated associations of two or more persons.
- Their members have limited personal liability for the obligations of the LLC.
- They are treated as partnerships for federal income tax purposes.
- At least two of the following corporate characteristics are lacking:
  — Limited liability
  — Free transferability of interests
  — Centralized management
  — Continuity of life

PB-14 provides guidance for U.S. LLCs that prepare financial statements in accordance with generally accepted accounting principles.

STANDARDS

Recognition of Assets and Liabilities

- When an LLC is formed by the combining of entities under common control or by conversion from another type of entity, assets and liabilities should be initially stated at the amounts at which they were stated in the financial statements of the predecessor entities (i.e., treated in the same manner as a pooling of interests).
- An LLC that is subject to U.S. federal, foreign, state, or local taxes (including franchise taxes) must account for those taxes in accordance with FAS-109 (Accounting for Income Taxes), including accounting for a change in tax status.

Financial Statement Display

- A complete set of financial statements must include the following:
  — Statement of financial position
  — Statement of operations
  — Statement of cash flows
  — Notes to financial statements
- Disclosure is required of changes in members' equity for the period, either in a separate statement or in notes to the financial statements.
- The equity section of the statement of financial position is referred to as "members' equity." Information about the different classes of members' equity is required, including the amount of each class, stated separately, either in the financial statements (preferable) or in notes to the financial statements (acceptable).
- If the members' equity is less than zero, the deficit should be reported, even though the members' liability may be limited.
- If the LLC maintains separate accounts for components of members' equity (e.g., undistributed earnings, earnings available for withdrawal, unallocated capital), disclosure of these accounts is required in the financial statements or notes.

- If the LLC records amounts due from members for capital contributions, such amounts receivable should generally be presented as deductions from members' equity, with the very limited exception of instances where there is substantial evidence of ability and intent to pay within a reasonably short period.
- Comparative financial statements are encouraged, but not required. Any exceptions to comparability must be disclosed in the notes to the financial statements.
- If the formation of an LLC results in a new reporting entity, APB-20 (Accounting Changes) should be followed with regard to a change in reporting entity (i.e., retroactive restatement of comparative statements).

Disclosures

- The following information is required to be disclosed:
  — Description of any limitation of members' liability
  — The different classes of members' interests and the respective rights, preferences, and privileges of each class
  — The amount of each class of members' equity included in the statement of financial position
  — If the LLC has a limited life, the date on which the LLC will cease to exist
- In the first year after an LLC is formed by the combining of entities under common control or by conversion from another type of entity, notes to the financial statements must disclose that fact and the transaction(s) giving rise to the LLC.

CHAPTER 31
STOCK ISSUED TO EMPLOYEES

CONTENTS

IMPRESS Cross-References	**31.02**
Overview	**31.03**
SOP 76-3: Accounting Practices for Certain Employee Stock Ownership Plans	**31.04**
Background	**31.04**
Standards	**31.05**
SOP 93-6: Employers' Accounting for Employee Stock Ownership Plans	**31.06**
Background	**31.06**
Standards	**31.07**
Accounting for Leveraged ESOPs	**31.07**
Purchase of Shares	**31.07**
Release of ESOP Shares—General	**31.08**
Release of ESOP Shares—Direct Compensation of Employees	**31.09**
Release of ESOP Shares—Satisfaction of Other Employee Benefits	**31.09**
Release of ESOP Shares—Replacement of Dividends on Allocated Shares When Such Dividends Are Used to Service Debt	**31.09**
Determination of Fair Value	**31.09**
Dividends on Unallocated ESOP Shares	**31.10**
Dividends on Allocated ESOP Shares	**31.10**
Redemption of ESOP Shares	**31.10**
Reporting of Debt and Interest—General	**31.10**
Reporting of Debt and Interest—Direct Loan	**31.11**
Recording of Debt and Interest—Indirect Loan	**31.11**
Recording of Debt and Interest—Employer Loan	**31.11**
Earnings per Share	**31.12**
Accounting for Nonleveraged ESOPs	**31.15**
Purchase of Shares	**31.15**
Dividends	**31.15**

Redemptions	**31.15**
Earnings per Share	**31.15**
Income Taxes	**31.16**
Accounting for Pension Reversion ESOPs	**31.16**
Disclosures	**31.16**
Examples	**31.17**
Illustration of a Common-Stock Leveraged ESOP with a Direct Loan	**31.18**
Illustration of a Common-Stock Nonleveraged ESOP	**31.25**
FTB 97-1: Accounting under Statement 123 for Certain Employee Stock Purchase Plans with a Look-Back Option	**31.28**
Background	**31.28**
Standards	**31.29**
Illustration of Look-Back Option without Dividends	**31.29**
Illustration of Look-Back Option with Dividends	**31.30**
FTB 97-1 Questions and Answers	**31.30**
AIN-APB 25: Accounting for Stock Issued to Employees: Accounting Interpretations of APB Opinion No. 25	**31.33**

CROSS-REFERENCES

1999 GAAP IMPLEMENTATION MANUAL: Chapter 30, "Stockholders' Equity"

1999 MILLER GAAP GUIDE: Chapter 46, "Stock Issued to Employees"

1999 MILLER GAAP IMPLEMENTATION MANUAL: EITF: Chapter 28, "Stock Compensation to Employees and Others"

CHAPTER 31
STOCK ISSUED TO EMPLOYEES

OVERVIEW

Stock issued to employees may include compensation (compensatory plan) or may not include compensation (noncompensatory plan). A *compensatory plan* is one in which services rendered by employees are partially compensated for by the issuance of stock. The measurement of compensation expense included in compensatory plans is the primary problem encountered in accounting for stock issued to employees.

The following pronouncements are the sources of GAAP for stock issued to employees that are included in the highest level of authority in the SAS-69 hierarchy:

APB-25	Accounting for Stock Issued to Employees
ARB-43	Chapter 13B, Compensation Involved in Stock Option and Stock Purchase Plans
FAS-123	Accounting for Stock-Based Compensation
FIN-28	Accounting for Stock Appreciation Rights and Other Variable Stock Option or Award Plans
FIN-38	Determining the Measurement Date for Stock Option, Purchase, and Award Plans Involving Junior Stock

The following additional sources of GAAP that are in lower levels of the SAS-69 GAAP hierarchy are discussed in this Manual:

SOP 76-3	Accounting Practices for Certain Employee Stock Ownership Plans
SOP 93-6	Employers' Accounting for Employee Stock Ownership Plans
FTB 97-1	Accounting under Statement 123 for Certain Employee Stock Purchase Plans with a Look-Back Option
AIN-APB 25	Accounting for Stock Issued to Employees: Accounting Interpretations of APB Opinion No. 25

SOP 76-3: Accounting Practices for Certain Employee Stock Ownership Plans

BACKGROUND

An employee stock ownership plan (ESOP) is an employee benefit plan sponsored under the provisions of the Employee Retirement Income Security Act (ERISA) of 1974. An ESOP can be either a qualified stock bonus plan or a combination of a qualified stock bonus plan and a money purchase pension plan. In both cases, the ESOP is expected to invest primarily in "qualifying employer securities."

At the time SOP 76-3 was issued, there were two essential differences between an ESOP and other qualified stock bonus plans. First, the ESOP generally is permitted to borrow money for the purpose of purchasing the employer's stock. Second, the allowable investment tax credit percentage that the employer can claim may increase by as much as 1.5% if that amount is contributed to the ESOP.

In borrowing money for the purpose of purchasing the employer's stock, the ESOP typically would borrow from a bank or another commercial lender. The employer shares purchased could be outstanding shares, treasury shares, or newly issued shares. The ESOP would hold these shares until they were distributed to employees. The shares may be allocated to individual employees even though the actual shares may not be distributed until a later date. In some cases, the ESOP would issue notes to existing shareholders in exchange for their stock.

The employer typically collateralizes the ESOP debt by pledging the stock (purchased from the debt proceeds), and by either guaranteeing or committing to make ESOP contributions sufficient to service the related debt. The employer's annual contribution to the ESOP is tax-deductible (subject to certain limitations). The employer's annual contribution is used to fund (1) amortization of the debt principal, (2) interest payments on the debt, (3) working capital needs, and (4) other expenses. If the employer's annual ESOP contribution exceeds items 1–4, the excess can be used to purchase additional employer securities.

SOP 76-3 was issued because several accounting questions arose relating to ESOPs that borrowed money from a bank or other lender to acquire shares, or that issued notes directly to existing shareholders in exchange for their shares.

STANDARDS

The provisions of SOP 76-3 were largely superseded by SOP 93-6 (Employers' Accounting for Employee Stock Ownership Plans). However, shares acquired by an ESOP before December 31, 1992, or shares acquired after that date that were committed to be released before the beginning of the year in which SOP 93-6 was adopted, can continue to be accounted for under the guidance in SOP 76-3.

If the employer has either guaranteed or committed to funding the ESOP in a manner sufficient to cover debt service payments, the related debt (i.e., obligation of the ESOP) is to be recorded as a liability on the employer's balance sheet. The AcSEC concluded that the employer's guarantee or commitment was in substance the assumption of the ESOP's debt; as such, the related debt amount should be shown as a liability in the employer's financial statements.

The offsetting debit that the employer records upon recognizing a liability for the ESOP's debt is to shareholders' equity. The employer does not recognize the assets of the ESOP; employees of the ESOP—not the employer—own these assets.

As the ESOP makes payments on its debt, the employer is to reduce its liability. As the employer reduces its liability, the offsetting credit is to shareholders' equity. Symmetry should exist between the liability for ESOP-related debt and the corresponding entry to shareholders' equity.

The annual ESOP contribution (or contribution commitment) that the employer makes is recognized as an expense. This requirement applies to all ESOPs—whether the ESOP has borrowed money from a bank or another lender or has issued a note directly to existing shareholders for their shares. The employer's contribution or contribution commitment is recognized in the year it was made, regardless of whether such contribution is concurrently used to reduce the ESOP's debt.

The expense is to be divided between interest expense and compensation expense, and the employer should disclose the interest rate and terms of the ESOP's debt in its financial statements (since SOP 76-3 essentially views such debt as that of the employer).

The employer should treat all shares held by the ESOP as outstanding for the purpose of calculating the employer's earnings per share (whether or not the shares have been allocated to individual employees). The employer should charge all dividends pertaining to shares held by the ESOP to retained earnings.

If the employer receives any additional investment tax credit (ITC) as a result of an ESOP contribution, such incremental ITC is to be recorded as a reduction in income tax expense in the year that the applicable ESOP contribution is made. This accounting treatment applies regardless of the method generally utilized by the employer in accounting for the ITC (flow-through or deferral) for property acquisitions.

SOP 93-6: Employers' Accounting for Employee Stock Ownership Plans

BACKGROUND

An employee stock ownership plan (ESOP) is an employee benefit plan described by the Employee Retirement Income Security Act (ERISA) of 1974 and the Internal Revenue Code of 1986. An ESOP can be either a qualified stock bonus plan or a combination of a qualified stock bonus plan and a money purchase pension plan. In both cases, the ESOP is expected to invest primarily in stock of the sponsoring employer.

SOP 73-6, which was issued in December 1976, primarily provided accounting and reporting guidance for leveraged ESOPs. SOP 93-6, which supersedes it, must be applied for ESOP shares acquired after December 30, 1992; at the company's discretion, it can be applied to ESOP shares acquired before December 31, 1992. Alternatively, SOP 76-3 can continue to be applied to ESOP shares acquired before December 31, 1992. A number of changes affecting ESOPs occurred between the release of SOP 76-3 and the issuance of SOP 93-6. For instance, Congress passed a number of laws affecting ESOPs, and numerous regulatory changes in this area have emanated from the Internal Revenue Service and from the U.S. Department of Labor. A number of these changes sparked a substantial growth in the number of ESOPs. Not only has the number of ESOPs grown, but also their complexity has increased. ESOPs are now formed for a number of different purposes:

1. To fund a matching program for one or more employee benefit plans of the sponsor (e.g., 401(k) savings plan, formula-based profit-sharing plan)
2. To raise new capital or to create a market for the existing stock
3. To replace benefits lost from the termination of other employee benefit plans (e.g., retirement plans, other postretirement benefit plans)
4. To help finance a leveraged buy-out
5. To be used by owners to terminate their ownership interests in the entity on a tax-advantaged basis
6. To be used as a deterrent against hostile takeovers

The financing of ESOPs also has changed significantly since SOP 76-3 was issued. When SOP 76-3 was issued, ESOP borrowing was typically from an outside lender. In today's environment, it is not unusual for an ESOP to be internally leveraged (the ESOP borrows from the employer sponsoring the ESOP, with or without an outside loan to the employer). In addition, some ESOPs use dividends on shares held by the ESOP largely to fund required debt payments. When SOP 76-3 was issued, most debt repayments were funded through employer contributions.

Finally, the AcSEC issued SOP 93-6 to resolve some continuing controversies regarding the measurement of compensation cost and how dividends on shares held by the ESOP should be treated. These two issues had been problematic since the issuance of SOP 76-3.

STANDARDS

The conclusions in SOP 93-6 apply to all ESOPs, both leveraged and nonleveraged. SOP 93-6 provides guidance to the employer that sponsors the ESOP. Accounting guidance for the ESOP itself can be found in the AICPA Audit and Accounting Guide titled *Audits of Employee Benefit Plans* (see *Miller GAAS Guide* for coverage of this AICPA Accounting and Auditing Guide).

The accounting for leveraged and nonleveraged ESOPs are discussed separately on the following pages. In addition, pension reversion ESOPs, the disclosures required by SOP 93-6, and the required method of transition from SOP 76-3 to SOP 93-6 are covered.

Accounting for Leveraged ESOPs

A leveraged ESOP borrows money to acquire shares of the employer sponsoring the ESOP. An ESOP may borrow either from the employer sponsor or directly from an outside lender. The shares acquired from the debt proceeds initially are held in a suspense account (i.e., they are not immediately allocated to the accounts of employees participating in the ESOP). The ESOP's debt is liquidated through (a) contributions of the employer to the ESOP and (b) dividends on the employer's stock held by the ESOP. As the ESOP's debt is repaid, shares are released from the suspense account. Released shares must be allocated to participants' accounts by the end of the ESOP's fiscal year.

Purchase of Shares

The ESOP may purchase either newly issued shares or treasury shares from the employer. The employer should record the issuance or sale of shares to the ESOP at the time it occurs, based on the fair value of its shares at that time. The offsetting debit is to unearned ESOP shares, a contra-equity account, which is to be shown as a separate line item on the employer's balance sheet.

In some cases, the ESOP may acquire shares of the employer through secondary market purchases. Even in this case, the employer should debit unearned ESOP shares for the cost of the shares purchased by the ESOP. If the ESOP is internally leveraged (i.e., the ESOP has borrowed from the employer), the offsetting credit recorded by the employer is to cash. If the ESOP is externally leveraged (i.e., the ESOP has borrowed directly from an outside lender), the offsetting credit recorded by the employer is to an appropriately titled debt account.

Release of ESOP Shares—General

ESOP shares are released for one or more of three purposes: (1) to compensate employees directly, (2) to settle a liability for other employee benefits, and (3) to replace dividends on allocated shares when these dividends are used to pay debt service.

The allocation of shares to employees typically is based on employee service. The number of shares to be released for each period (quarter or year) of employee service is usually specified in ESOP documents. As employees provide services, the release of ESOP shares is earned (hence they are committed to be released whether or not they have yet to be legally released). ESOP shares are legally released for distribution to participant accounts when debt payments are made.

When shares are committed to be released (which may occur before the shares are legally released), unearned ESOP shares should be credited for the fair value of the shares to be released. The offsetting debit depends on the purpose for which the ESOP shares are being released. If the committed-to-be-released shares relate to employee compensation, the debit is to compensation cost. If the committed-to-be-released shares relate to the settlement of a liability for other employee benefits, the debit is to employee benefits payable. If the committed-to-be-released shares are to replace dividends on allocated shares, the debit is to dividends payable.

When shares are committed to be released, the offsetting credit to unearned ESOP shares is recorded based on the cost of these shares. Therefore, in most cases, the debit for committed-to-be-released shares, which is based on fair value, will differ from the credit for these same shares, which is based on cost. This difference is accounted for as a debit or credit to shareholders' equity, typically through the use of the additional paid-in capital account.

Release of ESOP Shares—Direct Compensation of Employees

As employees provide services over the accounting period (quarter or year), they ratably earn the right to receive ESOP shares. In essence, the commitment to release shares occurs ratably throughout the period. Therefore, compensation cost should be measured based on the average fair value of the stock over the relevant time period. Compensation cost recognized in previous interim periods should not be changed to reflect changes in the stock's fair value in later interim periods in the same fiscal year.

Release of ESOP Shares—Satisfaction of Other Employee Benefits

In some cases, an employer will settle its liability to provide other employee benefits by allocating shares of stock held by the ESOP to participant accounts. For example, some employers may allocate ESOP shares to satisfy a commitment to fund a 401(k) plan or a profit-sharing plan. The employer should recognize the expense and the liability for employee benefits (e.g., 401(k) contributions, profit-sharing contributions) in the same manner as if the ESOP was not used to fund the benefit. The employer should debit the liability account (for employee benefits) and credit unearned ESOP shares, when ESOP shares are committed to be released to settle the liability. The number of shares to be released depends on the amount of the liability and the fair value of the ESOP shares at the time the liability is settled.

Release of ESOP Shares—Replacement of Dividends on Allocated Shares When Such Dividends Are Used to Service Debt

Dividends on shares of stock already allocated to participants' accounts can be used to service debt. However, if dividends on allocated shares are used in this manner, unallocated shares with a fair value equal to the dividends diverted must be allocated to participants' accounts. When shares are committed to be released to replace the dividends on allocated shares used for debt service, the employer should debit dividends payable. In addition, only those dividends that pertain to shares already allocated are charged to retained earnings.

Determination of Fair Value

A number of the provisions of SOP 93-6 require the use of the fair value of the employer's stock. The fair value of such stock is the amount that would be received in a sale, in the normal course of business, between a willing buyer and a willing seller. If the stock is publicly traded, the market price of the stock is the best estimate of fair value. If the employer's stock is not publicly traded, the employer's best estimate of fair value should be used.

Dividends on Unallocated ESOP Shares

Dividends declared on unallocated ESOP shares are not charged against retained earnings by the employer. If dividends on unallocated shares are used for debt service, the employer debits debt and/or interest payable (the credit is to cash). In some cases, dividends on unallocated shares may be paid to participants or added to participants' accounts. In these cases, the offsetting debit is to compensation cost.

Dividends on Allocated ESOP Shares

Dividends declared on allocated ESOP shares are charged against retained earnings by the employer. The employer can satisfy its liability for the distribution of dividends in one of three ways: (1) by contributing cash to participant accounts; (2) by contributing additional shares, with a fair value equal to the amount of the dividends, to participant accounts; or (3) by releasing ESOP shares held in suspense, with a fair value equal to the amount of the dividends, to participant accounts.

Redemption of ESOP Shares

Employers are required to offer a put option to holders of ESOP shares that are not readily tradable (required for both leveraged and nonleveraged ESOPs). The employer is required to purchase the employee's stock at its fair value at the time the put option is exercised. The employer would record its purchase of the employee's stock in a manner identical to the purchase of treasury shares.

Reporting of Debt and Interest—General

The employer's accounting for ESOP-related debt and interest depends on the type of ESOP debt. The three types of ESOP-related debt can be described as follows:

1. *Direct loan*—The loan is from an outside lender to the ESOP.

2. *Indirect loan*—The loan is from the employer to the ESOP, and the employer borrows a comparable sum from an outside lender.
3. *Employer loan*—The loan is from the employer to the ESOP. There is no related outside borrowing by the employer.

Reporting of Debt and Interest—Direct Loan

The ESOP's liability to the lender should be recorded by the employer (in essence, the ESOP's debt is treated as the debt of the employer). In addition, accrued interest payable on the loan is recorded by the employer. Cash payments that the employer makes to the ESOP, which are to be used to service debt payments, are recorded as a reduction in the related debt and the accrued interest payable amounts. The employer should record the reduction in these two liability accounts when the ESOP remits a loan or interest payment to the lending institution. The source of the cash contribution from the employer to the ESOP does not affect this accounting treatment (i.e., the accounting treatment is as specified above, regardless of whether the source of cash is an employer contribution or dividends on ESOP stock).

Recording of Debt and Interest—Indirect Loan

Because the employer borrows from an outside lender, the employer obviously records this borrowing as a liability. In addition, in the case of an indirect loan, the ESOP has borrowed from the employer (typically an amount equal to what the employer has borrowed from an outside lender). Although the employer has a loan receivable from the ESOP, the employer does not recognize this asset in its financial statements. Since the employer does not record the loan receivable, the employer also does not recognize interest income. The employer may make a cash contribution to the ESOP for the purpose of funding the ESOP's debt repayments—concurrent payments from the ESOP back to the employer. Neither the cash contribution from the employer to the ESOP nor the concurrent debt repayment from the ESOP to the employer is recognized in the employer's financial statements.

Recording of Debt and Interest—Employer Loan

The employer has made a loan to the ESOP, and the employer has not borrowed a comparable amount from an unrelated lender. Although the employer has a note receivable, it is not recognized in the employer's financial statements. Therefore, interest income also is not recognized. (The ESOP's note payable, and related interest cost, also are not recognized in the employer's financial statements.)

Earnings per Share

Shares that are committed to be released are treated as outstanding in computing both basic and diluted earnings per share (EPS). Shares not committed to be released are not treated as outstanding in either computation.

ESOPs holding convertible preferred stock may encounter the following unique EPS issues (however, some complexity in this area has been reduced by the issuance of FAS-128 (Earnings per Share)):

1. How to compute the number of shares outstanding for the application of the if-converted method
2. How earnings applicable to common stock in if-converted computations should be adjusted for the effects of dividends on allocated shares used for debt service
3. Whether prior periods' EPS should be restated for a change in the conversion ratio

Convertible Preferred Stock—Number of Common Shares Outstanding The number of common shares that would be issued on conversion of preferred stock, where the convertible preferred stock is committed to be released, should be considered outstanding for the purpose of applying the if-converted method. This treatment applies to the computation of both basic and diluted EPS (assuming the effects are dilutive).

A participant's account balance may contain convertible preferred stock when it is withdrawn. The participant may be entitled to receive either (*a*) common stock or (*b*) cash with a value equal to (1) the fair value of convertible preferred stock or (2) a stated minimum value per share. The common stock that would have been issuable (upon conversion) may have a fair value that is less than the fair value of the convertible preferred stock or less than the stated minimum value per share. If this is the case, the participant will receive common stock or cash with a value greater than the fair value of the common stock that would have been issuable given the stated conversion rate. The presumption is that any shortfall will be made up by the issue of additional shares of common stock. However, this assumption can be overcome if past experience or a stated policy indicates that any shortfall will be paid in cash.

When the employee applies the if-converted method, the number of common shares issuable on assumed conversion is the greater of:

1. The shares issuable at the stated conversion rate *or*
2. The shares issuable if participants were to withdraw the convertible preferred shares from their accounts

The shares issuable if participants were to withdraw the convertible preferred shares from their accounts is to be computed as the ratio of:

1. The average fair value of the convertible stock or, if greater, its stated minimum value *to*
2. The average fair value of the common stock

Convertible Preferred Stock—Adjustment to Earnings If employers use dividends on allocated shares to pay debt service, earnings applicable to common shares should be adjusted for the purpose of applying the if-converted method. Earnings applicable to common stock would be adjusted for the difference (net of tax) between:

1. The amount of compensation cost reported *and*
2. The amount of compensation cost that would have been reported if the allocated shares had been converted to common stock at the beginning of the period

Convertible Preferred Stock—Changes in Conversion Rates Earnings per share for prior periods should not be restated for changes in conversion rates.

Accounting for income taxes Differences between book ESOP-related expense and the ESOP-related expense allowed for tax purposes may result from the following:

1. The fair value of committed-to-be-released shares is different from the cost of these shares *and/or*
2. The timing of expense recognition is different for book purposes than for tax purposes

In either case, the guidance in FAS-109 is to be followed. The tax effects of differences between book and tax reporting are to be recognized as a component of stockholders' equity (i.e., these differences do not give rise to deferred tax assets and liabilities).

If the cost of shares committed to be released exceeds their fair value, the expense deductible for tax purposes will exceed the book expense. The tax effect of this difference should be credited to stockholders' equity. If the cost of shares committed to be released is less than their fair value, the expense deductible for book purposes will exceed the expense deductible for tax purposes. The tax effect of this difference should be charged to stockholders' equity to the extent that prior credits to stockholder's equity that are related to cost exceed the fair value of shares that were committed to be released in previous years.

Dividends paid on ESOP shares frequently result in a tax deduction. The tax-advantaged nature of ESOPs is a contributing factor behind their growth. The tax benefit of tax-deductible dividends on allocated ESOP shares is to be recorded as a reduction in income tax expense from continuing operations.

Accounting for terminations If an ESOP is terminated, either in whole or in part, all outstanding debt related to the shares terminated must be repaid or refinanced. The ESOP may repay the debt through one or more of the following sources:

1. Employer contributions
2. Dividends on ESOP shares
3. Proceeds from selling suspense shares, either to the employer or to another party

The share of suspense shares to the employer is limited. The employer can purchase only those shares that have a fair value equal to the applicable unpaid debt. Any shares that remain must be allocated to participants' accounts.

For example, if the ESOP sells suspense shares and uses the proceeds to repay the debt, the employer would account for this transaction as follows:

1. Debit the book value of the debt and the accrued interest payable that relate to the shares being terminated.
2. Credit unearned ESOP shares for the cost of the shares being terminated.
3. Debit or credit any difference between employer contributions and dividends on ESOP shares to paid-in capital.

If the employer reacquires the suspense shares, the employer should account for the purchase in a manner similar to the purchase of treasury stock. The employer debits treasury stock based on the fair value of the suspense shares acquired (on the date the employer reacquires them). The employer credits unearned ESOP shares based on their cost. Any difference between the cost and the fair value of the suspense shares reacquired is assigned to paid-in capital.

If the fair value of the suspense shares on the termination date of the ESOP is greater than the ESOP's unpaid debt, the remaining suspense shares are released to participants. The release of these remaining suspense shares to participants is charged to compensation cost. The charge is equal to the fair value of the shares released to participants, determined as of the date the ESOP-related debt is extinguished.

Accounting for Nonleveraged ESOPs

A nonleveraged ESOP is less complex than a leveraged ESOP, and the accounting guidance on it is less complex and less voluminous. An employer contributes shares of its stock or cash to the ESOP for the benefit of employees. If the employer's contribution is cash, the ESOP uses the cash contribution to purchase employer securities. The employer shares that are donated or acquired by the ESOP may be outstanding shares, treasury shares, or newly issued shares. The shares held by the ESOP are allocated to participants' accounts; they are held by the ESOP and are distributed to employees at a future date (e.g., termination, and retirement). Shares obtained by the ESOP must be allocated to individual accounts by the ESOP's fiscal year-end.

Purchase of Shares

The employer records compensation cost based on the contribution that the terms of the plan require the employer make to the ESOP in the reporting period. Compensation cost includes the fair value of shares contributed, the fair value of shares committed to be contributed, cash contributed, and cash committed to be contributed.

Dividends

The employer should record a charge to retained earnings for dividends declared on shares held by a nonleveraged ESOP, with one exception to this requirement: Dividends on suspense account shares held by a pension reversion ESOP are to be accounted for in a manner similar to dividends on suspense account shares held by a leveraged ESOP.

Redemptions

As was the case with leveraged ESOPs, the employer is required to provide ESOP participants with put options if the employer shares held by the ESOP are not readily tradable. If a participant exercises his or her put option, the employer is to record the reacquisition of its stock from the participant in a manner similar to the purchase of treasury stock.

Earnings per Share

In general, all shares held by a nonleveraged ESOP are to be treated as outstanding by the employer in computing its earnings per share, with one exception: Suspense account shares of a pension reversion ESOP should not be treated as outstanding until they are committed to be released to participants' accounts.

Income Taxes

Compensation cost for financial reporting purposes may be accrued earlier than it is deductible for tax purposes, which creates a FAS-109 temporary difference.

Accounting for Pension Reversion ESOPs

An employer may terminate a defined benefit pension plan and recapture excess pension plan assets, although such a reversion of pension plan assets exposes the employer to an excise tax on the reversion of the pension assets. The employer may avoid some of the excise tax by transferring the pension assets to an ESOP (either new or existing, either leveraged or nonleveraged). The ESOP uses the (reverted) pension plan assets to acquire shares of the employer or to retire ESOP-related debt.

The ESOP may use the pension assets it receives to acquire shares of the employer. If the shares are acquired from the employer (either new shares or treasury shares), the employer would debit unearned ESOP shares (the offsetting credit is to common stock or treasury stock). If the shares are acquired on the secondary market, the employer would still debit unearned ESOP shares (the offsetting credit is to cash).

The ESOP may use the pension plan assets received on the reversion to repay debt. If this is the case, ESOP shares will be committed to be released from the suspense account. The guidance for leveraged ESOPs should be followed in determining the appropriate accounting. For instance, the employer will record the reduction in debt as it is repaid. The employer also will reduce the account "unearned ESOP shares" as these shares are committed to be released. How these committed-to-be-released shares are used determines the offsetting debit (see the earlier discussion on this issue for leveraged ESOPs).

Disclosures

An employer that sponsors an ESOP (both for leveraged and nonleveraged plans) is required to make the following disclosures:

1. A description of the ESOP, employee groups covered, the method of determining contributions, and the nature and ef-

fects of any significant changes that would affect comparability across periods

2. The accounting policies followed by the ESOP, which include the method of determining compensation, the classification of dividends on ESOP shares, and the treatment of ESOP shares for earnings per share computations
3. The amount of compensation cost for the period
4. As of the balance sheet date, the number of (*a*) allocated shares, (*b*) committed-to-be-released shares, and (*c*) suspense shares
5. As of the balance sheet date, the fair value of unearned ESOP shares
6. The existence and nature of any repurchase obligation (if such an obligation exists, the fair value of shares already allocated that are subject to the repurchase obligation)

Shares an ESOP acquires before December 31, 1992, can continue to be accounted for under the provisions of SOP 76-3. For employers that elect to continue to account for these "old shares" under SOP 76-3, the disclosures required by items 2 and 4 above need to be made separately for shares accounted for under SOP 93-6 and SOP 76-3. Also, the fair value of unearned ESOP shares as of the balance sheet date (item 5) does not have to be disclosed for "old shares."

For leveraged and pension reversion ESOPs only, the following additional disclosures are required:

1. The basis for releasing shares
2. How dividends on allocated and unallocated shares are used

Examples

Appendix A of SOP 93-6 provides a number of detailed examples on the application of this Statement. Accounting is illustrated for the following types of ESOPs: (1) a common-stock leveraged ESOP with a direct loan, (2) a common-stock leveraged ESOP used to fund the employer's match of a 401(k) savings plan with an indirect loan, (3) a common-stock nonleveraged ESOP, (4) a convertible-preferred-stock leveraged ESOP with a direct loan, and (5) a convertible, preferred-stock, leveraged ESOP used to fund a 401(k) savings plan with an employer loan. Appendix A of SOP 93-6 also presents an example of an ESOP termination and of the required ESOP note disclosures. The first illustration that follows is a simplified example of the accounting for a common-stock leveraged ESOP with a direct loan; the second illustration is for a common-stock nonleveraged ESOP.

31.18 *Stock Issued to Employees*

Illustration of a Common-Stock Leveraged ESOP with a Direct Loan

Neal and Neel (N&N) establish a common-stock leveraged ESOP with a direct loan on January 1, 1999. Relevant information regarding the ESOP is as follows:

1. The ESOP borrows $2,500,000 from an outside lender at 8% for four years. The proceeds are used to purchase 50,000 shares of newly issued N&N stock that has a market value of $50 per share.
2. The ESOP will fund the debt service with cash contributions from N&N and with dividends on the employer stock it holds.
3. Dividends on all shares of stock held by the ESOP, allocated and unallocated, are used for debt service.
4. N&N makes cash contributions to the ESOP at the end of each year.
5. The average market price of N&N's common stock during each year is as follows: 1999, $54; 2000, $47; 2001, $56; 2002, $60.
6. At the end of each quarter, N&N pays dividends of $.50 per share on its common stock. Therefore, dividends on ESOP shares are $100,000 per year (50,000 shares x $.50 dividend per share per quarter x 4 quarters per year). Since dividends on allocated shares are used for debt service, N&N must provide the ESOP with additional shares of common stock. The number of additional shares of common stock required is determined by dividing the dividends on allocated shares by the average market price of N&N's stock.
7. Both principal and interest payments on the ESOP's debt are due in equal annual installments at the end of each year. Yearly debt service is as follows:

Table 1—Debt Service

Year	Principal	Interest	Total Debt Service
1999	$ 554,802	$200,000	$ 754,802
2000	599,186	155,616	754,802
2001	647,121	107,681	754,802
2002	698,891	55,911	754,802
Total	$2,500,000	$519,208	$3,019,208

8. The number of shares of N&N stock released to participants' accounts each year is as follows:

Table 2—Shares Released for Compensation and Dividends

Year	Dividends	Compensation	Total
1999	0	12,500	12,500
2000	532	11,968	12,500
2001	893	11,607	12,500
2002	1250	11,250	12,500

The number of shares released for dividends is determined by dividing the amount of dividends on allocated shares (which are being used for debt service) by the average market price of the common stock during the year in question. For example, in the year 2000, 12,500 shares of common stock were allocated. Dividends on these 12,500 shares are $25,000 (12,500 shares x $2 per year). Dividing $25,000 by $47 (the average market price of N&N's common stock during 2000) results in the issuance of 532 shares during 2000 to replace the dividends on allocated shares used for debt service. In this example, the remaining shares are released as compensation to ESOP participants.

9. Shares released and allocated are based on total debt service payments made during the year (both principal and interest). Since 25% of debt service payments are made in each year, 25% of the shares (12,500) are released each year. Shares released in a particular year are allocated to participants' accounts during the next year. See Table 3.

Table 3—Shares Released and Allocated

Year	Cumulative Number of Shares Released	Cumulative Number of Shares Allocated	Average Shares Released	Year-End Suspense Shares
1999	12,500	0	6,250	37,500
2000	25,000	12,500	18,750	25,000
2001	37,500	25,000	31,250	12,500
2002	50,000	37,500	43,750	0

10. N&N's income before giving effect to the ESOP is as follows: 1999, $2,600,000; 2000, $2,800,000; 2001, $3,100,000; 2002, $3,200,000.

11. All interest cost and compensation cost are charged to expense each year.

31.20 *Stock Issued to Employees*

12. Excluding ESOP shares, the weighted average equivalent number of shares outstanding is 2,000,000 each year.
13. N&N's combined statutory tax rate is 36% each year.
14. The only book/tax difference is that associated with the ESOP.
15. No valuation allowance is necessary for any deferred tax asset.

The following tables and journal entries illustrate the results of applying SOP 93-6.

Table 4—Summary of the Effects of Applying SOP 93-6

Year	Principal	Unearned ESOP Shares	Paid-In Capital	Dividends	Interest Expense	Compensation Expense	Cash
Notes:	(1)	(2)	(3)	(4)	(1)	(5)	(6)
1999	$ 554,802	$ (625,000)	$ (50,000)	$ 0	$200,000	$ 675,000	$ (754,802)
2000	599,186	(625,000)	37,500	25,000	155,616	562,496	(754,802)
2001	647,121	(625,000)	(75,000)	50,000	107,681	649,992	(754,802)
2002	698,891	(625,000)	(125,000)	75,000	55,911	675,000	(754,802)
Total	$2,500,000	$(2,500,000)	$(212,500)	$150,000	$519,208	$2,562,488	$(3,019,208)

Notes:

(1) Principal paid and interest expense from Table 1.

(2) The credit to unearned ESOP shares is calculated by multiplying the number of ESOP shares released each year (12,500) by the cost of these shares to the ESOP ($50 per share).

(3) The debit or credit to paid-in capital is computed by multiplying the number of ESOP shares released each year (12,500) by the difference between the average market price per share (for the particular year) and the cost per share ($50). For example, in 1999 this calculation resulted in a $50,000 credit [($54 – $50) x 12,500].

(4) The dividend amount is calculated by multiplying the cumulative number of shares allocated (see Table 3) by the dividend per share, $2 per year.

(5) Compensation expense is computed by multiplying the number of shares released for compensation (see Table 2) by the average market price per share (for the particular year).

(6) The cash disbursed each year comprises a yearly contribution of $654,802 and $100,000 of dividends. Also note that this amount equals the yearly debt service.

Table 5—Tax Computations

	1999	2000	2001	2002
Current provision:				
Income before ESOP	$2,600,000	$2,800,000	$3,100,000	$3,200,000
ESOP contribution	(654,802)	(654,802)	(654,802)	(654,802)
ESOP dividends	(100,000)	(100,000)	(100,000)	(100,000)
Taxable income	$1,845,198	$2,045,198	$2,345,198	$2,445,198
Multiplied by 36%	664,271	736,271	844,271	880,271
Deferred provision:				
Reduction in unearned ESOP shares for financial reporting	$ 625,000	$ 625,000	$ 625,000	$ 625,000
Related tax deduction (1)	554,802	599,186	647,121	698,891
Difference	$ (70,198)	$ (25,814)	$ 22,121	$ 73,891
Tax rate	36%	36%	36%	36%
Deferred tax expense (benefit)	$ (25,271)	$ (9,293)	$ 7,964	$ 26,601

Notes:

(1) The tax deduction in computing the deferred income tax provision is equal to the amount of the principal repayment.

Table 6—Reconciliation of Effective Tax Rate to Provision for Income Taxes

	1999	2000	2001	2002
Pretax income	$1,725,000	$2,081,888	$2,342,327	$2,469,089
Tax at 36% (statutory rate)	621,000	749,480	843,238	888,872
Benefit of ESOP dividends (1)	0	(9,000)	(18,000)	(27,000)
Effect of difference between average fair value and cost of released shares (2)	18,000	—	27,000	45,000
Provision as reported	$ 639,000	$ 740,480	$ 852,238	$ 906,872

Notes:

(1) Computed by multiplying the yearly ESOP dividend amount (see Table 4) by the statutory tax rate, 36%.

31.22 Stock Issued to Employees

(2) Computed by multiplying the number of shares released during the year (12,500 each year) by the difference between the average market value during the year and the cost of the ESOP shares and then multiplying this amount by the statutory tax rate. This computation is as follows for 1999: [12,500 x ($54 – $50) x 36%]. This amount cannot be negative; therefore, this amount is zero during any year in which the cost of the ESOP shares exceeds the average market value during the year (e.g., year 2000).

Table 7—Tax and EPS Computations

	1999	2000	2001	2002
Income before ESOP	$2,600,000	$2,800,000	$3,100,000	$3,200,000
Interest expense	(200,000)	(155,616)	(107,681)	(55,911)
Compensation expense	(675,000)	(562,496)	(649,992)	(675,000)
Pretax income	$1,725,000	$2,081,888	$2,342,327	$2,469,089
Provision for income tax:				
Currently payable	$ 664,271	$ 736,273	$ 857,774	$ 880,271
Deferred	(25,271)	(9,293)	7,964	26,601
Shareholders' equity (1)	0	13,500	(13,500)	0
Total	$ 639,000	$ 740,480	$ 852,238	$ 906,872
Net income	$1,086,000	$1,341,408	$1,490,089	$1,562,217
Average shares outstanding (2)	2,006,250	2,018,750	2,031,250	2,043,750
Earnings per share	$ 0.54	$ 0.66	$ 0.73	$ 0.76

Notes:

(1) Calculated by multiplying the shares released during the year (12,500) by the excess of ESOP cost over the average market value of the stock ($50 – $47) and then multiplying this amount by the statutory tax rate (36%).

(2) Calculated by adding the cumulative average number of shares released in each year (see Table 3) to the weighted average number of common shares otherwise outstanding.

Journal Entries

January 1, 1999 (Date N&N Establishes the ESOP)

Cash	$2,500,000	
Debt		$2,500,000

[To record the ESOP loan]

Unearned ESOP shares (contra-equity)	$2,500,000	
Common stock and paid-in capital		$2,500,000

[To record the issuance of 50,000 shares to the ESOP at $50 per share—the fair value of the stock at the time it is issued]

Stock Issued to Employees **31.23**

December 31, 1999

Interest expense	$200,000	
Accrued interest payable		$200,000
[To record interest expense]		

Accrued interest payable	$200,000	
Debt	554,802	
Cash		$754,802

[To record the debt payment. The cash disbursement consists of $100,000 of dividends (none of which is charged to retained earnings in 1999, because none of the shares has yet to be allocated) and $654,802 of additional employer contributions to the ESOP.]

Compensation expense	$675,000	
Paid-in capital		$ 50,000
Unearned ESOP shares		625,000

[To record release of 12,500 shares at average fair value of $54. The ESOP's cost is $50.]

Deferred tax asset	$ 25,271	
Provision for income taxes	639,000	
Income taxes payable		$664,271

[To record income taxes for 1999; see Tables 5–7 for the computations of these amounts]

December 31, 2000

Interest expense	$155,616	
Accrued interest payable		$155,616
[To record interest expense]		

Accrued interest payable	$155,616	
Debt	599,186	
Cash		$754,802

[To record the debt payment. The cash disbursement consists of $100,000 of dividends ($25,000 of which is charged to retained earnings in 2000 (see Table 4)) and $654,802 of additional employer contributions to the ESOP.]

Retained earnings	$25,000	
Dividends payable		$25,000

[To record declaration of a $2.00-per-share dividend on 12,500 allocated shares]

Compensation expense	$562,500*	
Dividends payable	25,000	
Paid-in capital	37,500	
Unearned ESOP shares		$625,000

31.24 *Stock Issued to Employees*

[To record the release of 12,500 shares (11,968 for compensation and 532 for dividends) at an average fair value of $47 per share. The per-share cost is $50.]

---
* $4 rounding difference

Deferred tax asset	$ 9,293	
Provision for income taxes	740,480	
Paid-in capital		$ 13,500
Income taxes payable		736,273

[To record income taxes for the year 2000; see Tables 5–7 for the computations of these amounts.]

December 31, 2001

Interest expense	$107,681	
Accrued interest payable		$107,681

[To record interest expense]

Accrued interest payable	$107,681	
Debt	647,121	
Cash		$754,802

[To record the debt payment. The cash disbursement consists of $100,000 of dividends ($50,000 of which is charged to retained earnings in 2001 (see Table 4)) and $654,802 of additional employer contributions to the ESOP.]

Retained earnings	$50,000	
Dividends payable		$50,000

[To record declaration of a $2.00-per-share dividend on 25,000 allocated shares]

Compensation expense	$650,000*	
Dividends payable	50,000	
Paid-in capital		$ 75,000
Unearned ESOP shares		625,000

[To record the release of 12,500 shares (11,607 for compensation and 893 for dividends) at an average fair value of $56 per share. The per-share cost is $50.]

---
* $8 rounding difference

Provision for income taxes	$852,238	
Paid-in capital	13,500	
Deferred income taxes		$ 7,964
Income taxes payable		857,774

[To record income taxes for 2001; see Tables 5–7 for the computations of these amounts.]

December 31, 2002

Interest expense	$55,911	
Accrued interest payable		$55,911

[To record interest expense]

Accrued interest payable	$ 55,911	
Debt	698,891	
Cash		$754,802

[To record the debt payment. The cash disbursement consists of $100,000 of dividends ($75,000 of which is charged to retained earnings in 2002 (see Table 4)) and $654,802 of additional employer contributions to the ESOP.]

Retained earnings	$75,000	
Dividends payable		$75,000

[To record declaration of a $2.00-per-share dividend on 37,500 allocated shares]

Compensation expense	$675,000	
Dividends payable	75,000	
Paid-in capital		$125,000
Unearned ESOP shares		625,000

[To record the release of 12,500 shares (11,250 for compensation and 1,250 for dividends) at an average fair value of $60 per share. The per-share cost is $50.]

Provision for income taxes	$906,872	
Deferred income taxes		$ 26,601
Income taxes payable		880,271

[To record income taxes for 2002; see Tables 5–7 for the computations of these amounts]

Illustration of a Common-Stock Nonleveraged ESOP

Melton, Inc., establishes a common-stock nonleveraged ESOP on January 1, 1999. Melton is to contribute 15% of its pretax profit before ESOP-related charges as of the end of each of the next four years. The ESOP will use this contribution to purchase newly issued shares at the current market price (the year-end price, since contributions to the ESOP are made at year-end). Melton's stock price at December 31 of each year is as follows: 1999, $52; 2000, $49; $2001, $54; 2002, $63. With the exception of these new facts, all of the relevant facts are identical to the assumptions used in the previous illustration. The following table and journal entries illustrate the results of applying SOP 93-6.

Table 1—Summary of the Effects of Applying SOP 93-6

Year	Compensation Expense	Dividends	Number of ESOP Shares Purchased	Cumulative ESOP Shares
Notes:	(1)	(2)	(3)	(4)
1999	$390,000	$ —	7,500	7,500
2000	420,000	15,000	8,571	16,071
2001	465,000	32,143	8,611	24,682
2002	480,000	49,364	7,619	32,301

Notes:
(1) Compensation expense is equal to pretax profit before ESOP-related charges multiplied by 15%.
(2) Dividends are equal to cumulative ESOP shares, as of the beginning of the year, multiplied by the annual dividend per share, $2.
(3) The number of ESOP shares purchased is computed by dividing the yearly employer contribution (i.e., compensation expense) by the year-end market price of Melton's common stock. For example, in 1999, 7,500 shares are purchased ($390,000/$52 per share).
(4) Cumulative ESOP shares are shares held at the beginning of the year plus shares purchased during the year.

Journal Entries

December 31, 1999

Compensation expense	$390,000	
Common stock and paid-in capital		$390,000

[To record Melton's contribution, the sale of shares to the ESOP, and compensation expense]

Provision for income taxes	$795,600	
Income taxes payable		$795,600

[To record income taxes at 36% on taxable income of $2,210,000 ($2,600,000 of pre-ESOP income less $390,000 of compensation expense)]

December 31, 2000

Compensation expense	$420,000	
Retained earnings	15,000	
Common stock and paid-in capital		$420,000
Dividends payable		15,000

[To record Melton's contribution, the sale of shares to the ESOP, declaration of dividends, and compensation expense]

Dividends payable	$15,000	
Cash		$15,000

[To record the payment of dividends]

Provision for income taxes	$856,800	
Income taxes payable		$856,800

[To record income taxes at 36% on taxable income of $2,380,000 ($2,800,000 of pre-ESOP income less $420,000 of compensation expense)]

December 31, 2001

Compensation expense	$465,000	
Retained earnings	32,143	
Common stock and paid-in capital		$465,000
Dividends payable		32,143

[To record Melton's contribution, the sale of shares to the ESOP, declaration of dividends, and compensation expense]

Dividends payable	$32,143	
Cash		$32,143

[To record the payment of dividends]

Provision for income taxes	$948,600	
Income taxes payable		$948,600

[To record income taxes at 36% on taxable income of $2,635,000 ($3,100,000 of pre-ESOP income less $465,000 of compensation expense)]

December 31, 2002

Compensation expense	$480,000	
Retained earnings	49,364	
Common stock and paid-in capital		$480,000
Dividends payable		49,364

[To record Melton's contribution, the sale of shares to the ESOP, declaration of dividends, and compensation expense]

Dividends payable	$49,364	
Cash		$49,364

[To record the payment of dividends]

Provision for income taxes	$979,200	
Income taxes payable		$979,200

[To record income taxes at 36% on taxable income of $2,720,000 ($3,200,000 of pre-ESOP income less $480,000 of compensation expense)]

FTB 97-1: Accounting under Statement 123 for Certain Employee Stock Purchase Plans with a Look-Back Option

BACKGROUND

FAS-123 (Accounting for Stock-Based Compensation) states that the objective of the fair value method of accounting for stock-based compensation is to estimate the fair value of the equity instrument—based on the stock price and other measurement assumptions at the grant date—that is issued in exchange for employee services. This objective also applies to the fair value measurement of grants under a compensatory employee stock purchase plan (ESPP) and is the basis for Illustration 9 of FAS-123.

A *look-back option* is a feature that provides the employee a choice of purchasing stock at two or more times (e.g., an option to purchase stock at 85% of the stock price at the grant date or at a later exercise date). Section 423 of the Internal Revenue Code provides that the employee will not be immediately taxed on the difference between the market price of the stock and a discounted purchase price if the following requirements are met:

- The option price is not less than 85% of the market price when the option is granted or when the option is exercised.
- The choice does not have a term in excess of 27 months.

FAS-123 establishes criteria for evaluating whether an ESPP qualifies for noncompensatory treatment; if it does, the employer is not required to recognize compensation expense. If an ESPP satisfies *all* of the following criteria, the discount from market price to the employee is not stock-based compensation and simply reduces the proceeds from issuing the shares of stock:

- The plan incorporates no option features.
- The discount from the market prices does not exceed the greater of (*a*) a per-share discount that would be reasonable in an offer of stock to stockholders or others or (*b*) the per-share amount of stock issuance costs avoided by not having to raise a significant amount of capital by a public offering of the stock.
- Substantially all full-time employees meeting limited employment qualifications may participate on an equitable basis.

A look-back option is one feature that causes an ESPP to be considered compensatory. In reaching this conclusion, the FASB observed that a look-back option can have substantial value, because it enables the employee to purchase the stock for an amount that *could be* significantly less than the market value at the date of purchase. A look-back option is not an essential element of a plan aimed at promoting broad employee stock ownership; a purchase discount also provides incentive for participation. Based on these observations, the FASB concluded that broad-based plans that contain look-back options cannot be treated as noncompensatory.

STANDARDS

FTB 97-1 responds to three questions concerning how Illustration 9 of FAS-123 applies to the different types of ESPP plans with look-back options described above. Following are a recap of Illustration 9 of FAS-123 and an analysis of the three questions and the FASB's response.

Illustration of Look-Back Option without Dividends

On January 1, 2000, Company S offered employees the opportunity to purchase its stock at either 85% of the current price ($50) or 85% of the price at the end of the year when the options expire. For purposes of valuing the option, expected volatility is assumed to be .30, and the risk-free interest rate for the next 12 months is 6.8%.

The value of this look-back option can be estimated at the grant date by combining its two components, as follows:

1. 15% of a share of nonvested stock
2. 85% of a 1-year call option held with an exercise price of $50

The option holder will receive value of at least 15% of a share of stock upon exercise, regardless of the stock price after the grant date. In this example, the stock price is $50 when the grant is made. If the price falls to $40 and the option is exercised at that price, the holder pays $34 ($40 x .85) and receives value of $6, which is 15% of the market price at the date of exercise. On the other hand, if the market price increases to $60, the holder can purchase stock at only $42.50 ($50 x .85) and receive value of $17.50 ($60 – $42.50).

Using an option-pricing model to value the look-back option under the stated assumptions (e.g., .30 expected volatility and 6.8% risk-free interest rate) results in the following:

15% of a share of nonvested stock ($50 x .15)	$ 7.50
Call on 85% of a share of stock with an exercise price of $50 ($7.56 x .85)	6.43
Total grant date value	$13.93

This calculation is based on the idea that the value of the look-back option consists of two components: (1) the 15% reduction from a $50 market value ($7.50) and (2) 85% of a call option with an exercise price of $50. The $7.56 figure in the second component is the value of the call option as computed by an option-pricing model.

Illustration of Look-Back Option with Dividends

This example assumes the same facts as in the previous case, except that Company S pays a 2.5% annual dividend quarterly (i.e., .625% per quarter). Calculation of the value of the look-back option is similar to the calculation in the previous illustration, except that the components are *reduced to reflect the dividends that the holder of the option does not receive* during the term of the option. The value of the two components of the option is calculated as follows:

15% of a share of nonvested stock ($50 x .15 x .9754)	$ 7.32
Call on 85% of a share of stock, $50 exercise price, 2.5% dividend yield ($6.78 x .85)	5.76
Total grant date value	$13.08

The first component is the minimum benefit to the holder, regardless of the price of the stock at the exercise date. The second component is the additional benefit to the holder if the stock price exceeds $50 at the exercise date. The $6.78 in the second component is the value of the call option as computed by an option-pricing model.

FTB 97-1 Questions and Answers

Question 1: Illustration 9 of FAS-123 provides the only specific guidance on measuring the compensation cost associated with an award under a compensatory ESPP with a look-back option. Is the fair value measurement technique described in that illustration applicable to all ESPPs with a look-back option?

Answer: No. The measurement approach in FAS-123, Illustration 9, was intended to illustrate how the fair value of an award under a basic type of ESPP with a look-back option could be determined at the grant date by focusing on the substance of the arrangement and valuing each feature of the award separately. The fundamental components of a look-back option may differ from plan to plan, affecting the individual calculations. For example, the illustration in FAS-123 assumes that the number of shares that may be purchased is fixed at the grant date based on the grant date stock price and the amount the employee elects to have withheld (Type A plan). Some plans (e.g., Type B plans) do not fix the number of shares that the employee is permitted to purchase, requiring modification to the determination of fair value.

Question 2: How should the Illustration 9 measurement approach be modified to determine the fair value of an ESPP award plan with a Type B look-back option (i.e., the plan does *not* fix the number of shares that an employee is permitted to purchase)?

Answer: In a Type A plan, the number of shares an employee is permitted to purchase is limited to the number based on the price of the stock at the origin of the agreement. For example, if an employee had $4,250 withheld from salary, and the plan permitted him or her to purchase shares at 85% of the $50 current stock price, he or she could purchase 100 shares, as follows:

$$\$4{,}250 / (85\% \times \$50) = 100 \text{ shares}$$

In a Type B plan, the employee is permitted to purchase as many shares as the $4,250 withheld will permit. If, for example, the market price falls to $30, the employee is not limited to purchasing 100 shares and may actually purchase 167 shares, determined as follows:

$$\$4{,}250 / (85\% \times \$30) = 167 \text{ shares}$$

Following the FAS-123, Illustration 9, approach of combining the components of the plan, and using the same underlying assumptions as in that illustration, the value of the Type B option is calculated as follows:

15% of a share of nonvested stock ($50 x 15%)	$ 7.50
One-year call on 85% of a shares of stock, exercise price of $50 ($7.56 x 85%)	6.43
One-year put on 15% of a shares of stock, exercise price of $50 ($4.27 x 15%)	.64
	$14.57

This Illustration is the same as that presented earlier (the "no dividend" case) with the addition of a third component: a one-year put option on the employer's stock, valued with a standard option-pricing model. The same assumptions are applied. This has the effect of adding $.64 to the value of the option, raising the total to $14.57 ($7.50 + $6.43 + $.64).

Total compensation is measured at the grant date based on the number of shares that can be purchased using the total withholdings and the grant date market price, rather than on the potentially greater number of shares that may be purchased if the market price falls. For example, in the above Illustration, an employee who had $1,275 withheld could purchase 30 shares based on the grant date price [$1,275/($50 x .85)], and total compensation expense recognized for that employee would be $437 (30 x $14.57).

Question 3: The characteristics of Type A and Type B plans are incorporated into other types of ESPP plans with a look-back option. The measurement approach in Illustration 9 of FAS-123 for a Type A plan, as modified by Question 2 of FTB 97-1 for a Type B plan, forms the basis for determining the fair value of the award under the other types of ESPP with a look-back option. What additional modifications are necessary to determine the fair value of awards under other types of ESPP?

Answer: The fair value of an award under an ESPP plan with a look-back option with multiple purchase periods (Type C plan) should be determined in the same manner as an award under a graded vesting stock option plan. Such awards under a two-year plan with purchase periods at the end of each year would be valued as having two separate options, both starting with the initial grant date and having different lives (12 and 24 months, respectively).

This same approach should be used to value ESPP awards with multiple purchase periods that incorporate reset or rollover mechanisms (Type D and Type E plans). At the date the reset or rollover mechanism becomes effective, the terms of the award have been modified. This is, in substance, an exchange of the original award for a new award with different terms. Similarly, an election by an employee to increase withholdings (Types F, G, and H plans) is a modification of the terms of the award, which is similar to an exchange of the original award for a new award with different terms.

FAS-123 indicates that a modification of the terms of an award that makes it more valuable should be treated as an exchange of the original award for a new award. In substance, the employer repurchases the original instrument by issuing a new instrument of greater value and incurs additional compensation cost for that incremental value.

A Type I plan permits an employee to increase withholdings retroactively. An employee may elect not to participate, or to participate at a minimal level, until just before the exercise date. This makes it difficult to determine when there is a mutual understanding of the terms of the award and, thus, when the grant date actually occurs. In this situation, the later date when the employee remits an amount to the company should be considered the grant date for purposes of valuing the option.

Changes in compensation resulting from salary increases, commissions, or bonus payments are not plan modifications and do not represent changes in the terms of the plan. The only incremental compensation cost is that which results from the additional shares that may be purchased with the additional amounts withheld.

AIN-APB 25: Accounting for Stock Issued to Employees: Accounting Interpretations of APB Opinion No. 25

Question: Should a corporation account for plans or transactions if they have characteristics similar to compensatory plans adopted by corporations, but are established or financed by a principal stockholder?

Answer: If the principal stockholder's intent is to maintain or enhance the value of his or her investment by entering into such an arrangement, the corporation benefits from the plan by the retention of, as well as the possible improved performance of, the employee. In this case, the benefits to the principal stockholder, the corporation, and the employee stockholder are inseparable. The economic substance of this type of plan is substantially the same whether the plan is adopted by the corporation or by a principal stockholder. The corporation should account for the plan as a contribution to capital by the principal stockholder, with an offsetting charge accounted for in the same manner as for a compensatory plan adopted by the corporation. Compensation cost should be recognized as expense in one or more periods, in accordance with APB-25.

CHAPTER 32
TROUBLED DEBT RESTRUCTURING

CONTENTS

IMPRESS™ Cross-References	32.02
Overview	32.03
FTB 80-2: Classification of Debt Restructurings by Debtors and Creditors	32.04
Background	32.04
Standards	32.04
FTB 81-6: Applicability of Statement 15 to Debtors in Bankruptcy Situations	32.04
Background	32.04
Standards	32.05
FTB 94-1: Applicability of Statement 115 to Debt Securities Restructured in a Troubled Debt Restructuring	32.05
Background	32.05
Standards	32.05
PB-5: Income Recognition on Loans to Financially Troubled Countries	32.06
Background	32.06
Standards	32.06

CROSS-REFERENCES

1999 MILLER GAAP GUIDE: Chapter 48, "Troubled Debt Restructuring"

1999 MILLER GAAP IMPLEMENTATION MANUAL: EITF: Chapter 30, "Troubled Debt Restructuring"

1999 MILLER GAAP FOR NOT-FOR-PROFIT ORGANIZATIONS: Chapter 2, "Overview of Current Pronouncements"; Chapter 6, "Liabilities"

CHAPTER 32
TROUBLED DEBT RESTRUCTURING

OVERVIEW

Debt may be restructured for a variety of reasons. A restructuring of debt is considered a troubled debt restructuring (TDR) if the creditor, for economic or legal reasons related to the debtor's financial difficulties, grants a concession to the debtor that it would not otherwise consider. The concession may stem from an agreement between the creditor and the debtor, or it may be imposed by law or court.

A loan is impaired if, based on current information and events, it is probable that the creditor will be unable to collect all amounts due according to the contractual terms of the loan agreement.

The following pronouncements are the sources of GAAP for a troubled debt restructuring that are included in the highest level of authority in the SAS-69 hierarchy:

FAS-15	Accounting by Debtors and Creditors for Troubled Debt Restructurings
FAS-114	Accounting by Creditors for Impairment of a Loan

The following additional sources of GAAP that are in lower levels of the SAS-69 GAAP hierarchy are discussed in this Manual:

FTB 80-2	Classification of Debt Restructurings by Debtors and Creditors (Level B)
FTB 81-6	Applicability of Statement 15 to Debtors in Bankruptcy Situations (Level B)
FTB 94-1	Application of Statement 115 to Debt Securities Restructured in a Troubled Debt Restructuring (Level B)
PB-5	Income Recognition on Loans to Financially Troubled Countries (Level C)

FTB 80-2: Classification of Debt Restructurings by Debtors and Creditors

BACKGROUND

FAS-15 defines *troubled debt restructuring* as a restructuring in which the creditor, for economic or legal reasons related to the debtor's financial difficulties, grants a concession to the debtor that the creditor would not otherwise consider.

STANDARDS

Question: In applying FAS-15, can a debt restructuring be a troubled debt restructuring (TDR) for a debtor but not for a creditor?

Answer: Yes, a debtor may have a TDR even though the creditor does not have a TDR. The debtor and creditor individually apply FAS-15 in light of the specific facts and circumstances to determine whether a particular restructuring constitutes a TDR. Paragraph 7 of FAS-15 is particularly helpful for creditors in determining whether a particular restructuring is a TDR for debtors and creditors. FAS-15 establishes tests for applicability that are not necessarily symmetrical between the debtor and the creditor, particularly when the debtor's carrying amount and the creditor's recorded investment are different amounts.

FTB 81-6: Applicability of Statement 15 to Debtors in Bankruptcy Situations

BACKGROUND

Some confusion arose over the applicability of FAS-15 to bankruptcy situations, prompting the issuance of FTB 81-6. On the one hand, FAS-15 indicates that it applies to TDRs consummated under reorganization, arrangement, or other provisions of the Federal Bankruptcy Act or other federal statutes. On the other hand, FAS-15 indicates that it does not apply to situations in which liabilities are generally restated under federal statutes, a quasi-reorganization, or corporate adjustment.

STANDARDS

Question: Does FAS-15 apply to TDRs of debtors involved in bankruptcy proceedings?

Answer: FAS-15 does not apply to debtors who, in connection with bankruptcy proceedings, enter into TDRs that result in a general restatement of the debtor's liabilities.

FTB 94-1: Application of Statement 115 to Debt Securities Restructured in a Troubled Debt Restructuring

BACKGROUND

FTB 94-1 was issued to clarify a perceived inconsistency between FAS-114 and FAS-115 (Accounting for Certain Investments in Debt and Equity Securities). This problem came to light during the FASB's discussion of the applicability of FAS-115 to Brady bonds that were received in a TDR. The term *Brady Bonds* refers to bonds issued to financial institutions by foreign governments under a program designed by Treasury Secretary Nicholas Brady in the late 1980s to help developing countries refinance their debt to those institutions.

If FAS-115 did not apply to a debt security that was restructured in a TDR involving a modification of terms before the effective date of FAS-114, then the impairment provisions of FAS-114 and FAS-115 would not apply, leaving the accounting to be handled in accordance with FAS-15, which would not require the recognition of the time value of money or the security's fair value.

STANDARDS

Question: For a loan that was restructured in a TDR involving a modification of terms, does FAS-115 apply to the accounting by the creditor if the restructured loan meets the definition of a *security* in FAS-115?

Answer: FAS-115 applies to all loans that meet the definition of the term *security* in that Statement. Therefore, any loan that was restructured in a TDR involving a modification of terms, including loans restructured before the effective date of FAS-114, are subject to the requirements of FAS-115.

PB-5: Income Recognition on Loans to Financially Troubled Countries

BACKGROUND

Many bank loans to financially troubled countries meet the criteria for accrual of losses in accordance with FAS-5 (Accounting for Contingencies). In those situations, banks should establish loan loss allowances by charges to income.

If a financially troubled country suspends interest payment, banks with outstanding loans from such a country should suspend the accrual recognition of interest income. Such financially troubled countries may later resume interest payments. Guidance on accounting by a creditor for the receipt of interest payments from a debtor that had previously suspended interest payments is included in the industry audit guide titled *Audits of Banks*.

STANDARDS

When a country becomes current as to principal and interest payments and has normalized relations with the international financial markets, assuming the allowance for loan losses is adequate, the creditor may recognize interest on an accrual basis. Even if these conditions are met, the bank should not automatically return the loan to accrual accounting status. Some period of payment performance generally is necessary to make an assessment of collectibility before returning the loan to accrual status.

1999

MILLER

GAAP IMPLEMENTATION MANUAL CPE PROGRAM

TAKE YOUR CPE TEST ONLINE!
www.hbpp.com

HARCOURT BRACE PROFESSIONAL PUBLISHING

A Division of
Harcourt Brace & Company
SAN DIEGO   NEW YORK   CHICAGO   LONDON

Registered with the National Association of State Boards of Accountancy as a sponsor of continuing professional education on the National Registry of CPE Sponsors. State boards of accountancy have final authority on the acceptance of individual courses. Complaints regarding registered sponsors may be addressed to NASBA, 150 Fourth Avenue North, Suite 700, Nashville, TN 37219-2417, (615) 880-4290.

INTRODUCTION

Thank you for choosing this self-study CPE course from Harcourt Brace Professional Publishing. Our goal is to provide you with the clearest, most concise, and most up-to-date accounting and auditing information to help further your professional development, as well as the most convenient method to help you satisfy your continuing professional education obligations.

This CPE program is intended to be used in conjunction with your *1999 Miller GAAP Implementation Manual*. This course has the following characteristics:

> **Prerequisites:** None
> **Recommended CPE credits:** 10 hours per module
> **Level of Knowledge:** Basic
> **Field of Study:** Accounting

The *1999 Miller GAAP Implementation Manual* Self-Study CPE Program is designed to provide 10 hours of CPE credit if the test is submitted for grading and earnS a passing score.

In accordance with the standards of the National Registry of CPE Sponsors, each credit hour awarded for this program is based on 100 minutes of average completion time. Credit hours are recommended in accordance with the Statement on Standards for Formal Continuing Professional Education (CPE) Programs, published by the AICPA. CPE requirements vary from state to state. Your state board is the final authority for the number of credit hours allowed for a particular program, as well as the classification of courses, under its specific licensing requirement. Contact your State Board of Accountancy for information concerning your state's requirements as to the number of CPE credit hours you must earn and the acceptable fields of study. This course is not currently recognized in Mississippi, North Carolina, or Florida.

To receive credit, complete the course according to the instructions on page 33.04. Each module costs $64.00. Payment options are shown on the answer sheet.

Each CPE test is graded within two weeks of its receipt. A passing score is 70% or above. Participants who pass the test will receive a Certificate of Completion to acknowledge their achievement. The self-study CPE Program offered in conjunction with the *1999 Miller GAAP Implementation Manual* will expire on December 31, 2000. Participants may submit completed tests for the program until that date.

Instructions for Taking This Course

Each module consists of chapter learning objectives, reading assignments, review questions and suggested solutions, and an examination. Complete each step listed below for each module you want to submit for grading:

33.04 *Self-Study CPE Program*

1. Review the chapter learning objectives.
2. Read the assigned material in the *1999 Miller GAAP Implementation Manual*.
3. Complete the review questions, and compare your answers to the suggested solutions.
4. After completing all assigned chapters in the module, take the examination, writing "true," "false," or the corresponding multiple-choice letter (a–d) to indicate your answer on the appropriate line on the answer sheet.
5. When you have completed the examination, remove the answer sheet, place it in a stamped envelope, and send it to the following address:

> *Miller GAAP Implementation Manual* CPE Coordinator
> Harcourt Brace Professional Publishing
> 525 B Street, Suite 1900
> San Diego, CA 92101-4495

Be sure to indicate your method of payment on the answer sheet.

SELF-STUDY CONTINUING PROFESSIONAL EDUCATION

Accounting Policies and Standards

After completing this section, you should be able to:

- Understand the purpose and scope of FASB Technical Bulletins and AcSEC Practice Bulletins.
- Describe the disclosure requirements for the sale or purchase of tax benefits through tax leases.

Read Chapter 1 of the *1999 Miller GAAP Implementation Manual*. Answer review questions 1 and 2 on page 33.09.

Advertising

After completing this section, you should be able to:

- Understand the appropriate accounting treatment for advertising costs.
- Identify instances where advertising costs may be capitalized.

Read Chapter 2 of the *1999 Miller GAAP Implementation Manual*. Answer review questions 3 and 4 on page 33.09.

Bankruptcy and Reorganization

After completing this section, you should be able to:

- Describe the financial reporting requirements for entities in reorganization under the bankruptcy code.
- Understand the accounting for foreclosed assets.
- Understand the accounting for preconfirmation contingencies in fresh-start reporting.

Read Chapter 4 of the *1999 Miller GAAP Implementation Manual*. Answer review questions 5–7 on pages 33.09–33.10.

Business Combinations

After completing this section, you should be able to:

- Understand many of the implementation issues of APB-16 (Business Combinations).

- Be able to apply the guidance of the Accounting Interpretations of APB-16 to business combinations

Read Chapter 5 of the *1999 Miller GAAP Implementation Manual*. Answer review questions 8 and 9 on page 33.10.

Contingencies, Risks, and Uncertainties

After completing this section, you should be able to:

- Understand the disclosure requirements for certain risks and uncertainties.
- Describe the accounting and reporting requirements for environmental remediation liabilities.

Read Chapter 7 of the *1999 Miller GAAP Implementation Manual*. Answer review questions 10–12 on page 33.10.

Financial Instruments

After completing this section, you should be able to:

- Describe the accounting and financial reporting requirements for foreign debt/equity swaps.

Read Chapter 10 of the *1999 Miller GAAP Implementation Manual*. Answer review question 13 on page 33.10.

Foreign Operations and Exchange

After completing this section, you should be able to:

- Understand the foreign currency accounting and financial statement presentation for investment companies.

Read Chapter 11 of the *1999 Miller GAAP Implementation Manual*. Answer review question 14 on page 33.10.

Income Taxes

After completing this section, you should be able to:

- Apply the guidance of the FAS-109 Implementation Guide for accounting for income taxes.
- Apply the recognition and measurement principles of FAS-109 for income tax provisions and related tax assets and liabilities.
- Understand the disclosure requirements in relation to accounting for the investment tax credit.

Read Chapters 12, 15, and 17 of the *1999 Miller GAAP Implementation Manual*.
Answer review questions 15–17 on page 33.10.

Investments in Debt and Equity Securities

After completing this section, you should be able to:

- Understand the meaning of "substantially the same" in the professional literature for holders of debt instruments.
- Describe the applicability of FAS-115 to various types of investments.
- Apply the requirements of FAS-115 to various types of investments.

Read Chapter 18 of the *1999 Miller GAAP Implementation Manual*.
Answer review question 18 on page 33.10.

Leases

After completing this section, you should be able to:

- Determine the appropriate interest rate to use in lease present value calculations.
- Understand the accounting for the residual value of a lease.
- Account for operating leases with scheduled rent increases.

Read Chapter 19 of the *1999 Miller GAAP Implementation Manual*.
Answer review question 19 on page 33.10.

Long-term Construction Contracts

After completing this section, you should be able to:

- Understand the revenue recognition principles for construction-type and other contracts where services are performed in accordance with a buyer's specifications.

Read Chapter 20 of the *1999 Miller GAAP Implementation Manual*.
Answer review question 20 on page 33.10.

Pension Plans

After completing this section, you should be able to:

- Understand the common practice issues employers encounter when applying the guidance of FAS-87 to pension plans.
- Understand how defined contribution pension plans report separate investment fund option information.

- Be able to apply the guidance of FAS-88 when an employer is accounting for the settlement or curtailment of a defined benefit pension plan or for termination benefits.

Read Chapters 22 and 23 of the *1999 Miller GAAP Implementation Manual*. Answer review questions 21–23 on page 33.10.

Personal Financial Statements

After completing this section, you should be able to:

- Understand the accounting principles used in preparing personal financial statements.
- Understand the financial reporting requirements for personal financial statements, including related disclosures.

Read Chapter 24 of the *1999 Miller GAAP Implementation Manual*. Answer review question 24 on page 33.10.

Postemployment and Postretirement Benefits Other than Pensions

After completing this section, you should be able to:

- Determine the types of benefits to which the requirements of FAS-106 apply.
- Understand the implementation issues for FAS-106.

Read Chapter 25 of the *1999 Miller GAAP Implementation Manual*. Answer review questions 25 and 26 on pages 33.10–33.11.

Results of Operations

After completing this section, you should be able to:

- Determine when an event or transaction should be considered an extraordinary item.
- Understand the accounting for the gain or loss on the sale of a portion of a line of business that is not considered a segment.

Read Chapter 27 of the *1999 Miller GAAP Implementation Manual*. Answer review question 27 on page 33.11.

Stockholders' Equity

After completing this section, you should be able to:

- Understand when treasury stock transactions may require the recognition of revenues or expenses

- Understand accounting and financial reporting for limited liability companies and limited liability partnerships

Read Chapter 30 of the *1999 Miller GAAP Implementation Manual*.
Answer review question 28 on page 33.11.

Stock Issued to Employees

After completing this section, you should be able to:

- Describe the accounting practices of certain employee stock ownership plans under SOP 76-3.
- Understand an employer's accounting for employee stock ownership plans under SOP 93-6.
- Understand the accounting under FAS-123 for certain employee stock purchase plans with a look-back option.

Read Chapter 31 of the *1999 Miller GAAP Implementation Manual*.
Answer review question 29 on page 33.11.

Troubled Debt Restructuring

After completing this section, you should be able to:

- Understand the consistency of classification of debt restructurings by debtors and creditors.
- Understand the relationship between troubled debt restructurings and bankruptcy situations.
- Explain the application of FAS-115 to debt securities structured in a troubled debt restructuring.

Read Chapter 32 of the *1999 Miller GAAP Implementation Manual*.
Answer review question 30 on page 33.11.

REVIEW QUESTIONS

1. Describe the kinds of guidance that FASB Technical Bulletins can be expected to provide.
2. What disclosures are required for the sale or purchase of tax benefits through tax leases?
3. What are the two exceptions to the general rule that advertising costs be expensed as incurred?
4. What conditions must be met for direct-response advertising costs to be capitalized?
5. Describe the accounting for the costs incurred to close duplicate facilities when a company acquires an investment in a second company and the investment is accounted for by the equity method.

6. Describe some examples of transfers or exchanges between entities under common control that would not be subject to the requirements of APB-16.
7. What are the steps in determining an organization's reorganization value in a reorganization plan?
8. Describe the accounting for professional fees related to a reorganization.
9. What disclosures are required for entities that are exiting Chapter 11 proceedings and are adopting fresh-start reporting?
10. List the areas of significant risks and uncertainties for which SOP 94-6 addresses disclosure requirements.
11. What conditions should be met in order for an organization to be required to disclose information about concentrations?
12. What factors should be considered when developing an estimate of environmental remediation liabilities?
13. What factors should be considered in determining the fair value of the equity investment/net asset received in a foreign debt/equity swap?
14. What conditions can give rise to a foreign currency gain or loss?
15. Does FAS-109 require separate deferred tax computations for each state and local tax jurisdiction?
16. Describe the disclosures required if a change in an enterprise's tax status becomes effective after year-end, but before the financial statements are issued.
17. Describe the accounting for tax differences relating to the amortization of goodwill.
18. How should a financial statement preparer account for equity securities that do not have readily determinable fair values?
19. Describe the appropriate accounting for an operating lease with a scheduled rent increase.
20. Describe the accounting treatment of an anticipated loss on a construction-type or performance-type contract.
21. Under what circumstances could an employer revise a schedule of amortization of unrecognized prior service cost from a specific retroactive defined benefit pension plan amendment?
22. Discuss whether an employer may immediately recognize actuarial gains and losses relating to a defined benefit pension plan instead of delaying their recognition.
23. What criteria under FAS-88 determine whether a pension plan settlement has occurred?
24. Describe the basic financial reporting requirements for personal financial statements.
25. Discuss whether the assumed discount rate used to measure an employer's postretirement benefit obligation should be the same rate as is used to measure the employer's pension obligation under FAS-87.

26. Under what conditions would a postretirement plan be considered a frontloaded plan?
27. Describe the accounting for the gain or loss from the sale of a portion of a line of business that is not considered a segment under APB-30.
28. How should assets and liabilities be recorded in a limited liability company that is formed by combining entities under common control or by converting from another type of entity?
29. What obligation does an employer have to holders of ESOP shares that are not readily tradable?
30. Describe how a debt restructuring can be a troubled debt restructuring under FAS-15 for a debtor, but not for a creditor.

SUGGESTED SOLUTIONS

1. FASB Technical Bulletins provide the following kinds of guidance:
   - To clarify, explain, or elaborate on an underlying standard
   - To provide guidance when application of a standard for a particular situation may differ from its general application
   - To address areas not directly covered by existing standards

2. Because alternative accounting practices may exist in the accounting for the sale or purchase of tax benefits through tax leases, the accounting policy and practice followed should be disclosed. The disclosure should include the method of accounting for those transactions and the method of recognizing revenue and allocating income tax benefits and asset costs to current and future periods.

3. The two exceptions to the general rule that advertising costs be expensed when incurred are as follows:
   - Certain direct-response advertising costs may be capitalized.
   - Expenditures for advertising costs that are made subsequent to the recognition of revenues related to those costs are capitalized and charged to expense when the related revenues are recognized. For example, if an entity enters into an agreement where it is responsible for reimbursing some or all of its customer's advertising costs, the entity would recognize the advertising expense concurrently with the recognition of revenue that arises from the reimbursement of the costs.

4. Direct-response advertising must meet two conditions in order for costs to be capitalized. First, the primary purpose of the advertising must be to generate sales, and these sales must be capable of being traced specifically to the advertising. Second, the direct-response advertising must result in probable future economic benefits.

5. The costs incurred to close duplicate facilities of an acquiring company in a business combination that is accounted for by the equity method should be charged to expense in determining net income. These costs should not be treated as part of the cost of the acquired company, which should include only the direct costs of the acquisition.

6. APB-16 does not apply to a transfer of net assets or to an exchange of sales of entities under common control. Examples of these transactions excluded from APB-16 are as follows:
   - A parent may transfer the net assets of a wholly owned subsidiary and liquidate the subsidiary.
   - A parent may transfer its interest in several partially owned subsidiaries to a new wholly owned subsidiary.
   - A parent may transfer its ownership or the net assets of a wholly owned subsidiary for additional shares issued by a partially owned subsidiary of the parent.
7. Generally, the reorganization value in a reorganization plan is determined through the following steps:
   - Consideration of the amount to be received for assets that will not be needed in the reconstituted business
   - Computation of the present value of cash flows that the reconstituted business is expected to generate for some period into the future
   - Computation of the terminal value of the reconstituted business at the end of the period for which future cash flows are estimated
8. SOP 90-7 requires that professional fees related to a reorganization are to be recognized as incurred and categorized as a reorganization expense. Establishing a liability for professional fees upon filing for bankruptcy or capitalizing the fees and then offsetting them against the discharge of liabilities in the reorganization plan are not acceptable practices under SOP 90-7.
9. Disclosures that are required for entities that are exiting Chapter 11 proceedings and are adopting fresh-start reporting are as follows:
   - Adjustments to the historical amounts of assets and liabilities
   - The amount of debt that has been forgiven
   - The amount of prior retained earnings or deficit that is eliminated
   - Matters that are significant in determining the reorganization value, such as methods used to determine the reorganization value, sensitive assumptions used, and assumptions about conditions that are expected to be different from current conditions
10. SOP 94-6 requires disclosure of significant risks and uncertainties that confront entities in the following areas: nature of operations, use of estimates in the preparation of financial statements, certain significant estimates, and current vulnerability due to certain concentrations.
11. Financial statements should disclose concentrations if all of the following conditions are met:
    - The concentration existed at the date of the financial statements.
    - The concentration makes the enterprise vulnerable to the risk of a near-term severe impact.
    - It is reasonably possible that the events that could cause the severe impact will occur in the near future.
12. Developing an estimate of environmental remediation liabilities involves consideration of many factors, including the following:

- The extent and types of hazardous substances at the site
- The range of technologies that can be used for remediation
- Evolving standards of what constitutes acceptable remediation
- The number and financial condition of other potentially responsible parties and the extent of their responsibility for the remediation

13. The following factors should be considered in determining the fair value of the equity investment/net assets received:
    - Similar transactions for cash
    - Estimated cash flows from the equity investment or net assets received
    - Market value (if available) of similar equity investments
    - Currency restrictions affecting:
      — Dividends
      — The sale of the investment
      — The repatriation of capital

14. The following conditions can give rise to a foreign currency gain or loss:
    - The value of securities held, based on current exchange rates, differs from the securities cost.
    - The amount of a receivable or payable at the transaction date differs from the amount ultimately received or paid upon settlement, or differs from the amount receivable or payable at the reporting date based on current exchange rates
    - The amount of interest, dividends, and withholding taxes at the transaction date differs from the amount ultimately received or paid, or differs from the amount receivable or payable at the reporting date based on current exchange rates
    - Expenses accrued at the transaction date(s) differ from the amount ultimately paid, or differ from the amount payable at the reporting date based on current exchange rates
    - Forward exchange contracts or foreign exchange futures contracts need to be marked to market.

15. FAS-109 would, as a general rule, require separate deferred tax computations for each state and local tax jurisdiction if there are significant difference between the tax laws of the different jurisdictions involved. As a practical matter, many state and local income taxes are based on the U.S. federal income tax and, accordingly, aggregate computations of deferred tax assets and liabilities may be appropriate.

16. A change in tax status that is effective after year-end but before financial statements are issued should not be recorded in the financial statements of the previous year. However, the previous year's financial statements should disclose that the tax status will change in the subsequent year and should disclose the effects of the change, if material.

17. Deferred taxes are not provided for temporary differences related to positive goodwill for which amortization is not deductible for tax purposes or unallocated negative goodwill.

18. In accounting for an equity security that does not have a readily determinable fair value, a financial statement preparer should apply the guidance of APB-18 (The Equity Method for Investments in Common Stock) as follows:
    - If the investment qualifies for the equity method of accounting, that method should be used.
    - If the investment does not qualify for the equity method, the investment should be accounted for using the cost method, adjusted to reflect other-than-temporary declines in fair value.

    However, investments made by insurance companies should follow the guidance of FAS-60 (Accounting and Reporting by Insurance Enterprises).

19. The effects of scheduled rent increases that are included in the calculation of minimum lease payments should be recognized on a straight-line basis over the lease term unless some other systematic and rational allocation basis is more representative of the time pattern in which the leased property is used.

20. When current estimates for a construction-type or production-type contract indicate that the total contract revenues and costs will result in a loss, a provision for the entire loss on the contract should be made. This applies regardless of whether the contract is accounted for using the percentage-of-completion method or the completed-contract method. The provision for loss should be made in the accounting period in which the loss becomes evident.

21. Once a schedule of amortization of unrecognized prior service cost is established, it should be revised only if one of the following three conditions occurs:
    - The pension plan is curtailed.
    - Events indicate that the period that the employer will receive benefits from a retroactive plan benefit is shorter than that initially estimated.
    - Future economic benefits have been impaired.

    Under no circumstances should unrecognized prior service costs be recognized more slowly than originally planned. In other words, the amortization schedule may only be shortened, not lengthened. In addition, the amortization schedule should not be revised due to variances in the expected service lives of employees.

22. An employer may recognize actuarial gains and losses immediately instead of delaying their recognition if all of the following conditions are met:
    - The method must be used consistently.
    - The method must be applied to all gains and losses (both on pension plan assets and on pension plan obligations)
    - The entity's policy to immediately recognize gains and losses must be disclosed.

23. FAS-88 specifies three criteria that define when a pension plan settlement has occurred. A *settlement* is defined as a transaction that:
    - Is irrevocable,
    - Relieves the employer (or the pension plan) of the primary responsibility for a pension plan obligation, and

- Eliminates significant risks related to the pension plan obligations and plan assets used to bring about the settlement.

24. The basic financial statements that are prepared when presenting personal financial statements are the following:
    - Statement of financial condition
    - Statement of changes in net worth
    - Notes to the financial statements

    Presentation of comparative statements with one or more prior periods is optional.

25. The discount rates used to measure the postretirement benefit obligation and pension obligation do not necessarily need to be the same. Measuring both obligations requires a discount rate chosen to reflect the interest rate on a high-quality debt instrument of a duration similar to that of the benefit obligation. Accordingly, a different discount rate may be appropriate because the timing of expected payments under the postretirement benefit plan may differ from the expected timing of pension payments.

26. A postretirement plan would be considered frontloaded if all, or a disproportionate portion of, expected benefits to be received under the plan are attributed to the employees' early years of service. The employee group as a whole is evaluated in determining whether the plan is frontloaded.

27. The gain or loss from the sale of a portion of a line of business that is not considered a segment under APB-30 should be calculated using the same management principles that would be used if it were a segment of a business. These gains or losses are not extraordinary items, but they may require separate disclosure in a manner that does not result in their being confused with discontinued operations or extraordinary items.

28. When a limited liability company is formed by combining entities under common control or by converting from another type of entity, assets and liabilities should be initially recorded at amounts at which they were stated in the financial statements in the predecessor entities. In other words, they should be treated as they would be in a pooling of interests.

29. Employers are required to offer a put option to holders of ESOP shares that are not readily tradable. The employer is required to purchase the employee's stock at its fair value at the time the put option is exercised.

30. A debtor and a creditor individually apply the provisions of FAS-15 in light of the specific facts and circumstances to determine whether a particular restructuring constitutes a troubled debt restructuring. The FAS-15 tests are not necessarily symmetrical between the debtor and the creditor, particularly when the debtor's carrying amount and the creditor's recorded investment are different amounts.

Examination for Continuing Professional Education Credit

1. *Multiple choice:* Which of the following professional guidance would not be likely to be found in a FASB Technical Bulletin?
   a. Clarification of an existing standard
   b. Application of a general standard to a specific industry
   c. Guidance for areas not covered by existing standards
   d. Change in the accounting requirements from an existing standard

2. *True or false:* All Notices to Practitioners that were issued by the AICPA have been superseded and are no longer part of the GAAP hierarchy.

3. *Multiple choice:* When should the cost of purchasing television time to air an advertisement be expensed?
   a. When the advertisement is aired
   b. When the advertising time is purchased
   c. Over a period of time that the benefit of the advertisement is expected to be realized
   d. When the cost of producing the advertisement is incurred

4. *True or false:* For direct-response advertising costs to be capitalized, the direct-response advertising must result in probable future economic benefits.

5. *True or false:* APB-16 (Business Combinations) generally excludes from its scope transfers of net assets between entities under common control.

6. *Multiple choice:* How should the costs incurred to close duplicate facilities of an acquiring company accounted for under the equity method be treated for accounting purposes?
   a. Charged to expense
   b. Included as part of the cost of the asset
   c. Capitalized and amortized over a period not to exceed 40 years
   d. Recorded directly as a reduction of the acquiring company's stockholders' equity

7. *Multiple choice:* Which of the following is the correct accounting treatment for professional fees related to a reorganization?
   a. Expensed as incurred and reported with reorganization expenses
   b. Estimated and accrued for at the date of filing for bankruptcy

c. Recorded as a liability and offset against debt discharged in the reorganization plan
d. Recorded as a deferred charge and amortized after the entity emerges from Chapter 11

8. *True or false:* Prepetition liabilities should not be reported on the balance sheet of an entity operating under Chapter 11.

9. *True or false:* The reorganization value of an entity in a reorganization plan is designed to approximate the fair value of the entity's assets, and it should conform with the amount that a willing buyer would pay for these assets.

10. *Multiple choice:* Where should the effects of debt forgiveness be reported by an entity that is exiting Chapter 11 and adopting fresh-start reporting?
    a. In the predecessor entity's financial statements, as part of income from operations
    b. In the predecessor entity's financial statements, as an extraordinary item
    c. In the new entity's financial statements, as part of income from operations
    d. In the new entity's financial statements, as an extraordinary item

11. *True or false:* Disclosure regarding estimates in the financial statements would not be required if the effect of a change in an estimate would not have a material effect on the financial statements.

12. *Multiple choice:* Assuming the disclosure conditions of SOP 94-6 are met, which of the following situations involving estimates is likely to require disclosure?
    a. Capitalized computer software costs
    b. Litigation-related obligations
    c. Environmental remediation-related obligations
    d. All of the above

13. *True or false:* Disclosures about concentrations would not be required if a concentration did not exist at the date of the financial statements.

14. *Multiple choice:* Which of the following costs should *not* be considered as part of an environmental remediation liability?
    a. Performance of remedial actions under Superfund requirements
    b. Government oversight costs
    c. Fees paid to outside law firms for work related to remedial activities
    d. Costs of routine environmental compliance

15. *True or false:* The development of an estimate of environmental remediation liabilities should not take into consideration the number and financial condition of other potentially responsible parties.

16. *True or false:* The measurement of a remediation liability should be based on enacted laws and adopted regulations, and it should not anticipate possible changes in these laws and regulations.

17. *True or false:* A foreign debt or equity swap should be measured at its fair value on the date it is agreed to by both parties.

18. *True or false:* The amount of dividend income on securities denominated in a foreign currency is recognized as income on the ex-dividend date and is converted into the functional currency using the exchange rate on that date.

19. *True or false:* When an interest-bearing security is sold between coupon dates, the difference between the recorded interest receivable and the foreign currency received, translated into the functional currency at the current exchange rate, represents a realized gain or loss.

20. *True or false:* The provisions of FAS-109 do not need to be considered for income taxes of state and local tax jurisdictions.

21. *Multiple choice:* For which of the following would amortization *not* result in the provision of deferred taxes for temporary differences?
    a. Goodwill
    b. Customer lists
    c. Trademarks
    d. None of the above

22. Which of the following elections should *not* be considered as a tax-planning strategy under FAS-109?
    a. Election to file a consolidated return
    b. Election to claim either a deduction or a tax credit for foreign taxes paid
    c. Election to forego carrying an operating loss back and only carrying that loss forward
    d. Election to change at a future date from C corporation status to S corporation status

23. *Multiple choice:* Which of the following would generally be included in the scope of FAS-115?
    a. An unsecuritized loan
    b. Limited partnership interest not currently available on a securities exchange
    c. Short sales of securities
    d. Convertible preferred stock that is redeemable

24. *Multiple choice:* How should the effect of a scheduled rent increase in an operating lease, which is included in the calculation of minimum lease payments, be recognized?
    a. On a straight-line basis over the lease term

b. At the time the scheduled rent increase occurs
c. On an effective interest method basis over the lease term
d. Either a. or b., at the option of the lessor or the lessee

25. *Multiple choice:* An agreement to perform under a contract for a price to be determined on the basis of a defined relationship to the costs incurred is known as a:
    a. Fixed-price contract.
    b. Cost-type contract.
    c. Time and materials contract.
    d. Unit price contract.

26. *True or false:* When current estimates indicate that a loss will be incurred on a contract that is accounted for by the completed-contract method, a loss provision is not required to be provided until the contract is completed.

27. *Multiple choice:* Which of the following is *not* a valid condition for decreasing the amortization period of unrecognized prior service cost?
    a. The period during which benefits will be received from a retroactive plan benefit is shorter than was initially estimated.
    b. The pension plan is curtailed.
    c. The future economic benefits have been impaired.
    d. The expected service lives of employees have decreased.

28. *True or false:* An employer is precluded from immediately recognizing actuarial gains and losses relating to a defined benefit pension plan.

29. *Multiple choice:* Purchasing nonparticipating annuity contracts to cover vested pension benefits is an example of a pension plan:
    a. Settlement.
    b. Curtailment.
    c. Suspension.
    d. Termination benefit.

30. *Multiple choice:* Which of the following bases of accounting should be used when preparing personal financial statements in accordance with generally accepted accounting principles?
    a. Cash basis
    b. Accrual basis
    c. Modified accrual basis
    d. Income taxes

31. *True or false:* The discount rates used to measure an employer's obligations for postretirement benefit plans and pension plans must always be the same.

32. *Multiple choice:* Acme, Inc., requires that employees must render 20 years of service to receive benefits under its deferred compensation contract. John Smith has already rendered 12 years of service at the date of entering into the contract, for which he is given credit toward the 20-year requirement. If no portion of the benefit vests until he has achieved the full 20 years, which of the following would represent the appropriate accounting treatment?
    a. The total obligation under the contract should be accrued over Smith's remaining 8 years of service.
    b. On the date the contract is entered into, a "catch-up" accrual for the 12 years of service Smith has already rendered should be recorded.
    c. No accrual should be recorded until Smith achieves 20 years of service.
    d. The entire amount of the obligation should be recorded on the date that the contract is entered into.

33. *True or false:* The gain or loss from the sale of a portion of a line of business that does not qualify as a segment under APB-30 should be treated as an extraordinary item.

34. *Multiple choice:* How should amounts that an enterprise pays to a shareholder be handled, pursuant to an agreement precluding that shareholder from purchasing additional shares?
    a. They should be capitalized as an asset and amortized over a period of 40 years.
    b. They should be capitalized as an asset and amortized over the life of the agreement.
    c. They should be expensed as incurred.
    d. They should be recorded as additional paid-in-capital.

35. *True or false:* When a business enterprise converts to a limited liability company, its assets and liabilities should be recorded at fair value, with any net change in equity recorded as part of paid-in capital.

36. *Multiple choice:* The equity section of a limited liability company is referred to as:
    a. Shareholders' equity.
    b. Participants' equity.
    c. Partners' equity.
    d. Members' equity.

37. *Multiple choice:* A holder of shares in an ESOP that are not readily tradable exercises his or her put option to sell the shares to the employer. At what value is the employer required to purchase the employee's stock?
    a. At the employee's allocated basis
    b. At fair value at the time the put option is exercised

c. At fair value at the time the shares are allocated to the employee
d. At book value per share

38. *Multiple choice:* An ESOP that borrows money to acquire shares of the employer sponsoring the ESOP is known as a:
   a. Leveraged ESOP.
   b. Non-leveraged ESOP.
   c. Participating ESOP.
   d. Compensatory ESOP.

39. *True or false:* Broad-based employee stock purchase programs that contain look-back options cannot be treated as noncompensatory.

40. *True or false:* For a debt restructuring to be treated as a troubled debt restructuring under FAS-15, it must be treated as a troubled debt restructuring by both the debtor and the creditor.

CPE ANSWERS

1. _____	21. _____
2. _____	22. _____
3. _____	23. _____
4. _____	24. _____
5. _____	25. _____
6. _____	26. _____
7. _____	27. _____
8. _____	28. _____
9. _____	29. _____
10. _____	30. _____
11. _____	31. _____
12. _____	32. _____
13. _____	33. _____
14. _____	34. _____
15. _____	35. _____
16. _____	36. _____
17. _____	37. _____
18. _____	38. _____
19. _____	39. _____
20. _____	40. _____

1999 Miller *GAAP Implementation Manual* CPE Program

Please record your CPE answers in the space provided on the left and return this page for scoring. Simply place the completed answer sheet in a stamped envelope and mail it to:

GAAP Implementation Manual **CPE Coordinator**
Harcourt Brace Professional Publishing
525 B Street, Suite 1900
San Diego, California, 92101-4495

METHOD OF PAYMENT

❑ **Payment enclosed ($64.00).**
(Make checks payable to Harcourt Brace & Company.)
Please add appropriate sales tax.
Be sure to sign your order below.

Charge my:
❑ MasterCard   ❑ Visa   ❑ American Express

Account number _____

Expiration date _____
Please sign below for all credit card orders.

❑ **Bill me.** *Be sure to sign your order below.*

NAME _____

FIRM NAME _____

ADDRESS _____

PHONE ( ) _____

CPA LICENSE # _____

ISBN: 0-15-606739-0

TO ORDER: Call Toll-Free 1-800-831-7799   Signature _____

See the reverse side of this page for the CPE evaluation.

Copyright © 1998 Harcourt Brace & Company. All rights reserved.

GAAP Implementation Manual CPE Evaluation

1. Were you informed in advance of the:
   a. Objectives of the course? Y N
   b. Experience level needed to complete the course? Y N
   c. Program content? Y N
   d. Nature and extent of preparation necessary? Y N
   e. Teaching method? Y N
   f. Number of CPE credit hours? Y N

2. Do you agree with the publisher's assessment of:
   a. Objectives of the course? Y N
   b. Experience level needed to complete the course? Y N
   c. Program content? Y N
   d. Nature and extent of advance preparation necessary? Y N
   e. Teaching method? Y N
   f. Number of CPE credit hours? Y N

3. Was the material relevant? Y N

4. Was the presentation of the material effective? Y N

5. Did the program increase your professional competence? Y N

6. Was the program content timely and effective? Y N

Please make any other comments that you feel would improve this course. We appreciate the time you take to complete this questionnaire. Be assured that all of your comments will be considered carefully.

_____
_____
_____
_____
_____
_____

Copyright © 1998 Harcourt Brace & Company. All rights reserved.

INDEX

A

Accelerated cost recovery system
  number of years for recovery deduction, 1.08
  tax leases, 1.05
Accounting policies and standards, 1.01 et seq.
Accounting Principles Board, rescission of statements of, 1.05–1.07
Accounting Standards Executive Committee (AcSEC), practice bulletins, 1.07–1.12
Accretion, foreign operations and exchange, 11.08–11.09
Accumulated benefit obligation, pension plans, 22.18–22.20, 22.24–22.25
Acquisition, development and construction (ADC), receipt of residual profit by financial institutions, 1.09–1.12
Additional minimum liabilities, pension plans, 22.14–22.17, 22.29
Advertising
  generally, 2.01 et seq.
  amortization, 2.03 et seq.
  communication of advertisements, 2.04
  defined, 2.04
  direct-response advertising, 2.03, 2.04, 2.05–2.09, 2.11–2.12
  disclosures in financial statements, 2.10
  measurement of costs of direct-response advertising, 2.07–2.08
  primary and secondary revenues, probable future economic benefits of direct-response advertising, 2.11–2.12
  probable future economic benefits of direct-response advertising, 2.06–2.07, 2.11–2.12
  production of advertisements, 2.04
  realizability of capitalized direct-response advertising, 2.09
  tangible assets, capitalization and depreciation of, 2.10
  tracing sales to direct-response advertising, 2.05–2.06
Aerospace equipment. *See* Construction contracts
AICPA Statements of Position. *See* Cross-Reference, pp. xxxvi–xxxvii
AICPA AcSEC Practice Bulletins. *See* Cross-Reference, p. xxxvii
Amortization
  advertising, costs of, 2.03 et seq.
  foreign operations and exchange, 11.08–11.09
  retirement benefits, 25.17
Annuity contracts, pension plans, 22.33
Architects. *See* Construction contracts
Asset reversion transactions, pension plan settlements and curtailments, 23.17, 23.32–23.33
Available-for-sale securities, 18.15 et seq.

B

Balance sheet classification
  generally, 3.01 et seq.
  life insurance, purchases of, 3.04–3.05
  long-term debt agreement with subjective acceleration clause, 3.04
Bankruptcy and reorganization. *See also* Foreclosed assets
  generally, 4.01 et seq.
  balance sheet reporting, 4.08–4.10
  cash flow, statements of, 4.10–4.11
  consolidated financial statements, 4.11
  disclosures, 4.07, 4.13
  earnings per share, calculation of, 4.11
  financial reporting, 4.07 et seq.
  fresh-start reporting, 4.11 et seq., 4.25–4.26
  income statement, 4.10
  interest expenses, treatment on income statement, 4.10
  interest income, treatment on income statement, 4.10
  legal summary of reorganization process, 4.04–4.06

Bankruptcy and reorganization *(cont.)*
  preconfirmation contingencies, fresh-start reporting, 4.25–4.26
  prepetition liabilities, compromise of, 4.08
  professional fees, treatment on income statement, 4.10
  reorganization value, determination and allocation of, 4.06–4.07, 4.12
  troubled debt restructuring, 32.04–32.05
  value of assets, eligibility for fresh-start reporting, 4.11–4.12
  voting shares, eligibility for fresh-start reporting, 4.11–4.12
Brokers and dealers
  closely held securities brokers and dealers as public or nonpublic enterprises, 29.05
  residual value of leased assets, 19.12
Business combinations
  generally, 5.01 et seq.
  autonomy of combining parties, 5.09, 5.17–5.18, 5.22
  common control, entities under, 5.23
  common stock, issuance of, 5.05, 5.09–5.10
  compensation contracts, 5.20
  completion of business combination, time for, 5.07–5.08
  consummation date for business combination, 5.07
  contingency agreements, 5.18–5.20
  contingent shares, issuance of, 5.11
  defined, 5.03
  disclosure for pooling of interests, 5.15
  downstream mergers, 5.05
  duplicate facilities, closing of, 5.04–5.05
  exchange ratio, formula for determination of, 5.06
  general management representations, contingency for, 5.19
  income taxes, 12.08–12.10
  internal costs, accounting for, 5.21
  minority interests, 5.05.5.15–5.16
  multiple parties, involvement of, 5.23
  mutual or cooperative enterprise, conversion to stock ownership, 5.05–5.06
  option to exchange shares, 5.18
  part-purchase, part-pooling election, 5.11–5.12
  pension plans, 22.10, 22.16–22.17, 22.28, 22.34–22.36
  pooling of interests combination, 5.03 et seq.
  proprietorships and partnerships, 5.16–5.17
  purchase method combination, 5.03
  retirement benefits other than pensions, 25.21
  sale of stock, requirement of, 5.21
  significant assets, disposal of, 5.14–5.15
  stock options, issuance of, 5.20–5.21
  subsidiaries, 5.12–5.13, 5.15–5.16, 5.22
  tender offer, initiation of, 5.06–5.07
  10 percent ownership, 5.07
  termination of combination plan, 5.09
  treasury stock, reacquisition of, 5.13–5.14
  unregistered securities, registration of, 5.21–5.22
  voting common stock, 5.08, 5.10–5.11, 5.13, 5.14, 5.16
  warrants, issuance of, 5.10–5.11

C

Callable debt securities, classification as held-to-maturity securities, 18.11
Capitalization of advertising costs, 2.03 et seq.
Cash flow
  bankruptcy and reorganization, 4.10–4.11
  debt and equity investments, 18.20
Certificates of deposit, 18.08
Change orders, construction contracts, 20.08
Changing prices, 6.01 et seq.
Closely held businesses, personal financial statements, 24.06, 24.08
Closely held securities brokers and dealers as public or nonpublic enterprises, 29.05
Colleges and universities, accounting for compensated absences, 1.08–1.09
Comments on proposed technical bulletins, 1.04–1.05

Compensated absences, accounting by colleges and universities, 1.08–1.09
Compensation contracts, business combinations, 5.20
Completed-contract. *See* Construction contracts
Conservation. *See* Environmental remediation liabilities
Consolidations. *See* Business combinations
Construction contracts
 generally, 20.01 et seq.
 anticipation of losses, 20.10
 basic contract price, revenues, 20.08
 change orders, revenues, 20.08
 claims, revenues, 20.08
 combination of contracts, 20.06–20.07
 costs, 20.09
 income, 20.09
 measurement of progress, 20.07
 options and additions, revenues, 20.08
 profit center, contract as, 20.06–20.07
 revenues, 20.07–20.08
 revision of estimates, 20.10
Consulting services. *See* Construction contracts
Contingencies. *See also* Environmental liabilities
 generally, 7.01 et seq.
 business combinations, 5.11, 5.18–5.20
 concentrations, vulnerability from, 7.05–7.06
 estimates, use of, 7.04–7.05
 nature of operations, description of, 7.04
 significant risks and uncertainties, disclosure of, 7.03 et seq.
Copyrights. *See* Intangible assets
Current value accounting, 6.01 et seq.
Customer lists, income taxes, 12.09

D

Dealers. *See* Brokers and dealers
Debt, extinguishment of. *See* Extinguishment of debt
Debt and equity investments
 generally, 18.01 et seq.
 available-for-sale securities, 18.15 et seq.
 callable debt securities, classification as held-to-maturity securities, 18.11
 cash flows, statement of, 18.20
 certificates of deposit, 18.08
 convertible debt securities, classification as held-to-maturity securities, 18.11
 convertible preferred stock, 18.09
 deferred tax assets, recognition of, 18.21–18.22
 derivative instruments, use to hedge securities, 18.17
 fair values, lack of readily determinable, 18.07–18.08
 forced sale of held-to-maturity securities by regulator, 18.13
 guaranteed investment contracts, 18.08
 held-to-maturity securities, 18.09 et seq.
 installment payments, 18.14
 insured loans, 18.07
 interest rate swaps, 18.17
 interim financial statements, 18.20–18.21
 "isolated, nonrecurring, and unusual . . . that could not have been reasonably anticipated," 18.14
 "major" business combinations and "major" dispositions, 18.12–18.13, 18.23
 marketability of equity security, change in, 18.15–18.16
 market prices, valuation in absence of, 18.22–18.23
 mortgage-backed interest-only certificates, classification as held-t0-maturity securities, 18.12
 mortgage derivative products, classification as held-to-maturity securities, 18.11–18.12
 net unrealized holding gain or loss on trading securities, disclosure of, 18.21
 options on securities, 18.07
 periodic evaluation of ability to hold security to maturity, 18.09
 pledge of held-to-maturity securities as collateral, 18.10–18.11
 puttable debt securities, classification as held-to-maturity securities, 18.11

Debt and equity investments *(cont.)*
  repurchase agreements or securities lending agreement, held-to-maturity securities as subject to, 18.11
  restrictions on sale of stock, 18.09
  restructured loans, 18.07
  retirement benefits other than pensions, 25.19
  short sales of securities, 18.08–18.09
  "substantially the same for holders of debt instruments," defined, 18.04–18.06
  temporary or other-than-temporary declines in fair value of debt securities, 18.19–18.20
  tender offer, sale of held-to-maturity securities in response to, 18.13
  trading securities, 18.15, 18.16, 18.18
  transfers between available-for-sale and held-to-maturity categories, 18.17–18.19
  trusts, financial statements issued by, 18.09
Deferred compensation contracts, 22.05–22.06, 25.05–25.06
Dental care, retirement benefits other than pensions, 25.19–25.20
Derivative instruments, use to hedge securities, 18.17
Direct-response advertising, 2.03, 2.04, 2.05–2.09, 2.11–2.12
Disability benefits, retirement benefits other than pensions, 25.04–25.05
Disclosures
  advertising, costs of, 2.10
  bankruptcy and reorganization, 4.07, 4.13
  business combinations, pooling of interests, 5.15
  limited liability companies and partnerships, 30.07
  personal financial statements, 24.08–24.09
  stock issued to employees, 31.16–31.17
Discount rates
  pension plans, 22.22–22.25
  pension plan settlements and curtailments, 23.14–23.15
  retirement benefits other than pensions, 25.06–25.07, 25.19
Dividends
  foreign operations and exchange, 11.09
  stock issued to employees, 31.10, 31.15

E

Electronic equipment. *See* Construction contracts
Employee stock ownership plans (ESOPs). *See* Stock issued to employees
Energy credit, tax leases, 1.05
Engineers. *See* Construction contracts
Environmental remediation liabilities
  generally, 7.06 et seq.
  allocation of liability, 7.13–7.15
  costs included in measurement of liabilities, 7.11–7.12
  estimation of liabilities, 7.09–7.10
  financial statement presentation and disclosure, 7.15–7.19
  future events or developments, 7.12–7.13
  identification of potentially responsible parties, 7.13
  loss contingencies, disclosure, 7.17–7.19
  measurement of liabilities, 7.10–7.13
  offsets, financial statement presentation, 7.15
  potential recoveries, impact of, 7.14–7.15
  probability that liability has been incurred, 7.08
  recognition criteria, 7.08
Equity investments. *See* Debt and equity investments
Equity method of accounting for investments in common stock
  generally, 8.01 et seq.
  intercompany profits and losses, elimination of, 8.04–8.05
  partnerships and joint ventures, 8.05
  transition issues, 8.05
  unrealized losses on marketable securities, 8.04
Estimates
  contingencies, 7.04–7.05
  environmental remediation liabilities, 7.09–7.10

Excess benefit pension plans, pension plans, 22.20–22.21, 22.27–22.28
Excise taxes, pension plan settlements and curtailments, 23.32
Extended warranties, recognition of revenue and costs of separately priced, 28.03–28.04
Extinguishment of debt
 generally, 9.01 et seq.
 common or preferred stock, extinguishment through exchange for, 9.04
 warrants, exercise of, 9.05
Extraordinary items, results of operations, 27.06–27.07

F

Families. *See also* Personal financial statements
 income taxes, family-owned farming businesses, 12.06
FASB Implementation Guides. *See* Cross-Reference, p. xxxix
FASB Technical Bulletins. *See* Cross-Reference, p. xxxiii–xxxv
FASB Statements and Interpretations, application of, 1.04. *See also specific topics*
Federal Home Loan Mortgage Corporation, receipt of preferred stock, 21.03, 21.04
Financial instruments
 generally, 10.01 et seq.
 foreign debt/equity swaps, 10.04–10.06
Foreclosed assets
 generally, 4.22 et seq.
 applicability, 4.22
 assumption that assets are held for sale, 4.22–4.23, 4.24
 defined, 4.22
 held for sale, assets as, 4.22–4.24
 unpaid debt, assets as subject to, 4.24
 value of assets held for sale, 4.23–4.24
Foreign debt/equity swaps, 10.04–10.06
Foreign operations and exchange
 generally, 11.01 et seq.
 accretion and amortization, 11.08–11.09
 cash, 11.11
 coupon dates, purchase or sale of interest-bearing securities between, 11.05–11.06, 11.08
 dividends, 11.09
 expenses, 11.10–11.11
 financial statement presentation, 11.11–11.12
 foreign currency accounting for investment companies, 11.03 et seq.
 forward exchange contracts, 11.11
 interest on security denominated in foreign currency, accrual of, 11.08
 investment companies, foreign currency accounting for, 11.03 et seq.
 liquidity of foreign markets, 11.12
 market value of security at valuation date, 11.06–11.07
 receivables and payables, 11.10
 sales of securities, 11.07
 size of foreign market, 11.12
 taxes, withholding of, 11.09–11.10
 valuation of securities, 11.12
Forward exchange contracts, foreign operations and exchange, 11.11
Fresh-start reporting, bankruptcy and reorganization, 4.11 et seq., 4.25–4.26
Frontloaded plans, retirement benefits other than pensions, 25.09–25.10
Future interests and similar assets, personal financial statements, 24.07

G

General price-level accounting, 6.03
Goodwill
 income taxes, 12.08–12.10
 step transactions, 13.04
Guaranteed investment contracts, pension plans, 22.33–22.34

H

Health care coverage, retirement benefits other than pensions, 25.05 et seq.
Held-to-maturity securities. *See* Debt and equity investments
Husband and wife. *See* Personal financial statements

I

Implementation Guides (FASB). *See* Cross-Reference, p. xxxix
Incentive payments, leases, 19.13
Income taxes
　generally, 12.01 et seq.
　allocation of tax expenses between pretax income from continuing operations and other items, 12.10
　business combinations, 12.08–12.10
　change in tax status, 12.07–12.08
　customer lists and trademarks, temporary differences related to, 12.09
　deductible differences and carryforwards, 12.08–12.09
　disallowance of expenses, 12.05
　disclosure of significant components of income tax expense attributable to continuing operations, 12.10
　family-owned farming businesses, use of accrual method, 12.06
　goodwill, 12.08–12.10
　interim financial reporting, changes in tax rates, 15.03–15.04
　leases, change in income tax rate, 19.08
　personal financial statements, 24.07–24.08, 24.09
　quasi-reorganizations, 12.06–12.07
　recognition and measurement, 12.06–12.07
　reversal patterns of existing temporary differences, scheduling of, 12.04 et seq.
　savings and loan associations, base-year tax reserves, 12.06
　scheduling, 12.04–12.06
　state and local jurisdictions, separate deferred tax computations for, 12.05
　state income taxes, deduction of, 12.06
　stock issued to employees, 31.13–31.14, 31.16
　tax-planning strategies, 12.12–12.14
　transition after adoption of FAS-109, 12.10–12.12
Installment payments, debt and equity investments, 18.14
Insurance. *See* Life insurance
Intangible assets. *See also* Goodwill
　generally, 13.01 et seq.
　internally developed intangibles, 13.04
　pension plans, 22.17
　personal financial statements, 24.06
　reorganization value, 4.12
　trademarks, income taxes, 12.09
Interest
　bankruptcy and reorganization, 4.10
　receivables and payables, 14.01 et seq.
Interim financial reporting
　　generally, 15.01 et seq.
　　income tax rates, changes in, 15.03–15.04
Interpretations, Accounting Principles Board. *See* Cross-Reference, p. xxxviii
Inventory
　generally, 16.01 et seq.
　intercompany transfers of LIFO inventories, elimination of profits resulting from, 16.03–16.04
Investment companies, foreign currency accounting for, 11.03 et seq.
Investment tax credits
　generally, 17.01 et seq.
　disclosures required, 17.03–17.04
　Revenue Act of 1971, accounting methods allowable under, 17.04
　tax leases, 1.05
Issuance of practice bulletins, 1.07–1.12
Issuance of technical bulletins, 1.04–1.05

J

Joint ventures, equity method of accounting for investments in common stock, 8.05

L

Leases
　generally, 19.01 et seq.
　brokers, residual value of leased assets, 19.12
　cumulative effect of retroactive application of FAS-13, 19.08
　defined, 19.03
　fiscal funding clauses, 19.05

"have published annual financial statements," transition requirements of FAS-13, 19.09
incentive payments, 19.13
income tax rate, effect of change on leveraged leases, 19.08
leveraged leases, 19.08, 19.13
money-over-money leases, 19.13–19.14
operating leases with scheduled rent increases, 19.10, 19.12–19.13
present value of minimum lease payments, interest rate used in calculating, 19.06
residual value of leased assets, 19.06–19.07, 19.11–19.12
sublease, loss on, 19.07
transition requirements of FAS-13, 19.09
wrap-leases, 19.14
Life insurance
balance sheet classification, 3.04–3.05
pension plan, funding of, 22.08
personal financial statements, 24.05, 24.08
retirement benefits other than pensions, 25.08–25.09, 25.12
Limited liability companies
generally, 30.05–30.07
disclosures, 30.07
financial statements, 30.06–30.07
recognition of assets and liabilities, 30.06
Limited liability partnerships
generally, 30.05–30.07
disclosures, 30.07
financial statements, 30.06–30.07
recognition of assets and liabilities, 30.06
Line of business, sale of
pension plan settlements and curtailments, 23.08–23.09, 23.11–23.12, 23.16–23.17
results of operations, 27.07
Liquidity of foreign markets, 11.12
Loans for acquisition, development and construction (ADC), 1.09–1.12
Long-term construction contracts. *See* Construction contracts

Look-back option, employee stock purchase plan (ESPP) with, 31.28–31.33
Lump-sum cash payments, pension plan settlements and curtailments, 23.05

M

Maintenance contracts, recognition of revenue and costs of separately priced, 28.03–28.04
Medicare reimbursement rates, retirement benefits other than pensions, 25.08
Mergers. *See* Business combinations
Minority interests, business combinations, 5.05.5.15–5.16
Money-over-money leases, 19.13–19.14
Mortgage-backed interest-only certificates, classification as held-to-maturity securities, 18.12
Mortgage derivative products, classification as held-to-maturity securities, 18.11–18.12
Multiemployer plans, retirement benefits other than pensions, 25.20–25.21
Mutual or cooperative enterprise, conversion to stock ownership, 5.05–5.06

N

Net periodic pension cost, 22.07–22.08, 22.13–22.15, 22.26–22.27, 22.36
Net worth, statement of changes in, 24.04
Noncancelable commitments, personal financial statements, 24.07, 24.09
Nonmonetary transactions
generally, 21.01 et seq.
Federal Home Loan Mortgage Corporation, receipt of preferred stock, 21.03, 21.04
Not-for-profit organizations, pension plans, 22.34
Notices to Practitioners, 1.07–1.12

O

Offsets
environmental remediation liabilities, 7.15

Offsets *(cont.)*
  pension plan settlements and curtailments, 23.23–23.26
Opinions, application of, 1.04
Options
  business combinations, exchange of shares, 5.18
  construction contracts, 20.08
  personal financial statements, 24.05
  securities, 18.07

P

Parents and subsidiaries
  business combinations, 5.12–5.13, 5.15–5.16, 5.22
  pension plans, 22.34
  pension plan settlements and curtailments, 23.08
  retirement benefits other than pensions, 25.25
Partnerships. *See also* Limited liability partnerships
  business combinations, 5.16–5.17
  equity method of accounting for investments in common stock, 8.05
Patents. *See* Intangible assets
Payables
  foreign operations and exchange, 11.10
  interest on, 14.01 et seq.
  personal financial statements, 24.07
Pension plans. *See also* Pension plan settlements and curtailments
  generally, 22.01 et seq.
  accumulated benefit obligation, 22.18–22.20, 22.24–22.25
  actuarial valuations, 22.26
  additional minimum liabilities, 22.14–22.17, 22.29
  all or almost all inactive participants, 22.10, 22.14
  amount and timing of pension plan contributions, 22.12
  annual and interim reports, 22.28–22.29
  annuity contracts, 22.33
  business combinations, 22.10, 22.16–22.17, 22.28, 22.34–22.36
  changes in pension laws, 22.25
  classes of assets, 22.13
  combination of pension plans, 22.29–22.32
  deferred compensation contracts, 22.05–22.06
  discount rates and compensation levels, 22.22–22.25
  division of pension plans, 22.33
  excess benefit pension plans, 22.20–22.21, 22.27–22.28
  federal executive agencies, 22.05
  financial reporting date, 22.15–22.16, 22.26–22.27
  guaranteed investment contracts, 22.33–22.34
  health care benefits, provision of postemployment, 22.06–22.07
  intangible assets, 22.17
  investment fund option information, reporting of, 22.04–22.05
  life insurance assets, pension plan funded with, 22.08
  market-related value of plan assets, 22.12–22.14
  measurement date, 22.15–22.16, 22.26–22.27
  minimum pension liability, 22.14
  multiple formulas, use of, 22.18–22.20
  net periodic pension cost, 22.07–22.08, 22.13–22.15, 22.26–22.27, 22.36
  new pension plan, establishment of, 22.37
  nonbenefit liabilities, 22.27
  non-U.S. pension plans, 22.05, 22.36–22.37
  not-for-profit organizations, 22.34
  parent–subsidiary arrangements, 22.34
  pension reversion ESOPs, 31.16
  prior service costs, 22.10–22.11
  projected benefit obligation, 22.18–22.21, 22.26
  projected unit credit method, 22.17–22.18, 22.21–22.22
  Puerto Rico, pensions plans in, 22.37
  recognition of gains and losses, 22.14–22.15
  regulated operations, employers with, 22.06
  restating of disclosures, 22.28
  retroactive plan amendments, 22.09, 22.10–22.12
  service periods of employees, 22.10

state and local governmental units, 22.05
substantive commitment requiring recognition of pension benefits beyond those defined in written formula, 22.22
territories of U.S., pensions plans in, 22.37
top-hat pension plans, 22.20–22.21, 22.27–22.28
transferable securities, inclusion in plan assets, 22.08
unrecognized net assets and obligations, 22.38–22.39

Pension plan settlements and curtailments
generally, 22.39, 23.01 et seq.
annuity contracts, defined, 23.09
asset reversion transactions, 23.17, 23.32–23.33
defined, 23.04
discount rates, 23.14–23.15
excise taxes, 23.32
expected years of future service, reduction of, 23.09–23.12
implicit annuity interest rates, 23.15
incorporation and subsequent spin-off of pension plan, 23.17–23.19
individual nonparticipating annuity contracts, settlement of pension benefit obligation with, 23.05–23.06
intercompany transactions, partial recognition, 23.09
limited-term annuities, 23.06
line of business, sale of, 23.08–23.09, 23.11–23.12, 23.16–23.17
lump-sum cash payments, acceptance of, 23.05
market-rated value of plan assets, 23.14
measurement date, 23.13–23.15
negative plan contributions, 23.05
offsets, 23.23–23.26
parent and subsidiaries, 23.08
participating annuity contracts, 23.06–23.07
permanent inactivity of plan participants, 23.23
recognition of settlement gain or loss, 23.04–23.06, 23.13–23.14, 23.21
simultaneous settlement and curtailment, 23.19
successor pension plans, establishment of, 23.10–23.12
supplemental early retirement benefits, 23.30
temporary employee layoffs, 23.10
temporary suspension of pension plan, 23.10
termination indemnities, 23.30
termination or suspension of pension plan, 23.22, 23.26–23.31
unrecognized net assets, 23.15–23.16, 23.20, 23.22–23.23
unrecognized prior service cost, 23.21–23.22
unusual nature and infrequency of occurrence criteria, 23.31

Percentage-of-completion. *See* Construction contracts

Personal financial statements
generally, 24.01 et seq.
accrual vs. cash basis, 24.04
closely held businesses, investments in, 24.06, 24.08
comparative financial statements, 24.04
current values and amounts, 24.05 et seq.
disclosures, 24.08–24.09
financial condition, statement of, 24.04
future interests and similar assets, 24.07
income taxes, 24.07–24.08, 24.09
intangible assets, 24.06
life insurance, investments in, 24.05, 24.08
marketable securities, 24.05
methods of presentation, 24.04
net worth, statement of changes in, 24.04
noncancelable commitments, 24.07, 24.09
options, 24.05
payables and other liabilities, 24.07
real estate, 24.06
receivables, 24.05

Pollution. *See* Environmental remediation liabilities

Pooling of interests, business combinations, 5.03 et seq.

Practice Bulletins (AICPA AcSEC), purpose and scope, 1.07–1.12. *See also* Cross-Reference, p. xxxvii
Prices, changing, 6.01 et seq.
Product maintenance contracts, recognition of revenue and costs of separately priced, 28.03–28.04
Professional fees, bankruptcy and reorganization, 4.10
Profit participation for funding of acquisition, development and construction (ADC), 1.09–1.12
Projected benefit obligation, pension plans, 22.18–22.21, 22.26
Projected unit credit method, pension plans, 22.17–22.18, 22.21–22.22
Proprietorships, business combinations, 5.16–5.17
Puerto Rico
  pensions plans, 22.37
  segment reporting, 29.04
Puttable debt securities, classification as held-to-maturity securities, 18.11

Q

Quasi-reorganizations, income taxes, 12.06–12.07

R

Rabbi trusts, 25.18
Real estate, personal financial statements, 24.06
Receivables
  foreign operations and exchange, 11.10
  interest on, 14.01 et seq.
  personal financial statements, 24.05
Redemptions, stock issued to employees, 31.10, 31.15
Regulatory agency ruling, applicability to annual reports, 27.05–27.06
Release of shares of stock issued to employees, 31.08–31.09
Reorganization. *See* Bankruptcy and reorganization
Rescission of statements of Accounting Principle Board, 1.05–1.07
Research and development costs generally, 26.01 et seq.

stock issued to acquire results of research and development arrangement, 26.04
Research bulletins, application of, 1.04
Residual value of leased assets, 19.06–19.07, 19.11–19.12
Resource Conservation and Recovery Act (RCRA). *See* Environmental remediation liabilities
Restructured loans. *See also* Troubled debt restructuring
  debt and equity investments, 18.07
Results of operations
  generally, 27.01 et seq.
  extraordinary items, 27.06–27.07
  line of business, sale of portion of, 27.07
  regulatory agency ruling, applicability to annual reports, 27.05–27.06
  start-up activities, costs of, 27.04–27.05
Retirement benefits. *See also* Pension plans; Pension plan settlements and curtailments
  generally, 25.01 et seq.
  active employees, contributions by, 25.07
  adoption of FAS-106, 25.24–25.27
  amendments to health care plan, 25.06
  amortizing gains and losses, 25.17
  attribution period, commencement of, 25.06, 25.08, 25.10–25.11
  business combinations, 25.21
  captive insurance company, investment contract with, 25.18–25.19
  credited service period, commencement of, 25.10
  curtailments, 25.11–25.16
  debt or equity securities, issuance by employer, 25.19
  deductible, increase in, 25.16–25.17
  deferred compensation contract, 25.05–25.06
  dental care, 25.19–25.20
  disability benefits, 25.04–25.05
  discount rates, 25.06–25.07, 25.19
  frontloaded plans, 25.09–25.10
  health care coverage, 25.05 et seq.
  health care insurance, premiums for purchase of, 25.07
  life insurance benefits, 25.08–25.09, 25.12

Medicare reimbursement rates, 25.08
multiemployer plans, 25.20–25.21
negative plan amendments, 25.11–25.16
nominal credited service period, 25.11
one-plan vs. two-plan accounting, 25.19–25.20, 25.22–25.23
parent and subsidiary companies, 25.25
rabbi trusts, 25.18
substantially equivalent replacement plans, 25.20–25.21
termination of plan, 25.21–25.22
Return, right of, 28.01 et seq.
Revenue recognition where right of return exists, 28.01 et seq.
Risks. *See* Contingencies

S

Savings and loan associations, base-year tax reserves, 12.06
Segment reporting
generally, 29.01 et seq.
closely held securities brokers and dealers as public or nonpublic enterprises, 29.05
defined, 29.01
insuring entity as "customer" of health care facility, 29.04–29.05
Puerto Rican operations, 29.04
territories of U.S., 29.04
Service periods of employees, pension plans, 22.10
Ships. *See* Construction contracts
Short sales of securities, 18.08–18.09
Start-up activities, costs of, 27.04–27.05
Statements and Interpretations (FASB), application of, 1.04. *See also specific topics*
Statements of Position, AICPA. *See* Cross-Reference, pp. xxxvi–xxxix
Statistics, probable future economic benefits of direct-response advertising, 2.06
Stock and stockholders. *See also* Stock issued to employees; Treasury stock
generally, 30.01 et seq.
business combinations, stock options, 5.20–5.21

equity of stockholders, 30.01 et seq.
extinguishment of debt through exchange for common or preferred stock, 9.04
limited liability companies, accounting and reporting by, 30.05–30.07
limited liability partnerships, accounting and reporting by, 30.05–30.07
research and development arrangement, stock issued to acquire results of, 26.04
takeover attempt, costs incurred in defense against, 30.04–30.05
Stock issued to employees
generally, 31.01 et seq.
convertible preferred stock, 31.12–31.14
debt and interest related to ESOP, 31.10–31.11
disclosures, 31.16–31.17
dividends, 31.10, 31.15
earnings per share, 31.12–31.14, 31.15–31.16
employee stock purchase plan (ESPP) with look-back option, 31.28–31.33
fair value of shares, 31.09–31.10
income taxes, accounting for, 31.13–31.14, 31.16
leveraged ESOPs, 31.06 et seq., 31.18–31.25
look-back option, employee stock purchase plan (ESPP) with, 31.28–31.33
nonleveraged ESOPs, 31.15–31.16, 31.25–31.27
pension reversion ESOPs, 31.16
principal stockholder, establishment or financing of compensatory plan by, 31.3
purchase of shares, 31.07–31.08, 31.15
recording of debt and interest related to ESOP, 31.11
redemptions, 31.10, 31.15
release of shares, 31.08–31.09
reporting of debt and interest related to ESOP, 31.10–31.11
termination, accounting for, 31.14
Sublease, loss on, 19.07
Subsidiaries. *See* Parents and subsidiaries

34.12 Index

Successor pension plans, establishment of, 23.10–23.12
Superfund provisions. *See* Environmental remediation liabilities
Supplemental early retirement benefits, pension plan settlements and curtailments, 23.30
Suspense shares, employee stock ownership plans, 31.14
Suspension of pension plan, 23.22, 23.26–23.31

T

Takeover attempt, costs incurred in defense against, 30.04–30.05
Taxation. *See also* Income taxes; Investment tax credits
  foreign operations and exchange, 11.09–11.10
  pension plan settlements and curtailments, excise taxes, 23.32
  reorganization, fresh-start reporting, 4.12
  tax leases, 1.05
Technical Bulletins, purpose and scope, 1.04–1.05. *See also* Cross-Reference, pp. xxxiii–xxxv
Tender offers
  business combinations, 5.06–5.07
  held-to-maturity securities, sale of, 18.13
Termination of pension plan, 23.22, 23.26–23.31
Territories of U.S.
  pensions plans, 22.37
  segment reporting, 29.04
Test market results, probable future economic benefits of direct-response advertising, 2.07

Top-hat pension plans, 22.20–22.21, 22.27–22.28
Tracing sales to direct-response advertising, 2.05–2.06
Trademarks. *See* Intangible assets
Trading securities, 18.15, 18.16, 18.18
Transport vessels. *See* Construction contracts
Treasury stock
  business combinations, 5.13–5.14
  purchase at price higher than market price, 30.04–30.05
Troubled debt restructuring
  generally, 32.01 et seq.
  applicability of FAS-115, 32.05
  bankruptcy proceedings, debtors involved in, 32.04–32.05
  debtors and creditors, classification of debt restructurings by, 32.04
  financially troubled countries, income recognition on loans to, 32.06
Trusts, financial statements issued by, 18.09

U

Uncertainties. *See* Contingencies

V

Vessels. *See* Construction contracts

W

Warranties, recognition of revenue and costs of separately priced, 28.03–28.04
Warrants
  business combinations, 5.10–5.11
  extinguishment of debt, 9.05
Wrap-leases, 19.14